Process
Family Therapy

Family Therapy
Theory, Practice, and Technique

Vincent D. Foley, Ph.D.   SERIES EDITOR

Process
Family Therapy

An Eclectic Approach to Family Therapy

Marvin Snider, Ph.D.

Foreword by Vincent D. Foley, Ph.D.

ALLYN AND BACON

Boston   London   Toronto   Sydney   Tokyo   Singapore

To my family: my late parents, Harry and Yetta Snider,
my wife, Faye, and our children,
Craig and his wife, Melinda,
Beth and her husband, Michael

Managing Editor: Susan Badger
Senior Editorial Assistant: Dana Lamothe
Editorial-Production Administrator: Rowena Dores
Editorial-Production Service: Spectrum Publisher Services
Cover Administrator: Linda Dickinson
Composition and Manufacturing Buyer: Louise Richardson

Copyright © 1992 by Allyn and Bacon
A Division of Simon & Schuster, Inc.
160 Gould Street
Needham Heights, Massachusetts 02194

Library of Congress Cataloging-in-Publication Data

Snider, Marvin.
    Process family therapy : an eclectic approach to family therapy /
Marvin Snider : foreword by Vincent D. Foley.
        p.   cm. — (Family therapy)
    Includes bibliographical references and index.
    ISBN: 0-205-13261-8 :
    1. Family psychotherapy.   I. Title.   II. Series.
    [DNLM: 1. Family therapy — methods.   WM 430.5.F2 S672p]
RC 488.5.S62   1991
616.89′156 — dc20
DNLM/DLC
for Library of Congress   91-26185
                                                                CIP

Printed in the United States of America
10 9 8 7 6 5 4 3 2 1   96 95 94 93 92 91

Contents

Foreword

In our series we have so far dealt with theoretical issues such as Bowen theory and structural theory. In addition, we have examined substance abuse and a family approach to the complex area of the borderline patient, offering some concepts relating to techniques for effective treatment. This volume is an attempt to give a total picture of theory, practice, and technique. It is an integrated work presenting the reader with a complete picture of family therapy by an experienced clinician in the field.

My interest in family therapy began in the early 1960s when I first saw Dr. Peter Laqueur doing multiple family therapy at Creedmore Hospital in New York. It became my main interest in 1967 when I was at the Menninger Foundation and saw Salvador Minuchin do marvelous things with a family of Kansas farmers.

In 1968 I went to Boston University to complete work in a doctoral program and began to see a wide range of families. At that time I had the good fortune to have a skilled, sensitive supervisor named Marvin Snider who guided me in those early stages. Dr. Snider brought to students the rare combination of theoretical understanding and clinical experience, both always in short supply.

In 1970 I returned to New York and finished my study of the field at the Ackerman Family Institute. During that time I had the opportunity of meeting most of the leaders in the field and of studying with them or having them as supervisors. Murray Bowen, Virginia Satir, Jay Haley, and Peggy Papp were some of the people who were at Ackerman at that time (1970–1972). Dr. Ackerman himself was my supervisor until his untimely death in June 1971.

Of all the people at Ackerman, Menninger, and Boston University, Dr. Snider was the one who helped me the most to put together the field of family therapy. He moved me from being tentative and uncertain to having confidence in what I was doing.

When I was asked to produce a series of texts covering the field of family therapy, I wanted to deal with ideas, issues, and specific techniques. Above all, however, I wanted to give students and practitioners a text that would integrate the whole arena of family therapy and serve as a guideline. It would have to be the work of one person who knew family therapy in both theory and practice. I thought of Marvin Snider as one of the few people capable of producing such a volume. Fortunately, he was available and interested.

Process Family Therapy is the work I had envisioned in my original proposal for the series. It is the critical volume for the series because it is the one that brings together the various elements of the field and gives them coherence.

My goal for the series was that we would produce texts that would present readers with a complete, objective, and comprehensive knowledge of the field. Central to this goal was a volume that one could hand to a reader and say, "Read this and you will understand how a therapist does family therapy: what one needs to know, how to proceed, and above all the rationale for it." *Process Family Therapy* is the text that fills that description. I think it will become a standard work for all those who teach family therapy or supervise the efforts of those who do.

Vincent D. Foley, Ph.D.

Preface

The setting was the pediatric service of a general hospital. The year was 1959. I was a psychologist working in a unit concerned with the treatment of children with behavior problems that included school phobia, learning problems, bedwetting, unmanageable behavior, depression, and difficulty adjusting to chronic physical illness such as diabetes.

My training in individual therapy was not accomplishing what I thought it should. I asked, "Is it me? Is it the nature of the problem? Or maybe I'm not using the right approach." My frustration led me to question what else might make a difference.

One day I was sitting in my office waiting for a patient. My office door faced the waiting room and happened to be open. My attention was attracted to an angry mother who charged into the waiting room with her reluctant offspring in tow. She was quite upset and appeared to be chastising him. I started to wonder how much such interactions affected the way a child related to illness and to what extent illnesses might be affected by difficult and persistent interactions between children and parents. I also wondered what impact a child's illness had on a parent, especially if it was chronic, potentially life-threatening, or debilitating or required a lot of care.

My musings were interrupted by the appearance of my patient. Later that day my thoughts returned to the issue of the relationship between illness, behavior, and family relationships. The obvious place to start seemed to be the relationship between the presented child and the child's parents, but this was too limited when I thought of the importance of sibling relationships and how parents related to them. This led to the conclusion that the family was the place to start.

At the time, it was common practice in child psychiatry clinics and mental health agencies for the child to be seen separately by one therapist and the parent, usually the mother, by another therapist, usually a social worker. I experienced this approach in my training and was not satisfied that it accomplished what was needed.

The next step that made sense was to see the parents and children together. Although this seemed reasonable, it raised my anxiety about how to cope with several people at the same time. My anxiety heightened as I thought, "What if they start to fight? What should I do? What if a parent hits a child? What if I find that the parents have problems? What if . . . ? What if . . . ?"

It became clear that I had to develop some way of thinking, some kind of approach that would enable me to determine the nature of the problem and how to develop a constructive working relationship. Such considerations, experiences, and developments in my practice over the next 30 years led to the evolution of my thinking and clinical practice, the subject of this book.

My experience and training led me to the conviction that an eclectic approach was the preferable way of being a family therapist. This includes incorporating knowledge from various "schools" of family therapy and from allied disciplines in the social and natural sciences. This book differs from most others in the field in the emphasis placed on being eclectic in practice. To do this requires that therapists have a clear sense of their own values, belief systems, and personalities and know how to blend all of these to make the best use of their potential for being effective therapists. This is a difficult but most rewarding challenge as a therapist and as a person.

Organization of This Book

The introductory chapter describes the evolution of Process Family Therapy, my theoretical base, in three stages. Stage I describes the beginning phase. Stage II describes the development of the theoretical and practical base. Stage III compares how the more familiar approaches to family therapy and the one presented in this book provide a perspective on family functioning and their different approaches to family therapy.

The second chapter describes the core concept of therapeutic culture and the components that define its development. A case illustration is included. The next eight chapters describe each of the components in more detail and include case illustrations and a guide for their application to clinical practice.

The last two chapters describe the application of Process Family Therapy. Chapter 11 describes the philosophy and method. Chapter 12 describes a special adaptation of the Milan method of interviewing and includes two case illustrations.

Gender reference is managed by alternating the use of male and female pronouns in consecutive chapters.

Acknowledgments

This book could not have been written without the help and assistance of many people. The seeds of this work began during my tenure in the

Department of Pediatrics at Massachusetts General Hospital. Dr. Nathan Talbot, Chief of the Service, and Dr. Richard Kearsley, Director of the Child Behavior Problem Program, both provided a supportive atmosphere for work on families with behavior problems. The next important step came from my work at McLean Hospital. Alfred Stanton, M.D., Psychiatrist-in-Chief, and Irene Stiver, Ph.D., Chief Psychologist, provided a sympathetic environment for me to treat families at a time when this form of therapy was relatively new. I owe a special debt of gratitude to Jacob Christ, M.D., who was Chief of the Outpatient Department at McLean Hospital where I spent the greater portion of my time. Dr. Christ was very helpful and challenging and, most of all, provided an environment where exploration and development were encouraged and nurtured. Bill and Carol Layfield, their staff, and the many therapists at Liberty Street Associates were catalysts for me as we worked with families both on an outpatient basis and in a residential treatment setting for families. This continued when the organization became the Institute for Family and Life Learning and later the Institute at Newton, an outpatient mental health clinic.

I am indebted to my colleagues, Arnold Miller, Ph.D.; Hyman Kempler, Ph.D.; and Beverly Bader, Ed.D., for their constructive feedback in reviewing earlier parts of this book. I also want to acknowledge that Henry Grunebaum, M.D., and Richard Chasin, M.D., inadvertently played a paradoxical role in this books' being written, about which they are unaware. Most of all, I am indebted to my wife, Faye Snider, M.S.W., L.I.C.S.W. This book would not have been possible without her help and support, both technical and emotional. She generously accepted the many hours and inconveniences that writing this book took from our relationship. In addition, her help in editing greatly contributed to improved readability.

Vincent Foley, Ph.D., editor of a series on family therapy, was most helpful and encouraging in reviewing the text. I am also very indebted to Executive Editor Susan Badger and Dana Lamothe, Editorial Assistant, for their help in getting this book published. Editing by Barbara Russiello at Spectrum Publisher Services significantly enhanced the readability of this book.

Last, but not least, I owe a large debt of gratitude to the many families I had the privilege of working with over the years and for their allowing me the opportunity to gain the knowledge and experience that is described in this book.

About the Author

Dr. Marvin Snider received his Ph.D. from Boston University and his M.S.W. from the University of Michigan. His book presents the development of theoretical approach and its clinical application over the past thirty years that he has been involved in the practice of family therapy. In 1967 he spent six weeks visiting the major centers in which family therapy was being practiced, which include the Mental Research Institute in Palo Alto, California, with Don Jackson, Jay Haley, Fred Ford, et al.; the National Institute of Mental Health with Lyman Wynne and his staff; the Ackerman Family Institute in New York City; Eastern Pennsylvania Psychiatric Institute with Ivan Boszormenyi-Nagi, Jim Framo, Gerald Zuk and others; and the Albert Einstein Medical Center.

Snider was a founder of the Society for Family Therapy and Research in Boston in 1968 and its first president. he is also a charter member of the American Family Therapy Association and was chairman of the membership committee for the first six years of the organization. He is also a member and approved supervisor of the American Association of Marriage and Family Therapists. He has lectured and consulted extensively in family therapy and currently has a private practice in family therapy in Newton, Massachusetts.

About the Editor

Vincent D. Foley, Ph.D. was born and raised in New York. He studied marriage and family therapy at the Menninger Foundation, the Ackerman Family Institute, and Boston University, from which he received his Ph.D.

He has taught at St. John's University, in Jamaica, New York, and has conducted workshops in Israel, Mexico, Ireland, England, and France on alcoholism in the family. He is a fellow and supervisor in the American Association for Marriage and Family Therapy and a charter member of the American Family Therapy Association.

Dr. Foley is in private practice in New York City.

CHAPTER ONE

The Evolution of an Approach to Family Therapy

In family therapy we punctuate context. This led me to the idea of presenting the material in this book in the context in which it has developed. This chapter provides that perspective.

Introduction

As an individually trained therapist, I was confronted with the complex challenge of shifting from focus on the intrapsychic world to incorporation of the psychosocial interactional realities of the family and how they affect one another.

I got involved in family therapy in 1959, just as the field was beginning to evolve. There was not very much literature or any formal training available. As a result, I went through three stages in my development. The first was in developing an immediate way to work with families. The second was to organize a theoretical base for my work and the methodology to implement it. The third was to integrate the ballooning developments in the field as they evolved.

Stage I: Getting Started

Once it became clear to me that working with families made sense, I realized that the challenges of working with an individual are multiplied both by the number of people in the family and by the complexity of their interactions. I found that I had to answer the following questions.

1

Who in the Family Have Problems?

My training dictated that the problem resides in the person who seeks help. If a therapist determined that a person in her client's life needed therapy, she would refer the person to another therapist. Psychoanalytic doctrine would discourage, if not prohibit, the therapist from seeing a "significant other." One of the things I learned early in my explorations was that the person who presents with a problem may not have the most significant problem and may, in fact, manifest the least of the problems in her family. This first came to my attention when I found my work with children was not going satisfactorily.

I was working with an 8-year-old boy, Charles, who was having a behavior problem in school. We communicated well enough in therapy. He was cooperative and bright and understood what was happening and what needed to be done. He made gains and then would regress. In the course of one of our sessions, it became clear that he was worried about the arguments his parents were having. This led to the hypothesis that his anxiety about his parents was, in some way, interfering with his progress.

I saw the parents in the context of giving and getting feedback about the status of Charles's behavior. In the course of this discussion, it became clear that there were significant marital problems. I discussed with them how the issues between them were affecting their son. I suggested that resolving their differences would be helpful to him. Fortunately, they welcomed the suggestion, which resulted in a shift in the treatment strategy to couple therapy. Approximately three months later, after significant improvement in their relationship, the parents reported surprise and pleasure at the great improvement in their son's school behavior.

This was one example of what became a common occurrence when the presenting problem was secondary to the underlying problem. This led to my interest in determining what significance to attach to how the identified patient was designated. I increasingly found that identification of the presented patient was determined more by family politics than on who needed help. Often, a dysfunctional parent could not acknowledge the need for help. When this happened, another family member, usually a child, would be designated as the identified patient. Sometimes this designation was imposed, and other times it was self-imposed, usually unconsciously.

When I was on the staff at McLean Hospital, I saw cases where the hospitalized adolescent was not the one most in need of help. In a typical case, a 17-year-old adolescent was hospitalized for being unmanageable at home. Underlying dynamics revealed that the adolescent became the focus to protect the dysfunctional parent. Such experiences led me to pay a lot of attention to determining who has what kind of problems in the family, both as individuals and in relation to each other.

What Is the Nature and Severity of the Problem?

It was clear to me that an effective and efficient treatment strategy required a keen understanding of what problems were present and at what level of severity. Also of concern was whether the problems were interrelated. Consider the case of a 12-year-old diabetic, Sam. The presenting problem was difficulty in stabilizing the illness because of the child's inability to follow a medical prescription for diet and insulin management. Sam's mother expressed her anxiety about his condition by infantilizing him; she insisted on giving him his insulin shots and on excessive supervision of his diet. He expressed anxiety and frustration about having diabetes, his mother's hovering over him, and problems with behavior at school. The father sided with his son and reprimanded his wife for being too protective. Over time, the mother's involvement with Sam and her difficulty in coping with her anxiety led to distancing from her husband. Their joint inability to cope respectfully with these differences was expressed in chronic marital conflict.

This case illustrated a common situation where there were several intertwining problems that evolved from a family's difficulty in adequately coping with a crisis. Effective intervention depended on assessing the nature and severity of each of these problems: diabetes, diet management, behavior problems, and marital problems. This determination gave rise to the next development in my thinking.

What Is the Interrelationship between Problems?

Analysis of the above case illustrated how problems can be interrelated. I will discuss my thinking at the time. The mother had a lot of guilt about her son's having diabetes. In addition, the emotional distance from her husband contributed to her overinvestment in her son's illness. Because Sam was an only child, his mother already had an enhanced investment in his care. Her anxiety was heightened by the potentially life-threatening situation if he did not receive proper care. Unwittingly, the mother fostered an overdependence at a time when Sam was beginning to feel more independent. Sam's conflict was further heightened by his father's siding with him. This analysis led me to decide on a treatment plan that first addressed the way the parents' differences in relating to Sam's medical problems were contributing to tensions in their marital relationship. Separation of the medical management issues from couple issues enabled the parents to develop a mutually compatible way to help their son move toward achieving the degree of independence he sought. This, in turn, enabled him to be more responsible in managing his diet and insulin shots. The behavior problems were eliminated, and his school performance improved.

What Combinations of People Should Be Involved in Therapy?

Cases like those just mentioned helped me clarify the concept of who should be in therapy. It was clear that the unique nature of individual and relationship problems and their attendant priorities would contribute to determining who should be involved in therapy and that the process of the therapeutic work would contribute to determining what problems should be addressed.

As in the aforementioned case of Sam, the diagnostic evaluation pointed to the couple's relationship as the first priority in treatment. In parallel with this effort, I did individual work with Sam. At a later time, the success of these separate efforts made it possible to have family meetings that resulted in the resolution of other problems not related to the diabetes.

How Motivated Are Family Members to Work on the Problem?

As I considered who should be involved in therapy, it became clear that such a determination did not mean much unless the relevant participants were motivated. The treatment plan in the case of Charles and his family was possible because it was clear upon evaluation that all family members were committed to working on the problems. Had this not been the case, a different approach would have been necessary. If the father had not been available for therapy, the treatment strategy may have been to work with the mother in coaching her how to relate to her husband in a way that might have enlisted his participation and support. This might have also included coaching Charles in how to relate to his father in a more meaningful manner.

What Resources Do Family Members Have, Singly and Collectively, for Resolution of Identified Problems?

Once motivation was established, I determined that the next concern was identification of resources that could be utilized in service of problem and conflict resolution. I defined a *resource* as any characteristic of an individual, relationship, or environment that could be mobilized to have a positive impact on changing the dysfunctional behavior. In the case of Charles and his family, the available resources included the caring that family members had for each other, intelligence, desire to have relationships with one another, a lot of positive premorbid history as a family, and Charles's competence in reading and music and his interest in history. In addition, he was attractive and had a good sense of humor.

In Sam's case other kinds of resources could include friends or relatives who made a good adjustment to a similar illness, support of role models that are respected, ability to follow instructions, and positive self-concept. I looked for anything that had the possibility of changing or interrupting the destructive pattern of behavior.

Does the Therapist Have the Needed Interest and Resources to Help the Family Deal with Its Problems?

Attention to availability of a family's resources led to the desirability of doing the same assessment on the therapist. I felt I had a dual responsibility in the treatment of a family. The first is diagnosis of the problem and designing a treatment program to resolve the problem. The second is responsibility to determine whether I had the interest, commitment, and resources necessary to implement the treatment plan.

One component of resources is the assessment of the match between the needs of the family and the personality, skill, and cultural background of the therapist. In the case of Charles, I was working with a family of a different cultural background than my own. I was from an upper-middle-class background; they were from the working class and of a different religion. I believe my therapy was successful with them because I was able to relate to their needs in the context of their cultural reality.

Compatibility between therapist and client(s) is a combination of skill, chemistry, and circumstance. A therapist may be very skilled and still have trouble establishing rapport with a family because of age, sex, color, or any other characteristic that has a strong negative meaning either for the client or therapist. Examples of interfering circumstances include the negative relationship to the referral source of the client (e.g., school or court), coercion from family members, timing, and the context in which therapy is conducted (therapy interferes with other family commitments).

What Is an Appropriate Strategy for Resolving the Dysfunctional Problems Derived from These Questions?

In my experience, I had the option of working with a family in two major ways.

Expert

In this role, I function in a more directive and paternalistic manner by virtue of having the knowledge and skills to provide information to clients on how to solve their problems. This approach may be more frequently needed in severely dysfunctional families.

Consultant

In this role, I aid the family in discovering the issues and solutions to their problems. This method is likely to be more useful for families who have adequate resources that can be utilized but do not know how to use them. This was the case with the families of Sam and Charles. In both cases I was able to help them discover what the problems were and work out a way to resolve them.

I have the additional option of whether to relate to members of the family on a one-to-one basis in the context of the group or as a group. In the expert option, the primary interaction is between the therapist and one or more family members. There is less emphasis on interaction between family members than when I am in the role of consultant.

As a consultant, I relate to the family as a group in a manner that encourages the family to interact with each other as they provide me with the requested information. In this manner I gain information on two levels at the same time: issues in conflict and direct observation of how the family members interact. I obtain information regarding what alliances and subgroups exist, and on what basis, in the family. Frequently, information gained through such observation contradicts what the family describes.

This framework of questions provided the starting point for my work with families and provided the jumping-off point for the next stage of development.

Stage II: Early Developments in Process Family Therapy

My experience from Stage I demonstrated that working with families was productive, challenging, and exciting. At that time literature on the subject was sparse, and I was aware of only a few people working with families. Most immediate was Fred Duhl, who worked next door in adult psychiatry. We shared experiences both on an individual basis and in the context of a weekly conference, where we talked about theory and cases.

The basis for my theoretical thinking emerged from a range of experiences. I drew upon my graduate clinical training; my experience in social psychology in group dynamics, leadership, attitude theory, and general systems theory; and my undergraduate background in math and physics. My thinking was also stimulated by work in anthropology, in particular, how different cultures were organized and how such organization determined in what way people viewed and valued their world and their interaction with one another.

The bubbling of this thinking led me to ask, What accounts for an effective working relationship between the therapist and a family? It occurred to me that the challenge in the therapy setting is how two cultures, that of the therapist and that of the family, can come together to form a new joint therapeutic culture. This concept is the subject of Chapter 2.

I felt an important insight would be derived from looking at how families define their value system and the rules that guide their individual behavior and at how they will relate to each other and the outside world. I defined dimensions that I found useful in understanding families in the therapy context (Chapter 5).

I also felt it was important to recognize that families, like individuals, go through developmental sequences. What evolved was a way to account for sequences of individual development in a context where all members of the family were simultaneously in multiple stages of development, and I wondered how this multiplicity affected their interactional patterns. This developmental sequence concept is discussed in Chapter 7.

Focus on developmental sequences led to the recognition that I needed to pay attention to how a person or a family moves from one sequence to another. I had to try to account for differences in how people approached such changes and what kind of problems they encountered in doing so. This evolved into an approach that involves five steps in how people cope with life events: anticipation, adaptation, stabilization and maintenance, termination and mourning, and integration. These transition issues are discussed in Chapter 8.

At one point during graduate school, I worked in a program on economic behavior at the University of Michigan. During this time I had some exposure to cost-benefit analysis. Later, in the course of my career as a family therapist, the thought occurred to me that it might be productive to look at family dynamics from a cost-benefit point of view. This work is presented in Chapter 9.

The theoretical base for doing family therapy was one step in an analytical process. Successful therapy is, in part, the result of the therapist's development of a circular interchange among his thinking, the diagnostic formulations, the interventions that are made, and feedback from the family. This circular process is examined in Chapter 11.

The choice and development of techniques I use came from a variety of sources. One of the limitations of the normal interviewing context is that people are keenly tuned to the desire to protect their image. As a result, there is a lot of opportunity for censorship in how and what information is provided. Such considerations led me to look for ways of gaining information that minimized this opportunity.

I came across one such approach when I visited Lyman Wynne's group at the National Institute of Mental Health (NIMH) in 1967. Hanna Kwiatkowska (1967a&b), a member of his staff, developed a technique for obtaining diagnostic information on families by having each member of the family do a series of drawings. She asked for information in a way that produced a lot of information that was less susceptible to censorship. This process is discussed in Chapter 11.

I developed another approach for gaining information via family interaction exercises. Family involvement in tasks is most useful when done in the presence of the therapist. This permits firsthand observation.

One such technique that I evolved provides a great deal of information about a family in a brief period of time and does not involve asking any questions. I refer to this technique as "interviewing without questions"; it involves giving a family a series of tasks to accomplish in various combinations. This and related task or activity techniques are described in Chapter 11.

Families express their individuality in many distinctive ways. One is in the kind of rituals they observe and in the way they do them. Hearing about or observing their rituals is a useful source of information. The understanding and use of rituals are discussed in Chapter 11.

The use of genograms as demonstrated by the work of Guerin (1976), McGoldrick and Gerson (1985), and others has become a very useful tool in therapeutic work with individuals as well as with families. The ways I have used and adapted genograms are described in Chapter 11.

The work of the Milan group provides the basis for another opportunity to obtain information in a way that inhibits censorship. This involves an adaptation of their technique of circular questioning. Family members are asked to respond to questions as they believe other family members would answer. This technique is described in Chapter 12.

Stage III: Relationship of Process Family Therapy to a Sampling of Established Models

Talking about the family is like the well-known tale about blind men and the elephant. Each man developed a different concept about the elephant based on which part of the elephant he touched. Similarly, each family therapist has her own view of the family and how to relate to it, depending on her orientation. I will now present my work in contrast to some of the more commonly referred to approaches.[1] I considered each orientation in

---

[1]Boszermenyi-Nagy, *Contextual Family Therapy* (1986), Bowen, *Family Systems Therapy* (1978), Jackson, et al., Mental Research Institute of Palo Alto (1968a & 1968b), Minuchin, *Structural Family Therapy* (1974), and Haley, *Strategic Family Therapy* (1969, 1976).

two ways: what it reveals about how families cope with core necessary functions and how it approaches therapy.

The problem I faced was how to make a reasonable comparison from a common reference point. The Gurman and Kniskern handbook (1981) served this purpose as a starting point because each perspective is written by a practicing proponent, and each of the authors addresses the same questions. Original references were used as needed.

I apologize in advance for any injustice that comes from trying to compare the essence of extensive work in the limited available space. I decided that the advantages of making such a comparison outweighed the disadvantages. My intent was to be as evenhanded as possible. Attention was addressed to the basic characteristics of these views without any attempt to address the variations developed by various proponents.

For purposes of differentiation, I decided to call my approach "Process Family Therapy."

Conceptualizations about Family Functioning

There are certain fundamental processes that each family must define and achieve for the family to function and achieve its objectives. These include:

1. Defining a value and belief system, implicitly or explicitly
2. Communicating in appropriate ways
3. Distinguishing between individual and joint needs
4. Organizing and accomplishing necessary functions to implement transitions in life cycle developmental sequences, which involves development and management of resources and the ability to cope with appropriate points of transition
5. Resolving differences consistent with individual and family needs

Definition of Value and Belief System
Two people bring to marriage their individual value and belief systems. A basic task for survival in a marriage is the development of a joint value and belief system. The value and belief system is both a road map for how the world is perceived and a guide for where the couple would like to go. Failure to accomplish such definition becomes a source for a difficult marriage and turbulent family relationships.

The Contextual Family Therapy orientation deals explicitly with how families define values and goals. Process Family Therapy (Chapter 4) includes an operational definition of values and beliefs and describes significant variables thought to affect how they are formed and the ways in which they are subject to change. None of the other four approaches to family therapy considered in this chapter explicitly defines values and goals.

Communication Style

A necessary outcome of any attempt by two or more people to communicate is the definition of mutually acceptable means for how to conduct their relationship. Role theory provides a useful guideline. Briefly stated, role theory posits that every person functions in a variety of functional positions. In the family, roles include parent, spouse, child, and sibling. Each of these positions carries with it the evolution of three kinds of behaviors for occupation of the position to continue: those that must be performed, those that must not be performed, and the remainder, which are permitted but not required or prohibited. For example, in order to continue in the parent position, parents are required to provide for the welfare of their children and prohibited from abusing them; everything else is permitted.

The same concept applies to the development of how people communicate with each other. Every relationship develops required, prohibited, and permitted ways for relating. I shall now show how the various approaches to family therapy differ in the attention paid to this topic.

Contextual Family Therapy.   This approach does not directly address how communication styles are established in a family. One can infer from their discussion of relational ethics that a basic need in communication is the regard for other family members' feelings and needs. It is assumed that a viable way of communicating will emerge in families when they are able to negotiate their needs in a context of fairness.

Family Systems Theory of Bowen.   This approach also does not directly deal with the ways family members define how they will communicate. Bowen's emphasis on the balance between intellectual and emotional functioning suggests that appropriate communication can occur only when this balance exists. The degree of success in communication affects the degree to which appropriate autonomy (individuation) and togetherness (fusion) are achieved among family members. Other implications for communication capability are reflected in the Bowenian concepts of triangulation, nuclear family emotional process, family projection process, and emotional cutoff.

Mental Research Institute Interactional View.   This approach explicitly addresses communication process in the family. In this view the family has a responsibility to develop rules that enable functioning in a sufficiently stable manner (homeostatically) that includes the ability to cope with internal conflicts and external changes. Other communication interests of concern are the nature of circular causality, the evolution of the double-bind hypothesis, and the symmetrical or complementary nature of all human communication. Watzlawick, Jackson, and Beavin (1967) extended the work of Bateson in developing five axioms of pragmatic communication. Satir (1967) contributed to communication considerations in her description of dysfunctional families and the nature of their differences. This includes not being able to share hopes, fears, and expectations, to disagree, to give clear messages, to give constructive feedback, or to ask direct questions.

Structural Family Therapy.   This perspective views communication as the product of the family's social structure, through which an individual functions and expresses herself. Another aspect of this structure is the development of regulating codes of behavior. These result in operational patterns through which people relate to one another to perform necessary functions.

Strategic Family Therapy.   A communicative act is viewed as an agreement between two or more members about how to relate to a particular function, that is, how to resolve a difference or express anger. Problems are the result of a breakdown in this process. One way this appears to happen is directly as a consequence of conflict in managing communication, both within a given hierarchy and especially between competing hierarchies.

Process Family Therapy.   Family communication is the resultant of the interaction of values, beliefs, goals, resources, status in developmental sequences, ability to make transitions, and the benefit-cost balance.

Distinguishing between Individual and Joint Needs

Family therapy theorists have different ways to distinguish between individual needs, which will be described.

Contextual Family Therapy.   These therapists address this issue in multiple ways. Paramount is the concept of relational ethics that is concerned with fairness between people and focuses on both individual and joint needs. The concept of fairness implies consideration for all concerns. The negotiation process that results from the determination of fairness adds emphasis to the importance of addressing joint needs.

Further support for this distinction is accomplished in their concern with trustworthiness. To be trustworthy involves valuing a relationship. To have a successful relationship requires respect for another person's needs. To accomplish this requires that both individual and joint needs are considered.

Individual needs are addressed in a unique way in the concept of legacy and the debt, entitlements, and merit accumulations that are involved in it. This is in contrast to relational corruption, which is a violation of trust in a relationship. This is referred to as *entitled unfairness,* in which a person is lured into expecting a caring relationship and is then treated badly. The individual needs that go with separateness are not viewed as conflicting with needs for intimacy. Autonomy is achieved through consideration of relational equitability.

Family Systems Theory.   This conceptualization places greater emphasis on the identification of individual needs than on joint needs. Differentiation is a basic concept that refers to the ability of an individual to maintain appropriate separation between her intellectual and emotional systems. The interest in dealing with this separation is expressed in the belief that in human relationship systems there is a balance that is never static between autonomy (differentiation) and togetherness (fusion) forces.

The concept of fusion defines the situation where the boundaries between individual and joint needs become blurred. Increased anxiety leads to greater fusion between the intellectual and emotional systems.

Mental Research Institute Interactional View.   One criterion of healthy family functioning is the balance between separateness and togetherness in pursuit of established rules to achieve cooperative functioning. This enables the family to maintain a homeostatic level of functioning in spite of the problems that may confront it. To accomplish homeostatic functioning involves a balance of individual and joint needs.

Structural Family Therapy.   One way this point of view addresses the distinction between individual and joint needs is implicit in the therapists' underlying belief that the whole and the parts in a system can be meaningfully explained only in terms of the relationships among the parts. The therapists also believe that the psychological structure of the individual is interdependent with the individual's social structure, (the medium through which the individual functions and expresses herself). Their primary concern is on the way a family is organized to accomplish its necessary functions. The implication is that a good organization that successfully performs its needed functions will adequately attend to individual needs.

Strategic Family Therapy.   The distinction between individual and joint needs cannot be considered apart from the context in which they occur and the functions they serve. The primary focus is on how family functioning gets expressed in problems. Individual problems are seen as manifestations of disturbances in the family. This would suggest that failure to find a way to attend to the joint needs of the family as a unit with the needs of the individual will be expressed in individual pathology. In essence, the individual often is the thermometer of family functioning. Her aberrant behavior says that something is wrong, but not necessarily what is wrong.

Process Family Therapy. I address the distinction between individual and joint needs in many different ways. In Chapter 3 I discuss how each social entity (therapist and family members in various combinations) develops its own framework for what to look at and how to interpret what it experiences. When individual frameworks present conflicting conclusions, the family is tested to find solutions that attend to both individual and joint needs.

In Chapter 5 I discuss values, beliefs, and goals that are defined and held both by individuals and by any other social collective such as a couple, children as a group, and the family as a group. Problems develop when there is conflict in these areas between any two or more social units. Means for blending individual needs into joint needs are described in Chapter 5 in the section on negotiations.

Chapter 6 is concerned with defining resources both on an individual basis and in relation to whatever social collectivities are relevant in the family. Chapter 7 describes the concept of developmental sequences. This includes sequences that apply both to individuals and to significant groupings in the family. Chapter 8 considers how people make transitions at various points in the life cycle, both as individuals and in various groupings. Chapter 9 looks at how the benefit-cost balance affects individual behavior in relationship to how this balance gets accomplished in a group.

Family Organization
Families organize themselves in different ways. Each approach has its own way of viewing families.

Contextual Family Therapy. The criteria for functioning in the family revolve around the flexibility that is achieved in resolving the imbalances in fairness that result from the concepts of legacy, ledger of merit, and indebtedness. Parental responsibility serves as the basic and essential reference point. The child's accountability increases as her capacity to reciprocate increases. Problem solving is accomplished through the intent to balance the ledger through respectful give-and-take.

Family functioning runs into trouble when a revolving slate of invisible filial loyalties occurs. Problems also develop when there is a lack of commitment to balancing the ledger or when relational corruption, as previously defined, occurs. Parental responsibility is the cornerstone for maintaining multilateral oscillation of fairness imbalances.

Family Systems Theory. Effective family functioning is dependent on a balance between intellectual and emotional functioning. Such functioning breaks down and symptoms develop when the system is stressed beyond its ability to adapt. Family members seek emotional distance to reduce the anxiety of too much closeness rather than in service of differentiation. Difficulty in family functioning is also expressed in the concept of the family projection process, in which the undifferentiation of the parents is transmitted to the children. This limits the next generation's capacity to achieve differentiation.

Too much stress can imbalance the adaptive mechanism of the family. This results in the emergence of symptoms. The nature of the symptom that develops tends to be an exaggeration of the mechanism that originally was used to preserve the balance.

Mental Research Institute Interactional View.   Effective family functioning occurs when a family is able to define rules that enable the family to perform necessary survival functions. These include mechanisms for coping with internal conflicts and external changes. This is done in the context of seeking a balance between autonomy of its members and maintaining a sense of family that includes reciprocity, mutuality, and connectedness.

Structural Family Therapy.   The structural organization of a family refers to the relational patterns that evolve from the composite of influences from its traditions, culture, and socioeconomic status as they are adapted to meet the functional requirements of the family. Members of the family system structure their relationships to meet the requirements necessary for family functioning. Each family develops a repertoire of structures to carry out these functions. Families develop codes for regulating behavior. The structural dimensions of transactions in families include definition of boundaries, description of coalitions, and ways family members influence the outcome of an activity. Every interaction contains varying degrees of these dimensions.

Strategic Family Therapy.   A contributing characteristic to a family's functioning well is clarity in hierarchical relationships and the absence of cross-generational coalitions. Another contributing factor is the family's ability to adjust to the developmental transitions that occur within the family life cycle in a manner that is consistent with biological dictates and cultural practices. A symptom in the identified patient represents a disturbance in the entire family and a misguided attempt to change an existing difficulty.

Process Family Therapy.   In this view the family's organizational structure is guided by the values, beliefs, and goals (Chapter 5) that are defined and held. This structure is also a reflection of what form is needed to traverse the developmental sequences (Chapter 7) that family members, individually and collectively, need to accomplish. Also influencing the shape this structure takes are the availability of access to needed resources (Chapter 6) and the benefit-cost balance (Chapter 9) in either acquiring the resources or accomplishing developmental sequences.

How Differences Are Resolved

A necessary skill for successful relationships is the ability to resolve differences to the joint satisfaction of all participants. Family therapists approach this in different ways.

Contextual Family Therapy. Family members resolve differences through negotiation of differences in loyalty and fairness issues. This process is enhanced in a trustworthy environment that is free from distortions of unconscious loyalty issues.

Family Systems Theory. Stability in family functioning is, in part, achieved by maintaining a low level of anxiety that results from a balance between forces toward autonomy (differentiation) and forces toward togetherness (fusion). When this is accomplished, family members are able to define and relate to their differences in a constructive way. Disruptions to this capability occur when the family's ability to relate is diminished and attempts to cope are expressed in such ways as triangulation, family projection process, and emotional cutoffs.

Mental Research Institute Interactional View. Family members renegotiate the rules that define how they function homeostatically as a family when such rules become dysfunctional. To accomplish this requires finding a balance between separateness and togetherness. Difficulty in dealing with differences arises when members are not able to communicate in mutually respectful ways. These aberrations in the communication process are described by Sluzki and Bevin's (1965) typology of dyads and by Watzlawick, Jackson, and Bevin's (1967) axioms regarding the pragmatics of communication.

Structural Family Therapy. When a family system's structural organization experiences difficulty in accomplishing necessary functioning for one or more of its members, differences are resolved by redefining the regulating codes. This may involve changes in one or all three of the major dimensions of transactions: definition of boundaries, power relationships, and the nature of alignments.

Strategic Family Therapy. Families who have trouble negotiating their differences often express such difficulty in the form of symptoms, generally through an identified patient. Such focus often masks difference difficulties in other members of the family. Once this process is started, the identified patient learns to continue to behave in ways that reinforce the identified patient status.

Process Family Therapy.   One important consideration in dealing with differences is to be able to define them clearly. Such definition is related to understanding the values, beliefs, and goals (chapter 5) that in some combination may underlie differences. One source of difficulty is the tendency to assume that family members share a common orientation in these areas. An additional consideration that can give rise to differences is the presumption that family members share a common reference point in how they interpret their experience. Every family member develops her own orientation in how to do this (Chapter 3). Various considerations that affect how differences are resolved are discussed in Chapter 6. An added determinant in resolution of disagreements is their level of importance. How much is to be gained by attending to them, relative to the effect of the process on satisfactory resolution (Chapter 9)?

Approaches to Family Therapy

Two considerations are addressed: goals to be achieved in therapy and what approach is used in conducting therapy.

Goals to be Achieved in Therapy

Contextual Family Therapy.   A major goal is to facilitate the clients' ability to move toward trustworthy relationships (rejunctive action) and to aid family members in achieving self-motivated relational integrity. The goal also is to interrupt the ties to invisible loyalty and to be open to new options. Also of interest is facilitating family members' thinking about and recognizing unused trust resources in their relationships. An additional concern is to achieve age-appropriate power and role structures in the family.

Family System Therapy.   The goal of therapy is to reduce anxiety in the emotional field and to improve the functional level of differentiation. This contributes to the increased adaptability of the family system.

Mental Research Institute Interactional View.   The goal of therapy is removal or amelioration of presenting symptoms.

Structural Family Therapy.   The goal of therapy is to find solutions to problems by changing the underlying systemic structure that is viewed as giving rise to the presenting symptoms.

Strategic Family Therapy. The goal of therapy is removal or amelioration of presenting symptoms.

Process Family Therapy. The goal is to help families define the core issues that underlie the presenting problems, define the options and consequences that are involved in resolving these problems, aid them in developing their capacity to make their own decisions, design the means to monitor that these decisions are properly implemented, and generalize the competence gained in this experience to other problems.

How Therapy Is Conducted

Contextual Family Therapy. The therapist helps clients to develop relational commitments and balances of fairness. This involves being able to assert their own views and to hear those of others (multilateral perspective of fairness), both to develop trustworthiness and to become accountable for their own goals. Therapy is not time limited. The approach is elicitive, not prescriptive. The therapist does not attempt to put things in a better light, such as through relabeling. She demonstrates balanced input through multidirectional partiality. She does not prescribe tasks on an interactional or power basis. The essence of therapy is functioning that leads to a balance of individuation and fair accountability. Therapy does not focus on pathology but on how such behavior affects relational trust. The goal of increased trustworthiness is achieved by improved capacity for open negotiation on ledger issues and the exploration of loyalty and legacy issues.

Family Systems Therapy. The family evaluation consists of a review of history in three areas: presenting problem, nuclear family, and the families of origin of husband and wife. The final step in the evaluation is to define an objective for family work. Focus is placed on getting the family members to define the quality of their emotional system rather than on exploring the symptom. An attempt is made to get all family members to appreciate that they react and contribute to the tension in the family. Family group therapy is considered useful in reducing family anxiety and in improving levels of differentiation, but not in dealing with basic changes in the underlying fusion of the emotional system.

The therapist seeks to increase the level of differentiation in at least one person. The expectation is that this will stimulate similar behavior in others. At times, the therapist finds that seeing the couple or whole family together can impede a family member's work toward a better level of self.

For a period of time, working with the couple was the major treatment unit. This was expanded to multiple family therapy, which involved working with three or four couples. The belief is that couples also learned through observation of other couples' therapeutic work.

The objective in working with a couple is to learn about the emotional process that exists in the family, while the therapist stays detriangled from their emotional process. This requires the therapist to relate to the emotional process without taking sides. When this is done, the belief is that the couple will automatically move toward some form of resolution.

Another belief about emotional systems results from the process of couple therapy; when one spouse increasingly functions as a better-defined self, the other spouse tends to undermine the effort. A challenge to the therapist is not to get triangled into supporting the protests of the other spouse.

In a later development of this approach, therapeutic efforts shifted emphasis to differentiation of self in relation to one's family of origin. This resulted in more sessions with spouses seen separately. With this came the awareness that what a person did between sessions was a contributing factor in successful family-of-origin work, and this awareness resulted in more time between sessions. This was based on the belief that fusions that exist in nuclear families are the result of unresolved fusion in the spouses' respective families of origin. The expectation is that success in differentiation in the original family will be followed by a greater ability for differentiation in the nuclear family.

Mental Research Institute Interactional View.   Therapy involves some combination of individual, couple, family, and extended family that may include multiple generations. The therapist may work individually or with a cotherapist. The length of therapy varies from the ten-session limit in the Brief Therapy Center to extended therapy, depending on need. Greater emphasis is placed on shorter than on long-term therapy. The therapist is expected to maintain control of the session. To this end, specific techniques have been developed that include the devil's pact, advertising instead of concealing, symptom prescription, self-fulfilling prophecies, reframing incomprehensible behavior, substituting a more desirable suspicion for an existing suspicion, system prescription, and benevolent sabotage (Gurman and Kniskern, 1981, pp. 296–299).

In the initial part of therapy, the role of the therapist is to establish rapport, gain needed information for defining the problem, set treatment goals, and design treatment interventions that are compatible with the client's motivation. In the middle phase of therapy, the focus is on conceiving and conducting behavioral interventions aimed at instigating second-order change. At the end of therapy, the goal is to gain closure around what was accomplished and to add support and encouragement for continued growth. The way this is done is tailored to what will best enable clients to incorporate this message. An objective in therapy is to accomplish changes in structure or transactional patterns by stimulating second-order change. Importance is placed on the therapist's providing acknowledgment and validation of progress achieved by the client(s). Knowing what not to say is as important as knowing what to say.

Structural Family Therapy   This approach to therapy focuses primarily on problem solving and involves anyone who shares the problem or may be able to contribute to its solution. Therapy is an ecological balancing act that takes into account every resource in the ecosystem of the family while the therapist disrupts, maintains, and creates new organizational structures. The therapist usually starts with a joint session with all those involved in the problem and may or may not later work with subgroups. In families where joint sessions are not possible, the therapist may meet concurrently with different subgroups of the family who are not able to negotiate with each other. Sequential sessions with a subgroup are held when an issue needs to be resolved before therapy with the whole family can continue. The structure of the process of therapy is flexible in terms of the number of therapists involved, who participates, and the length and frequency of interviews.

The therapist's objective is to develop relational contexts that allow, stimulate, and provoke change in transactional patterns related to the presented problem. The therapist may encourage family members to interact with each other, facilitate engagement, or promote interaction between the therapist and family members. The therapist may function as a participant, observer, advisor, commentator, or director.

The major techniques of therapy fall into three categories: creation of a transaction, joining with the transaction, and restructuring the transaction. Creation of a transaction includes *structuralization,* the way a therapist organizes the family to perform a task; *enactment inducement,* the process by which the therapist encourages the family to behave in their habitual patterns of relating; and *task setting,* the assignment by the therapist to carry out a prescribed transactional operation.

Joining with the transaction involves tracking, accommodation, and mimesis. Tracking involves the therapist's use of the symbols families use in their communication to communicate with the family. Joining in communication using their symbols provides a way to influence a family.

In accommodation, the therapist joins the family by respecting their rules for communication. In this way, the therapist tries to enter the family's supporting network as a means to encourage change.

Mimesis is the therapist's attempt to join with the family by adopting its manner of speaking, body language, or other modes of communication. It can also be done by conveying personal experiences, traits, or interests that are similar to those of the family.

Restructuring involves techniques concerned with changing the structure of transactions in two broad categories: (1) system conflict, which involves problems resulting from competing needs of family members or the ecosystem, and (2) structural insufficiency, which involves problems that result from a lack of structural resources to meet functional needs of the system such as finances, social support, and needed skills. There are three basic types of restructuring: system recomposition, symptom focusing, and structural modification. System recomposition produces structural change by adding to or taking away from the existing system in which the problem is involved. Symptom focusing approaches change directly through the symptom and utilizes techniques from strategic therapy. Structural modification is concerned with how the composition of the ecosystem affects the alignment of relationships and the boundary and power structures within and among the systems and their subsystems.

Strategic Family Therapy.   The therapist assumes responsibility for defining the structure of the therapeutic process, which includes anyone relevant to the problem within or outside the family. The therapist meets with any combination of people dictated by the nature of the problem. Meeting with an individual client is discouraged. Strategic therapists tend to follow a brief therapy model, with therapy often lasting less than six months. Most strategic therapists space sessions early in therapy weekly and then space them more widely as termination approaches. The Milan group tends to average a month between sessions. Their belief is that the family needs time for systemic change to take place. Most therapists employ posttreatment follow-ups to ensure that positive change occurs.

Decisions about therapy are the responsibility of the therapist. Frequently therapists encourage family interaction but maintain control when this happens. Treatment that fails is viewed as the therapist's responsibility, not the family's. Successful treatment is credited to the family to reinforce the likelihood that the positive effects of the treatment will last.

Therapists focus more on family dynamics than on how their interventions bring about change. They embrace any technique, however illogical, if it has the prospect of being useful. They are symptom focused and behaviorally oriented. The client's understanding of her motivation is considered of little value. Therapists focus on present behavior rather than on past history. The main therapeutic tools of this therapy are tasks and directives. The most effective task is one that uses the presenting problem to effect a change in the family. Tasks are usually designed to be carried out between sessions. Therapists also use structural interventions such as attempting to unbalance family systems by joining with one or more members on a conflictual point, fortifying generational boundaries, and supporting members at particular times to accomplish a specific objective.

Therapists tend to use family resistance to achieve change by redefining the problem or reframing it. An important technique is the paradoxical intervention, which undermines the family's struggle with change. Therapists tend to ascribe positive motives to their clients, which facilitates clients' cooperation. It places familiar patterns in a new context to increase the potential for receptivity to change.

Process Family Therapy.   The starting assumption in working with a family is that the therapeutic relationship will be a partnership. This is modified when it is determined that the client system has different needs (Chapter 11). Participation is determined jointly by the therapist and the family. Differences in opinion provide an opportunity to model conflict resolution. The initial focus is on the presenting complaint. In evaluating the problem, the therapist determines whether to focus solely on the presenting complaint or to focus on its symbolic meaning embedded in underlying problems that get expressed in other ways. After making this determination, the therapist evaluates resources (Chapter 6). The therapist also reviews the family's culture, their relevant values, beliefs, and goals, their observational frame for interpreting behavior, their definition of relevant social units, the status of their various social units in traversing developmental sequences, their ability to deal with transitions, and the nature of their benefit-cost balance for investing their energies. This information becomes the basis for determining an intervention strategy that is negotiated with the family.

Therapeutic work focuses on the present unless it is clear that historical material is in the way of current functioning. Therapy also includes exploration of intergenerational issues over time until the impeding issues are defined and resolved. In the course of conducting therapy, the therapist functions in various roles as needed: guide, consultant, advisor, mediator, and limit setter.

Termination in the usual sense is not included. When the reason for seeking therapy is adequately addressed, therapy is interrupted, with one or more follow-up sessions planned. After that point, the family is free to seek help on an as-needed basis. A more detailed discussion follows in Chapter 11.

Discussion

From this review of the different approaches to family therapy, I find that they fall into two groupings. The first group includes the Contextual and Family System approaches. They have in common their interest in understanding and working with the quality of the family environment beyond the immediacy of that dictated by the presenting complaint. They view intergenerational issues as relevant and relate to them as needed. Implicit in their view is that by attending to the larger underlying issues they attend to the presenting complaint and increase the probability of developing enough competence to avoid problems in the future. These orientations have evolved from a psychoanalytic background.

The other three approaches — Mental Research Institution (MRI), Structural, and Strategic — have in common dealing only in the present, focusing on the presenting problem, and making therapy as brief as possible. There has been a lot of cross-fertilization between these approaches. Major influences in their approach stem from the work of Gregory Bateson and Milton Erickson.

The purpose of providing this overview was to provide a context for the work that is presented in this book. The Process Family Therapy approach falls somewhere between the two groupings described above. I see this approach as combining attention to intergenerational interests and attention to the quality of the family relationships, as needed, when focusing on the current presenting problem. The remainder of the book describes the theory and practice of Process Family Therapy.

Summary

In this chapter I described the development of Process Family Therapy in three stages: initial conceptualizations, development of a theoretical base, and comparison to other approaches to family therapy.

CHAPTER TWO

Therapeutic Culture

This chapter developed from my conviction that I needed to pay more attention to how the interaction between myself as therapist and the client system affects the outcome of therapy. I found it was helpful to consider how the success of the therapeutic relationship is dependent on the ability of the participants (therapist and clients) to merge their respective person or cultures into a common therapeutic culture.

THEORY

Historically, the focus in clinical work was on the client: the presenting problem, quality of relationships, nature of family history, and satisfaction in work and leisure activities. Also included was assessment of his character structure, goals for therapy, and attitudes toward therapy. With the advent of family therapy, interest broadened to encompass how family relationships affected the presenting problem. This also included attention to whether the presenting problem was the core difficulty or whether it was the expression of problems in the family, marital problems, addictions, or protection of other family problems.

In psychoanalytic perspective, the therapist was expected to provide an atmosphere where the therapist's personality was intended to be kept out of the therapy. The client was provided with a blank screen on which to project his conflicts. An additional concern to the therapist's technical competence was to keep any countertransference from interfering with the therapy.

Family therapy and its many variations broadened the focus of attention to the context in which the presenting problem occurs, shifted to a more interactional style with client(s), and encouraged the therapist's use of his own history and personality, as well as the realization that the therapist is part of the therapeutic process, not outside it.

Therapists vary in their orientation from a determinist perspective to a constructivistic one or some combination of the two. Those therapists who function from a determinist orientation are concerned with defining the underlying reality of the client system. The constructivists believe that in therapy we are dealing with multiple realities — not just the one defined by the therapist or any part of the client or external system.

My own position is somewhere in the middle. I believe that one of the functions that the therapist serves is to help a family define a reality that is compatible for all concerned. To do this involves facilitating the family members' ability to respect one another's different perspective of reality rather than to judge it. This sets the stage for a family defining a common reality from which to relate to one another.

In this chapter I define and discuss the *therapeutic culture,* which is a product of family characteristics and circumstances; the orientation of the therapist; the goals to be achieved; and the environment in which the assessment takes place. The therapeutic culture is a dynamic entity like a kaleidoscope; each shift in perspective provides a different perspective on the family.

Definition of Therapeutic Culture

In my view the therapeutic relationship is the attempt of two individual social units to determine if one unit, the therapist, can help the other, the client, to change or eliminate a perceived dysfunction in a part of the individual or the family system. How well this gets accomplished is a function of whether a therapist and a client are able to define a mutually acceptable therapeutic relationship, that is, a therapeutic culture. A challenge to both parties — and the primary responsibility of the therapist. It means taking into account the culture each brings while creating an amalgamation of both suitable to defining and accomplishing therapeutic goals. I use the term *culture* to refer to the way in which a social unit defines the ethics, goals, customs, rituals, and rules of how they will relate to each other.

Therapists are sensitive and mindful of the need to define and understand the unique characteristics that each family brings to therapy. What gets too little attention is what a therapist also brings of his own culture to a meeting with a client. I call this the *therapist's culture.* He comes with a blending of two cultural influences: his personal history and his professional training (education in theory, ethics, and technical skills).

A therapeutic culture is an evolutionary process. Like any living organism, it requires that specific needs be met for its continued existence. In therapy, a main requirement is that family members and the therapist have the ability to identify and adapt to changing needs over time. I recommend the following to assure the adaptive process:

1. That the needs of each participant be acknowledged by other participants.
2. That the rules for interaction of social entity members be acceptable to all participants.
3. That there be a safe environment that encourages support for self-expression.
4. That all people involved participate in the definition of acceptable goals for therapy.
5. That the focus of therapy be on issues, not on personal attack.
6. That there be attention to evidence of progress toward the goals of therapy.
7. That there be respect for differences between therapist and client and between family members.
8. That the tools for resolving differences are satisfactory to all participants.
9. That therapeutic goals are best achieved when understanding the nature of a problem is followed by disruption of a destructive pattern and replacement by a more constructive one. This involves directed means for implementing change and monitoring procedures to track progress.
10. That attention and respect are given to cultural background and biases that result from gender differences.
11. That the task of determining whether these objectives are achievable is primarily the responsibility of the therapist.

Commonly, family assessment and the development of a treatment plan focused on characteristics of the family, such as motivation, the nature of the problem, their willingness to participate, payment of fees, and willingness and ability to relate to the stresses of the therapeutic process. More attention is warranted on the context in which this assessment takes place and the impact of the process on therapy. This involves considerations such as whether seeking help is voluntary, whether the therapist was selected or assigned, the financial impact of the therapy, whether or not being in therapy is viewed as demeaning or enriching, and what impact seeking therapy has had on other aspects in the life space.

External Influences on Individual Practice and How They Impact the Therapeutic Culture

Agency Policy
When a therapist is practicing in the context of an agency, the agency defines the selection of clients a therapist sees based on the presenting problem, the expected duration of therapy, and the fee. In this setting, clients

do not have the option of selecting their therapist. The family also has the disadvantage of not being able to negotiate directly with the agency's policymakers.

In contrast, a family seeking therapy privately has the choice to select who the therapist will be. This puts the family on a more equal footing with the therapist. Each party to the therapy, family or therapist, has the option to decide whether there is an acceptable fit. In the private setting the therapist defines his own operating policy. This permits direct negotiation on how the therapy relationship will be defined.

Third-Party Payers' Influence

When payment for services is made by other than the recipient of such services, an added cultural influence has impact. Insurance companies have their own culture and agenda. In the name of quality of care and cost effectiveness, they determine what they will pay for what kind of services from what kind of providers. The family covered by insurance does not have any say in their policy except their choice of an insurance carrier. When such insurance is obtained in a group plan, the choice of carrier and range of benefits are determined by the employer. Some employers provide more than one option for their employees, usually a very limited selection. This leads to an atmosphere where the therapist and the family may join in being at odds with the insurance company about how much and what kind of care should be given.

Third-party payment carries with it a number of problems. The options for a family seeking help are more limited when they are dependent on insurance.

An added difficulty for insurance carriers is those clients who use the insurance because it has the illusion of being free. Such people often stop therapy when benefits run out if their reason for being there is not a compelling one.

A third difficulty is that the accountability for the therapy is divided between the family and the insurance company. In addition, there are times when there are conflicting points of view on how accountability is assessed. This happens when the family has a need for therapy that the insurance company does not cover.

Another problem concerns confidentiality. Often subscribers are reluctant to use their insurance for therapy when they have a concern that doing so will prejudice how they are viewed at work. Those families who do not have the option to pay out of pocket find themselves at potential risk.

Governmental Policies

Legislatures take as part of their responsibility passing legislation related to protecting the health of their constituents. This includes laws relating to public health, licensing, health insurance, and mandated benefits. Agencies that implement these laws set their own policies, which significantly affect how mental health services are provided. This can include federal, state, and local agencies concerned with public health, child welfare, and medicaid. Such actions constitute another cultural influence that affects the context of how and what therapy will be delivered, for how long, and who will pay.

An added problem is the monitoring of therapeutic services that such agencies may choose to enforce. Oftentimes, judgments are made about the delivery of services by administrative personnel who have little, if any, clinical background. Policies that meet administrative needs frequently adversely affect clinical practice in a way that can be similar to what happens with insurance carriers. This can be distracting for the therapist in an agency who may have to deal with conflicting regulations from insurance carriers and state agencies.

Community Attitudes and Standards

Seeking help for psychological problems continues to be viewed in a negative light by significant groups in the population. As a result, many people may approach seeking therapy with varying degrees of clandestine behavior. Such attitudes can affect their willingness to seek mental health services. It is still not uncommon to hear, "I should be able to solve my own problems."

Significant Reference Groups

Some families define their culture from within and are relatively impervious to outside influences and standards. For these families the decision to seek therapy would not be affected by outside considerations. More commonly, families are subject to the influence of significant reference groups regarding the definition of their values and how they behave. Religious affiliation, social class, and occupation are examples of significant cultural influences outside the family that impact on whether and how a family relates to therapy.

Formation of Therapeutic Culture

Negotiating a Context for Therapeutic Culture

Phone Contact

The evolution of a therapeutic culture usually starts with a phone call from a member of the family to the therapist. An experienced therapist recognizes the importance of the first contact. The therapist is alert for clues that tell him the nature of the problem, how receptive and cooperative the family is likely to be, and whether or not the client's needs seem appropriate for therapy. Such choice could be related to the therapist's felt area of competence or to the type of problem or personality with which he likes to work. The complement of this is the beginning of the family's vigilance for assessing the quality of the therapist, whether they trust his competence, and their comfort in working with him.

A person other than the prospective therapist taking the phone call can heighten the family's anxiety because they are delayed in making the needed immediate connection. This can be a problem when there is ambivalence for getting into therapy, or when it is difficult to make the call.

The disadvantages in having an intermediary handle the initial therapeutic request can be minimized by proper training. Such a person should provide a cordial receptive atmosphere in which only essential information — name, address, telephone number, method of payment — is requested. Staff personnel should not be asking potential clients for a statement of their problem.

My preference is for the therapist to make the appointment directly. Doing so gives the therapist important information while conveying a manner that is supportive and caring.

How much information to obtain regarding the nature of the problem and the family situation is a matter of personal preference and style. I prefer to limit gathering information to what is needed to determine who will be seen initially. I believe it is to the mutual advantage for both family and therapist to assessing the viability of a working relationship face-to-face. In this context, the first session is an evaluation or consultation, during which both parties determine whether proceeding further is mutually desirable. In general, I let the caller indicate who is to be seen first, if he has a preference. Otherwise, I usually start with the largest relevant social unit: couple, dyad, family, or extended family.

An additional way to enhance communication both on the phone and in person is to pace the manner and content of speaking to what appears comfortable to the potential client. This involves the speed and tone of speaking and the level of language. Using technical language with people who have a limited experience with therapy provides a barrier to establishing a relationship. It carries the message of difference that is usually experienced by the potential client as being one down.

Office Setting As Context
The first message a family gets when they come to the office for therapy is through the nature of the physical surroundings, which carries its own messages. The quality of the furniture and the way in which offices are decorated contribute to setting a tone. It leads to hypotheses about whether the management and staff care about the environment in which they work. Overhead fluorescent lights create a different lighting atmosphere than

incandescent lamps. Comfortable furniture suggests consideration as do appropriate and current magazines. Finally, cleanliness is another way in which respect is conveyed. Old coffee, overflowing wastebaskets, and general disorder convey a sense of disregard.

It is important for clients to feel that they are treated with respect and consideration. This is especially the case when part of the problem is a feeling of inadequacy. The safest way to proceed is to start with formality and to negotiate for informality, if that is desired. This is accomplished by addressing adult clients by their last name unless they request otherwise. At times, the intent to create a friendly atmosphere by the use of first names can be received as belittling, especially when staff members are referred to by their last names. This carries the message of a double standard.

Another way of communicating respect is to start the appointment on time. When this is not possible, appropriate acknowledgment should be made for the late start. Do not keep a client waiting while the receptionist or therapist is having an extended phone conversation or a converstion with a co-worker. Should such a conversation need to be conducted, then the client should be acknowledged and told that the appointment will start as soon as possible.

Clients are generally concerned about their confidentiality. They will be alert to clues about privacy. One concern would be casual exposure of client names through exposure to names on records or observation of appointment schedules. Hearing the receptionist or staff members use client names in a manner that could easily be heard in the waiting room is inappropriate and can be unsettling. Likewise, hearing staff members discuss cases, especially if they do it in a hostile or belittling manner can provoke anxiety about respect.

Conducting therapy from behind a desk creates a barrier both physically and emotionally. It also emphasizes and heightens the power relationship in which the therapist is one up from the client. For some, it may give the message that the therapist is insecure and needs to protect himself by sitting behind a desk. It is not likely to encourage a feeling of trust and openness.

Another way distance can be communicated is when the therapist uses a chair that is significantly different from all the other chairs. This is another way in which the therapist can communicate the one-up feeling. Such a differential may be necessary for the therapist, because of physical needs and the length of time he is in his office. Any negative impact, should there be any, can be minimized by some form of acknowledgment.

Dress

The first thing a family sees when meeting a therapist is how he is dressed. Physical appearance carries a message. The therapist who dresses differently from the norm needs to be aware of the message of deviance that may or may not be helpful. For some families it might be a positive message and for others, a negative one. Dressing in the expected manner is the safest way, even if it is different than the cultural style of the family. Dressing in a style that fits the socioeconomic status of the client population can carry the message of being one of them and thereby promote their confidence in his ability to understand their reality. A hippie appearance in a conservative middle-class neighborhood or a three-piece suit in a working-class neighborhood will convey the initial message that the therapist is not from their world and is less likely to understand their problems or to arouse a sense of trust.

Application of Double Standards on Behavior
A therapist may expect his client to be on time without showing the same courtesy in return. The issue is not whether the therapist is able to stay on schedule, but rather his showing due acknowledgment when he runs late. This can be effectively communicated by indicating to the client that there are times when getting closure is more important than strict adherence to a time schedule and that the same consideration would be shown them as needed. This turns what could be an act of disregard into a matter of respect for clients.

Therapists are used to giving feedback to families but may find it hard to accept critical or negative feedback from them. Such sensitivity in the therapist runs the risk of undermining the family's confidence that he is any better able to cope than they are.

Negotiating Time of Appointment
It is often common practice, when making an appointment to present a time at the therapist's convenience. This can carry the implication, even though it is not intended, that the clients are expected to arrange their lives to make the appointment. Another approach is to negotiate appointment times, conveying respect for the availability of all concerned.

Negotiating Length of Session
A carryover from psychoanalytic work has been the custom of the 50-minute hour. I find that people differ in the time frame in which they comfortably work. For some people an hour is too long, for others it is too short, and for many it is a comfortable working period. The therapeutic relationship is enhanced when families feel that their individual needs are being addressed. I am comfortable working in a flexible time frame and have had clients who found two-, three-, and even four-hour working blocks preferable. This is especially useful when people are coming from long distances.

An added consideration is when too high a priority is attached to having the course of therapy be determined by the clock. This can be disruptive if not destructive. This is particularly the case if it results in having to send a family away when significant material has surfaced without sufficient time to achieve needed resolution in some form, even if only on a temporary basis. Confidence in the predictability that such consideration will take place encourages families to trust and to take greater risks, which are key to successful therapy.

Problems in Negotiating a Fee

The discussion of money can have different meanings such as a measure of worth, power, success, and status. The matter is relatively simple when the feasibility of the fee is realistically evaluated by the client at the very beginning. In a client's eagerness to gain the services of a desired therapist, he may be unrealistic in assessing what can be managed over the time period the therapy is likely to take. When this happens, financing therapy becomes an increasing burden to the client and interferes with the process.

Discussion of the fee is stressful when a desired service may not be available because of inadequate financial resources. This problem is minimized when the family is dealing with a social agency that has a sliding fee scale. The issue is more complex in a private practice setting. This is especially the case when a person with limited means seeks private care from a recommended therapist. A therapist who accepts a reduced fee without adequately resolving any feelings he may have about it may let these feelings leak out into the therapy in an adverse way. This will be a problem especially under circumstances when such fee reduction results from the financial need of the therapist to continue with a client that he might not otherwise want to.

Adding to the burden of a family in trouble is the felt rejection that results when the fee is prohibitive. If they stretch beyond their means, they impose a financial burden on themselves. If they have to go elsewhere, then they have to deal with feelings of rejection. This is likely to stir up feelings of diminished self worth and anger at the therapist and at the system that creates such feelings.

An added problem results when a person enters therapy without adequate attention to financial management for the therapy after the insurance runs out. Failure to pay attention to this matter on the part of both the therapist and the family creates a problem for both parties. The therapeutic culture that was carefully crafted can be jeopardized.

The alternative choice of stopping therapy or the frustration of starting with a new therapist creates its own problems. Precipitous interruption of therapy at such points would be destructive. I believe that in such situations the therapist should not terminate therapy until ample opportunity has been provided to deal with their (therapist and family) joint responsibility in not having paid adequate attention to financial realities. I feel this should be done on whatever basis necessary, reduced fee or for no fee. I take this view because I feel that the therapist has the primary responsibility to insure the financial viability of the therapeutic relationship.

Family-Therapist Interaction

Exploratory Phase

The beginning of the therapeutic culture is the first contact between a family member and the therapist. Each contact, whether on the phone or in person, provides information to the therapist and the family that gets utilized in determining whether the relationship will continue from both points of view. This exploratory phase continues until both the family and the therapist agree to a mutually satisfactory definition of their working relationship—the critical mass that marks the formal start of the work of therapy. This includes, in addition to the negotiations mentioned previously, a statement of the presenting problem, immediately relevant history, and some agreement on the initial treatment plan, which initially includes who will be seen at what frequency and with what focus. The therapeutic culture is not static but a dynamic evolution of a relationship between the participants.

Trust-Building Phase

The second phase concerns the development of trust and confidence that the therapeutic culture holds promise as a viable means for problem solving. This phase continues until enough work is accomplished in therapy to demonstrate that the therapeutic culture is working.

When the road to building trust contains too many obstacles or requires too much energy, therapy is likely to be terminated either in the form of a conscious or subconscious decision by family and/or therapist. Such action may take the form of the therapist becoming less sensitive and supportive, the client becoming oppositional or disengaged, or of canceled appointments by either party. It is important that these feelings be directly confronted by either party and made part of the issues of therapy so that the prospects are excellent that the problems will be solved and the therapeutic culture strengthened.

Failing this, the conclusion may be reached that therapy should be terminated. This could result from the conclusion that adequate work had been done, that insufficient motivation exists for further work, or that an adequate therapeutic culture had not been established. It is incumbent on the therapist not to view such an occurrence as the family's problem, that is, that they are resisting therapy. The therapist should not lose sight of the principle that every relationship is the product of those who participate in it. I believe it is in the best interest of the therapist to consider openly and jointly with the client what each contributed to their impasse to see whether correction is sufficiently possible to continue the relationship.

I find it useful to look at what is happening in the relationship when the therapy stalls. Usually some kind of transference issue is involved. In one case a client was having a hard time dealing with hostility in the workplace. He was discouraged and was considering stopping therapy because nothing was happening. I suggested that we review what was happening in the therapy relationship. After some discussion it became clear that he was angry at me and was not able to express his feelings for fear of rejection, which was a replay of the situation with his father. The connection between all of these events became clear, which freed the client to break his mind-set and risk new patterns of behavior that proved to be the start of achieving mastery.

Working Phase

The major work of therapy is accomplished in the working phase. Its success depends on maintaining the climate of the therapeutic culture in a form satisfactory to the therapist and the family. This involves the capacity of the participants to adapt constructively to the repeated destabilizing of the therapeutic culture and of the family culture as therapeutic issues get addressed. Progress in therapy involves interrupting old and destructive patterns and replacing them with new and more satisfactory patterns. The time between the attempt to give up an old pattern and the replacement of it with an uncertain new pattern is a critical period. It is a time of heightened vulnerability. One task of the therapist is to facilitate the incorporation of new ways of thinking and/or behaving before emerging anxieties that are stimulated by the therapeutic process undermine the viability of the therapeutic culture. Considerations important in dealing with transitions are discussed in Chapter 8.

Closure Phase

The next phase involves the process of closure. There are two major objectives in this phase. The first is integration of new learning gained in the previous phase. This objective begins with the explorative phase and is well on its way to being incorporated by the relevant social unit in this phase. This involves the definition and interruption of destructive patterns and replacing them with more constructive ones. It also involves the definition of specific ways of implementing such changes and how to monitor progress to ensure that desired changes occur or how to make corrections to ensure that they do occur.

The second objective is to prepare for the interruption of the therapeutic culture. It involves reinforcing the family's confidence in their own abilities to continue the learning and nurturance outside of therapy. It also involves coping with the mourning that results from ending a relationship that was an important stabilizing resource for them.

Integration Phase

I do not believe in using the concept of termination because it implies that therapy has a final and fixed ending. I prefer an interruption of therapy for a period to test out how well their new learning is working. If they find that they do not need any further learning that therapy provides, they continue on their own until they experience a time when further consultation is desired. The basic message is for them to go as far as they can on their own and to seek help when they run out of their own resources. I reinforce the value that doing this is an act of strength and the way to expand their ability to cope on their own.

I have had many clients who went through the termination route in previous therapy. Whether or not they were correct, they walked away with the notion that once they terminated therapy they should not have to come back. If they did, it carried the aura of having failed.

When a client enters this phase, I gradually move from weekly to bi-weekly, then monthly sessions to give time to apply the acquired learning so that they gain confidence in their own ability to cope. After arriving at the point of monthly meetings, I negotiate a three- to six-month interruption for a vacation from therapy to test out their functioning on their own for an extended period. After that point they return for a "checkup." If things are going well, or if their confidence is shaky, we do some work to reinforce their gains. I then give them another period to integrate their learning before scheduling another review session. If this does not seem necessary, then no set appointment is made, with the understanding that they are free to call at whatever point they have exhausted their own resources. I sometimes use the metaphor of being the "family doctor" for their emotional life. All of these decisions are made in partnership with clients when they are capable of such participation. If they are not able to do so, the therapeutic culture is defined to provide needed support until they are better able to function on their own.

Obtaining Information for Development of a Treatment Program

The combined concepts in the chapters that follow provide the basis for diagnosis and treatment planning. Each of the following chapters describes a concept in detail that provides an important contribution to help facilitate the development and maintenance of the therapeutic culture.

Chapter 3 emphasizes the importance of having a clear framework that provides a guide for what and how to gain information.

Chapter 4 provides a guide for determining what social units are most in need of attention. The concept of social unit (SU) is introduced to facilitate a generic reference to any size of social entity from an individual to the family as a whole.

Chapter 5 is a guide to determining what road map the family follows in guiding its behavior as expressed through the clients' values, beliefs, and attitudes.

Chapter 6 provides a guide for assessment of resources that may be called upon to help accomplish therapeutic goals.

Chapter 7 calls attention to identifying the pattern of developmental sequences (DSs) in the various social units (SUs) of the family. The objective is to determine how well SUs are traversing these sequences and how doing so affects the developmental sequences of others. This provides information on resources and problems in the family.

Chapter 8 addresses the importance of attending to how family members cope with transitions. These are essential to a therapist's understanding because high vulnerability generally accompanies times of transition.

Chapter 9 focuses on the importance of attending to the balance between the benefits gained from experiences relative to the cost of obtaining them. Benefits that are too costly to obtain lose their charm and are replaced by those that have a more rewarding balance between benefits and cost. When this does not happen, attention is directed to determine why this is the case.

Chapter 10 reminds us that the definition of *problem* has many aspects that should be considered in making a diagnosis.

Concurrent with these considerations, I address the issue that the therapist has the task of being aware of how these same issues in his own cultural bias may affect his observations or his conclusions.

To make the concept of the therapeutic culture viable, I will now use a case illustration to demonstrate how to think about the therapeutic culture using the aforementioned concepts.

I started this case with about four years of clinical experience in the early 1960s and before family therapy emerged as a respectable treatment modality.

CASE ILLUSTRATION

I will discuss this case from three perspectives: observations, clinical commentary from the professional culture, and perspectives from my personal culture point of view.

The Manly family was composed of Allen, 50; Audrey, 48; John, 19; Brian, 17; Larry, 15; and Mark, 12. Allen is a philosophy professor, and Audrey was a homemaker. John was a sophomore at a nearby college. He presented as a typical college student. He was undecided about whether to major in art or math. Brian and Larry are at an alternative school. Both identified with the drug culture, had a strong interest in music, and were very much into counterculture interests. They both had shoulder-length hair and in my first meeting with them were dressed in railroad overalls. Mark seemed to be following in the footsteps of Brian and Larry.

Impact of External Influences on Therapeutic Culture

I saw this family in private practice. They paid for the therapy with insurance and their own funds when the insurance ran out. A significant external influence that impacted on the therapeutic culture was that therapy was an acceptable thing to do in their community.

Evolution and Development of the Therapeutic Culture

Initial Contact

Observations

My first contact with the family was in 1966 with a phone call from Mrs. M. She had a powerful voice and came across in an assertive manner. She requested couple therapy. She indicated that her husband was reluctant but would participate. They had an ongoing struggle in their marriage. She was exasperated at his passivity and passive-aggressive behavior. She also was angry at his attempts to get the boys to side with him. He often made disparaging remarks to them about her. Appointments were made both for the couple and for the family.

Commentary

As noted earlier, I usually do not get much information on the phone beyond the nature of the problem, a brief overview of the family situation to determine who should come to the first interview, motivation for therapy, and financial capability for private therapy.

My first impression of Mrs. M was of an aggressive woman who freely expresses her feelings and sounds as if she usually gets what she wants. There was a lot of anger in her voice. I was wondering whether I wanted to get involved with someone who would be emotionally draining and a family where there would likely be stormy sessions. This was the beginning assessment of how such characteristics would affect development of the therapeutic culture.

Professional Culture.   I happened into doing family therapy before there was much literature on family therapy and before any of the established points of view emerged. What evolved from the composite of my training in the natural sciences, social work, and psychology was an eclectic orientation. My theoretical orientation at the time was based on the assumption that behavior is purposive. To understand and modify behavior, the therapist needed to know what major influences were involved and how people affected one another.

Theoretically, I drew on psychoanalytic theory and other personality theories that included elements from social learning, neo-Freudians, Murray's personology theory (1936), Lewin's field theory (1951), and Murphy's biosocial theory (1932). I also drew from motivation and attitude theory, group dynamics, and cybernetics. From the family therapy literature of the time, I had the early work of Ackerman (1966), Bowen (1957), and the Mental Research Group in Palo Alto (Jackson, 1968b). From this potpourri of background, I gradually fashioned a theoretical road map that guided me in what I looked at and how I made sense of it.

I was committed to having a theoretical framework as a frame of reference that was open to modification as need and experience warranted it. My individual and group clinical training and experience had broadened my skills and tolerance for relating to a wide range of affect. Initially, I was a little apprehensive about working with very dysfunctional and challenging families but decided that I needed to learn to cope with them to become an effective clinician. When I encountered a family with a major conflict between the parents, I saw them both individually and as a couple before I would focus on family issues. I did this because I felt that the potential battling of the parents in the family session would be more disruptive than helpful. In retrospect, I believe this rationale has merit in some situations, but not in all. An added consideration in this approach is that it was a way of coping with my discomfort. Children are quite familiar with their parents fighting. When these fights erupt in a session, they provide the therapist with an opportunity to interrupt the pattern and help them learn more productive ways to cope. Since then, I let the client decide which family members to include in the first interview unless I see some clear contraindication that might sabotage the outcome.

My objective in this first interview is to determine the definition of the problems at two levels. I start with the manifest problem(s) and then seek to determine if there is an underlying problem and what it is. Usually the core problem manifests itself in a variety of symptoms. I am also interested in determining for whom the presenting symptom is a problem, who is involved in it, and who has what motivation for participating in therapy. I am also interested in determining what resources can be called upon to address the problem.

Personal Culture.   I am the younger of two children. My sister is four years my senior. My father was of working-class background with no formal education. My mother was the dominant force in the family. My parents had a working relationship in which there was little overt conflict. I grew up in a family where conflict was dealt with on a low-keyed level and the expression of anger was not encouraged.

Evaluation of Presenting Problem

Observations

The presenting problem was Mrs. Manly's frustration with her husband. She was angry and totally frustrated with his failure to follow through on his commitments, his passive-aggressive behavior, his lack of respect for her, and his undermining her relationship with the children. She felt that he constantly undermined her authority and would often say disparaging things about her to the children such as "She was crazy," "She is too demanding," and "She should be put away." Mr. M felt she was too intense in her reactions, got to be a nag when she wanted something, and was hypercritical and too unsympathetic and unsupportive of him and what mattered to him.

Mr. Manly and the children had difficulty dealing with Mrs. Manly's affect. They felt she was overly intrusive in managing their lives and in what she expected from them. Mrs. M felt that a major part of the problem was her husband's lack of involvement in the home and with the children. His open disrespect, criticism about how she expressed her feelings, and undermining her attempts at setting standards and exercising discipline were major problems. She felt that this gave the children confusing messages and undermined their respect for her.

Mr. Manly came to therapy reluctantly and only to pacify his wife. As noted earlier, he did not feel that they should be airing their differences in public. It was no surprise that the children reflected the same attitude. Of the children, the oldest son, John, was more sympathetic to his mother's view but was not comfortable actively supporting her for fear of being put in the same position as his mother. Once they agreed to come to therapy, their focus was on Mrs. M as the problem.

Commentary

This is a stuck system in which the parents are at an impasse. Mr. Manly has difficulty acknowledging his feelings and taking responsibility for his actions. He copes with his feelings through the filter of intellect. He usually exhibits an even demeanor, which he values as the appropriate way to behave. He gains support for this view in contrast to the volatility of his wife. He grew up in the environment of an entitled child who often was not held accountable for his behavior.

Mrs. Manly is bothered by her inability to control her emotions and resents the superior position her husband portrays. She grew up in an environment in which she felt emotionally victimized by her mother. In significant ways the marriage was a continuation of the emotional climate in which she grew up. She is angry at the chronic way her views and feelings get discounted by family members, while at the same time she is expected to nurture them.

The children get caught in the cross fire between the parents and vacillate between joining in with their father when their own frustrations are consonant with his and attempting to distance themselves from both parents. The lure of the drug culture provided a convenient additional outlet.

Professional Culture.   This is a long-standing marital conflict that dates back to the beginning of the marriage. They came to it with significant unresolved issues. A major issue in their marriage was their inability to relate to their different styles in managing their emotionality and the continual battering of each other with unresolved family-of-origin issues. They never developed an effective way to respect and resolve their differences in a mutually satisfying manner. The children grew up in an adversarial atmosphere and were consistently caught in the power struggles between the parents.

Personal Culture.   From the first meeting on with this family, there was always a high state of tension in our sessions. I found working with this family demanding and draining. Prior to this I had not encountered a family that chronically carried such a high level of tension. One of the things that I learned from my work with them was how to cope in such an environment. At times I got pretty frustrated and angry at their chronic bickering. From this experience I learned how to cope with my own feelings in a way that had minimal impact on the therapy. At first I was spending as much time managing my feelings as I was trying to help them manage theirs. One of the ways I did this was to let them know what impact their way of expressing their feelings had on me and using this to try to help them get some perspective on how they were affecting each other.

Social Entity Characteristics

One objective in an evaluation is to identify the significant social units in the family and in what way they should be related to in therapy.

Observations

The major social units in the family were father, mother, each of the children, the marital relationship, the father and the sons, and the children as a group. A striking omission in this family is the absence of an enduring social unit that included the mother and the children. At fleeting times there was a semblance of a transient identity of a social unit with one or more of them. They tended to be brief and never lasted long enough to develop an enduring identity.

The social units that were the primary focus in the therapy were the father, the mother, the marital relationship, and the father and sons. The last one gained its importance in therapy because of the way it created tension in the marriage.

Mr. and Mrs. Manly came to the first interview. He presented a distinguished appearance with his neatly trimmed, light gray beard, neat, dark, three-piece suit, and soft-spoken manner. In contrast, Mrs. Manly was a stocky woman who dressed casually and had a frenzied appearance that was consistent with the intensity of her expressed hurt and anger. It was quickly very clear that this couple was in a long-standing power struggle and stuck in virtually all developmental sequences of their marriage: ability to communicate, sexual relationship, division of labor, managing money, child rearing, religious practice, and general life-style. They agreed their marriage was difficult from the very beginning. Mrs. Manly expressed her frustrations with anger in a loud and, at times, screeching voice in a foreboding manner, which, according to Mr. Manly, indicated she was going crazy. He dealt with his frustrations through silence, a sense of righteousness, and passive-aggressive behavior that totally frustrated his wife.

Commentary

Professional Culture.   I concluded that the major social units in the family were Mr. Manly, Mrs. Manly, the couple, the children as a group, and weakly defined and shifting social units of each parent with the children. Both parents attempted to get the children to ally with each one against the other. These efforts failed and contributed to maladaptive developmental sequences of parent and child relationships. The children would read the father's silence and pasive-aggressive behavior as being helpless and defend him, as well as be critical of the mother. Siding with the father created another kind of problem. The mother was the primary source of nurturance in the family. Siding with their father put them in a guilt-provoking situation when they were not angry at their mother in their own right. There was no winning, and they were not able to find a satisfactory way to deal with their dilemma. This contributed significantly to dysfunctional DSs with both parents.

The children had poor role models for coping with difference and conflict. They resented living in a war zone and dealt with these feelings by distancing themselves from parental values and life-style. They mimicked their father's hostility toward their mother and their mother's mistrust toward their father.

Personal Culture. I felt bad for the viselike pain in which the couple were locked. I felt particularly bad for the children, who in important ways were distracted from attending to their normal developmental sequences because of the hostile and unstable emotional environment. I had to be ever alert that my regard for their situation did not unduly interfere with the therapy.

Values, Beliefs, and Goals Assessment

Observations

The values important to Mr. and Mrs. Manly on which they agreed were religion, education, and interest in children and less on material acquisition. Mrs. Manly placed a high value on intellectual and emotional communication. Mr. Manly valued intellectual discussion, particularly on philosophical issues. He viewed communication about feelings as inappropriate and a demonstration of weakness. He felt that people should keep their feelings to themselves and solve their own problems. Mr. Manly felt that everybody in the family should do their own thing, but it was a wife's role to manage the home and organize people to get things done, such as helping out with meals and getting chores done. His value system did not include participation in child care, except to voice criticism when he did not like the way his wife was treating the children.

Mr. Manly believed that his wife's way of expressing her feelings was neurotic. When she would get very frustrated and angry, he would call her crazy and tell her she should be in a mental hospital. He saw himself as being victimized by her. She saw him as being insensitive and incapable of expressing feelings. He believed the children were doing OK in adolescence, whereas she was very concerned about problems Brian and Larry were having in dealing with authority and in social relationships. She was also concerned about their involvement in drugs. He disagreed with her on both issues and saw it as her making problems where they did not exist. Denial was his frequent companion.

Mr. Manly's primary goals were focused on his work. He also valued his goal of providing financially for the family, which he felt was accomplished satisfactorily. He left the management of money up to his wife. His goal for a pleasant family life did not include any major responsibility for making it happen. Mrs. Manly's goal was primarily on home and family. She did not begin to attend to personal goals until her children finished high school.

Commentary

Professional Culture.   It was difficult to be clear about what Mr. Manly's values were because of the inconsistency between what he said and the way he behaved. This was complicated by his reluctance to be clear about his values. My attempts to clarify what he was saying gained a response of vague statements. In one interview we were talking about disciplining children. He made a statement to the effect that as adolescents they should be allowed to make up their own minds much more than his wife thought. When I tried to clarify how far he would permit that, he responded with vague generalities, and I felt he was reacting as though I was treating him as his wife did.

I made a conscious effort to be as supportive as I could whenever possible. One way that usually was effective was to acknowledge the positive aspect of his motivation when I had some sense of it and then ask him to consider that what he was trying to communicate was not coming across in the desired way. I then asked him to see whether he was doing anything to contribute to this happening. Sometimes, this was successful, and sometimes, it was not.

Differences in their belief systems were far more a problem than were differences in their values. They perceived the world quite differently but from a similar perspective. They both tended to view the world through the lens of being a victim. This was always a problem when it occurred within the family setting, which was often. I had to be aware of the likelihood that I would be seen as another victimizer when I had to ask either of them to consider something they were not comfortable facing, such as finding a common way to look at the same situation.

One such instance was a discussion around an argument about how to manage a situation in which Brian had violated his mother's request not to use her knives in the workshop. Mrs. Manly was furious at the disrespect for her request, and Mr. Manly felt the request was unreasonable because no harm was done. It took some effort to separate the two issues and help them find an acceptable resolution.

Another problem surfaced in the evalution of their goals and associated priorities. His manifest goal of highest priority was his work, followed by his hobby of cabinetmaking. He also professed a high priority on family that was not consistent with his behavior, as demonstrated by his difficulty in coping with relationships with all members of his family. He was most comfortable in solitary activities. He enjoyed his teaching except when he had to deal with students on a one-on-one basis. Such behavior reflects a level of anxiety and vulnerability that would likely get expressed in resistance to therapy.

Mrs. Manly's goals up to the early part of therapy were focused on family. As problems developed with her children in adolescence and as her marital problems intensified around these problems, she increasingly felt that she had failed. This growing awareness only heightened her frustration and the intensity with which she expressed it. My therapeutic work within the family context and later with her as an individual focused on helping her define a more positive self-image that was not so heavily dependent on what other people thought.

Personal Culture.   My value system was similar to Mrs. Manly's and I found it easier to communicate with her. It was a fairly common experience in my efforts with Mr. Manly to be accused of siding with his wife or treating him as she did when I would ask him to consider something. As a result of such interchanges, I had to be careful not to let my frustration undermine my ability to relate to him. I worked hard at being patient and usually succeeded. At other times I could empathize with how threatened he felt when emotional demands were made on him or when his competence was being challenged.

Resource Assessment

Six areas of resource assessment are described in Chapter 6: personal and group characteristics, ability to communicate and express affect, ability to negotiate, cultural content, assessment capability, and influence of history and past experience. This assessment started with the first phone call and continued throughout therapy. I will briefly describe the major resources in each of these areas.

Observations: Personal and Group Characteristics
There was a high level of intellectual capability in all members of the family. There was a shared interest in music by all of them. The mother was

the only one who did not play a musical instrument. She had a broad interest in art and literature. They were all skilled in various forms of crafts and building skills. They were socially conscious and would often engage in intellectual debates about social and political issues. Their creativity in working with things did not generalize to relationships.

Commentary

Professional Culture.   Periodic discussion of one of these interests and events manifestly unrelated to therapy provided an opportunity for joining with the family and helped to define our relationship in a broader context than only in therapy. It also gave them an added sense of me as a person. It helped in a nonverbal way to indicate that I could appreciate them as people, not just clients.

Personal Culture.   I was comfortable and experienced in dealing with families that possessed similar interests in music, social consciousness and political issues. Paying attention to their positive resources helped me maintain a more balanced perspective about them as people. This kind of family reinforces my concern about the importance of my finding ways to keep a balanced perspective on a family. In dealing with families with a lot of pain and problems, it is all too easy to form a distorted view of them.

Observations: Communication Ability
The mother was the communication hub in the family. It was common for family members to communicate through her, especially when they were at odds with one another. Oftentimes Mr. Manly would communicate to his wife through the boys when he wanted to avoid dealing with her. The boys would go to their father when they knew that their mother would give them a hard time about what they wanted. They would go to her for support or when they needed help in solving a problem. Playing one parent off against the other was a common occurrence. Mrs. Manly did a great deal of nurturing and influencing via her culinary efforts. She was described as creative and an excellent cook.

Commentary

Professional Culture.   This family did not do well in their ability to influence one another in positive ways. The major impact family members had on each other was in negative communication. Shame, anger, and guilt were major ways of communicating. There was little capacity for empathy or sympathy. The father used silence as a major way to vent his anger when he did not feel he could match the mother's expression of wrath. Expressions of caring and validation were usually in short supply. The family attempted to use me in the way they related to each other. They frequently tried to communicate through me to another family member. I would handle such attempts by helping them experience that they could talk to each other directly in a productive way.

Personal Culture. At times it became wearing to deal with all of the indirect and nonverbal communication. Through experience with this family, I gained an added appreciation for the problems that can arise when things that matter cannot be dealt with in a safe and open atmosphere. I had to be careful that my sympathy, empathy, or, at other times, anger did not unduly undermine my responsibilities as a therapist.

Observations: Ability to Negotiate

This family did not usually negotiate well. Attempts to negotiate a division of labor started with reluctant agreement and usually wound up with varying degrees of indifference and frequent failure to honor commitments. The mother was usually the one to organize such efforts, and the father was the leader in undermining them, with the boys following in his tracks. The mother's reactivity would be intense and dramatic, which only gave the rest of the family further reason to justify their behavior.

Commentary

Professional Culture. Decision making was difficult because content issues frequently resulted in power struggles where everybody wound up frustrated and angry. Decisions that did get made were most often made unilaterally by one parent or the other. Mr. Manly's decisions tended to be guided more by what he wanted than by what was practical; Mrs. Manly tended to be more realistic about what was possible. One source of their fighting was his making a decision that she felt was unrealistic. Often this led to a nonproductive battle. Periodically the merits of the situation were more critical than their power struggles, and they were able to make and carry out joint decisions. One such situation occurred when Brian got hurt in an accident that required hospitalization. They were able to work together in making decisions during the crisis about his care. Once he was out of danger, their power struggle resurfaced around how to help Brian recuperate.

Each spouse often functioned at an extreme — he with his silence and passive-aggressive behavior and she with her shrill intensity and loud voice. At times she would get so upset she would turn red from her pain, frustration, and fury. I was often told by other staff people in distant parts of the office that they could hear her yelling. At the other end of the continuum, it was not uncommon to see her husband expressing his boredom and/or anger by making shadow figures with his fingers when beams of sunlight happened to cross his path during a session. He did this during the course of discussion without apparent awareness or concern for how it appeared.

Personal Culture.   Because of my own reactions, I continually had to monitor my reactions to their behavior. Doing so forced me to look at my own reactions and history in dealing with such behaviors and at how it affected my ability to be helpful to them. I had to separate out what it stirred up in me regarding such extremes of behavior. It would often be tempting to impose my values, beliefs, and needs for comfort on this family. I learned to monitor my reactions to keep focused on the merits of what was happening and to be sensitive to when my own vulnerabilities were being stimulated. I gradually learned to define and set limits on the intense interchanges that were becoming destructive. I also learned how to nurture budding events that had a chance of being constructive. Moreover, I found out that setting limits was welcomed by the couple. It helped to give them some measure of safety.

Observations: Cultural Background

They were a family with strong allegiances to their value system and the heritage of their extended family. Sunday dinners were an important family ritual. Everyone was expected to be there. Failure to do so was to risk the mother's wrath. The father in his own unique way quietly supported this value. Much as they bickered with each other, looking out for one's own kind also was valued highly. Support for expression of ideas and feelings was encouraged and supported.

Commentary

Professional Culture.   Sunday dinners were their one activity that had any semblance of relating in a cooperative manner that carried with it a sense of being a family. At times this did not work, and family dinners became a battleground that usually resulted in the children leaving and the parents continuing the battle. However, these events were sufficiently meaningful that the negative occasions did not interrupt the family ritual. An important part of history taking and casual conversation was to learn what part of their cultural background had special meaning for them in either a negative or positive manner. At times I was able to use this information to gain their attention and motivation in therapy. Part of my success in doing this shifted the source of authority from me to their own value system. When doing this put them in touch with their own value conflict, it did not work as well.

Personal Culture.   One of the personal gains from dealing with cross-cultural issues is that it stimulates my looking at how I relate to my own cultural background. In this case I became aware of the difference in values regarding accountability for one's behavior. In this family the parents gained a sense of well-being when they adhered to the dictates of their religion. I came from a background where the individual was more accountable to himself for his sense of well-being. This awareness helped me to avoid presuming that they should follow my value system.

Observation: Assessment Capability

Mr. Manly had poor capacity for self-assessment. He had a distorted view of how he came across to others and had a hard time accepting his part in family tensions. The more threatened he was, the more he saw her as the "crazy" one. Mrs. Manly was much more realistic in her self-assessment, which at times got distorted when she regressed to a victim position. Mr. Manly's assessment of others was not much better than his self-assessment. Mrs. Manly was quite insightful in her ability to read other people's behavior. With guidance she did well in being able to define and test assumptions she made about other people.

Commentary

Professional Culture.   A major challenge in the therapy was to help this family recognize the distortions that were rampant in the family. To accomplish this required breaking the mind-sets that did not permit taking in new information. The next step was to help them learn to respect and identify differences. This was followed by attention to how to resolve these differences so that all participants could relate to the resolution. Difficulty in accomplishing this created many tense momens in therapy. At times, such difficulty got expressed as "If you're not with me, then you are against me." These reactions at times threatened the viability of the therapeutic culture.

Personal Culture.   I value being open to new information through reading and discussion. This contributed to my frustration when I ran up against the rigidity of a seemingly impenetrable long-standing mind-set. At the same time, I could also appreciate the vulnerability that the mind-set protected.

Observations: History and Past Experience

Both parents had significant negative modeling experiences in their families of origin. In both families there was a lot of marital conflict. His mother was the dominant force in that family, which his father reinforced by his passivity and deference to his wife. Mrs. Manly also experienced conflict with one parent or the other. Because of this and her competence, she was expected to be a parent surrogate to her younger siblings.

Mr. Manly had a strong positive history in academic achievement as a student and as a professor. He was quite competent in using his intellect when his emotional needs were not involved. He also had difficulty constructively applying his analytical ability to interpersonal relationships. This often got him in trouble in faculty meetings.

Although Mrs. Manly did not have the same degree of academic training, she had a history of being intellectually sharp and incisive in her thinking and observations in her interpersonal relationships. She did well in managing crisis situations such as emergencies and accidents. Mr. Manly tended to become immobilized if the best course of action was not immediately apparent to him.

Commentary

Professional Culture.   One binding force that kept this family together during the years of their marriage prior to their coming to therapy was their legacy and loyalty to having an intact family. This commitment superseded the abuse they inflicted on each other. Complementing this was the hostile dependency they developed on each other. The fear of the unknown was more compelling than the tensions between them.

Mr. Manly's success in his work gave him an area in which he could feel successful. At times I was able to use his work experience as a metaphor for how he might apply the learning gained there to coping with the family situation. Over the years, Mrs. Manly gradually got involved in participating in organizational activities quite successfully. These successful experiences provided a similar opportunity for utilizing past learning.

Negative experiences provided another source for developing resources. This was done by focusing on the interruption of destructive patterns. This involved the joint understanding of the negative experiences that all family members had had and how they had developed and contributed to family problems. Their confidence in resolving problems increased every time they were able to identify and interrupt a destructive pattern and replace it with a more constructive one, even if it was only temporary. Such occasions helped to maintain a positive feeling about the therapeutic culture even when there was periodic regression.

Personal Culture.   As I thought about this family, I was glad that I did not run into them when I was much less experienced. I probably would have found them far more threatening. I learned from past experience the importance of staying non-reactive and keeping focused on core issues.

Developmental Sequences Assessment

One of my initial and ongoing concerns in working with families is to determine the significant developmental sequences for each of the major social units and how they relate to the dysfunctional relationships in the family. In doing this I also attend to those developmental sequences that appear distorted or are absent when they should be present.

Observations

In phase one of my contact with this family, it was striking that all of the major developmental sequences of this couple were in trouble: how they communicated, their sexual relationship, division of labor, child care management, and management of finances. The same was generally true of the children. All of them were having significant difficulty in coping with their major developmental sequences (school, friends, and family relationships).

Commentary

Professional Culture. The review of the developmental sequence pattern of this family provides striking testimony regarding why this family is in difficulty. Each person was preoccupied with struggles in her own developmental sequence and therefore had few resources to help others. Under such conditions the needs of other social units become an additional burden.

Evaluating a family through the wide-angle lens of developmental sequences provides an overview of how family members in various combinations are coping with the variety of objectives of concern to each social unit. Also of interest is how each social unit's progress affects the developmental sequences of other social units. A case in point in this family was the difficulty the parents had in dealing with the developmental sequence of communication with one another. This difficulty affected the evolution of their relationship to their children, which in turn affected how the children dealt with each other and their relationships outside of the family.

Shifting from a wide-angle lens to a telephoto lens provides perspective on where a given social unit is having difficulty in traversing a particular developmental sequence. When this lens is turned to the parents' ability to form constructive ways to communicate with each other, I found the problem started at the beginning of the relationship. They both were very needy and had difficulty forming relationships. She was attracted to his intellectual and seemingly confident manner and was flattered by his interest. She was particularly vulnerable because she had had a lot of disappointments in relationships. He was attracted to her quick mind, wit, warmth, and nurturing.

Neither of them was able to do much anticipatory work about the potential in the relationship beyond presuming that what felt good would continue. They had little experience in adapting to relationships and had poor role models for doing so. They started to have children shortly after their marriage. Developmental sequences related to children and Mr. Manly's pursuit of his career took priority. Contributing to this shift in priorities was the fact that they were easier to face than dealing with their relationship issues.

My attempts to help them address the negative ways they had stabilized in the developmental sequence of communication threatened the viability of the therapeutic culture. There was a massive accumulation of many years of hurt and anger stemming from their failure to learn how to respect differences and to find mutually satisfactory ways to resolve them. One obstacle was the threat of giving up the security of old established ways of coping for the vulnerability and risk of new ways.

My contribution to the development of strain in the therapeutic culture came from my frustration and diminishing patience with Mr. and Mrs. Manly in how they approached this work. I was able to help them break new ground in developing more constructive ways to relate. They were never able to sustain it long enough and gain enough confidence in this new way of communicating to be able to weather the storm of the day-to-day crises that occurred. I was aware enough of my difficulties so that I did not totally sabotage the therapy. In spite of this turmoil, they took two steps forward and in a varying manner took one to three steps backward. Gradually, they made a modest net gain. When there is pervasive dysfunction across social units and within social units, my priority shifts from dealing with the manifest issues to what underlying sources are giving rise to the generalized level of dysfunction. This gets addressed at some combination of individual and couple therapy, with some involvement of family therapy as warranted. In this case the initial primary thrust was on couple therapy, with family sessions as needed.

One of the challenging aspects of working with developmental sequences is sorting out the myriad sequences that are engaging family members in all different combinations of social entities in the family. The first objective is to identify the most significant ones. Second, the goal is to determine whether core issues underline problems across developmental sequences. In this family one such problem was their adversarial mode of communication, which made any kind of negotiations difficult.

Personal Culture.   At first I was overwhelmed at the pervasiveness of their problems in coping with developmental sequences. The problem became much more manageable once I recognized that many of them were tied to deficient self-images and to core issues around communication and the ability to respect their differences. I also found it helpful to draw upon some of my own experiences in overcoming obstacles in moving through developmental sequences. I was reminded of one such incident in my adolescence when my fear of letting my needs be known almost destroyed a friendship.

Managing Transitions Assessment

Another way to gain understanding of problems in developmental sequences is by looking at the points of transition as described in Chapter 6. I look to see if there is any pattern across sequences where there are difficulties in anticipating change, adapting to it when it occurs, developing a stable way to relate to the change, and adjusting to endings when valued relationships or experiences end.

Observations
Mr. and Mrs. Manly had difficulty in anticipating events. She did reasonably well in adjusting when an event would occur. He had a harder time doing so. He did well in finding a stable way to adjust to the onset of an event to which he had to relate. She was a bit more pragmatic. She was able to develop stabilized ways of functioning that were more responsive to how she affected other people. Both Mr. and Mrs. Manly had a hard time with the loss of relationships. The children had difficulty with anticipating coming events and in developing stable ways to adjust to their onset. John, the oldest child, did better than the others but shared the same basic difficulty.

Commentary

Professional Culture. The negative mind-sets that Mr. and Mrs. Manly had about each other interfered with their ability to anticipate events realistically based on the merits of the situation. She did reasonably well in adjusting when an event would occur. His anxiety about dealing with conflict and rejection would get in the way of his judgment. He would find a way that worked for him and stick with it, even if it caused some discomfort.

Mrs. Manly had difficulty dealing with losses that tapped unfinished work with various losses, particularly of her father. Also contributing to her struggle with losses was her difficulty in making friends. Mr. Manly also had difficulty with losses, in part because it was not easy for him to form relationships. One of the ways he dealt with this was to get involved in activities that were solitary. When his withdrewal created problems in his family or with his colleagues, it would compound the problem further.

Personal Culture.   The amount of pain and struggle in this family often became exhausting. I coped with the strain I experienced in two ways. I made sure I scheduled their sessions at a time when I had the emotional reserve to deal with them. I learned this early in my work with them, when I was reviewing difficulties in early sessions. At one point I realized that I was meeting with them at the end of the day when I was low on reserves. This led me to see them when more energy would be available. Sessions became easier after doing this. The second thing I did was to consult with colleagues when I felt the pressure building. This helped me keep my perspective.

Cost-Benefit Balance Assessment

Observations

This concept provides some added perspective on why troubled marriages stay together. The benefits for Mr. Manly were clear. He had a well-maintained home, gourmet meals, fresh laundry, and a companion and sexual partner when he would relate appropriately. Earning a living did not have any major negative impact because it was something he enjoyed doing. The major negative aspect was when he had to put up with his wife's demands and emotionality. For him, clearly the benefits outweighed the cost of obtaining them.

For Mrs. Manly the benefits included having a home and children, a major fulfillment of her goals. The major negative aspect was the lack of support from her husband and the negative modeling he provided to the boys by frequently denigrating her in front of them and behind her back. She was especially pained when she heard her husband's words coming out of her children's mouths.

Commentary

Professional Culture.   It appears that the cost-benefit balance for Mr. Manly coming to therapy was predicated on reducing the emotional pressure he felt from her and the presumption that it would help her to see that the problem was hers. He hoped that she would see that if she would be more cooperative and control her feelings better, then everybody would be happy. On this basis, he seemed willing to participate. As therapy progressed and he increasingly became aware that he had to look at his contribution to the problem, the cost-benefit balance gradually shifted to the negative side. He gradually withdrew under the cover that the therapy would not work and that I was not seeing the real situation.

She envisioned marriage as a partnership. Instead she had to manage both the home and the children on her own. Although less than she desired, it would have been far more manageable if she did not have to contend with his criticism and undermining of her authority. The emotional abuse exacted a great price. For her the cost-benefit balance was clearly on the negative side. The option to leave did not seem to offer any relief, and the prospect that she might have to resort to it made her feel even worse. She felt her one realistic option was to see if therapy could make a difference.

One aspect of the cost-benefit balance for the children that will be discussed here is in relationship to their parents. They had four choices: identify with their father, identify with their mother, try to play a neutral role, and distance themselves from both. The benefit of siding with their father is that they would have his support and have a lot more freedom to do what they wanted to do. They also knew that they would still have their mother's caring except at times of arguments. The negative side of siding with their father was having to put up with their mother's anger and demands. They also had to deal with the degree that anger that was generated by their father was directed at them.

Siding with her would mean loss of some degree of the freedom that had become important to them. It would not be clear that they would have to deal with any less of her anger. Siding with her would also alienate their father, who was already more distant than they would like. They would also not like getting more of his occasional references to their being like their mother. The positive side of siding with her would be that they might have fewer hassles with her. However, they also had some concerns about her becoming too dependent on them. The net result was that the cost-benefit balance of siding with their mother was clearly on the negative side.

The option for the children to play neutral was not a real possibility. If they did that, it would bring them the combined negatives of both parents with few redeeming benefits. Trying to distance themselves from both would make things only worse.

Personal Culture.   In view of Mr. Manly's ambiguous withdrawal from therapy, I felt it was important to look at the extent to which I may have contributed to the partial breakdown in the therapeutic culture. I reviewed the various ways I tried to relate to his evolving concern. I tried being very supportive. I gave acknowledgment to his views whenever I could. I made sure he had an opportunity to have his feelings heard and acknowledged. I concluded that together we could not find enough ways for him to benefit from the process to offset the emotional cost that he experienced as necessary to obtain it.

The other option was to see whether I could reduce his experience of the cost that went with therapy. I found that I was not able to have any significant or lasting impact on his entrenched values and beliefs about therapy and his marriage. Contributing to the problem was my limited success in relating to him. This only increased his anxiety level because he was caught between his established beliefs and the times he felt trusting of me, which made him feel more vulnerable.

Mind-Set as an Impediment to the Development of the Therapeutic Culture

Ellen Langer (1989) in her book on mindfulness eloquently describes the dynamics that are involved in mindless and mindful behavior. From this vantage point, therapy involves the process of helping clients move from destructive, mindless behavior to mindful behavior. With this in mind, I will briefly address the importance of the therapist being aware of the mind-sets that he and the family bring to therapy, which relate to each participant's openness to receiving information. Inability to take in new information is a commitment to repeating old patterns for the family. When the therapist has a closed mind-set, it leads to sabotage of what might otherwise be a viable therapeutic culture.

Observations
In this case and as often happens in situations like this one, I find a basic dysfunction in the ability to process information. When this occurs, the prevailing mind-set acts like a filter for how the incoming information is processed. It is like a camera that receives light through a lens that distorts the image. Such distortions result in misinterpretations of events that interfere with a person's ability to negotiate relationships. Such experiences undermine confidence in the self-concept and reinforce the negative mind-set that continues to be reinforced. When this becomes the predominant mode of relating, the mind-set will stay mired in its dysfunction.

Professional Culture.   Mr. Manly's mind-set included confidence in his intellectual ability but fear of taking the risk to expose it to criticism, such as in publications. This also gets expressed in family relationships when he commits to doing something to avoid conflict and then does not follow through as promised or does something different without consulting those affected. This occurred when he promised his wife he would remodel their bathroom in a particular way. With the belief that he would avoid conflict, he changed the plans with the contractor without discussing it with her. This led to a horrendous battle, during which he viewed himself as victim.

Mrs. Manly's mind-set was that she was not appreciated, and she tended to take expressions of difference as rejection. When family members did not like a particular meal, she would likely interpret this as rejection, with little room for hearing it as an expression of preference. In a similar manner, if her advice was not followed, she would tend to hear it as low regard for her point of view. Her mind-set for approaching relationships was the expectation that she would not be liked.

Personal Culture.   I had to be careful of my own mind-set about the family preventing me from taking in information that would change my views of them. One example was my having to be cautious that I did not presume that Mr. and Mrs. Manly were so entrenched in their ways that no change was possible. I also had to be careful of the mind-set that led me to bring assumptions and biases about behavior to my relationship with this family that would get in my way of accepting information that was contradictory to these views.

Overview of the Development of the Therapeutic Culture

Thus far I discussed some of the highlights of information gained in my assessment of the Manly family. I will now present an overview of our therapeutic culture as it evolved through its various phases.

Phase I: Exploration

One of my first impressions was that it would be a challenge to engage this family in therapy. This turned out to be the case because the only person motivated for therapy was Mrs. Manly. The children came under pressure and without any goal on their part.

We were able to negotiate a working contract on the administrative details of therapy: time of meeting, frequency of meeting, and fee. We also were able to work out who would attend, the presenting problem, and goals for the therapy. One of the contributing factors to defining the therapeutic culture at this point was that I was experienced and of similar age and cultural background to the couple.

Phase II: Establishing a Working Relationship

During this phase I was able to further solidify the therapeutic culture. I was able to gain enough trust from the couple to begin therapeutic work. I accomplished this by being able to define myself as being relatively unbiased and as having the goal of improving their relationship. Part of my accomplishing this was my ability to avoid being seduced by the efforts each one made to bring me to his or her point of view. I also was able to provide an atmosphere of safety, which meant that no person was going to be allowed to beat up another person emotionally in our sessions. I was also able to react to hostile challenges in a constructive way that they did not experience as defensive. My basic way of relating to them was to validate their feelings and help them define ways to solve their differences that were acceptable to all concerned. I was also mindful of not being judgmental about value differences, particularly with Mr. Manly.

During this phase I developed a good therapeutic relationship with Mrs. Manly. Mr. Manly continued to participate but was also skeptical and critical of the therapeutic process. He softened somewhat over time.

Phase III: Therapeutic Work

Major accomplishments of this phase included some limited improvement in their ability to negotiate differences. Mrs. Manly developed a stronger sense of her own identity and was better able to stand up for her point of view with her husband and children, the children learned how to get less involved in parental battles, and the parents improved their management of behavior problems such as poor grades, skipping school, and failure to do their chores. A new but tenuous level of improved stability in the family evolved after about a year and a half of therapy. The situation began to deteriorate at this point for two reasons. The first was that the two middle children left home for school. Brian went away to college, and Larry went to an alternative high school in another part of the state. As Mrs. Manly became better able to express her emotions, it put more pressure on Mr. Manly to look at his contribution to the marital and family problems. This was very threatening to him. Efforts to be supportive at this point were not successful. He gradually regressed to earlier patterns of resistance to therapy and passive-aggressive behavior in the family, such as agreeing to do things and then not following through on his commitments.

The therapeutic culture that had become more firmly established during the 18 months when progress was being made came apart. Mr. Manly was more resistant and attended less often. When I asked him to consider his contribution to their problems, he viewed it as siding with his wife. The alliance we developed earlier disappeared. The support he accepted earlier was now viewed as manipulating.

Phase IV: Therapeutic Closure and Follow-up

Shortly after the breakdown in family therapy, the couple separated at Mrs. Manly's initiative. Mr. Manly was resistant but went along with it.

Eventually the couple divorced. Mrs. Manly went back to college, obtained a graduate degree, and was very successful in establishing herself in her field. I continued with her in individual therapy during the separation period. Over the following years I saw her for brief periods of work during crises. The oldest son established a comfortable relationship with both parents. The three younger children tended to side with their father and found living with him less demanding than living with their mother. They saw her on a regular basis. She continued to be the one they would go to with a problem or in a crisis. The sons followed their father's lead and did not want to participate in family therapy. One contributing factor to their position was that their father viewed such participation as disloyal.

Summary

In this chapter I described the various influences that impact on the development of the therapeutic culture both outside the therapy relationship and within it. The primary concept is recognition that the success of a therapeutic relationship is the product of the interaction of the cultures of the therapist and the family. The therapist is not outside the therapeutic process but an integral part of it. The therapist needs to be acutely aware of how the two cultures interact in pursuit of therapeutic goals. I illustrated in a case discussion how each of the concepts described in the chapters that follow contributes to the development of the therapeutic culture.

CHAPTER THREE

Observation and Assessment

In the course of my training and experience, I found the tendency to pay too little attention to what guides how an observer determines what she looks at and how she interprets what she sees and hears. This applies as much to the family as to the therapist. This chapter is intended to add some clarity to these processes.

Introduction

It is always disappointing when a family drops out of therapy. That was the case with the Starr family. There were five members in the Starr family. Sam, 45, the father, was a lawyer. He was graying, tall, slender, and intellectual, with a cool poker face that appeared to be guardian of his emotions.

Sara, 43, mother, was a teacher. She was tall, stocky, and intellectual. Her hair provided a broad frame for her face, which communicated a feeling of tension and anxiety. She spoke rapidly, and the tenseness of her body suggested she was sitting on a chair of upright nails.

Rick, 12, was slender and tall for his age. He generally sat quietly and mirrored the same emotional demeanor as his father. He was doing well in school after a shaky time in the sixth and seventh grades. At the time of the interview he did not pose any problem.

Sam, 10, was the emotional monitor of family. He was very sensitive to not hurting other people's feelings. His mother viewed him as being well adjusted because he always let her know the state of his feelings.

Stuart, 7, blond and blue-eyed, mirrored the emotional demeanor of his mother. He usually looked uncomfortable, was fidgety, and resisted making eye contact with me. He frequently looked to his mother as though to get a cue on where he stood and how to proceed. He was the identified client because of his behavior problems in school.

The mother was clearly in charge of the emotional environment in the family. Both parents were highly invested in the intellectual achievements of their children.

I saw this family for nine sessions and often had the feeling that I was a rodeo rider who was trying to hang on and on the verge of being thrown. The parents would present their problem and then appear to switch seats, become cotherapists, and debate how the therapy should be managed.

The relationship felt tense from the very beginning. In reviewing this case, my attention was drawn to evaluating the interaction between the family and me. I carefully reviewed what my observations were and how I was affected by them. This led me to evaluate other cases in a similar way to better understand on what basis I made observations, how I used this information, and how the product of such observations affected families. This involves understanding the observation process and the way the resulting data are utilized in the assessment process. These considerations are the subject of this chapter, with the Starr family for illustration.

My first reactions to the Starr family were mixed. Although I had been successful with families like this before, I was also aware that I probably would have to struggle with the parents over who would manage the therapy before they would accomplish very much. My initial efforts to deal with this issue were successful until the parents' anxieties about their problems were stimulated. As their anxieties and my frustration increased, I was reminded of other times when I had similar difficulties. I had to be careful not to put the responsibility on the family by labeling them as "resistant." I had to focus on what was preventing them from being able to address their concerns. As the therapy progressed, I considered whether I was doing something that was making the therapy difficult. I wondered whether my observations were faulty or whether my way of making assessments was the problem. I first discuss issues involved in the observation process and then follow this with a discussion of the assessment process.

Observation Process

The Observer and the Nature of Reality

Two important developments have evolved in the last 15 years in family therapy.

Observer Is Part of the System
The way a family relates in a therapy session is the product of the interaction of the therapist and the family. There are no observers in the sense that someone views the process without having any impact on what occurs. There are only reporters on how experienced events are interpreted, whether from a therapist's or a family member's point of view. How each reporter interprets what she sees is a function of both an event that occurs and the frame of reference within which it is interpreted. For the therapist this is

the combined product of her training, experience, the context within which she operates, and the personal meaning that the family's interaction stimulates in the therapist.

For a family member reporter, the experience may be a function of the person's place in the family, relationship to the presenting problem, attitude about being in therapy, nature of the therapy setting, and attitude toward the therapist.

There Are as Many Realities as There Are Observers

There is not an "objective" single reality. It is a natural inclination for the observer to assume that what she perceives is "the" reality — what really happened. Maturana (1978) and others have cogently argued that there is not one reality but as many realities as there are reporters. Even this is an understatement. Actually there are as many realities as there are reporting states. A therapist may report her impression of the same family session quite differently at different times. This could be due to additional experience with a family, new experiences of the therapist, reflection of personal stress, or many other factors.

The same is true for each family member and for the family as a group. Much of what gets discussed in a family session is the disagreement about what was the reality of a given event. Most of the heat in such discussions stems from the underlying acceptance of the concept that there is only one reality: what is perceived is what is! The therapeutic challenge is to move from differences on who is right and who is wrong to the recognition that once an event has passed the issue becomes how to resolve the different perceptions that family members may carry of the same event.

What practical significance derives from these two developments? Bateson (1972) reminded us that the way the therapist uses power affects what happens. What is observed and how it is interpreted will significantly affect how clients respond. In Keeney & Ross's (1985) view, what we perceive and know is a product of our participation with the observed. Von Foerster (1981) urges us to focus on the observing system as much as the observed.

The impact of the therapist reporter is addressed by Bateson (1972) in his concern with the ethics of observing:

> *In order to "know," one must first make a distinction. The act of making a distinction itself suggests a choice or preference. A therapist's view of a symptom therefore presupposes a particular preference, intent, and ethical base. This perspective suggests that any description says as much or more about the observer as it says about the subject of description.*

Such a view is reinforced by Keeney and Ross (1985) who would not want us to forget that the boundaries of any unit of observation are always drawn by an observer. Observers with their distinctions are always part of the observed.

We need to recognize that a given event has no meaning except through the eyes of the reporter. What events are chosen from all those available in a given situation as subjects for reporting and how such reporting is made are products of many characteristics within the reporter, as outlined previously.

Consider a typical family therapy session. There are a myriad of discrete events that take place in the session: what is said to whom, nonverbal behavior, and sequences of behavior. At various points in the session, the therapist comments. In order to do this, the therapist elects to make certain distinctions about what is important to comment on and when to do it. In so doing, the therapist changes the course of family interaction and what will be observed. Once this happens, the therapist is part of the system. For the therapist to have a significant impact on the family's evolving a satisfactory resolution of dysfunctional relationships, a great deal depends on the therapist's perspective concerning conceptualization of what to observe end how to relate to her observations.

An additional point needs to be made regarding the responsibility of the therapist. The therapist who assumes the responsibility for the family to change defines a working environment that is likely to be more difficult than it need be. This results when the therapist puts herself in a position where she cannot control the events for which she assumes responsibility. This is compounded by the self-delusion that she knows the family's reality and what is best for them. To function adequately, each person has to define in what reality they wish to live and develop the means to accomplish it. This is necessarily the case because no matter how sage the therapist's recommendations may be, the person who lives the reality has to be able to integrate it into her total life space and be comfortable with the "package deal" end products.

Therapists' Assumptions in Making Observations

A contributing factor to problems in making observations is the assumption that the observer makes about what she is observing, whether that observer is the therapist or the family. In this section I explore the relevance of these assumptions.

What a Therapist Can Accomplish in Therapy

The most that the therapist can accomplish is to assist the family in finding their own solutions — to decide whether changes are needed, desired, possible, in whom, when, and how. This position may appear to understate the role and power of the therapist. The power for change is not in the therapist but in her ability to mobilize the resources in the family so that the recommended changes in current family behaviors are appropriate, possible, and worth the commitment it would take to accomplish them. This applies to unmotivated families as well. Their message is that their discomfort in their current situation is not sufficiently great to warrant the perceived risk that would be required to make the change. The successful therapist is one who has been able to assist a family to the position where the risk of changing is more attractive than continuing in the existing situation. This involves helping the family to decide whether changes are needed, desired, possible, in whom, when, how, and at what financial and emotional cost.

The Therapist Is Granted an Executive Function in a Family Interview — Maybe?

The therapist is seemingly granted executive function over a family interaction in the interview by the family on the presumption that it will lead to alleviating the presenting problem. Although this may be done intellectually at one level, families are often unable to implement this on an emotional level, which can easily result in a struggle between the family and the therapist. This was the case with the Starr family. At an intellectual level they presented themselves for help in dealing with their concern about Stuart. On an emotional level they regularly made comments about who should come to a session and what should be talked about. They sounded more like therapists than like a family presenting their concerns and feelings.

At an early part of the initial interview, the following interaction took place:

Mother: We are concerned about Stuart's behavior.

Therapist: Which behaviors are of concern to you?

Mother: He has trouble controlling his temper. The other night at dinner I corrected him on his manners. He got very upset. He started crying, threw his silverware and napkin on the floor, and stormed out of the room.

Therapist: How often does this happen?

Mother: Frequently.

Father: He also has a hard time getting along with the kids at school. The kids tease him and make fun of him when he gets frustrated and cries.

Mother: The teachers say he gets very frustrated when things don't meet his expectations. This often results in his crying and being teased. We are at wit's end! We need help in learning how to cope with his behavior.

Later in the session their emotions got expressed in their competition with me on how to manage the therapy.

Therapist: In our next session I would like to have the whole family attend so that I can get a sense of the family as a whole and Stuart's place in it.

Mother: I don't see what they have to do with Stuart's problem. They're on a very busy schedule. Besides, they won't want to come in.

Father: I think you should see Stuart alone.

Mother: I agree. I think we should wait a while before we have a family session. I think you [therapist] should work with Stuart on controlling his temper first.

Established Patterns of Behavior Will Continue

A significant new behavior usually arouses the conscious attention of the person performing it as well as those affected by it. Once some form of accommodation is made to it, the vigilance originally shown to the new behavior decreases and tends to be replaced by the presumption that it will continue to occur. This is followed by a resulting numbing of sensitivity to it. Ultimately, this numbing can result in such behaviors not being consciously experienced.

In the Starr family it became clear early in our relationship that they had an established behavior pattern of competing with me for how the therapy would be managed. It became clear that this pattern would not readily change after our discussion in which they rejected my perceptions.

It is apparent that their experience with me was equally frustrating when they seemed unable to get me to change my behavior regarding my part in the way that therapy was being conducted. I believe that a significant factor in their terminating therapy was based on their assumption that I would not change.

The presumption that established behavior patterns would continue was also seen in the interaction between Mr. and Mrs. Starr. She had repeated experience with her husband's attempts to minimize her concern about Stuart's problems at school. In one session she started to talk about her anxiety at Stuart's social isolation and his difficulty in dealing with frustration in school. She expressed anger at her husband's lack of interest in talking about the problem. In her presumptions that her husband would continue to ignore her feelings, she did not notice his attempt to speak to her concern.

The challenge to the therapist is to maintain her observational sensitivity for determining what established behavior patterns are relevant to the presenting problems. A related concern is what will contribute to motivation to change. This generally involves skills and knowledge for doing so and the compatibility of the change with what is going on in other parts of their lives.

The challenge to the family is to improve their observational capability, which is necessary to define and understand the persistent destructive patterns of behavior. Such capability is also necessary to understand the motivations of those family members involved in the dysfunctional behavior. This contributes to their ability to finding a way to interrupt them. This is accomplished with the assistance of the therapist if they are not able to so on their own.

The family faces an additional challenge with respect to the therapist. They need to maintain sensitivity in their observations when changes in the therapist's behavior signal to them that she is moving in a direction that appears alien to their goals. Ideally, the family should call such a departure to the attention of the therapist. The resolution of such differences is a significant determinant in building a therapeutic relationship and in providing a safe enough environment to risk attempting changes in behavior.

There Is Only One Explanation for a Given Set of Events

A problem in making observations is the tendency for the therapist to assume that her interpretation is the correct one. This most readily occurs when the collected observations all fit together. What can get easily overlooked is the possibility that there may be more than one explanation for the same set of observations that "all fit together." An added contributing factor is the bias that the observer (therapist or family member) brings to the situation. This stems from a combination of the observer's own experience history and the theoretical base that guides what the reporter observes and how she interprets the data.

In retrospect, I made the assumption that the Starrs' desire to be in control of the therapy was the result of their high achievement orientation and their felt assurance that they knew what needed to be done. When I got some distance from the events, another explanation became evident and more likely. If they had been so sure of the solution to their concerns, they would have implemented it and would not have sought therapy, or if they knew the solution but were unable to implement it they would have made their need known. The more likely explanation was that they expressed their anxiety over their felt failure in coping with Stuart and the resultant helplessness by attempting to be in control of the therapy. This is not unlike the drowning victim who fights his rescuer out of anxiety.

A similar situation is involved in the relationship between Mr. and Mrs. Starr. She assumes that he is not very responsive to her concerns because he does not take them seriously. Discussion of the matter in our session revealed that he behaved in this way because he presumed she would not take his comments seriously or that she would negate them, as she had often done in the past.

Motivations Can Be Assumed from Behavior

A common error in observing and evaluating behavior is to presume motivation from observed behavior. Such inclinations do not adequately take into account the recognition that a variety of motivations may account for a given observed behavior. A mother may reprimand a child for a given behavior because it is uncomfortable for her, is a danger to her child, would displease the father, or would cause problems for other children in family. Failure to determine which motivation was relevant would be a source of misunderstanding and conflict.

In the incident described previously in the Starr family, Mrs. Starr assumed her husband's motivation from how he attended to her concerns. She did not adequately attempt to determine what motivations might account for her observation of his behavior. She presumed that if he had minimized her concern in the past he would continue to do so for the same reasons in the future. Once she took this position, her ability to be open to observations with contrary data was diminished. What she learned in one of our sessions was that he was differently motivated in the therapy setting because he presumed he would get a better hearing with a third party present. He later revealed this to be the case because when the issue is discussed at home it is hard for him to be heard without his views being attacked.

Influences that Affect Observations

Many things affect how observations are made: observation of self by the observer, values and beliefs, theoretical orientation, goals of observation, abilities and resources for making observations, past personal experiences, and past successes and failures. This applies to both the therapist and the family because everyone present is constantly making observations.

The Therapist's Job Is to Be a Careful Observer of the Family

Once the therapist accepts the concept that the observer is part of the system, the field of observation is enlarged to include behavior of the therapist and the interaction between the therapist and the family.

The therapist has an obligation to develop a means for self-observation. This includes awareness of signs of anxiety felt consciously or indirectly through changes in attention span, mood, and body function (tensed muscles or perspiration, for example). An understanding of the source of these feelings can aid the therapist in properly attending to the needs of the family and constructively using her own experiences.

Other areas of potential bias in the therapist include differences in values, personality styles, and cultural background. Another objective for self-observation is sensitivity to when the therapist is unable to hear what is said or fails to observe significant behavior. This is likely to occur at an unconscious level with material that is threatening and out of the experience, interest, or competence of the therapist. A therapist can become aware of such information through review of audiotapes, videotapes, and case records.

For the novice or inexperienced therapist, self-observation is accomplished in the supervision process, which consists of direction in what is observed, how it is interpreted, and how to respond. For the more experienced therapist, this is accomplished through consultation on an individual basis or through peer groups. This is in addition to the need for the therapist to develop the ability for self-monitoring on an ongoing, session-by-session basis.

As noted earlier, it did not take long in my first interview with the Starr family to become aware that I was going to be in for a tug-of-war about how the therapy would be managed. This became clear as I observed the mixed messages between asking for help and trying to direct the therapy. This awareness reminded me that I needed to be especially careful in observing my own behavior as my frustration level increased. I also needed to be careful that my feelings did not bias what I did or did not observe, such as not giving adequate recognition to their behavior that went counter to my feelings.

An example of this point came in the middle of the third interview, when I was pursuing a discussion about Stuart's relationship with his brothers. Mrs. Starr interrupted me and said that she thought we should talk about why he was having difficulty with his peers and what she should do about it. This came after we had been having a tug-of-war about the way the therapy was going. I was feeling pretty frustrated at that point. My first reaction was to dismiss her request out of hand as more manipulation. My observing self was available and led me to take a more objective view. When I did, I could appreciate the validity of her request and proceeded to honor it.

Is the Therapist's Function to Bring about Change?

Implicit if not explicit in family therapy training is that the therapist's goal should be to bring about change or to prevent an undesired change from happening. There is potentially a major problem in this view because it is too easy for the therapist to presume to know how an individual, couple, or family should lead their lives. This is most presumptuous. Such a position carries the considerable risk of the therapist imposing her value system on the clients.

I believe a more appropriate function for the therapist is to assist a family to understand what is happening, define options for coping with the problem and the consequences that go with it, decide the option that best meets their needs, and assist them in learning new coping mechanisms as desired. Such an approach encourages a family to gain greater coping competence and confidence in their own abilities.

Theoretical Orientation

A therapist's theoretical orientation is a value and belief system designed to guide the therapist in what she observes and how she interprets such observations. It derives from the therapist's values and belief system as a person. Added to this is the value and belief system of professional training and experience, as discussed in Chapter 2.

A family seeking help provides a vast amount of behavior for observation. The task of the therapist is to learn what to observe, how to observe it, and how to make use of such observations in a way that will help a family satisfactorily cope with the issues that brought them to therapy.

In the natural sciences the implicit expectation in developing a theory is that if the right variables and how they interact can be identified and understood under all conditions, then the scientist can predict behavior that increasingly approaches certainty. When this happens, the theory becomes a law.

In the family therapy area, we are nowhere near this point. We have ideas about what variables are important and under what conditions. We have ideas about what affects the way people interact. We have become smarter in understanding how a therapist can affect what happens in a family. We have a lot of ideas about the therapy process: when it should start, with what kind of problems it should be concerned, when it should end and how the outcome should be measured. We have a long way to go to develop a unitary theory. Unlike the natural sciences, it may be that there are more ways than one to account for interaction between people.

As in the evolution of any area of knowledge, people develop different ways of accounting for the same phenomena; each orientation develops its disciples and indirectly, if not directly, attempts to proselytize its point of view. Those who become too entrenched in one or the other calling can limit their ability to gain insights from other points of view. This could result because the developer of a particular point of view does so within the framework of her own perspective and talents. A disciple may have other talents that would not have adequate opportunity to develop if the boundaries of a particular point of view are too restrictive.

In the natural sciences the observer has relatively less effect on what is observed, whereas in family therapy the therapist observer has a major impact on what is observed. For this reason a great deal of attention has to be paid to what affects the way a therapist observes and how she relates to her observations. As a result the domain of family therapy is not only about what happens in families but also about how interaction between a therapist and family affects the family's way of behaving — be it to bring about change or to help undesirable change from taking place.

Goals of Therapy

There are two kinds of goals in therapy. One focuses on how to conduct therapy; the other one is on therapeutic outcome. At this point I will discuss the latter.

One goal in a diagnostic session is to determine the nature of the problem in relation to the context in which it occurs. For this a wide-angle lens is needed. This leads the therapist into a process whereby she classifies observed behaviors into four categories (indication a problem exists, indication a problem may exist, there is no indication a problem exists, and indication a strength is present) in the course of interviewing the family. The basis for making these distinctions is guided by the therapist's theoretical orientation, as referred to previously.

Once a diagnosis is made and a treatment strategy is defined, an attempt is made to implement it. Evaluation of the intervention leads to the determination of to what degree problems are resolved and what kind of further therapeutic intervention is indicated, if any. The therapeutic process is characterized by an ongoing process of defining and redefining goals as observations and behaviors warrant. This process will be addressed in more detail later in this chapter.

In my work with the Starr family, the first session was characteristically focused on getting an overview of the family structure and values and in defining problem areas. As I did this, I also classified my observations into the categories noted previously regarding whether observed behaviors may or may not be indicative of problem areas. During this process I also made note of strengths in the family system that may be utilized in the future to aid in resolving dysfunctional areas.

My goals in the first session were accomplished when I obtained a sense of how the family was organized, the nature of the parental relationship, a definition of problem areas and areas of strengths, and a starting agreement with the family on the recommended course of therapy.

It was clear that the Starr family was organized around the emotional energy of Mrs. Starr's priorities. Mr. Starr's needs became a priority when he got sufficiently frustrated to demand they be considered. One of the problem areas was in the very strong emphasis that was placed on achievement in any endeavor and especially in academics. This blinding commitment at times overshadowed any sensitivity to the emotional impact of these expectations. The family did not have the means to cope with the conflicts that resulted.

Areas of strength included a strong commitment to the family, all members were bright, there were significant successes in each of their lives, and all family members were highly motivated to interrupt the existing pattern of expectations and relationships. The parents and I reached tentative agreement in the first session that family therapy was an appropriate way to attempt to resolve the existing family tensions.

The second type of goal in a diagnostic session concerns defining achievable goals based on the nature of the problem and the family's available resources for accomplishing them. These goals are best accomplished when the family participates in their definition.

Limitations and Resources of the Therapist

The limitations and resources of the therapist are a major factor in developing observation skills. This is a product of training and the personality of the therapist. This could include such qualities as the natural ability to communicate, the ability to put people at ease, the use of humor, ability to listen and empathize, and comfort in dealing with affect.

Initially, I felt that I had developed a good rapport with the Starrs because I was experienced, I had had the experience of raising children, I had the right credentials and track record, and I was able to talk in a language and behave in a manner with which they were comfortable. The difficulty in our relationship came when I was not able to find a mutually satisfactory way to deal with their competition for directing the therapy. Attempts to validate their views and include them in developing a therapeutic strategy were not sufficient to achieve the desired goals.

Past Personal Experiences

Past personal and professional — successful and unsuccessful — experiences color the enthusiasm with which the therapist and family approach new situations. The more a current observation draws on the negative experiences of the observer, the more likely that the ability to present an accurate representation of external events will become distorted. This is in addition to whatever biases are introduced by way of the personality and theoretical orientation of the therapist. Past positive experiences can also be a source of distortion when the therapist or family is premature in presuming tht the current situation is like a past successful one. The further presumption to follow is that what was appropriate in that situation is appropriate in the present one.

My first reaction to hearing about the Starr family's problem was that it sounded like so many other situations that I had worked with in the past. I found myself presuming what was likely to be the case. As I realized this, I was able to approach the first interview sensitive to not presuming undue similarity to other families with whom I had worked. This required keeping a sharp distinction between what I was observing and assumptions about what these observations indicated. I could not presume that the father's quiet manner meant that he was not as concerned with Stuart's problem as I had found in many other situations. It turned out that he shared his wife's concerns but deferred to her more volatile and assertive nature to be family spokesperson.

I also had to guard against letting past negative experiences influence how I approached this family. My past experience included many families with well-educated parents who were highly invested in their children's success to the point where the degree of their involvement interfered with achieving the goal they desired. It took some self-discipline to approach the Starrs without letting these past experiences unduly influence my evaluation of them. Had I not done this, I would have missed some important ways in which they differed from other families.

Assessment Process

All therapists have in common that they follow an assessment process as a guide in the way they conduct their therapy. Therapists differ widely in the degree to which this is a conscious process and in the content and method they use in therapy. Families also follow their own form of assessment process. The same principles that apply to how therapists conduct assessment also apply to family members. The primary differences are in the formal training and conscious application of these principles. Therapists will be more effective if they learn to make use of the ongoing assessment processes of family members.

In this section I discuss elements of the assessment process that are common to all therapists. It may also be instructive to the reader to keep in mind how these same assessment processes are conducted by families.

Assessment can be viewed as a circular process in which the adequacy of the outcome is a function of the degree to which each step is properly addressed, as shown in Figure 3-1. The components of the assessment are theoretical orientation, gathering information, formation of hypotheses, designing a test of the hypotheses, making an intervention, evaluation of outcome, modification of the hypotheses, checking the adequacy of the conceptual orientation, and repeat of the cycle until therapy goals are accomplished. I will illustrate this process using the Starr family.

Theoretical Orientation

As noted earlier, a therapist approaches a family with some form of theoretical formulation that provides a framework for determining what behaviors to attend to, how to interpret the observations, and what kind of interventions to make in what form to address therapeutic goals. Theory is a road map that guides the therapist in going from diagnosis to problem resolution. As with any road map, there may be more than one way to reach the same goal.

Historically, family therapy developed in one of two ways: (1) those in the first generation developed it from their own experience and those of their colleagues; (2) over time "schools" of family therapy practice developed that favored a particular way of thinking and conducting family therapy. Each school in varying degrees carried the implicit, if not explicit, message that its approach was *the* way to conduct therapy. Attitudes toward other approaches varied from tolerance to outright rejection.

Eclectic Approach

The therapist operating from this point of view recognizes that there are a variety of ways to do family therapy and that each approach has its

FIGURE 3-1 • *Assessment Process*

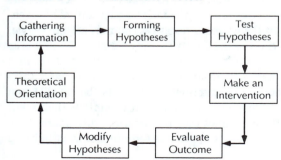

strengths and weaknesses. Such a therapist is also likely to prefer to operate from a "problem-oriented" point of view rather than from a "method oriented" point of view. In the problem-oriented view, the therapist considers what kind of intervention is most likely to be effective in coping with the defined dysfunctional behavior. To do this the therapist has to have a working knowledge of various approaches to family therapy. This can be an overwhelming expectation to the novice therapist as well as to the experienced therapist, when the challenges from a single orientation appear very demanding.

The therapist operating from an eclectic orientation faces the added challenge of not sacrificing depth of knowledge and skill from one orientation to have familiarity with other orientations. Because of this, a therapist can develop the eclectic approach only over enough time to permit acquisition of sufficient depth in knowledge and skill in the approaches that are utilized. Once achieved, this approach gives the greatest latitude for each therapist to creatively develop her own approach that best suits her talents and personality. Doing this provides the evolving therapist an opportunity to achieve her maximum potential as the result of using all her resources.

School-Oriented Approach

The implicit, if not explicit, goal for the school-oriented therapist is to operate from the method-oriented point of view. In this approach, the therapist considers how the preferred orientation and method of doing therapy can best be utilized for the resolution of dysfunctional behavior.

Such an orientation provides a clearly defined theoretical orientation and specified ways of intervention. This approach is likely to be easier to learn because of its more limited focus.

Goal: Each Therapist to Define Her Own Orientation

As noted earlier, a therapist is most likely to be effective when she puts together the best combination of theoretical orientation and a clinical intervention that makes the most use of the personal resources (humor, affective style, interests, etc.) the therapist brings to the family therapy training. What works well for one therapist may not work well for another therapist. I recall a conversation I had with Nathan Ackerman many years ago. We were talking about his unique therapeutic style and how his students "bombed" when they tried to mimic him. The challenge to trainees is not to mimic their mentors but to take from them the principles they demonstrate and adapt them to their own style. The effective use of self is a most important asset in being an effective family therapist.

Therapy as a Partnership

My underlying philosophy in working with families is to view the relationship as a partnership to the degree that families are capable of relating to it. Family members are involved in decisions that affect them, such as who comes to sessions, how long and how often they are held, what is discussed, and how the relationship is structured. When there is a disagreement, I let them know my feelings and the basis for them. From this we evolve a joint way of proceeding. Part of the reason for this approach is that it models ways to respect one another and constructive ways of communicating. This approach is modified to relate to the family's resources and ability to function. There are times when families are not able to relate adequately in a partnership model. Then my approach is modified to what the family needs to help them move to a level of functioning that meets their goals. This could involve a transition period where I function in a parent or executive role in service of modeling and education until they are able to assume these functions themselves.

My orientation starts with information that comes with the referral and with what is gained on the telephone. The first point of interest is to hear what the referral source and the family member calling for an appointment have to say. I am interested in hearing who is perceived to have what kind of problem, who is not perceived as part of the problem by virtue of not being mentioned, and the contextual orientation of the referrer or the parent making the call, that is, why she feels there is a problem and the process they went through in deciding to seek help.

The referral on the Starr family was made by the school psychologist. The mother called because of her concern about Stuart. She described him as an exceptionally gifted child who was having difficulty in school, behavior problems, and difficulty in peer relationships. It was clear that she placed a high value on achievement and was very identified with this child. Her manner of speaking suggested she was anxious, frustrated, and in search of immediate relief. She asked some questions about my credentials and then asked for an appointment as soon as possible. She portrayed her husband as feeling the same way but not with her degree of concern. She did not present any information about her other two sons in relation to the problem. She did not feel that her other sons had any impact on Stuart's problems.

Following the telephone call with the mother, I called the referring school psychologist. She saw Stuart as a very bright child who had trouble with authority and difficulty in relating to his peers. He was easily frustrated and readily broke down in tears, which made him the subject of ridicule by his peers. He dealt with this by excelling in his school. His achievement level was several grades ahead of his age, which provided a further basis for distance from his peers. She felt that the mother was overinvolved with Stuart and that Stuart was in a power struggle with his mother. The school psychologist found the mother very demanding, which was in part fueled by her experience as a teacher and her concern for how his behavior reflected on her.

I gave Mrs. Starr an appointment for her and her husband without Stuart at her request. She wanted to give background information before bringing him in.

Gathering Information

The second step in the assessment process is the gathering of information using the guidelines derived from the therapist's theoretical orientation in four areas: pertinent history, the content of what is or is not talked about, the way it is discussed, and the way in which family members interact with one another.

Content.   The nature of the content is accomplished by the therapist's questions and by comments initiated by the family. Attention is paid to whether the comments relate to thoughts or feelings and to whether a person speaks for herself, is coherent, sticks to the subject, speaks concretely or abstractly, and speaks in a linear or circular manner. Also of interest is how much insight a person has; whether they speak in first, second, or third person; sensitivity to other people's feelings; the kind of defenses used by the family members; areas of conflict; nature of coping mechanisms; areas of strength; self-concept, quality and quantity of relationships, how well they are able to directly address their concerns; and time orientation focus in past, present, or future.

A therapist's theoretical orientation determines whether and to what extent these content areas will be addressed. In contrast, family members' comments are likely to be guided by their comfort level in addressing matters of concern to them.

Therapists differ in the degree to which they focus on defining the kind and degree of pathology. This is also the case in how they approach the assessment of strengths and the nature of the life space in which a family functions. The therapist should not make the assumption that what is dysfunctional to her will be considered dysfunctional by the family or vice versa. The way in which a therapist attends to these areas of assessment can lead to the definition of different therapeutic contexts, which in turn will affect the kind of information that is obtained. Such considerations support the contention that a therapist is not outside the system but both an observer and participant within an evolving definition of a therapeutic system.

Process.   How informtion is communicated carries its own messages. Tone of voice, use of silence, facial expressions, gestures, eye contact, body movement, volume of voice, pacing of speech, and being late or missing appointments are some of the ways in which information about a family is communicated.

This process is not limited to how the family communicates. In the therapist's concern with obtaining a diagnosis and developing a treatment strategy, it is easy to forget that the diagnostic process is a circular process. During the therapy session, the family is making its own ongoing diagnosis of the therapist and evolving a determination of to what extent they can trust her and whether they choose to continue the relationship. The family develops its own orientation and criteria for how to observe and interpret what happens in their life space.

The therapist who becomes too complacent or self-absorbed runs a high risk of losing the family. When this happens the message is that in the therapist's concern with the clinical process, she lost touch with the family.

Interaction Patterns.   The ways in which family members interact with each other and with the therapist offer information that is much harder for a family to censor than what they talk about. In one family I noticed that before a child would answer one of my questions he would look at his mother as though to gain permission to speak and/or to look for cues as to how to guide his comments as he proceeded. In another family situation, I was curious to notice how the subject matter of discussion changed every time the father stroked his ear. It was informative to note in another family that I was interviewing in middle of February that no one bothered to remove the snowsuit of a 2-year-old child. The child appeared to make a quick survey of parents and siblings and without much hesitation made a beeline for an older sibling and held her hands up as a nonverbal plea to have her snowsuit removed. The parents appeared oblivious to the process.

In the Starr family, it was evident from the beginning of the first interview that Stuart and his father had difficulty making eye contact with Mrs. Starr when the content was emotionally charged. This observation gave a preliminary suggestion that the mother was the emotional hub in the family. This was confirmed as the therapy progressed.

Also noteworthy is how the therapist and family initially jockey for position. It takes many forms both for the therapist and the family. Each stance carries its own message. The ways of relating for the therapist include the omniscient authority, the parent, the teacher, the consultant, the judge, the friend, the colleague, and the enforcer. Each of these has its own implications for the therapeutic process.

A family may initially also present themselves in a variety of ways, including: "Everything is OK; we're not sure why we are here," "We're falling apart; fix us," "We are all OK except we have one bad apple; please fix her," "The outside world is treating us unfairly; make it better," and "We are embarrassed to be here; we should be able to solve our own problems."

It becomes the therapist's job to decide which way of defining the relationship is most appropriate for developing a constructive working alliance. The Starr family presented a combination of "We are all OK except we have one bad apple" and "We should be able to solve our own problems." I attempted to present myself as a consultant to competent people who needed some outside perspective. Part of the challenge I faced was dealing with their ambivalence toward these problems. Intellectually, I believed they wanted to be addressed in the way that I presented myself. At an emotional level they wanted me to fix things for them while at the same time resenting that they felt that way.

Ways of Obtaining Information.   One strategic choice open to the therapist is whether to gather information based on the present or on the past. The orientation followed is largely a matter of theoretical inclination. Therapists who are committed to the psychoanalytic view that present conflicts are the expression of unresolved conflicts from childhood are likely to proceed with collecting historical data. Therapists with interactional theoretical orientations are more likely to concentrate on data gathering in the present but are not necessarily limited to it.

I have found both orientations to have relevance. I integrate them by starting with a current focus and moving to a historical focus when it becomes clear that dealing in the present appears to be handicapped by past experiences. I go back and forth as needed until the desired progress in the present is achieved.

Information in either vein can be obtained in a number of ways.

Observation. Therapists need to develop acute observational skills. Milton Erickson attributed much of his success to his ability to be a keen observer of his patients. He would attend to their breathing patterns, facial expressions, changes in muscle tone, complexion, body language, and eye contact. Careful attention to such considerations and the way they change in interaction with family members or in reaction to the therapist can provide useful information that might otherwise be very elusive. People are far better able to censor their verbal behavior than they are their non-verbal behavior.

Interviews. This is the most familiar way to obtain information from the family in a variety of possible subunits, such as the marital couple, children alone, parent(s) and a child, a subunit of children, and members of the extended family or significant others. Which one or which combination of these interview units is utilized depends on the circumstances of each presenting situation.

In the Starr family, my preference was to meet with the whole family as the primary treatment unit because I felt that the underlying problems were issues that involved all family members, not just Stuart. The parents resisted this idea beyond the evaluation session. They did not feel that the other children should be involved. Although I did not agree with their evaluation, I went along with it with the expectation that, as in the past in similar situations, the merit of involving other family members would become apparent. At the time, I felt they needed to experience that their feelings were being respected.

This is another example of a basic principle of the therapeutic process. As noted earlier, therapy is a partnership that requires some constructive collaboration between partners. As in any partnership, when the needs of one partner are not adequately acknowledged and responded to appropriately, the partnership fails. Common to partnerships is that power is not equally held. What is important is that whatever form the relationship takes it can be successful only when the working relationship is acceptable to both parties. The therapy situation is no different. One of the goals for family therapy is to help a family learn how to use power constructively. Therapy provides a safe environment where these skills can be learned and practiced, given that the therapist provides a constructive model.

A significant obstacle in the Starr family therapy was the difficulty we had in developing a way to share power regarding how the therapy should be managed. Our difficulty in finding a mutually satisfactory solution was a significant factor in the breakdown of the therapy.

Some therapists believe that there is a danger in significant involvement with subunits because it may suggest bias or convey messages of rejection. Although I concur that insensitivity to the significance of who is interviewed with what frequency and in what context can present problems, I believe that the benefits that can be achieved outweigh the problems. In practice, there is likely to be little if any such difficulty if the therapist properly attends to keeping family members informed regarding how and why such choices are made and to addressing to any concerns that may arise. The danger is less in who is seen than in each family member feeling that she is treated respectfully.

Interview with Collaterals. Interviewing significant others of the family can be a valuable resource. They might include friends, family doctor, minister, school personnel, and neighbors. Such interviewing may be done with or without family members present. Which way it is done is a function of the individual situation and is not likely to present a problem as long as appropriate family members are consulted and feel that their wishes are properly addressed. In the Starr family, my interview with the school psychologist was most helpful in learning how they related in the school situation and was done with the parents' consent and support.

Testing. This is another way of gathering information and may be done on an individual basis or as a group, depending on the nature of the instruments involved. Testing has the important advantage that it becomes much harder to censor responses and give what a person may feel is the "right" answer to protect the desired image.

Another advantage of testing results from the norms upon which a test has been validated. The norms provide a basis for comparing the obtained test results against the population on which the test was developed. One potential complicating factor is whether the norms are appropriate for those being evaluated, such as people from different cultural groups.

Common personality tests used for evaluating individuals include the Rorschach, the Thematic Apperception Test (TAT), and the Draw-a-Person test. These tests have been adapted for family use. Margaret Singer adapted the Rorschach test for family use. The TAT is also adaptable for family use. Howells (1984) developed a family-oriented test similar to the TAT. Kwiatkowska (1967a, 1967b) was a pioneer in developing techniques for utilizing family art evaluations.

One of the concerns in the use of testing is the timing and sensitivity with which tests are applied. One of the problems that can occur results from the feeling of some clients that the testing is intrusive in that the client is giving information without being aware of what it is that she is providing. The potential for this being a problem is minimized when the therapist adequately orients clients.

Structured Tasks. A structured task is a prescribed activity that the therapist asks the family to do during the interview or as homework for the purpose of obtaining information on family dynamics, for giving the family a new understanding of their relationships, and/or for enabling the family to experience new ways to relate to one another.

A prescribed activity in the office may take various forms that include such activities as genograms, drawings, building blocks, games, role plays, and use of batacas (foam rubber bats). These activities are described in more detail in Chapter 11.

Homework activities may take any form: family meetings, family outings, trips to cemeteries, visiting relatives, vacations, games, and many others, limited only by the imagination of the therapist. Therapists have used such activities in different ways. Erickson was most innovative in sending individuals and couples on all sorts of excursions with no clear understanding about why or how they were supposed to relate to the task. He left to the client determining the meaning to be derived from the experience. Such exercises included climbing Squaw Peak, visiting a botanical garden, and talking to relevant others to gain a particular perspective. One point of these experiences was to discover and tap resources within themselves and in so doing challenge erroneous notions they had about themselves.

Minuchin and associates (1967) were innovative in the homework tasks they gave to families. Such activities gave families new perspectives and led to developing different ways to relate to each other. Haley (1971) and therapists operating from a strategic orientation use homework assignments to bring about change in family interactions through techniques similar to Minuchin's. In addition, they make use of paradoxical assignments. One such form derived from Erickson's (1973) work is where the therapist prescribes the symptom to help people gain control of symptomatic behavior.

The Bowenians utilize the technique of coaching their clients in how to relate to family members with whom they have unresolved issues. They are sent on assignment to relate to such people in ways they have not adequately achieved in the past.

I have presented some ways in which homework assignments have been utilized by some of the pioneers in the field. Disciples of these and other mentors have adapted these same principles in many innovative ways. The underlying key issue in the use of any homework assignment is that its effectiveness depends on it being based on a clear understanding of the family's problem(s), sensitivity to what they are able to handle, and tasks designed to provide some form of corrective experience. Assignments that do not meet these criteria are likely to set up the family for a failure experience and impede therapeutic progress if not handled appropriately.

Questionnaires. Self-administered questionnaires are another way to obtain information. They can be useful as a way to obtain background information and to identify problem areas for further evaluation in an interview. For some therapists and clients the use of such instruments is experienced as intrusive and disruptive to establishing rapport. As is the case with any way of relating, if the therapist is uncomfortable in what she is doing, it is likely to be ineffective, if not disruptive.

Family Photo Album. Another way of obtaining useful information is through the family photo album. Having the family take the therapist on a trip through the family's photo history is usually welcomed and can be most informative. It provides information about the past but also provides a forum for observing how the family members interact when such history is brought into the present. There may be a logistical problem in going through the album when there are a number of children, especially young ones, present. When this is not manageable as a group, it may be desirable to go through the photos with different family members. The receptivity of family members and the nature of the material give clues on how far to pursue this effort.

Talents and Accomplishments. Another source of information is through the talents and interests of family members. It generally is very informative to have clients bring in samples or recognition of their accomplishments, such as trophies, certificate of merit, and scout badges. This might include paintings, poetry, writings, crafts, photos awards, or any manner in which they may have expressed themselves. Such an activity often provides a perspective on a person's resources that might not otherwise be noticed. At times people may be initially reluctant to share this part of themselves.

However, once they get started, they often thrive on it and may allow the therapist to get to know them in a way they might not otherwise show.

Showing one's wares is done most easily on a one-to-one basis. When a family can have a "show and tell" as a unit, it can provide an opportunity for family members to discover one another in ways they hadn't appreciated. Such an exercise also has potential for illuminating rivalries and competence issues.

Evaluation of Obtained Data

One of the problems of gathering clinical data is how rapidly great amounts of information are accumulated. Each therapist faces the challenge of how to organize the material for greatest utility. As noted earlier, the theoretical orientation of the therapist largely determines what data are collected, how information is organized and evaluated, and what issues will be addressed.

Often families present a myriad of concrete symptoms. Coping with them can be overwhelming and confusing if an attempt is made to address them at face value. Therapy could become endless. The therapist's task becomes much simpler when she processes information at two levels: the manifest meaning of what is presented and what symbolic issues are expressed in the symptom. When this is done, it quickly becomes evident that core issues get expressed in a variety of seemingly different problems. When the therapy is focused on the core issues, significant progress is made in dealing with different manifestations of the same underlying problems. An example of this would be the different ways that dependency issues might be expressed.

Forming Hypotheses

The theoretical orientation becomes the basis for formulating hypotheses in which background information is utilized to account for symptomatic behavior. This may include hypotheses about what is happening and why it is happening. The hypotheses may relate to individuals, interaction between individuals, the relevance of the content area of family concern, the relationship between the various hypotheses.

In the case of the Starr family, I identified themes around achievement, control, management of affect, and others. From the initial information I formulated a number of hypotheses: the mother turned to Stuart for affection she did not get from her husband; the mother's emphasis on achievement in her children and Stuart, in particular, served the purpose of dealing with her own sense of inadequacy; expression of anger by both parents was equated with their felt incompetence. The consequences of these and other hypotheses led to the additional hypotheses that Stuart's unique circumstances provided the family with an outlet and focus for their tensions that served the purpose of avoiding confrontation with other issues. This only further impeded Stuart's developmental progress by placing on him intense academic and social pressure that he did not have the maturity to handle.

Designing a Test of Hypotheses

The next step in the assessment process is to test the formulated hypotheses. The therapist draws upon whatever collection of theory, tools, and techniques is in her repertoire — interviewing, exercises, homework — to test the validity of her hypotheses.

Ideally, the evolution of a hypothesis should be followed by a strategy for obtaining the necessary information to test the hypothesis. This process is enhanced when there is good clarity in what information will be collected and how it will be evaluated.

In the case of the Starr family, the initial interview was with Mr. and Mrs. Starr at her request. She thought it would be useful to give some history before an interview with Stuart or with the family as a unit. By the end of the phone contact I had begun to formulate hypotheses about Mrs. Starr's need for control, her insecurity, and the apparent overinvestment she had in the progress of her son Stuart. These impressions were enhanced during the first interview with Mr. and Mrs. Starr. In addition, it became clear that there were undefined difficulties in the relationship that were getting expressed through pressure on Stuart. Based on these impressions, I gained further information through the use of genograms, interviews with parents separately and together, family interviews, and interviews with Stuart alone and with each parent alone. I also gave homework assignments for the family. Mrs. Starr supplied me with a variety of test materials and reports from Stuart's school.

Test of Hypotheses

Part of the process in formulating hypotheses is to determine what data are needed to determine the validity of the hypothesis. Once these data are obtained, they provide the basis for evaluating the data's adequacy. If the hypothesis is supported by the data, it sets the stage for the therapist to design an intervention that will stimulate the family to modify their behavior in some form of corrective action.

If the hypothesis is not supported, then the therapist needs to review the accumulated data to formulate a new hypothesis and repeat the evaluation process described previously.

Critical to an adequate test of a hypothesis is to have a clear operational statement of what constitutes an outcome that would support or negate the hypothesis. Failure to do so could lead to a false-positive or false-negative outcome and the distortions that would result from it. An additional hedge against misinterpreting the data for testing a hypothesis is to attempt to account for the data that do not fit the hypothesis.

Designing and Implementing an Intervention

An intervention is a deliberate action or a decision to act or not to act by the therapist with the goal of providing a family with an experience that contributes to correcting satisfactorily dysfunctional behavior in the family system. Interventions are most likely to be effective when they are based on a clear understanding of the family context, the resources available in the family, the motivation to change existing patterns of behavior, the part that the symptomatic behavior plays in the functioning of the family system, what would be the consequences of interrupting existing patterns of behavior, and on whom.

Other factors that contribute to the success of an intervention are a trusting relationship with the therapist and the timing and validity of an intervention that is not too complex or time-consuming. Also relevant is that it does not interfere unduly with the clients' other priorities.

Trust and Timing of Intervention.   An intervention that is brilliantly conceived may well be ineffective, if not disruptive, if it is not introduced at a time when the family is likely to be receptive to it. An important part of receptivity to giving up old behaviors or trying new ones is to feel sufficient safety both with family members and with the therapist. Safety involves being able to risk looking bad or showing vulnerability and trusting that it will not be used against the person or otherwise negatively reflect on her or them. One of the difficulties I had with the Starr family was my inability to help Mrs. Starr feel safe enough to be able to show her vulnerabilities.

Face Validity of the Intervention.   No one is likely to participate in a behavior if it does not appear to have some form of face validity for some purpose. If I had told Mrs. Starr not to pay attention to Stuart's peer relationship problems because it was a developmental phase that would pass, she would have considered me incompetent and terminated therapy at that point. However, if I recommended to her that she change her way of behaving toward Stuart in a way that would make sense to her, then there would be a reasonable likelihood that she would follow through and respond accordingly.

Such a situation developed, which illustrates the matter of timing and face validity of interventions. This occurred when the Starrs expressed their frustration at not being able to cope with Stuart's temper tantrums when he got frustrated. Before I suggested an intervention, we discussed the context in which such events took place: when such behaviors occurred, under what circumstances, and with what impact on all concerned. When all of this was understood and the parents were satisfied that I adequately appreciated the situation, I made my recommendation of alternative ways they could relate to the situation. The underlying idea was to relate to Sturt's pain rather than focus on his behavior. They accepted the recommendation and implemented a way of relating that greatly reduced the problem.

Complex or Time-Consuming Interventions.   An intervention that is too complex or time-consuming has a high likelihood of failure, independent of how appropriate it might be from other considerations. When an intervention is too complex for the resources of the family, it is likely to heighten tensions related to competence in a system that is already having difficulty with this issue. A family is likely to attack the intervention rather than risk igniting further conflict. This would undermine their sense of safety and confidence in the therapist.

Interference with Other Priorities.   An intervention that is too time-consuming runs the risk of interfering with other priorities. This would make it easy to avoid investing the necessary energy in the intervention. This is likely to be especially appealing when the intervention requires facing an issue that has been avoided.

Involvement of People Unrelated to the Problem.   An intervention that involves people who are not originally presented as part of the problem is likely to be met with resistance. This difficulty is diminished when such inclusion is introduced within the comfort level of the participants and has the prospect of contributing to the elimination of the problem. A case in point with the Starr family was their resistance to including their other two sons in therapy. Their initial reaction was that they were not relevant to the problem. Although they reluctantly went along with the recommendation, they never accepted it. This became apparent in the various ways they undermined full participation in family meetings. My failure to adequately address their underlying concerns was another contributing factor to the premature termination of this therapy.

Evaluating the Outcome

Carefully developed hypotheses and brilliantly designed and implemented interventions can be fruitless exercises if they are not followed by a careful evaluation of the intervention outcome. It becomes easy to miss doing this in a family that is good at sliding from one issue to another, especially when the tension level rises. A therapist who succumbs to this can readily feel she is overwhelmed and losing control of the therapy. A related problem is when the therapist is too willing to take "flights into health" too readily.

Part of evaluating the outcome is determining whether the intervention occurred as intended and how the information gained from it reflects on the hypothesis. To what extent is it supported? Another aspect of such an evaluation is what new hypotheses are suggested by information gained from the intervention that was not anticipated.

Modifying Hypotheses

The results of an outcome evaluation lead to another round of hypotheses for various reasons: the original hypotheses were not supported, they were supported in part or whole and this led to new hypotheses based on the new findings, and the formulation of new hypotheses based on data gained from the intervention.

As hypotheses multiply from whatever source, the therapist is challenged to interrelate them in a way that can result in developing priorities for what issues will be addressed and in what manner. This is not a static process but one that is ongoing as new information and progress are achieved in the course of therapy.

When hypotheses are not supported, consideration should be given to evaluating to what degree an appropriate theoretical orientation has been utilized in formulating these hypotheses. In the Starr family, I was primarily operating from a strategic orientation. As we struggled in the therapy, it became clear that I needed to enlarge the conceptual base. I concluded that I needed to draw from a psychoanalytic frame of reference to deal with some mourning issues. I was in the process of doing this when therapy was terminated.

A GUIDE TO CLINICAL APPLICATION

Every therapist utilizes some theoretical frame of reference that guides what she observes and what questions she asks. The following questions are presented as a guide in how to apply the material in this chapter.

1. What concepts do you use as a basis for how you conduct an interview?
   a. Decide what theoretical orientation you will be using.
   b. If you are using an eclectic approach, review the major concepts in each approach to family therapy, and list those that have particular meaning to you. This should be done at two levels: conceptual and process. The same process applies from a single theoretical position.

   Do the same for other conceptual areas such as personality theory, group dynamics, individual therapy, group therapy, and sociology.

    c. Organize the accumulated concepts in some personally useful form.

  2. Develop operational guidelines for how you monitor the way you affect what you observe. This includes being aware of your own reactions and how they affect your observations.

  3. Monitor the following considerations in your interviewing:

    a. Make a clear distinction between your goals and the family's goals.

    b. Determine what goals are realistic for the situation.

    c. What kind of relationship does the family want — partnership, authoritative, or some other form?

    d. Pursue the explanation that best accounts for the observed data.

    e. Keep a clear distinction between what is observed and your interpretation of what is observed. Be especially careful about assuming motivations of clients or allowing them to do that with each other.

    f. Be aware of your own biases.

    g. Define goals for therapy that reflect compatible views of you and the family.

    h. Your approach to therapy should reflect knowledge of your own resources and limitations.

    j. Monitor what kinds of countertransference get stimulated with each client.

    k. At some point accumulated observations lead to hypotheses, which should not become conclusions until they are sufficiently tested using the process outlined in Figure 3-1.

  4. Consider the following in designing interventions:

    a. Sufficient trust was developed.

    b. Timing is appropriate.

    c. Intervention has sufficient face validity.

    d. It is not too complex or time-consuming.

    e. It does not interfere with other priorities.

    f. It does not involve people unrelated to the problem.

Summary

The challenge to all therapists is to have some organized way for determining how to help a family find a suitable resolution to the problems that brought them to therapy. This chapter presents a framework for understanding behavior, what to observe, how making such observations affects what is observed, how to account for what is observed, how to change existing patterns of behavior, how to evaluate the outcome of such efforts, and how to proceed on the basis of such information. In so doing, the therapist is able to keep a clear focus on where she is going and how she is going to get there and know when she has arrived. Attention is also addressed to how family members utilize their own form of the observation and assessment process and how it gets expressed in determining how they relate.

CHAPTER FOUR

Social Entity Concepts

I found the need to develop a generic reference for all levels of social groupings because they share common characteristics. I adopted social entity *(SE) as this generic reference.* This concept is the subject of this chapter.*

THEORY

Each individual is part of many social entities such as a couple, family, extended family, friendships, organizations, and some form of work relationship. Reference to the term *social entity* (SE) simplifies communication by permitting the use of the generic term rather than specifically listing each social entity to which a comment refers.

In this chapter I discuss three of the major social entity concepts in the family system: individual, couple, and family concepts. I describe the dimensions that I find useful in accounting for how a social entity gets defined. This includes the structure of the social entity concept, skills for assessing itself, coping skills, and impediments to the development of healthy social entity concepts. I also illustrate how the social entity formulation is useful in clinical application.

Part I: Definition and Dimensions of Social Entity Concepts

A social entity develops a concept of itself when it has enough history and experience to play a significant role in the lives of its members. This concept refers to the constellation of characteristics that each social unit has in itself.

Such a conceptualization provides a way of tracking how characteristics of relating in one social entity are expressed in another social entity and how

**Throughout this chapter and in the following chapters, the terms *social entity* and *social unit* are used interchangeably.*

they affect one another. For example, how does the self-concept of a person get expressed when he is part of a couple or participates in starting a new family unit? How a couple defines itself provides data on how they are likely to define themselves when they become a family and how they will define their concept when incorporating the extended family. These social entity concepts are circular in their impact on one another.

Families are composed of a variety of social entities that include individuals, parents as a couple, parents singly and/or jointly in combination with one or more of the children, the family as a whole, and one or more family members with one or more members of the extended family, especially grandparents. Each social entity defines its own unique characteristics, implicit or explicit, and how it will function. Each parent defines the relationship with each child in a unique way. When parents are together with one child, that relationship develops its own identity and operates differently with each child. The more significant a social entity is, the more clearly and broadly defined it will be, both to the participants and to others. These social entities vary in degree of development from little definition for a relationship that is casual to one that is very well defined, as in the case of a significant other. Knowledge of such relationship history is a potential resource for the therapist to draw on.

The social entity concept also permits an assessment of the degree of differentiation and maturity of the various existing SEs in a family. This yields information on available resources and problem areas. Significant relationships are defined by the presence of substantial data on the various dimensions of the social entity concept. This is in contrast to social entities which are only vaguely defined. When a SE, such as two siblings, has an ambiguous definition, it suggests that the relationship is a low priority for the participants involved. I find the concepts useful in defining the relative significance of the social entities in a family system and how they contribute to health or any existing dysfunction.

Social Entities Function in Multiple Modes

Each person has memberships in many social entities and is always engaged in juggling priorities regarding which social entity will be dominant at a given time. When a person is behaving in a given social entity context, they are referred to as operating in a particular mode, for example, individual, couple, family, parent-child, or boss-employee. This conceptualization provides a systematic framework for mapping the nature and quality of the various relationships in which a person is involved. In this book I am limiting the focus to family relationships.

Other concerns involve how flexible and adaptable family members are in shifting between different modes. How well are family members able to develop ways to function compatibly in one mode in the context of another? Can a husband pursue his interest in golf in a way that is compatible with couple needs? Can an adolescent deal with developmental issues of independence in a way that is compatible with being a cooperative member of a family? A related question is how conflict is managed when circumstances require operating in two incompatible modes at the same time. This would be the case when a mother wants to pursue a career that requires full-time work and at the same time wants to be home when her children come home from school. It is a similar dilemma for the father who has to choose between all-out investment in succeeding in his occupation and wanting to spend a lot of time with his family.

A person functions well when he feels comfortable in functioning compatibly in different modes such as husband, businessman, and father. Problems develop when a person functions in one mode in a way that interferes with relating in another mode and is not able to resolve the conflict. This is the case for the wife whose husband resents the amount of attention she gives her children when he is at home.

At times such problems develop when inadequate attention is given to how behaving in one mode will affect another one. An illustration is the man who is so absorbed in his work that he does not give consideration to how such behavior affects other modes, such as individual, husband, and father. Therapy would serve the purpose of helping him realize the implications of operating in conflicting modes and how to achieve greater compatibility between them. Such therapy might involve couple or family therapy, depending on the particular circumstances.

Static and Dynamic Dimensions of Social Entity

The social entity concepts under discussion can be described along two dimensions: a relatively static dimension that describes the nature of a social entity concept that endures over time, and a dynamic dimension that describes the way in which a social concept is subject to change (social entity concept balance).

A social entity, like any other viable entity, needs adequate nurturance to continue to exist in a healthy and satisfying manner. Breakdown or divorce occurs when the social unit concept balance is in a negative state over a sufficiently long period so that it drains whatever positive factors existed in the social entity concept. A marriage that has a positive core couple concept as a result of years of a reasonably good marriage will be able to endure a conflicted relationship (negative couple concept balance) to the degree that it does not overshadow the existing positive history. At some point the positives that held the marriage together become diluted by the persistence and intensity of the negative couple concept balance, which ultimately becomes a negative core couple concept and the end of the marriage unless the relationship is changed.

Self-Concept

Development of the Self-Concept
Self-concept refers to the composite way in which an individual perceives and values his physical, emotional, intellectual, and personality characteristics. The self-concept is an inner, evolving perception that takes place in a kaleidoscope of multiple interpersonal contexts. It evolves from a socially undifferentiated core at birth. With time and experience, a person undergoes an evolving sense of identity as a separate person. This may be positive or negative and is one of several entities shared with others, such as family, friends, and co-workers. Over time a positive self-concept results from identification of patterns that are functional and reinforced and become firmly established. Resistance develops to accepting information that contradicts the status of the existing self-concept. Dysfunctional self-concepts develop in a similar manner, evolving from consistent negative input. Such a self-concept, once entrenched, tends to develop behavior patterns that reinforce the negative sense of self.

Self-Concept Balance
Thus far I referred to the core component of the self-concept. The other component is the more transient part of the self-concept, which is a reflection of a person's immediate life experience. The relatively stable core of an established self-concept is regularly exposed to the ebb and flow of current life experiences. These experiences support the existing self-concept, raise questions about it, contradict it, or are irrelevant to it. The degree of impact these experiences have will depend on their intensity, degree of relevance to the existing self-concept, and the extent to which they support or contradict other current experiences.

When such experiences are primarily positive, they provide support for continuing the self-concept as is. Experiences that raise doubts about the definition stimulate evaluation regarding whether the current definition of the social entity needs to be modified. Experiences that contradict the existing self-concept create pressure to modify the self-concept or get expressed in defenses aimed at avoiding or negating such input. The degree to which such modification is likely to take place depends on the anticipated consequences that would result from such modification and the person's belief that the modified self-concept is justified and can be maintained.

I refer to this dynamic aspect of self-concept development as the *self-concept balance*. The state of a person's self-concept at any given point in time is the composite of the core self-concept and the state of the current self-concept balance, which will be the result of the difference between the self-enhancing and critical experiences.

A person's core self-concept may be one of inadequacy and unworthiness. However, he may be feeling pretty good about himself on a given day because of successes at work or other experiences. The half-life impact of such experiences may be very short because of the strength of his core negative self-concept. If the core concept is too negative, positive experiences are short-lived. This diminishes the likelihood that one success will be sufficiently sustaining to increase the possibility of other successes. It also affects whether a person has enough faith in his ability to persist through disappointment until success is again achieved. A core concept changes only after the transient self-concept develops some persistent valence and where the core concept is sufficiently permeable to accept and integrate new information.

In summary, the elements of self-concept balance are: nature of the core self-concept, the balance of incoming positive and negative life experiences, and the ability of the person to process these experiences and enable modifications to take place.

Couple Concept

Development of Couple Concept

The foundation for a positive couple concept is laid by the quality of the self-concepts with which two people enter a couple relationship. Success in this effort depends on each participant's ability to move from a life-style that focuses around individual needs (individual mode) to one that includes a balance between individual priorities and joint priorities (couple mode). The challenge is to be able to give up some degree of autonomy in exchange for the benefits of an intimate relationship.

This is a demanding experience under the best conditions. Traditionally in our culture, the transition was somewhat easier for women because in Gilligan's (1982) terms women are raised to have relationships as a priority. If they did not have careers or aspirations, then developing a couple relationship became all the more important. Such a situation might also carry with it greater economic dependence. These conditions may predispose women to being more receptive and adaptable in making the transition to a couple relationship.

According to Gilligan (1982), the situation for men presents a different challenge. A man's first priority in our culture is to achieve and secondarily he wants to have a relationship. For some, this achievement orientation spills over into at least the early years of dating, where achieving sexual conquests supersedes quality of relationship. As social maturity increases, a man approaches the prospect of a couple relationship with ambivalence that includes giving up the freedom to roam and the threatening prospects of taking on major responsibilities for the benefits of companionship, intimacy, and the desire to perpetuate his family heritage. When a man and woman bring to the couple relationship strong self-concepts and adequate social skills for negotiating a relationship, they have a good probability of evolving a mutually acceptable relationship.

People who enter a couple relationship with poor self-concepts are likely to feel they have little to offer and to feel needy. As such, they will compete for resources from which to negotiate a couple relationship. The result is apt to be an undesirable couple relationship fraught with many difficulties and the likelihood that the relationship will not survive or will continue with negative reinforcement to the negative self-concepts of the individuals involved.

Couple relationships can be described on a continuum. At one end is the couple who become fused to the degree that they do not function as individuals unless it cannot be avoided (Figure 4-1). For such couples their primary priorities are defined within the couple relationship. Individual priorities are minimal and secondary to the relationship. At the other extreme are those couples who for all intents and purposes live parallel lives. They essentially live their lives as they did when they were single but function as a couple when it is mutually convenient. Between these two extremes is a continuum in the balance between when the priority is to function as a couple (couple mode) and when functioning as an individual (individual mode) is the priority. I refer to this as the I-we balance.

Couples differ in their flexibility regarding the state of the I-we balance. For some couples, once the balance is defined, it remains relatively intact. For other couples the balance changes as developmental needs and circumstances warrant. One common source of difficulty is when a mutual

FIGURE 4-1 • *Couple Concepts*

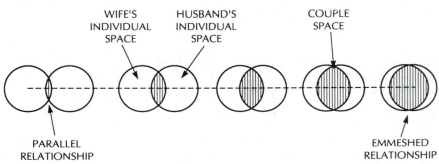

definition of the I-we balance changes so that the couple differ in their definition of this balance or change it in a different way. When one member wants to change the nature of the balance while the other wants to maintain the existing balance, the member who wishes to change is often viewed as creating a "problem." A common goal of therapy is to reestablish a mutually acceptable I-we balance.

Among the dimensions that define the couple relationship and the accompanying I-we balance are compatibility of values, tools for resolving conflict, and a mutually agreeable balance between their having individual identities and a collective identity.

Couple Concept Balance

The process between a couple in the evolution of the couple concept balance is parallel to that of what occurs in the self-concept balance. It has an additional layer of complexity that develops from the interaction of two self-concepts. From these two self-concepts emerges a core couple concept — the way each person views the nature of the couple relationship. Two people may view their relationship as basically good but at a given point may view it negatively because the couple concept balance is in a negative state, that is, the impact of the negative interactions outweighs the positive ones. In such a situation the strong core couple concept would likely lead to "kissing and making up," guided by the underlying belief in the relationship. However, this would not be the case if the negative couple concept balance continued for an extended period. Eventually, the weight of the continued negative imbalance would affect the core couple concept and also would affect their respective self-concepts. When this happens, the prospect for divorce increases. The kind and amount of imbalance that it would take to change the core couple concept would be the product of the history of the relationship and the nature of their individual self-concepts. A couple concept that is chronically in a negative state is likely to result in divorce, except where conditions exist that do not make this a viable option such as prohibitions against divorce, economic considerations, for the sake of the children, or the couple is locked into a sadomasochistic relationship.

Family Concept

Development of Family Concept

The family concept derives from the meaning that members of family place on identifying as a member of their family. Dimensions for defining a family concept include meeting aforementioned criteria for a couple concept, adequacy of generation boundaries, compatibility in values for parenting, ability of parents to work together effectively, respect for various family subunits (individuals, marital couple, and other appropriate constructive alliances), and freedom to have constructive emotional and intellectual expression.

The family concept is not static. It changes as the developmental needs of its members change. The couple become a family with the birth of their first child and develop a family concept for that unit. This concept will change with changing needs of both the parents and the child and the addition of other children.

Families in which the children are all of one sex are likely to have different family concepts than when the children are of both sexes. This is particularly the case when one parent has some special investment in having children of one sex. A father for whom perpetuating the family name is important will have a strong investment in having a son. For him having all daughters will have a different meaning than if there were children of both sexes.

The addition of other adults (grandparents, aunts, uncles, cousins, etc.) who live with the family will have an impact on the family concept. The degree to which this takes place depends on the strength of the parents and the degree to which they work in concert to achieve and maintain a desired family concept. If they abdicate this role by giving undue influence to another adult living with the family, such as a grandparent, then the family concept is likely to be unstable and negative, resulting in low affiliation by its members.

Another level of family concept derives when the nuclear family is viewed in the context of the extended family. Each person brings to the start of a new nuclear family the family concept model from their own nuclear family of origin.

Part of what determines the degree to which these different levels of family concept emerge is the degree to which they develop permeable boundaries that permit new information, values, beliefs, and opinions to be considered in a manner where differences can be respected and appreciated. This permits an emerging identity to another level of family concept that compatibly encompasses the culture of both families.

Each member of the family may have his own idea of what the family concept means to him. When there is a good deal of agreement across family members on the definition of the family concept, then there is likely to be a strong sense of cohesiveness in the family. Under these conditions family members are likely to have a strong influence on one another. When the reverse is true, the family members are likely to have weak identification with the family unit and be less responsive to family pressures.

Family Concept Balance

This concept parallels that of the individual and couple concept balances, with the added complexity that occurs when more people are involved. Each member of a family has his view of the family concept, with varying degrees of priority that such concepts play in his life. The nature of the family concept balance will depend on the state of the self-concept balance of family members, the state of the couple concept balance of the parents, and the concept balance of all other significant family subunits. Contributing to the quality of the family concept balance is how all family members are coping with their respective developmental sequences and how compatible they are with each other. A family that has a good family concept balance when the children are small will not necessarily have it when they are adolescents unless the family was able to adapt the family organization and their way of relating to the changing needs of both adult and child family members.

Members of a family vary in the priority that the various social concepts play in their lives. It may be the case that a father's first priority is his self-concept, the second the family concept, and the third his couple concept (marriage). The mother's first priority may be the family concept, the second her marriage, and third her self-concept. One child's self-concept may come first, followed by the family concept, and his third being his maternal extended family concept. The quality of the social entity concepts and that of their respective social entity balance concepts are interdependent. The degree to which this happens depends on the priorities attached to social units within the family relative to the priority attached to other influences outside the family, such as friends, organizations, and occupation.

One social entity has priority over another to the degree that its needs take precedence when there is conflict between the two. A person's first priority may come as a member of a family and secondarily be his self-concept. In such a situation a person gains his primary sense of identity from the family. He may be very proud of such membership and function well in that context. However, he has a low or uncertain sense of value when viewed as a separate individual. A man may have a low sense of self as an individual but have a very different sense of self as a marine. A man may feel that his responsibility to carry on the family tradition supersedes his individual desires. He may gain a sense of identity from such a posture, whereas he may have a low sense of self separate from it. Understanding the nature of the priorities by which a social unit concept gains and values identity is a valuable consideration in developing any intervention strategy.

Dynamic Equilibrium

Thus far in this chapter I discussed the social entity concepts of individual, couple, and family and the way in which they are maintained or change. These concepts do not exist independent of one another. Each social entity concept is functioning in parallel with other SE concepts (individual, couple, family friend, worker, etc.). When this state of ongoing activity continues within and between the various social concepts with no significant change in them or in the relationship between them, I refer to this as a state of dynamic equilibrium.

A challenge to a therapist is to determine whether and in what ways the state of equilibrium can be modified in pursuit of therapeutic goals. This involves determining where the sources of energy are that affect the family unit and how they are best utilized in therapy.

One consideration is to determine how the interaction between the momentum of past history and the quality of a current experience will affect future behavior. Past history provides the context for how each new experience is perceived: When a current experience is consistent with past experience, then the past context and perspective are reinforced. When the present experience conflicts with the past, then the social unit makes a decision inadvertently or by design as to whether the present experience warrants a change in the dynamic equilibrium of the resulting shift in the social entity concept. When the current experience neither reinforces nor conflicts with past experience, it provides an opportunity for experimentation until the behavior becomes identified as alien or compatible and reinforcing to the existing state of dynamic equilibrium and aimed at modifying it.

A marital couple may view their marriage as being in a chronic state of minimal satisfaction. At this level it has the appearance of staying the same over a period of years and hence has the appearance of being static. Closer scrutiny reveals that this chronic state has been the result of different content situations that on balance get experienced at the same level of minimal satisfaction. In such a situation the couple develops a context for viewing their relationship as one where they do not function very well as a couple.

Suppose the couple has a good weekend together. Consciously or unconsciously, they make a determination about how to interpret the event in the light of the historical context in which they have perceived the relationship. Does it represent a happy accident under ideal conditions that could not be achieved on a regular basis, or does it suggest that there have been changes in one or both of them that can lead to a qualitative shift in how the relationship is viewed? Should the latter possibility be the case, there is the challenge whether the new perspectives can be nourished and survive in the face of the historical momentum of a negative past. Therapy often facilitates experiencing the relationship in a more positive light. At a more critical level, it provides an atmosphere where these new perceptions can be nurtured and protected from being crushed by the negative momentum of the past until enough confidence is gained by the couple to realize that the existing context in which the relationship is defined can be modified to a more positive and enduring one.

Thus far I defined the general nature of the self, couple, and family concepts. I will now provide a more detailed description of social entity characteristics.

Part II: Characteristics of all Social Entities

Structural Characteristics

Purpose
Each couple or larger social entity exists to serve a purpose that may or may not be the same for each of its participants. A husband and wife may have quite different reasons for having a child. It may be to keep the family name alive, help with the farm or business, someone to love and be loved by, a means of economic survival as in the case of some welfare mothers, the joy and opportunity of raising one's own offspring, or for someone to care for them in their old age. The purpose behind the conception of a child is part of the context that affects how a child evolves into an adult.

The formation of a couple social entity serves its own purposes, which may include to legitimize the conception of a child, an arranged marriage by the parents to serve their needs, the thing to do, for economic or social position, desire to have a family, expression of love, and companionship. The purpose for which the couple relationship starts, at least initially, influences what form the social entity takes.

The formation of the family social entity derives from the needs of the individual and couple entities. Its success depends in part on the degree to which the parents have compatible purposes in mind for having a family. Also necessary is the availability of necessary emotional and material resources. This includes the ability to adapt to changing needs and maintain a balance between individual, couple, and family needs.

The extended family has a less clearly defined function beyond being a support system for the emerging families that derive from it. In the later periods of the life cycle of the family of origin, the second generation has the added responsibility for care of the first generation, as their ability to care for themselves diminishes.

Values, Beliefs, and Goals
Necessary to the effective functioning of any social entity is appropriate definition of values, beliefs, and goals. Such definition provides focus and direction for how a social unit is to function. These concepts are discussed in detail in Chapter 5.

All social entities have implicit or explicit goals. When goals are explicit, it increases the likelihood that they are more clearly defined. When goals are only implicit, there is a greater likelihood of problems developing because inadequate attention was paid to defining the process for accomplishing them. A couple may have the explicit goal of having a close, caring relationship and the implicit goal of having children some day. When the implicit goal is discussed and turns out not to be shared, problems result. This happened with one couple and resulted in their getting a divorce because they were not able to resolve their differences.

A social entity that does not have meaningful implicit or explicit goals is likely to be unstable and prone to be dysfunctional. This is the case of the individual who does not develop an occupation and some definition within that occupation. This is likely to result in occupational wandering and affect the quality of the self-concept as well as affect the developing couple concept.

Expectations

Implicit in holding values and in setting goals is that it will lead to satisfactions of one kind or another. These might include financial success, recognition by others, attainment of political office, or success in a relationship or as a parent. The realization of such expectations reinforces maintaining currently held values, beliefs, and goals or modifying them in ways that maintain the same outcome.

Failure to achieve the desired expectations becomes the basis for modification of values, beliefs, and goals. I saw a man who was promoted to an executive position. He came to this position with a value system tht involved relating in a direct and forthright manner when he had a conflict. He was sorely disappointed to find out that performing in this way in his new position did not work well. He concluded that he had to revise his value system regarding how to relate in his position. He modified his values in how he should communicate but not in the kind of executive he wanted to be.

In another situation an adolescent young man had a clear sense of how he should behave to be socially successful. This involved behaving in a macho manner. He quickly discovered that doing so violated his own ethics regarding respect for others and that rather than achieving social success it had the opposite effect. This led to a change in values and behavior that led to greater success.

Membership in Social Entities

Usually membership in the couple entity is determined by mutual choice of the participants. Exceptions to this are marital entities that result from the pressure to legitimize a pregnancy or from an arranged marriage.

Membership in the family social entity occurs either by birth or by choice. The latter option includes such cases as adoption, foster care, or informal inclusion of some person outside the nuclear family unit, such as an aunt, a grandparent, or any other person significant to the family.

The decision about who will have membership or who will be excluded from the family is a function of how it is organized. In paternally or maternally dominated families, one parent will be the primary decision maker. In other families, parents jointly decide on family membership. In some families, there are circumstances under which family members may be excluded. An extreme case is in the Orthodox Jewish family where a child is considered dead for marrying a person of another faith. This is marked by shiva, which is a ritual for mourning the dead.

Social Entity Boundaries

The psychological boundary of the social entity is defined by the strength and permeability of the boundaries that separate one social entity from another. Strength of a boundary is observed by the degree to which a social entity is able to implement the values it holds, especially when challenged. Permeability is the degree to which there is open communication across the boundary with other social units.

A family defines what behavior is required and prohibited in relating outside the family. This includes manners, dress, and ways to behave that will reflect family values. In extreme cases, a family may isolate itself as was the case with one family I saw. They said, "we don't care what other people say or do; we live by our own principles. The world is an evil place. We take care of our own and have as little to do with other people as possible."

More common is the situation where the boundary varies in its permeability from areas where it is closed to areas where it is very open. In one family the boundary was very closed on matters having to do with religion and sex. It was very open about subjects such as politics, science, and economics. The boundary was semipermeable when it came to the expression of affect. There were times when the expression of feelings was permitted. The same applied to accepting the expression of feelings from others toward the family.

Time Frame

Social entities vary in the length of time they exist. For the individual the time frame is birth to death. For the marital couple the time frame starts at marriage and ends with the death of one partner or by divorce. Also to be considered is the distinction between the formal and informal beginning of a social entity. In our present culture two people can live as a couple without the formality of marriage. At the other end of the spectrum, many marriages cease to function as a viable couple long before the formality of separation or divorce is entertained.

The boundary is less clearly defined for the family. It has a clear start with the birth of the first child. The ending time of the family entity is less clear. It could be when the last child leaves home, or it could end when only one member of the family survives. It gets further complicated in the case of abortion, merged families, divorces and living situations that involve a child rotating where he lives. In many families it is a state of mind in the form of an emotional connection independent of physical separation.

Wartime provides a striking example of how an emotional connection can be made when a parent is thousands of miles from his family. Parents who are off to war are felt very present through letters and through constant reference to how they would feel about what is happening in the family on a day-to-day basis. In contrast, a parent may be in the same room with the rest of the family, yet his presence is not felt because of his disengagement from what is going on around him by virtue of sleep, absorption in TV or newspaper, work, or other interests. I often see families where people regularly guided their thinking and feeling by memories of how departed family members would think, feel, or behave.

The absence of a clearly defined time frame for the existence of a social unit is often a source of conflict. Parents often want to extend the time frame for children to be part of the family unit beyond that which children desire. In our culture the press for a college education often facilitates the process, even when both parents and children are reluctant for the child to leave the family unit.

In recent years, the time frame of the family social unit developed an added dimension. Adult children who left the family return for one reason or another, usually related to needing economic support of the parents. When this is more than a brief interlude, it requires a redefinition of the family social entity concept that includes adult children. Such a unit is a challenge to parents and children to define what limits they will set regarding such dependence. Such a definition is further complicated when dependent grandparents are involved.

How Information Is Processed

Social entities vary in how they process information. There are people whose behavior is guided primarily by their feelings, whereas the behavior of others is guided by their intellect. In between are those social units whose behavior is guided by greater balance between their emotions and intellect. One couple I saw approached managing finances from both a cognitive and emotional point of view, but the cognitive considerations usually prevailed. The reverse was usually true with regard to children. They would consider both perspectives, but the emotional considerations usually prevailed. Life becomes more complicated when spouses operate on the assumption that they are communicating on the same level (emotional or cognitive) when they are on different levels.

Social entities vary in the level at which they process information. At one end of the continuum are those who relate primarily at the concrete level. At the other end of the continuum are those entities who relate at a more symbolic level. In one family the parents were arguing about the wife's expenditures on clothes. One source of the argument was that the wife was justifying why she needed to make a particular purchase. The husband was less concerned about the specific purchase than that it symbolized an irresponsible attitude about the use of money. Resolution was accomplished when the two issues were dealt with separately. They considered the merits of the specific purchase and worked on their differences in values about how decisions were made in the expenditure of money.

Another dimension that affects how social entities process information is on an impulsive-obsessional dimension. At the impulsive end, a social entity has a quick and often reflexive response. At the obsessional end is the social entity that needs to check out every detail and every assumption before any action can be taken. In one couple the woman tended to operate impulsively on the basis of instinct, whereas her husband was not likely to take action until he was sure about the validity and accuracy of his information.

Adequacy of Resources
Clarity in definition of values, beliefs, and goals will be of little value beyond academic interest if the resources for acting on them are not available. A parent may have a very clear concept of these characteristics and have read all the child development literature, but be of little avail if the parents do not have the emotional capacity to implement what they understand. The desire to have a family is a significant problem if the financial resources to support it are not available and if the emotional resources to invest the time and energy to develop and maintain relationships are not there.

Valence
Valence refers to the attraction that being a member of a particular entity has for the individual holding it. A parent or child who is not happy being a member of a family is in a very different place than the person who is happy to be a member of that social entity. The functioning of a marriage when a husband or wife wants out is going to be poor. In contrast when there is a desire to be a part of a social entity, its members will exert great effort to ensure that the unit functions in a satisfactory manner.

Rules
Rules provide the framework for how the business of the social unit is conducted to achieve its defined goals. This works best when the rules are designed to facilitate accomplishing mutually agreed-upon objectives. Problems develop when following the rules becomes too much of an objective

in itself rather than a means of accomplishing some function. Ideally, rules are modified as changing circumstances warrant.

When children are young, parents establish certain rules for their behavior appropriate to their age. This is in service of facilitating their development consistent with their level of physical and emotional maturity. If the rules for their behavior do not change to take into account changing needs and abilities, conflict and problems are likely to result. Problems will also develop when the rules do not provide the necessary structure and protection that children need at all stages of child development.

In a couple relationship, the rules take the form of agreements on how both spouses will participate in the relationship. It takes the form of a division of labor — who will shop, cook, pay the bills, and mow the lawn. It also takes the form of how a couple will cope with disagreements and express anger and affection.

Priority

Every person is a member of multiple social entities: individual, family, friendship, organization, and others. Each unit carries with it a level of priority in importance. With that level of importance goes the allocation of emotional and other resources necessary to function effectively as a member of that entity. When the demands of membership in various social units exceed the available resources (time, money, energy, etc.), choices have to be made regarding how these will be allocated. This in turn may precipitate a crisis that results in changing how a person functions in an existing social entity or, if necessary, terminating membership in it. When a man feels that meeting the needs of his spouse would not permit him to pursue his career in his desired way, he may ultimately choose to leave the relationship or set more modest career goals.

When both parents are working, they may not have sufficient time to spend with their children. When this becomes unsatisfactory, either out of choice or because of a child getting into trouble, one or both parents may be pressed to make changes in their priorities. This might involve spending less time at work and more time with family. The price of shifting priorities may threaten their membership in their work social entities but is consistent with giving the welfare of their children a higher priority.

Often such situations are managed by the secondary breadwinner, usually the mother, who would change her behavior. When this is not done with adequate consideration, it becomes a threat to the stability of the couple and family social entity.

Assessment Skills of the Social Entity

Critical for the healthy functioning of any social entity is the ability for self-assessment and implementation into corrective behavior. One of the skills necessary to accomplish this is the social entity's ability for developing a realistic assessment of its strengths and weaknesses.

Defining Source of Social Entity's Self-Worth

Necessary for appropriate assessment is that judgment of self-worth is made by the social unit itself rather than being defined primarily by other social entities. I frequently come across people in clinical practice whose assessment of themselves is primarily determined by how other people see them, with little or no value given to their own feelings. If their own assessment is contradicted by others, then they tend to accept their evaluation to be the reality. Ideally, a person receives input from others and evaluates it for whether it appears valid. If considered valid on its merits, then it is accepted. If not, it is rejected.

Ability to Separate Personal Performance from Outcome

Too often people do themselves a great disservice by basing the evaluation of their performance primarily on the outcome of a given event, where the outcome was determined by the combined performance of multiple people and events. What gets overlooked in such cases is that a given social entity may have performed very well, but the outcome was a failure because of other people or circumstances. When this happens, at best reinforcement for appropriate behavior is lost. At worst, the social entity views the negative outcome in the distorted sense of a personal failure.

Oftentimes in therapy, couples come with different levels of commitment to the process. I saw one such couple where after much struggle the couple decided on divorce. The woman, who was more committed to the therapy, felt that it was her failure because of the impending divorce. What she did not adequately appreciate is how hard she worked and how much she matured in the process. Although she intellectually appreciated that she could not make the therapy work all by herself, emotionally she held herself responsible for the outcome.

Ability to Learn from Experience

Many people operate from the frame of reference that making a mistake constitutes a failure. When this happens and their daily behavior is guided by fear of making mistakes, their lives become constricted and fear-ridden. For these people, the therapeutic challenge is to recognize that intellectual and emotional growth occurs by exploring new behaviors. Such exploration into new territory is likely to contain negative experiences. The goal is to help them realize that the problem was not in the negative experience occurring but in not learning from the experience so that it is not repeated.

Assessment of Strengths and Weaknesses

An important skill for a social entity is its ability to assess its strengths and weaknesses realistically. Such assessment is necessary to determine whether a social entity has the needed resources to accomplish desired goals. The high school senior who aspires to go to Harvard with a C grade point average sets a goal that is doomed to failure. The consistent practice of setting unrealistic goals that do not adequately reflect the strengths and weakness of the social unit feeds the development of negative core self-concepts and negative self-concept balances.

Coping Skills

Expression of Affect

Feelings are the lifeblood of any social entity. They are positive when needs and desires are met and negative when they are not. A healthy, functioning social entity depends on a balance between the generation of feelings and the way they are expressed. This involves the ability to accept and give positive and negative constructive expression of feelings.

Each social entity defines the rules and mechanisms under which feelings are expressible and the means through which they may be expressed. Families of Mediterranean heritage are commonly characterized as being emotionally expressive both in words and in gesture. The reverse holds true for white Anglo-Saxon Protestants, who frequently are seen as very controlled and limited in their emotional expression. I frequently hear adults describe their families of origin as, "We didn't express feelings in my family. My parents never argued. You were expected to keep your feelings to yourself."

In one family a woman was sent to her room as a child when she expressed anger. She was told not to come out until she could smile. In other families expressing what you feel when you feel it is the norm.

Management of Conflict

Conflict exists in any social entity as the product of competing needs, either within the social unit or between social units. A person may be in conflict on which job to take or how to terminate a relationship. A couple may be in conflict on how money is managed or how to discipline the children. A family may not be able to decide where to spend their vacation or how chores should be shared. A person may be in conflict between pursuing his career and his commitment to his family.

An easy temptation in coping with conflict is to focus on blaming self or others on why the problem exists. The net result of such efforts is only to add additional problems to those that already exist. A more constructive alternative is to focus on how to manage or cope with the conflict. Such an orientation carries the prospect that resolution is possible. An approach for managing conflict is described in Chapter 6.

Division of Labor

All social entities have a number of maintenance tasks to perform that are necessary to its continued existence. In the family, this includes such items as food, shelter, and income to purchase what they cannot do for themselves. Support for one social entity by another includes such situations as the child or elderly grandparent who lives with and is supported by the family, a divorce where a parent provides support for the other parent and children, a family on welfare that is financially supported by the state, and an agency that delivers meals for elderly people who are not able to cook for themselves.

In an intact family, the way the division of labor is managed plays a major role in determining its emotional and physical survival. The probability of a healthy functioning family is increased when each member contributes to the maintenance of the family in a way that feels equitable and appropriate to all concerned. One family that I worked with where this was not the case involved a mother who did not ask for or want other family members to participate in such tasks as laundry, cleaning up the kitchen after dinner, or helping with housecleaning, yet she complained about how overburdened and unappreciated she felt. The father was annoyed that his teenage son did not work during the summer, yet did nothing to see that he did. As a result, the children developed a sense of entitlement that contributed to heightened family tensions.

Part III: Impediments to Social Entity Functioning

In the last section I described the dimensions that define social entities. There are a number of impediments that interfere with a social entity's ability to achieve its goals, which I describe in this section.

Definition

An *impediment* is any act or event that interferes with the desired development or functioning of a social entity. It can occur in two forms: the absence of desired or needed events and the occurrence of disruptive events.

Absence of Desired or Needed Events

Financial Security

Money is a major consideration in determining the life-style a social entity will follow. The source of this money has great impact on the definition of the social unit. When the parents in a family are able to provide the necessary funds to support the family, they are able to define the character of the family social unit as they feel appropriate. When they are not able to provide sufficient funds and it becomes necessary to gain them from other sources, such as from welfare or from extended family, then the character of the family social unit changes. The ability of the nuclear family social entity to define its own integrity becomes diluted by the degree to which an outside funding source dictates how the family will live.

In the case of a family on welfare, its ability to determine how they will live, especially with respect to how money is spent, is directly influenced by a social agency through its representative, a social worker, and indirectly by policies defined by local, state, or federal governmental policies, WIC, school lunches, food stamps, housing policy, etc. This happens when a state sets standards and rates for medicaid, which are implemented by a local agency. In such situations the integrity of the family social unit boundary becomes somewhat blurred to incorporate the funding representative.

Similar problems of control over a nuclear family social entity occur when the funding source is from an extended family member. The absence of the formal authority when funding from a social agency is involved can be both an asset and a liability. It is an asset in the absence of all of the rules and regulations that are involved and in not having to deal with strangers, usually of different social and economic backgrounds. The liability can occur when the funding source attempts to dictate the life-style the family being subsidized follows and there is no recourse for appeal.

The pressure of making ends meet financially can also affect the definition of the family social unit when both parents are required to work for the economic survival of the family. The absence of both parents requires the introduction of substitute parenting, be it in the form of baby-sitters, day care, or extended family members. In any event this changes the character of the family social entity. Each of these participants adds his own contribution to the definition of the social entity. A child who is in day care five days a week has to integrate membership in two different "families" — the nuclear family and the day care family. The experience can be negative or positive, depending on the degree of contradictory messages that are received or the difficulty in resolving them.

When a divorce occurs, there are three social entities instead of the original family social entity: the children and the parent who has custody, the other parent and the children, and the terminated yet influential reference point of when the family was intact. Usually what was in the past becomes a reference point for how current life situations are experienced. This could be a positive or negative reference point. It could be positive when a child experiences the absence of parental fighting after the divorce. It could be negative when positive times with the absent parent are no longer possible the way they were. Financial security becomes an issue when money becomes a means of dealing with power and conflict issues that were likely the result of the divorce in the first place. This is commonly the case when the parent who does not have custody, generally the father, is the sole or major provider for children and the parent who has custody.

Emotional Security

Emotional security is necessary for the parents to meet their own needs and adequately perform their parenting functions. It is also necessary for children if they are to mature physically, intellectually, and emotionally and gain the skills necessary for adulthood.

One of the distinguishing characteristics in families is the power that goes with blood ties. Family members have little in common and have little affection for one another, yet the connection through blood generally commands a loyalty to one another not achieved under other circumstances. In one family I saw a man was very different from his brother in values, lifestyle, education, and success in career and social relationships. In addition, he did not like the kind of person his brother was. When his brother got in trouble, as he often did, my client was always there to help him. His explanation was simple: "He's my blood! He's my brother! I have to help him out when he gets into trouble." In one case a couple disputed an issue with the wife's brother. The husband felt that his view would not get proper consideration because "blood is thicker than water."

Feeling Loved and Respected

An essential ingredient for a healthy and strong self-concept derives from growing up in an atmosphere where one feels appropriately loved and respected appropriate to age, need, and stage of development. A mother who showers her child with love to make up for her own deprivation will give her child a distorted sense of self that will interfere with his normal emotional development. A father may do the equivalent by catering to and protecting his children from adversity so that they will not have to live the hard life he did. In so doing he deprives them of the life experiences that were significant to his success. Children from such experiences grow up with an inadequate sense of self as adults. One man put it very succinctly: "I don't want my children to suffer the way I did. So I make things easy for them." This came out in a family discussion around a young adult who had a poor self-concept, had experienced a series of repeated failures in school and work, and got into trouble with drugs.

Another aberration often occurs when a woman is not able to get what she needs emotionally from her husband and turns to her child to make up for the deficit. While less common, the reverse also occurs. This tends to parentify the child and interfere with the child's normal developmental path.

Fathers tend to have other ways to deal with their deprivations. One way this occurs is in families that develop traditions over the generations. This could be the case of a long history of lawyers, doctors, military officers, or a family business that was passed from generation to generation. The need to maintain the tradition can and often does result in a child having a great deal of pressure placed on him in service of this goal. Failure to achieve this goal can lead to rejection. In such cases, the individual is not permitted to have his own identity. Love is conditional and secondary to fulfilling a responsibility to family.

Another aspect of emotional security is expressed in the way parents permit their children to interact with the outside world. It starts with providing them with the necessary social skills for how to relate to other people and how to protect themselves physically and emotionally in the world outside the family. This starts at the age they begin to relate to other children and continues until the time they leave home to be on their own. Some children who develop a negative self-concept grow up with an attitude that the world is a dangerous place and that the only place they are safe is at home. Other children who grow up with a good self-concept have the necessary tools to pursue a happy and productive life.

Problems develop when the parents deal with their own deficiencies by not permitting or making it difficult for their children to leave home. This may take various forms: economic dependence on their earnings, guilt for not caring enough about family and thinking too much about their own needs, withholding economic or emotional support a child may need in leaving home, or dire predictions about the world outside of the home.

A key to competent functioning comes from learning the limits of what is possible, safe, and appropriate behavior. A child learns this as he grows up and learns to trust that his parents will protect him. A child quickly learns not to trust a parent who does not protect him from emotional or physical harm. This applies not only to small children but to children of all ages. The adolescent who is given too much freedom may enjoy it at one level but feel abandoned at another level. In one family a young adolescent girl talked about how helpful curfews were in helping her deal with social situations she was uncertain about how to manage. A young child learns to be reluctant to take risks partially as a result of growing up in an environment where the desire to take risks (e.g., participate in sports) was shrouded in terms of overtly emphasized possible dangers.

Physical security provides another basic contribution to emotional security. Having a safe and stable place to live becomes a cornerstone of a child's emerging identity. Addressing this need permits attention to be paid to other concerns. Many a child has found a sense of safety under his bed, under the covers, or in his closet. The importance of physical security extends throughout life. I frequently hear about adult children who are upset when parents wish to change the character of the room they grew up in long after they have left home. It appears that keeping their rooms the same offers a sense of emotional security as though it is always a place they can retreat to if needed.

Physical security also includes physical and emotional safety. This involves the absence of physical or sexual abuse. It also concerns freedom from inappropriate expectations for physical labor, either in terms of the kind of task or in the amount of work expected. I saw a single-parent family where the oldest child was expected to work part-time after school, have child care responsibilities, and help with meals and housekeeping. One difficulty in this situation was that this 13-year-old child was very competent and her mother functioned at a bare minimum level. The child's competence and her desire to take care of her alcoholic mother ultimately resulted in her emotional collapse.

A child who gets sexually abused by the father and is not able to enlist the mother's support and protection feels abandoned, betrayed, and mistrustful. To add to the problem, such children often feel that there must be something wrong with them for feeling the way they do.

Modeling

Modeling is the most potent form of teaching. Parents who provide a poor or contradictory model can inhibit or distort the appropriate development of a child's self-concept. All too common is the situation in which parents provide a contradictory model in which they do not practice the behavior they preach to be the standard they wish their children to follow. In such situations the message that will be followed is the behavioral one. Tensions develop when the parents expect the child to follow the verbal expectations, not what the parents demonstrate. Other kinds of tensions develop when the parents offer contradictory models of behavior. When both parents have an investment in the child modeling their behavior, the child is caught in a no-win situation.

In one family situation, the mother felt it was important that children be encouraged to express their emotions. The mother modeled such expression on both intellectual and emotional levels. The father disagreed with his wife. He felt that children should be respectful of their parents and keep their anger to themselves. However, he modeled different behavior and felt perfectly comfortable venting his anger when and how he felt it.

CASE ILLUSTRATION

I will briefly describe the major social entities of the Dale family at the beginning of therapy and then illustrate how the use of this concept is applicable in a clinical situation.

Overview of the Dale Family

The family consisted of Aaron, 42; Annette, 40; Charles, 17; and Carol, 15. Aaron was an executive in a real estate company who was completely absorbed in his work. He rarely was home for dinner and often worked on weekends. Annette worked as a restaurant hostess before her marriage and continued to have a variety of part-time jobs. Her major interests were in being a mother and homemaker. Charles was an average student in high school. He was bright but not very interested in academics. His major interests were cars, sports, and his social life. Carol was a high school sophomore. She was a good student and very absorbed in her social life.

Aaron and Annette were divorced after 16 years of marriage. The marriage occurred because of an unexpected pregnancy. The manifest reason for the divorce was a gradual buildup of emotional incompatibility between Aaron and Annette, which started with Aaron's felt obligation to "do the right thing" regarding the pregnancy. Shortly after the divorce, Annette moved to Florida to be near her family of origin, and he remained with the children in the Boston area. They stayed with their father because they did not want to disrupt their schooling and friendships.

The major significant social entities in this family at the time of entering therapy were the individuals, the couple, and the family.

Presenting Problem

Aaron and Annette originally sought therapy around marital problems. The major issues centered around her anger and feelings of abandonment because of his overinvolvement in his work. She also was bothered by his emotional distance from the family and the marriage in particular. They also had strong differences in how to relate to their children.

After a few months it became apparent that the hidden agenda in seeking therapy was to find a way to end the marriage. A divorce resulted, and the focus of therapy became mourning the marriage and adjustment of the family to the divorce. I will illustrate social entity concepts as they apply to the father and the family social entity.

Characteristics of Aaron's Self-Concept

Structure

Purpose
There were no significant circumstances related to Aaron's birth.

Primary Values, Beliefs, and Goals
He valued doing well in his profession, being a good father, and having a satisfactory marital relationship. He believed he was doing well in his work, was marginal as a father and was not doing too well in his marriage. His goals were to maintain his work performance, improve his relationship with his children, maintain an amicable working relationship with his ex-wife, and find a new mate.

Integrity and honesty were values he believed he accomplished. He also valued dealing openly and directly with his feelings and was aware he was not very successful at it. One of his goals in therapy was to improve his ability to be more aware and expressive of his emotions.

Other primary goals were success in his career and an improved relationship with his children. Before his divorce, he tried to make his marriage work. He continued to work in pursuit of all three goals.

Expectations
During the marriage, Aaron expected Annette to be more sensitive to his work needs and more respectful of the way he managed the expression of his feelings. He expected his children to be closer to him.

Boundaries
Aaron's work required that he be quite precise. In that environment he set very clear boundaries. He set limits on when and how he could be interrupted and carefully weighed information he received from other people. During his marriage he had a way of tuning out Annette when she would go after him emotionally. He was fairly open in his communication with his children, both in accepting information from them and in giving information to them.

How Information Is Processed
His primary mode of processing information was at an intellectual level. He had a long fuse and would relate information on an emotional level only when he had waited too long to address his accumulation of frustration. He tended to focus more on the conceptual level than on just the concrete issue of the moment. He was more inclined to be analytical than impulsive. When

Charles abused a curfew, Aaron focused on the principle that Charles did not honor his commitment rather than focus on how late he was.

He was aware of his difficulty in relating to what he was feeling and his inability to express his feelings appropriately. He was surprised to find out how often he did not know how he felt.

Adequacy of Resources
He had the necessary intellectual resources to meet his needs. He was deficient in matters that involved affection and intimacy. His major deficiency was the common occurrence of not being aware of his feelings. This frequently happened in confrontations with his ex-wife.

Valence
How well he took care of himself physically and emotionally was of major importance to him. Competence in his profession was very important to him.

Rules
A guiding implicit rule was to avoid emotional confrontations, particularly with his ex-wife. He did not spend money he did not have. He had to finish his work before he could relate to his family.

Priorities
Taking care of his personal needs was a high priority. During the course of the marriage, his work was his major priority, followed by his children and then his marriage.

Assessment Skills

Judgment from Within
Aaron usually functioned on the basis of his own judgment and tended to be resistant to accepting input that went contrary to his views, especially from his wife. During much of the marriage he was adamant and clear about what he felt was Annette's contribution to the marital difficulties, and he was resistant to any information to the contrary from any source.

Judgment of Personal Performance as Separate from Outcome
He evaluated his own performance on whether the desired outcome was achieved. It was difficult for him to value his performance when the negative outcome was not the result of his performance. An example of this was the occasion when he felt very good about the way he made a sales presentation. When his company did not get the contract because of other considerations

that had nothing to do with his performance, he felt he had failed. His own worth was solely defined by the outcome.

Ability to Learn from Experience

At times his rigid stance interfered with his ability to learn from experience. When his sense of competence became threatened he eventually was able to be more flexible and open to new learning. During the marital therapy that occurred prior to the divorce, he became aware of his difficulty in knowing how he felt and in expressing his feelings. As that awareness was integrated, he became more open to receiving constructive feedback.

Assessment of Strengths and Weaknesses

He had a realistic sense of his strengths and his weaknesses. He viewed himself as being bright, loyal, caring, committed, and tenacious in anything he undertook. He was aware of his difficulty in dealing with anger and his tendency to avoid dealing with his feelings. He also felt he tended to get too absorbed in his work at the expense of other priorities in his life.

Coping Skills

Expression of Affect

He did not feel comfortable expressing and receiving positive or negative feelings that showed any significant degree of intensity. He had little of it growing up and never acquired the ability to act differently.

Conflict Management

He was comfortable and competent in coping with problem-solving situations on an intellectual level. His ability to negotiate differences decreased as he became more upset, which was expressed in his becoming more entrenched and distant in his positions.

Division of Labor

In the case of the individual, division of labor refers to how well a person divides his energies to accomplish his defined goals. Aaron did not do very well in this area. He was overinvolved in his work to the degree that he did not devote the time and emotional energy necessary to develop the desired relationships in his marriage and with his children.

Getting and Giving Constructive Feedback

Aaron generally did well in giving and receiving constructive feedback on an intellectual level. However, receiving negative feedback did not necessarily mean that he would utilize it. He tended to be reluctant to change his views once he was committed to a particular point of view.

Impediments to the Development of His Self-Concept

Absence of Desired Experiences
He did not have a home environment that gave him the love and support that he desired. He had little support for developing his own identity.

Presence of Undesired Experiences
One major impediment to the evolution of his self-concept was his relationship to his parents. His mother was intrusive, demanding, and hypercritical. His father was largely absent, removed from daily events, and distant.

Another significant impediment was the unexpected pregnancy that resulted in an unwanted marriage, which he dealt with by distancing himself into his work.

Self-Concept Balance
The part of Aaron's self-concept that related to work was generally quite positive. He characteristically had many more positive experiences than negative ones. That portion that was related to his marriage was generally more negative than positive. The portion related to his children was more varied. Prior to the divorce, it was more negative than positive. This occurred for two reasons: a spin-off of the tension with his wife and his frequent unavailability because of his work. The net result was that he did not feel too good about himself. As he once put it, "At times like this, I feel like one leg is a lot shorter than the other one." He went on to explain that the imbalance between the parts of his behavior he regarded as good and those about which he was unhappy left him frequently feeling down on himself.

Characteristics of the Family Concept

Structure

Purpose
As noted earlier, the initial purpose of the marriage was to legitimize Annette's pregnancy. The purpose for the second child was to provide a companion for Charles and, they hoped, a daughter for Annette.

Values, Beliefs, and Goals
The parents did not espouse clearly defined values, beliefs, or goals.

Aaron demonstrated the value of hard work and "do your own thing." He also felt that children should be respectful of their parents. He felt the family as a unit was doing reasonably well.

The core of Annette's value system focused on attending to the emotional needs of her children. She also felt strongly about developing an identity as a family unit but gave it up early in the marriage when it was clear that the demands of Aaron's work overshadowed his concern about being with the family. She settled for developing a sense of identity with her children.

The children had a realistic assessment about the status of the marriage. They were not comfortable with the tension in their parents' relationship and were apprehensive about what would happen when they were together as a family. At times being together was enjoyable, but more often it would be unpleasant. This was complicated by uncertainty about being able to predict what would happen on a given occasion. Their goal was to keep a low profile and avoid family "together times" unless they could not avoid it or there was a prospect for positive outcome.

Expectations

There were not any clearly defined expectations as a family except the assumption that Aaron would provide financial support and that Annette would perform the usual mothering responsibilities. They operated in a manner where each person had his own personal expectations. The only general expectation that was shared was that the family provided a base from which to operate.

Membership

At the start of therapy, the membership of the Dale family consisted of father, mother, and two children, Charles and Carol. Since the divorce there were now two family units: the father and children, who were living together; and the mother, who was now living in Florida. This configuration was determined by two considerations: the children's wishes not to have to give up their existing living situation and the father's desire and ability to have them live with him. The potential for changing the family configuration always looms in the background as a means for solving problems. One such instance followed an argument that Charles had with his father about losing access to his car because he got a speeding ticket and did not tell him. Another such instance involved an argument between the parents when Annette was upset because she thought that Aaron was not spending enough time with Charles.

Boundaries

The family boundary was pretty open. Outsiders were readily welcomed. The children had a lot of opportunity and were encouraged to participate in interests outside the family. The family was open to hearing and respecting information from the outside world. There was also support for sharing resources and points of view outside of the family.

Struggles developed when outside values and ways of behaving were in conflict with those of the family. Common examples were use of profanity, standards of dress, and substance abuse of alcohol or drugs.

Neither parent was very close to his or her family. An added contributing factor for Annette was that her family lived a considerable distance away. The impact on the children was that they did not have much of a sense of extended family.

The Dale family was largely dependent on their own resources. The parents had friends but there were no people with a significant impact on the family. The children had their friends, but none of them was close to the family.

Time Frame
The time frame for the intact family was formally terminated by the divorce. However, for all practical purposes the emotional identification of the family as a unit terminated years earlier, when it became clear to the parents that their relationship would not survive.

The Processing of Information
The predominant mode for processing information was the intellectual level. The most common exception to this was when Annette got too frustrated. At that point information management shifted to the emotional level, which frequently involved other family members relating at the same level.

For the most part information was processed at a concrete level as opposed to symbolic management. When Charles fell behind in his homework, the emphasis was likely to be more on the specifics of what he was and was not doing than on the symbolic significance of why it was important that he did his homework.

Adequacy of Resources
The Dale family had the basic resources needed for being successful as individuals and as a family. This included intellect, health, financial means, experience, adequate social skills, and a modest level of social maturity. Their biggest difficulty was their lack of ability to utilize these resources in a manner that was meaningful to all concerned.

Rules
Among the rules that the Dale family evolved were: Keep your feelings to yourself. Do your own thing. Don't give father a hard time when he is not home for dinner or in the evenings. Back off when mother gets up tight.

Get homework done every night. The children were expected to fulfill their responsibilities for school. Children would perform their chores as required and be respectful to parents and other adults.

The covert rules included: Father would be around when he was able. Children could do chores when they got around to it. It wasn't safe to show your anger. Be respectful of authority.

Valence

The family concept was very high for Annette in spite of it being less important to Aaron. Up until the few years preceding the divorce, she was always hopeful and optimistic that family would become more important to Aaron. As the children grew older, the importance of the family increased for Aaron.

Priority

The priority on family life was highest for Annette. For Aaron and the children, individual priorities had a higher priority than the family concept.

Assessment Skills

Judgment from Within

The family did not appear to be unduly influenced by outside judgments on their status as a family. The absence of any strong identification as a family unit was expressed by being more self-focused.

Assess Performance Separate from Outcome

Family members had a difficult time separating what they individually contributed from how well they did as a group. On one family vacation they were determined to get along and have a good time. In spite of a lot of effort by all members of the family, things did not work out as they had hoped. One bad incident overshadowed all the positive efforts made and any good times they experienced.

Ability to Learn from Experience

The Dale family had a hard time learning from experience. The long-standing tensions in the family got in the way of the family being able to interrupt well-established patterns. This awareness was one of the considerations that brought them to therapy.

Realistic Assessment of Strengths and Weaknesses

This family had a much clearer understanding of their weaknesses as a family than they did of their strengths. This, in part, was a reflection of their difficulty in comfortably giving and receiving positive feedback from one another and was largely a reflection of the negative modeling by the parents.

Coping Skills

Expression of Affect
The Dale family was hampered by their limited ability to express anger or affection in sufficiently positive ways. Too often anger was expressed in destructive ways which involved attacking the person rather than the issue of the anger. Aaron tended to assume that his affection for his family was obvious. He tended to get irritated when he was challenged on this issue. Annette was the only member of the family who freely expressed her feelings. Often its value was lost when it was expressed in extremes.

Management of Conflict
The Dale family had not done well in developing this capacity. The model set by Aaron and Annette was characterized by differences of opinion that were not adequately respected. This contributed to their developing a less than adequate ability to resolve differences in a mutually satisfactory manner. The children mirrored the same problem. The result was that Aaron often resolved conflict by dictate. At other times Annette might dictate or get resolution through emotional explosion. Sometimes resolution was accomplished when the children badgered Annette enough that she would give in just to get them off her back.

Division of Labor
There was a great deal of tension in the family around division-of-labor concerns. Almost all of the responsibility for managing the children and the home was left to Annette. She was often angry at Aaron because he tended to be negligent or inconsistent in the responsibilities for which he was responsible in the home. Annette tended to indulge the children by being very inconsistent in holding them to fulfill the responsibilities for maintenance of the home. The net result was that she felt resentful, overburdened, and taken for granted.

Getting and Giving Feedback
The difficulty the family had in getting and giving constructive feedback within the family also applied to how they related to feedback from outside the family. When such feedback was contrary to family member perceptions, it was discredited for one reason or another. This applied primarily to Aaron and Charles. The women in the family were more vulnerable to negative feedback from others.

Manage and Do Not Judge

The Dale family tended to respond to conflict by engaging in an exchange of judgments about how somebody else had caused the problem. When this did not work and a person was backed into a corner, the tendency was to blame oneself. They had a hard time getting mobilized in how to correct a problem. They usually needed a cooling off period after an exchange of judgments before they could relate in a more constructive manner. In one incident Annette got very angry at the other family members because they were not picking up after themselves. This resulted in an angry exchange of judgments. Several hours after the argument, they were able to talk more constructively about their differences and find an improved way to resolve them.

Relationship Enhancement

Time to Nurture the Relationship. The more unsuccessful the family was in learning how to manage their differences, the less inclined they were to spend time together. This became a vicious cycle where a negative situation fed on itself. Failure to balance negative interactions with positive ones resulted in family members turning to other sources for such experiences. Annette was the least inclined to do so and was the one who kept trying to get the family to spend time together.

Balance between Other Social Entities and the Family. The more that family members experienced being together with a negative valence, the more their priorities went to other relationships. This resulted in the family social unit receiving little investment of emotional resources.

Respect and Support for Individual Differences. Individual differences in the Dale family were not tolerated well. In theory Aaron was pretty tolerant but in practice had a hard time dealing with values or behaviors that were at variance with his. He was furious that Charles did not think he should have to have a summer job.

Annette erred in going too far in the other direction. She tended to overindulge her children by catering to their wishes. She dealt with Charles's desire not to have a summer job from the view that he would have plenty of time when he would have to work when he is older, so do not rush him. She got little support from any source for respecting this opinion and other things that were important to her.

Balance Own Needs with Family Needs. There was a weak identification with the concept of being a family. For the most part each person did his own thing. They rarely did things as a family. The closest identification there was as a family unit was Annette and the two children, but it was loosely held. After the divorce, the family unit of father and the children was stronger but still loosely held.

Annette was the only one in the family who was able to put the interests of the family ahead of her own when it was needed. Aaron and the two children had a much harder time doing this. One Thanksgiving Annette was going to prepare dinner for their respective families. She took time off from work with difficulty to prepare for the event. She asked the other family members to make time available to help with cleaning the house, shopping, and other chores related to the event. Aaron begged off because he had too much work to do. Both children had their own reasons why they could not be available when needed. All three said they would help when they could, which turned out to be very little. This occurred because Aaron did not support her and she was not able to take a stand on her own.

Family Concept Balance

The result of significantly more continuous negative experiences as family than positive ones on a day-to-day basis contributed to a negative family concept balance. This provided further reinforcement to a less than positive core family concept.

Impediments to Social Functioning

Absence of Desired or Needed Experiences

The tensions previously described were expressed in an environment in which all family members felt an emotional insecurity that varied in degree from strong at times to little at other times. Aaron felt unloved and taken for granted by all members of the family. He experienced himself as being viewed primarily, if not solely, as the breadwinner. Annette did not feel she knew where she stood with Aaron during most of their marriage. She too felt taken for granted and unappreciated. The children did not get the emotional security and consistency they needed. Both parents came from families that provided poor models for developing a strong and positive family concept.

Presence of Undesired Experiences

The major destructive event that impinged on the family was the emotional tension between the parents, which ultimately involved the children, who developed the same ways of coping as did their parents.

Discussion

I will now illustrate how I applied these concepts in relating with the Dale family. My first step was to determine the significant social units in this family. On the basis of the data, I concluded the following:

1. Aaron had strong conviction and a clearly defined self-concept. Annette's self-concept was less clearly defined, with a strong element of insecurity about her own self-worth. Charles's self-concept on the surface mirrored the self-assurance and conviction of a clearly defined self-concept. This surface masked the insecurities and struggles characteristic of his adolescent stage of development. Carol's self-concept was characterized by the relative calm that often precedes adolescence.

2. The couple concept never developed very far. This appears to result from Aaron's commitment to "do the right thing" as a result of the pregnancy and the tensions that resulted from it. Contributing to their problem was the difference in their emotional style and their joint inability to find a mutually satisfactory way to deal with their differences. This established a pattern early in the marriage where attempts to resolve conflicts ended in arguments and each withdrawing in his own fashion. The children were the primary reason for the marriage lasting as long as it did. There were periods when the couple concept balance was positive, but it never endured long enough or often enough to have a significant impact on the core couple concept.

3. The family concept was never a high priority for any family member except as a fading ideal that for brief moments aroused some enthusiasm in the family as something that might be realized. The struggles between the parents usually contributed to dashing whatever hopes might be stimulated. The children's efforts to protect themselves only added to the problem when they coped by emotional withdrawal. In addition Aaron's workaholic tendencies added further frustrations and resulting tensions.

4. Before the divorce, there were primarily three major social units in the family: the couple, the mother and the two children, and the father. When the children were small, the social entity of the mother and children had a more positive parent-children concept. This positive sense of their concept diminished as they grew older. Contributing to this was Annette's difficulty adapting to the children's need to be more independent.

5. A major problem for this family was their difficulty in learning how to cope with relating to the different modes that were necessary as a member of the family. For Aaron the problem was to function in his work mode in a way that was consistent with his vocational aspirations, that did not interfere with operating in the parent mode, and that would not further complicate

the couple mode. His personal limitations in not being very aware of his feelings and his avoidance of conflict made it hard for him to shift to and function in the family mode. It was easy to cope with such frustrations by staying in the work mode, where the cost-benefit balance for the expenditure of his energies reaped more satisfying rewards.

Annette was most comfortable in the parent mode. Being able to respond to the needs of the children when they were young was gratifying and rewarding. During this period she had a heightened sense of a more positive self-concept. It became clear that it was not based on who she was as a person but primarily as a reflection of her behavior in the parent mode. Her struggles in the couple mode only reinforced her long-standing negative self-concept. This contributed to her difficulty in being able to adapt to the children's need for greater distance and independence. At one point she tried to cope with her deprivation and negative self-concept by engaging in an affair. It helped in the short run but only further contributed to her negative self-concept when she realized that this would not solve her problems and only added another reason to be down on herself.

Charles had to deal with the pressure of his emerging adolescence, which was complicated by the lack of security he felt from both parents. He was hurt by his father's distance and unavailability during much of his early years and his tendency to be overly strict and rigid when he was around. As a result, the father-son concept never developed much of a positive core concept. Charles had trouble with his mother's volatility and was threatened by being drawn into her disappointments with his father. This came as a result of the frequent times she would make disparaging comments about Aaron to him. His difficulty was further enhanced when she would accuse him of being just like his father when she was frustrated with him and her anger spilled over on him. The only comfortable mode for him was developing relationships outside the family.

With this background it was no surprise to find that Charles had a difficult time with the divorce that resulted in his choosing to live with his father. Part of what contributed to this choice was to maintain the stability of the familiar environment and the most nurturing relationships he had, which were outside the family. The positive spin-off was that the changed circumstances might permit development of a different relationship with his father, one that he once hoped he could have. This had not occurred thus far. Aaron's attempts at being the responsible parent have resulted in his vacillating between the extremes of being too permissive and too strict. Neither way of relating provides a base for developing the kind of relationship both father and son desire.

Carol coped with the emerging family scene by maintaining emotional distance from her mother increasingly as she grew older and was able to develop other nurturing and safer relationships. She learned a long time before the divorce that she could not expect much in the way of a father-daughter relationship and so did not harbor any conscious aspirations in that direction. As with her brother, she chose to live with her father for somewhat similar reasons. She also had awakened to the possibility that the hoped-for father-daughter relationship might yet come to fruition. She encountered the same experience in her father's first attempts as did Charles.

Carol never felt very close to her brother. The only significant relationship she had in the family was in the early years with her mother. As a result, she depended a lot on her own resources and the relationships she was able to develop outside the family. She had a stable, positive self-concept and a self-concept balance that supported it. She had little difficulty shifting relationship modes in the family under these circumstances.

6. I concluded that there were significant resources from which to draw to cope with existing problems. The resources included stable and relatively intact family members. There was ample motivation to improve relationships and the willingness to take some emotional risks. The continual disruptive conflict between parents was largely eliminated after the divorce. Most of their interactions were positive and cooperative.

Therapeutic Intervention Following Evaluation

From the evaluation, we defined therapeutic goals that included improvement of self-concepts, how to maintain a positive social unit concept balance as individuals and also in dyads between each parent with each of the two children, to be aware of the relationship mode in which they were operating and learning how to relate to multiple modes at the same time, and ways to resolve conflict when modes conflict.

The therapeutic plan involved working with the following social entities: individually with the father and the children as needed, the father and each of the children, and the father and both children. I spoke with the mother periodically on the phone and planned to meet with her when she was visiting. The decision about which social unit was seen was determined by the current issues facing the family. When there were no crises or compelling issues that required attention, I would focus on the social entity and the underlying issues that interfered with developing trust and with the needed skills in developing relationships, such as coping with the expression of feelings and how to resolve conflicts in ways that were satisfactory to all concerned.

Outcome of Therapeutic Intervention

The family was in ongoing therapy at the time this chapter was written. Progress to date includes: Aaron learned to be more aware of what he feels and is able to express his feelings in more appropriate ways. Both Charles and Carol are taking risks in relating to Aaron. Charles and Carol have started to develop and define a more satisfying relationship. Charles is learning to express his anger in more constructive ways. As a family, they are learning how to cope with differences and resolve conflict in more mutually satisfying ways. They are learning how to meet personal needs in the context of the family mode. When Charles first learned to drive, he would fight for permission to use the family car solely in terms of his own needs. After some family work, he learned how to deal with needs in the personal mode in the context of the family mode. When he wanted to use the car, he would state his need and then find out how this might mesh with other people's needs. If there was a conflict, he was learning how to meet his needs in a way that showed consideration for the needs of other family members. Although there remains more to be accomplished and incorporated, the members of the family have crossed the hurdle of seeing that more is possible than they originally thought.

A GUIDE TO CLINICAL APPLICATION

   1. Identify the relevant social entities:
   - Self-concept
   - Self-concept balance
   - Couple concept
   - Couple concept balance
   - Nuclear family concept
   - Nuclear family concept balance
   - Paternal extended family balance
   - Maternal extended family balance
   - Other relevant social entity concepts and how balanced they are in involving people outside of the family

   2. Determine how well defined SEs are and what priority they play in the presenting and diagnosed problems.

   3. Determine the SE's ability to make the transition between different modes.

   4. Determine the status of social entity concepts on the following dimensions:
   - Purpose
   - Values, beliefs, goals
   - Expectations
   - Membership inclusion
   - Boundaries
   - Time frame

- How information is processed
- Adequacy of resources
- Valence
- Rules
- Priority
- Assessment skills
- Ability to learn from experience
- Ability to assess its own strengths and weaknesses

5. Evaluate the dynamic equilibrium pattern.
   - Has there been a significant change in it?
     - If so, what precipitated the change?
     - What is the quality of the change?
     - How transitory is the change?

6. Evaluate the coping skills using the following dimensions:
   - Expression of affect
   - Management of conflict
   - Division of labor

7. Evaluate for presence of impediments to social entity functioning.
   - Absence of desired or needed events:
     - Financial security
     - Emotional security
     - Feeling loved and respected
     - Nature of modeling exposure

Summary

In this chapter, I explained a framework for defining concepts for every social relationship on both static and dynamic bases. I described dimensions that permit comparisons across different relationships. The concept of mode is utilized to refer to when a person is behaving in a particular social entity concept. Attention was given to problems that evolve when there is conflict in operating in different modes. The application of these concepts was provided in a case illustration.

CHAPTER FIVE

Values, Beliefs, and Goal Setting in Therapy

In my daily work I was struck by the contribution to my clinical work gained by considering the values, beliefs, attitudes, and definitions of goals of my clients. In this chapter I drew upon the literature from social psychology and describe how these concepts have application to clinical practice.

THEORY

In 1983, I participated in a couples conference in Boston that focused on four therapists' interview of the same couple. The therapists were Jim Framo, Peggy Papp, Normal Paul, and Carlos Sluzki. Observing the interviewing approach of these four therapists gave rise to a number of questions that resulted in this chapter.

Why does a therapist pick a particular approach? Why is it that different therapists working with the same client conceptualize the case differently? Framo (1982) was concerned with the resolution of unresolved conflict with the family of origin; for Paul (Paul & Paul, 1975), it was to obtain better self data; for Papp (1983), it was restoring balance in the couple's reciprocal relationships; and for Sluzki (1978), it was to define and extricate the conflicted interaction patterns in the couple.

Why does Peggy Papp work with fantasy and metaphor, whereas Norman Paul works with stressor tapes? Why is it that Carlos Sluzki does not want any background information before he meets a couple, whereas the other therapists felt it appropriate if not necessary to use such material?

What guides us to perceive and interpret the world around us in the way we do? One explanation is that the cumulated experience from whatever source — personal history, training, or professional experience — gets organized and expressed through our ever-evolving values, beliefs, goals, and attitudes. One of the distinguishing characteristics between people — and between therapists in particular—is the degree to which such perspectives change or become rigid. How open is a social unit to taking in new information? How able is a social unit to risk changing its values, beliefs, goals, and attitudes? The answer to these questions significantly influences the therapeutic process.

Before proceeding with these definitions, I would like to provide a clinical context for why I find these concepts useful. In a family session, a father was furious with his son for lying to him: "You should never lie, you should always be honest!" (value). What really annoyed him was that there was too much dishonesty in the world and in the family in particular (belief). The son accused his father of being a hypocrite because he often bragged about how he cheated on his income tax (a conflict between his value and his behavior). The son was challenging his father's predisposition to compromise his value when it was convenient (the son was challenging his father's commitment to his value of honesty).

In therapy the focus on the distinction between a value and a belief was useful in clarifying the ambiguity of expectations that the father had of his son in this instance but also led to how it created tensions between them in other situations.

In this chapter I discuss these concepts from four points of view: a description of the concepts, how they are utilized in clinical work, how I define them for myself, and a case illustration.

Values, Beliefs, Goals, and Attitudes

These concepts are used freely by both the professional and lay community. The problem with their use in any systematic way is the absence of any operational definition. I was surprised to find very little in the family therapy literature on this subject. The social science literature proved more productive. A number of years ago Milton Rokeach (1980), a social psychologist, did extensive work on this subject. For him, in essence, values are statements of *what ought to be,* statements of ideals, such as "A person should be honest." Beliefs are statements of *what was, is, or is expected to be,* for example, "Many people are dishonest when it suits their purpose." Attitudes are the behavioral expression of both values and beliefs, such as the predisposition to approach a given situation with honesty. Whether a person behaves this way will depend on the circumstances. I found this frame of reference useful conceptually, but it lacked sufficient operational definition for use in therapy. This led to my search for identification of operational dimensions that define these concepts for use by the clinician in understanding her clients and in the way she interacts with them. I found eight operational dimensions of values and beliefs useful in clinical practice.

Operating Structure

Subject Matter of Value or Belief

People hold values about what is important to them — religion, work ethic, abortion, or education, for example. Each value carries with it a belief about the degree to which it actually happens. To what extent does a person who values honesty perceive that it actually happens?

The relationship between values and beliefs can be circular. At times a held value can influence the belief that is held. This also works in reverse. A person who is committed to the work ethic is likely to hold the belief that she behaves consistent with it. When she gets compelling feedback that her belief does not match her value, she will have one of four responses: change her behavior or belief to fit her value, change her value, deny the discrepancy, or accept the discrepancy.

A man has the value that he should be able to solve his own emotional problems. He believes that therapy is not an appropriate mechanism to resolve his difficulties. His wife coerces him into therapy. When the experience becomes helpful, he could respond by changing his belief that therapy is an appropriate mechanism for solving problems, changing his value about having to solve his own problems, denying that therapy was the cause of the positive experience, or accepting that the therapy was helpful in a particular area but minimize it in a way that leaves the value untouched.

To Whom Does the Value or Belief Apply?

Does it apply only to the person who holds it or is it applied to people in general, men only, women only, or to another specific group? Is it consistently applied, or is there a double standard?

When Does the Value or Belief Apply?

Does it always apply or only under certain conditions? For instance, some therapists hold the value that both spouses should always be present in couple therapy except during the evaluation period, when the therapist should see each spouse separately at least once. There are those who believe that people are honest only when they have to be.

How Consistent Are Values and Beliefs with Behavior?

To what extent does a person who holds a particular value or belief act consistently with such views? People do not always behave consistently with their values. Some may express the value that people should not use drugs but in private frequently do so. Knowledge of the discrepancy between stated value and performance points to an area of vulnerability to change.

Discrepancies suggest the presence of conflict that is the breeding ground for change in values or attitudes. The conflict may be accounted for in weakly held values or beliefs, inability to act consistently with values or beliefs, and conflict with higher priorities. The knowledge of which mechanism may be operating contributes to understanding their susceptibility to change.

In one situation a man had a drinking problem that was inconsistent with his value that he should not drink. He explained that he was in an untenable situation. He was in a marriage that was not working, but he could not leave because he came from a family of divorce and saw what it did to them. He vowed he would never do that to his children. Adding to this problem was his religious conviction against divorce. He claimed the drinking helped him to cope with his frustrations. Understanding the relationship between his values and beliefs was a useful tool in helping him and his wife to improve their relationship.

How Intense Is the Commitment to a Value or Belief?

Commitment to a particular value or belief may range from none to intense and unwavering. It would seem reasonable to expect that the more fervently a value is held, the less likely the person is to take in contrary information. The existence of such a condition is likely to diminish the likelihood of change or influence. I found a striking example in a case I saw of a family that had a child involved in a cult. The young man of 20 was so committed to his value and belief in the cult's teaching that all information was received in one of two ways. When it fit the value and belief system of the cult, the information was accepted. When it went contrary to it, it was rejected as the work of the devil. There were no gray areas.

How Specific Is the Value or Belief?

Clinical experience consistently demonstrates that the more specific the subject matter of a belief, the greater the potential for change. Concreteness provides the necessary focus for providing information that would warrant a change. There is a greater chance of educating a teenager about the use of drugs when a specific drug that she used is the subject as opposed to drugs in general.

Source

The source of a value or belief may come from family tradition or cultural background involving religious, social, political, economic, ethnic, and educational roots. It may derive from an individual's needs and experiences that include modeling and experience with significant others or a combination of the other factors.

Evaluation

Inherent in each person's value system is an explicit or implicit ongoing assessment of whether a given held value should stay the same, be modified, or be eliminated from the existing value or belief system. Usually this occurs on a subconscious level. Such assessment may be experienced on an increasing level of discomfort that leads to gradual changes in values or beliefs. In one family case the parents entered therapy with strongly held values about strict discipline. Over the course of a year's therapy, their views gradually shifted. Toward the end of therapy, they were surprised to find how much their rigidly defined value system had shifted without their conscious awareness.

The evaluation process becomes more conscious when a person is confronted with a significant problem. In one family the presenting problem focused on an adolescent who was involved in drugs. The parents displayed a double standard by openly engaging in drug activity. They saw no difficulty in their position. They felt that the children could make their own decision about the use of drugs when they were older. After discussion in therapy, they came to the conclusion that their value system needed revision.

When Values or Beliefs Remain the Same
Values stay the same for one or more of the following conditions: holding a given value fits the desired image for the person holding it, experiences support holding it, new information supports holding it, and other values do not interfere with holding it. An illustration of this is seen in a father I saw in therapy who held the value that children should be treated with strict discipline. Holding such a value supported his image of being the good parent. When he got the desired response from practicing strict discipline, it supported his value that unites strong discipline and good parenting. The same parent feels his value is supported when he reads literature on parents and tough love. Finally, he is able to maintain his value because no other value he holds contradicts his doing so. He would have had a problem if he had another value that parents should let their children learn from their mistakes with minimal parent intervention.

When Values or Beliefs Change
Values and beliefs are often not static. They change when holding them no longer fits the needs of the people holding them. They change for a variety of reasons, such as changing needs or abilities, new information, changing priorities, undesired consequences for continuing to hold a value or belief, inability to behave consistently with the value or belief, and changing a value or belief for financial gain. Dissatisfaction alone with a held value or belief is not sufficient to result in a change. Staying with a familiar position, even if

unattractive, is appealing to many people in preference to taking an unfamiliar position.

One of the things that facilitates the taking of drugs is rejection of any information that does not support continued use. As a result, the only aspect of the evaluation process that is being used is the rejection of contrary information. In the case of the drug taker, the therapist may rapidly conclude from the client's rejection of information on the negative effects of drug taking that therapy for this problem would be pointless as long as the current values and beliefs prevailed.

A woman may get some indication that her spouse is having an affair but choose to ignore or avoid any information that supports this fear. Such apprehension occurs because verification of the relationship would require consequences the affected spouse was not ready to face.

In another context a man may agree with his wife that it would be nice if he were more open about his feelings. However, the therapist's judgment may indicate that the husband is likely to resist doing so as long as he did not feel he could trust that his wife would *not* use such disclosure against him at another time.

Interaction between Therapist and Client on Evaluation

The evaluation process for the therapist is concerned with whether a change in values or beliefs is desirable and/or possible. A client is likely to be concerned with evaluating whether she needs to change any of her values or beliefs and how such changes may affect the outcome of therapy. Her evaluation may also include her values and beliefs about the therapist and the therapy process, with concerns such as whether it accomplishes what she thinks should happen.

In the therapy context, the evaluation process proceeds on a parallel track by the therapist and the client. In a constructive therapy situation, the therapist and the client work collaboratively in the evaluation process. In an ineffective therapy situation, each party proceeds on her own way, often disagreeing or not communicating about their differences.

Flexibility

This dimension refers to whether a change in values or beliefs is possible. Other conditions that affect whether change will take place include the ability to accomplish the desired change and the consequences that may result from making it. Determination of a client's ability to shift from her value position to that of another is a significant factor in assessing how a client will respond to therapy.

From the Client's View

To what degree does the client believe that a change in value or attitude is possible? I once saw a person who was raised with the value and belief that drinking and dancing were evil. She wanted to change these views but felt they were too ingrained to do so. She tried on various occasions, but the guilt she experienced was too powerful. She concluded that the gain was not worth the effort.

From the Therapist's View

To what degree does the therapist believe that a change is desired, and what is the likelihood that such a change is possible? The therapist who attempts a therapeutic relationship when she does not believe that the client is able to shift positions is embarking on a trip destined to end in failure.

Priority

What priority does the client place on either maintaining or wanting to change a particular value or belief? A priority is a reflection of the extent to which holding a given value or belief serves an important function for the social unit holding it. The higher the priority to maintain or change, the greater the impact on the therapeutic process.

Purpose of Holding the Value

Values are held because they serve a purpose. It will be difficult to understand or seek to modify a value without understanding what purpose holding it serves. Therapists place a value on confidentiality because it contributes to providing an atmosphere of trust for a client. In one case a couple placed a value on letting their child know she was adopted and loved at every opportunity. They held this value as the result of being told by a counselor at an adoption agency that this would be helpful to the child. Knowing the source and purpose facilitated appropriate modification of this value.

Consequences of Holding a Particular Value or Belief

A major contributing factor to whether and how avidly a person holds a particular value or belief is the consequences that result from doing so. This affects not only whether a given value or belief is held but what impact holding it has on other values and beliefs held by an individual or another social unit.

A person may hold a value about abortion and be disposed to change it based on receiving new information. However, if making such a change would conflict with her strongly held religious or other beliefs, then she probably would not change her value system no matter how meritorious the argument to change it. Attempts to change values and beliefs should take into account how the change will affect the holding of other values and beliefs.

Determining the Basis for the Value or Belief

It can be hazardous to assume that logic will be necessarily sufficient to change values or beliefs. Efforts to change them through logic when they are based on emotion or faith are destined to end in failure. An example is the mother who refuses to believe that her son committed an act of violence even when confronted with clear evidence. To protect her belief in her son's innocence, she grasped at any explanation that would serve her purpose: there was an error, other boys made him do it, it was a case of mistaken identity, and more.

The reverse can be equally complicated. A parent often takes a stand on setting a limit on her child's behavior for a very clear and rational set of reasons. Often the right kind of emotional appeal can get a parent to modify her values and beliefs and significantly change or withdraw the established limits.

I had one situation where two parents believed that motorcycles were dangerous and held the value that they should be banned from the road. They had a great deal of statistical data and opinions from significant sources to back up their convictions. Their son mounted an impassioned plea over a period of time. Ultimately the parents relented on their position based more on their emotions that on any basic change in their values or beliefs. Once committed, they found ways to account for the discrepancy between their values and beliefs and their behavior.

There appears to be greater success when emotion is used to change values and beliefs that are based on logic. Interventions are likely to be more effective when they take into consideration what combination of logic and emotion is most likely to bring about the desired change.

Interaction between Values or Beliefs and Goal Setting

Major values get expressed in defining goals. Beliefs that arise from experience affect how goals are set and, as noted earlier, may lead to modification of values. I saw a man who held the value that there should be good communication in a marriage. He entered the marriage with clear goals on how to achieve it. After a year or two of relative harmony, repeated bickering and unresolved differences led to redefining the goal of communication. It got redefined to minimizing contact and avoidance of certain topics. The belief that good communication was possible was changed to the belief that peaceful coexistence could be achieved. The value of good communication in marriage did not change.

Goal setting is one way values get translated into behavior and beliefs. Success in accomplishing this reinforces holding the value, and failure to do so contributes to modifying it or eliminating it. Values change when there are sufficient negative experiences to make holding the value no longer viable and there is no other compelling reason to hold it. A person may value religion and believe in God and maintain this view even though they may suffer a series of painful experiences that would appear to contradict the concept of God.

The Holocaust was an example of such a situation. Many people could not reconcile the apparent contradiction that there could be a God and that she would allow such a thing as the Holocaust to occur. For some of these people, the value of religion and belief in God were rejected. Other people maintained their relationship to God by developing an explanation that did not force a change in their value and belief system.

Consistency between Values, Beliefs, and Goals

One indication of problems in a family occurs when there is an incompatibility between the explicit and/or implicit goals of family members between how they behave and their value and belief systems. Presence of contradictions heightens the probability that there are significant sources of dissatisfaction in a social entity (within an individual, between spouses or other family members). In one family I saw, a man was successfully running a business he inherited from his father. He wanted to be an artist and believed that he had the talent to do so but went into the family business to be "practical." He harbored a lot of sad feelings about not pursuing his goal. A partial resolution was achieved when he found a way to express his artistic interests within the business by taking responsibility for advertising and interior decorating.

Clarity of Goal Definition

Vaguely defined goals may reflect a number of possible conditions: weakly held values and beliefs, other conflicting commitments, lack of confidence in being able to achieve them and thus diminishing enthusiasm for clear definition, and lack of resources (time, money, importance, energy, or knowledge) to accomplish them.

Whether Goals Are Assigned Priorities

Insufficient clarity in setting priorities for goals is a potential cause of tension, conflict, frustration, and sadness. This generally occurs because energies are being dissipated into too many directions for the available resources, resulting in necessary tasks not being accomplished when needed. Feelings of helplessness and being overwhelmed are commonly felt under such conditions.

In one family, I saw the mother set very high standards for herself. She had a hard time asking for or expecting help from other family members. She had a laundry list of things that needed to be done but had difficulty in setting priorities. She frequently would jump from doing one thing to another. She was very scattered and chronically felt she never got enough done. She set unrealistic goals that derived from a distorted value that was modeled by her mother. This contributed to a distorted perception about how much she did get done. The result was a constant state of anxiety. Attempts by her family to help her set priorities were to no avail. Ultimately such frustrations leaked out into conflict with family members.

Problems in setting priorities on goals also manifest themselves in achieving long-term goals. This frequently happens in trying to juggle immediate short-term, and long-term goals. The ongoing challenge is to balance the need for immediate gratification versus achieving longer-term gratification.

I saw a typical example of this in a male sophomore college student who frequently found himself in a frustrating situation. On one occasion, he had to prepare for a test the next day, a paper due in a week, and a chemistry project by the end of the month, which was two and a half weeks away. He was feeling tired and frustrated when he got a call to play tennis, which he enjoyed. He had to struggle with how meeting his immediate need would interfere with being able to achieve his other commitments. This was a problem for him because he had a history of going with the pressure of the moment and not giving enough attention to the consequences of doing that on a regular basis.

Availability of Resources Needed to Accomplish Goals

Setting goals is one of the easier tasks for any social unit to accomplish, especially when accomplished without respect to how a particular goal may relate to setting of other goals. The task becomes more difficult when the goal is set on the basis of available resources (motivation, time, money, and appropriate knowledge and skills). Failure to address what resources are needed to accomplish a defined goal is a common problem.

In my experience, difficulty in adequately addressing the time required to accomplish a goal is the most common problem in dealing with resources for accomplishing a goal. People frequently grossly underestimate what time will be required and often have difficulty recognizing this as the problem. This may happen for a variety of reasons: lack of knowledge, interference from outside sources, underestimate of amount of energy needed, difficulty of task(s) involved, or mistakes.

One family I worked with got into a lot of trouble in planning a cross-country trip. A lot of their difficulty stemmed from their being unrealistic in their assessment of resources. The family included three children, aged 14, 10, and 7. The motivation for the trip came mostly from the parents, with some mild interest from the 14-year-old and little to no interest from the other two children. What little interest the younger children had quickly dissipated with long hours on the road and too little planning on how the children would stay amused under these conditions. The result was a lot of irritability and haggling between them. Often it infected the atmosphere and resulted in tension between all family members.

In planning the itinerary, the parents grossly underestimated the time it would take. This happened for various reasons: unexpected auto trouble, they could not drive as many hours a day as they planned, they stayed longer at some sites than they planned, they got lost a number of times, and they had not planned their itinerary carefully enough.

The time problem created money problems. Money problems in turn limited what they were able to do. This added to the tension. The accumulation of problems gradually eroded the level of enjoyment in the trip. What started out with an anticipation of a happy family going on a vacation deteriorated to a tired, unhappy family at war with each other by the time they got home with the resolve that they would never again take such a trip.

Impact of Values, Beliefs, and Goals on the Family Social Entity

I often find that by the time couples seek therapy they are a couple in name only. They do not have commonly shared values and beliefs as a couple. The same can be said for children in a family. Adolescents face the evolving challenge of to what degree they continue to be identified emotionally and intellectually as part of a family unit as they struggle to define themselves as a separate social entity. This differentiation process is significantly affected by the degree to which these adolescents' emerging views significantly contradict major family values, beliefs, and goals. When they are reasonably compatible with family mores, identification with the family entity is continued and probably enhanced.

When the individual's differentiation is not consistent with the family's values, beliefs, and goals, then the individual has a choice. She either succumbs to identification with the family unit and thereby forgoes an identity as a separate social unit, or she gives up her identification with the family unit in service of her identity. When such differences become incompatible without adequate tools to reconcile them, there is a split from the family. This may range in form from a total cutoff to one in which the individual physically remains part of the family but her identity is defined for practical purposes outside of the family.

I worked with a middle-class family that consisted of father, mother, 17-year-old son, and 14-year-old daughter. The father was a scientist who was very rigid in his values and beliefs and not very open to information, values, or beliefs not consistent with his views. He was a caring father but very restricted because of his inability to show or express his feelings.

The mother was a teacher who was very open and expressive of her feelings. She had her own value and belief system and was able to listen to and accept other views. She was constantly caught between the struggles of her husband and their son as the son searched for his own identity.

The son dealt with the struggle with his father by being very rebellious. Whatever his father valued or believed, he was the opposite. His father was religious, so he criticized his father's beliefs and defined himself as an atheist. His father was very careful about his appearance and valued cleanliness; the son's clothes would make him feel right at home on skid row, and his hair was long, uncombed, and unwashed. It was not necessary to see him to know of his presence because his failure to shower or wash his clothes resulted in his exuding a strong odor.

The father was politically very conservative; the son was far to the left. This was the pattern in most of the areas of their life. As a result, a great deal of tension existed between father and son. The mother was caught in the middle and constantly frustrated in her attempts to mediate their difficulties.

The outcome of failure for father and son to resolve their differences resulted in the son disavowing his identification with the family for all intents and purposes. He maintained a relationship with his family but in all other ways did not identify with the family as a unit. He married a woman of a different religious background, moved to the West Coast while his family lived on the East Coast, and lived a life-style very different from his parents'.

Application of the Value, Belief, and Goal Setting Concepts

Next I discuss the ways in which these concepts have general application and follow this with a case illustration.

There are a number of implications for the use of the value, belief, and goal setting concepts in the practice of therapy. One source of problems in therapy is not adequately attending to differences in value systems between members of a couple or family or between the client and the therapist. This can happen by not identifying the differences or by not helping the clients find a mutually satisfactory way to work with their differences.

Helping a couple become aware of their value system can in itself be a useful intervention in providing them with a clear understanding of the frame of reference by which they guide their behavior and judge themselves. There was the case of a couple who consulted with me about child management issues. They were arguing about differences in how to discipline their son for lying. They were operating on the premise that they shared the same value. Awareness that they had a difference in values interrupted the negative interaction. They were able to negotiate their differences and find a more mutually acceptable resolution of the conflict.

Identification of a couple's ideal for behavior can be an added tool in helping them come to grips with the discrepancy between ideal and actual behavior. A common illustration of this is the person who takes perfection as a standard for measuring behavior. Under these conditions, no level of performance would be adequate, with the accompanying experience of always falling short and feeling like a failure. Redefining the ideal—in the context where present performance was viewed as being an improvement over past performance and not against an idealized standard—led to greater satisfaction and accomplishment.

A belief was defined earlier as a statement of what is, was, or will be. Our clients commonly present with the desire to change a noxious reality. All we know at the outset is that they want something different than what they have. It is useful to determine whether the difficulty is because their behavior violates their value system or whether their value system is inconsistent with the existing reality. A person who lies may be unhappy because she violated her value about honesty or because she is angry at living in an environment where people are dishonest. Such clarification facilitates development of an appropriate treatment strategy.

One consideration in the modification of behavior in therapy is to determine whether a client's statement of belief is an expression of a value or a report of her experience. Making such a distinction will be useful in helping to clarify and define what the presenting problem is.

Knowing a person's value system gives another basis for predicting what direction a person's behavior will take and under what kinds of intervention it is likely to happen.

Each therapist has a belief system that accounts for how to approach therapy. This is a separate consideration from what ideal may be held for how to do therapy. Much of therapy is helping individuals to define and understand their belief systems, how they got that way, and how to work out conflicts with the belief systems of those with whom they have a relationship. Therapeutic interventions are efforts to change belief systems guided by the values held by the therapist that may or may not be shared by others. In the conference I referred to earlier where four therapists interviewed the same couple, Framo's interventions were in part motivated by his value that the client should communicate with parents about unresolved issues. Paul was guided by his values regarding how mourning issues should be dealt with in order to resolve problems in the couple's relationship.

Therapy also involves correcting distortions in belief systems. At one point the woman in a couple believed that her boyfriend was rejecting her because he was angry with her. This turned out to be a distortion when she learned that he needed to learn how to fend for himself after he had an operation before he could accept help from her.

Evaluation of goal setting in the therapy setting is useful in a couple of ways. One way is to determine to what extent the social unit has defined goals and how they are an adequate expression of their values and beliefs. This involves assessment of the realistic definition of the goals and the skill with which efforts are made to accomplish them.

Another useful way of evaluating goal setting is when values and beliefs are defined but no goal setting was defined. The absence of such behavior suggests that the goals for the social unit are defined by other social units. This leads to identification of the other social units and how their interaction is relevant to the problems that were the reason for the therapy.

Managing Conflicting Goals

How conflicting goals are managed gives clues to how important the values and beliefs are that are the basis for the goals. Values and beliefs that are readily modified or scrapped may indicate lack of self-confidence or commitment to achieving the expressed goals. It also is suggestive of the possibility that the values and beliefs held may be more an expression of what they feel they should be than reflecting their commitment to behavior. It also gives information about the self-confidence of the people involved and the extent to which they abdicate making such judgments, for example, the wife who reflects her husband's values and beliefs in service of a harmonious relationship and at the expense of enhancing her own identity.

An Example of a Therapist's Value and Belief System

Thus far the discussion focused on how understanding the values, beliefs, and goals of family members is useful in coping with their problems. The end product of professional training is a value and belief system that is the guide for how a therapist practices psychotherapy. It is essential for an effective practitioner to know what these guiding concepts are. Such conscious awareness provides the opportunity to test continually the validity of such values and beliefs. As new knowledge and experience are accumulated without such grounding and focus, it becomes easier to drift into a repetitious mindset that does not include evaluation of new information. To illustrate this point, I am presenting a sampling of the values and beliefs that guide my therapeutic practice; they derive from my personal history, training, and clinical experience. I do not presume that this should dictate how other therapists practice. However, I do feel that each therapist should have a clear and conscious definition of her own framework for the practice of psychotherapy.

Value System

Respect for the Client's View
A therapist should respect a client's right to have a point of view different from hers, even if the therapist is convinced it is detrimental. Failure to respect this invites a power struggle that undermines the possibility of a constructive therapeutic experience and can contribute to further diminishing the client's sense of self-worth. The problem is likely to get worse if the client accedes to the therapist's definition of truth at the expense of her own judgment. Such a situation encourages the client to depend on defining her own identity from the outside rather than developing and trusting her own judgment.

Helping a Client to Make Decisions
A major responsibility of a therapist should be to aid a client in making decisions by helping her define options and the consequences that go with them. Before this can be accomplished, the therapist may need to help the client resolve whatever obstacles are in the way that prevent appropriate coping. This may involve rebuilding self-esteem and confidence in her ability to cope by resolving the consequences of unresolved trauma due to rape, physical or emotional abuse, deprivations, or traumatic events such as accidents, death of loved ones, or other losses. A major step in accomplishing

this objective is helping the client discover and utilize their individual and collective resources.

One temporary exception to this value is when a client is not able to manage her own affairs by virtue of emotional incapacity. Under such circumstances, the therapist may undertake a more directive role until the client is more competent while making use of as many of the client's resources as possible.

Therapist's Self-Awareness of His or Her Limitations

A therapist should be aware enough of her own issues and limitations so that she can know when they interfere with her ability to help a client reach defined therapeutic goals. One way to achieve this when such problems surface is through consultation with a colleague. When this is insufficient or when the therapist, at the outset, recognizes that there may be too much difficulty dealing with the countertransference, the client should be referred elsewhere. Working with a cotherapist is another way to achieve the same perspective.

Respect for and Management of Another Therapist's View

A therapist should respect another therapist's point of view. When this information is received via a client, the therapist should not challenge the report of the other therapist's views without firsthand information. This is necessary because of the intentional or unwitting distortions that the client may introduce for one reason or another. Such reporting also has potential as a manipulation to avoid facing difficult issues. When such a difference involves violation of professional ethics as defined by a therapist's professional organization, the matter should be taken up with the therapist directly or be called to the attention of the therapist's professional organization or the licensing board. Which direction is followed will depend on the circumstances of the particular situation.

Develop a Therapeutic Strategy for Multiple Needs of a Social Entity

When the client is a couple, I should be prepared to work with the couple jointly and separately unless otherwise indicated. When meeting with the couple, the relationship should be my focus, that is, the client. When I see each of these spouses separately, I should relate to them as my client without being influenced by what impact my work will have on the other spouse. I repeat the same process with the other spouse and help her relate to her concerns, again without concern for whether it will be pleasing to the other spouse. To function this way requires that I am comfortable with the possibility of dealing with the potential problems that go with such a strategy. This includes dealing with secrets, coping with attempts at manipulation, distortion of comments in individual sessions used outside of therapy to heighten conflict, and competition for approval of the therapist and others.

Therapeutic Relationship As a Partnership

In most situations, the therapeutic relationship should be a partnership between the therapist and the client, including the way the therapy is conducted administratively concerning when sessions are held, how often they are held, length of session, cancellation policy, when and how fees are paid, management of children in the session, and phone calls. The partnership also extends to the content of the therapy — what subjects are discussed, when, and to what degree. When such discussions reach an impasse, they provide challenges to both the therapist and the client. The ability to resolve such differences will determine the viability of the therapeutic relationship.

Coping with Therapeutic Impasse

An impasse becomes an opportunity for growth in different ways for the therapist and for the client. For the therapist, the challenge is to determine to what degree her position is based on her own areas of vulnerability: personal issues or limitations in knowledge or experience. When these difficulties are addressed, it enhances the therapist's competence. Failure to face these issues contributes to undermining the competence and confidence of both the therapist and the client.

The therapist should persist with creative efforts to the point where it is clear that further progress is not possible or that what the client wants is unethical or inappropriate. Under such circumstances, therapy should be terminated and a transfer to another therapist considered. The client should be informed about why termination or transfer is being considered. The responsibility for such a decision should be jointly shared by the therapist and the client or appropriate other such as a parent when the client is a child. When the client is a child, she should share in this process commensurate with her ability to cope with it. At no time should the sole responsibility be placed on the client, that is, "the resistant client."

For the client, the impasse represents an opportunity to break an established destructive pattern. The challenge to the therapist is to provide a safe enough environment for the client to take the risk of vulnerability that will permit considering why she is reluctant to follow the lead of the therapist. When this is done with safety and support, it can help the client endure the heightened vulnerability that occurs between giving up an established pattern of behavior and developing a new, comfortable replacement. This also contributes to increasing the client's trust to take risks in the future. Failure to accomplish overcoming the impasse is likely to reinforce dysfunctional behavior and increase resistance to the therapeutic process.

A challenge to the client, with the help of the therapist, is to sort out to what extent she is reluctant to address issues presented by the therapist. The evaluation should also address the safety of the therapeutic environment and the adequacy of the match between the therapist and the client.

Commitment to Continuing Education

A therapist should be committed to increasing the scope of her knowledge and skills. The therapist should approach this with an eclectic orientation and avoid the tempting security of commitment to a singular school or point of view. Such an approach carries with it the challenge and burden of how to make choices among the many options and how to incorporate new information into an existing style of therapy. To do so requires developing ways to avoid stimulus overload and its attendant anxiety.

Therapist Should Develop Own Treatment Style

The processes outlined previously are a contributing factor to the value that each therapist should develop her own unique style and avoid any temptation to mimic a mentor or another therapist. This is accomplished by selecting from one's ongoing education the theory and technique that best suit the kind of therapeutic problems with which the therapist chooses to work. What works for one therapist may have the reverse effect for another therapist. When a therapist tries to relate in a way that is not compatible with her personality or way of communicating, she is likely to appear awkward and uncertain and undermine credibility with her client. Mimicking another therapist undermines a therapist's confidence in developing her own creative style and the confidence that goes with it.

Therapist Should Avoid Multiple Relationships with Clients

Usually a therapist should have only one kind of relationship with a client. When a therapist and a client relate to one another in more than one context, a possibility of role conflicts that may undermine both roles is likely. An example occurs when a client and a therapist also have a social relationship; it will probably inhibit the freedom of disclosure in the therapy and also impact on the quality of the social relationship.

This also may occur in any other dualities, such as therapist and teacher roles. A client may be inhibited from sharing vulnerabilities in therapy that may negatively reflect on her performance as a student.

The question for both participants in a duality is to assess whether the benefits warrant the involved risk. There are likely to be times when such duality is workable. In such situations both parties should develop some mechanism for monitoring when continuing the dual relationship is no longer feasible.

Therapeutic Intervention for the Largest Relevant Social Entity

The basis for this value is most clear when the presenting symptom is a reflection of some underlying issue in a family. It was just such a situation that got me started in working with families, which I described in Chapter 1.

This experience led me to expand my thinking to the value that as a therapist I should design an intervention to work with the largest social unit relevant to the therapeutic goal. I would then shift the treatment unit as it became clear that work with a subunit such as the couple or an individual was indicated.

Therapeutic Program Should Include the Means for Implementing Change

For some therapists the goal in therapy is insight, with the presumption that it will lead to desired change. For others the goal is knowing what and how to change behavior in a desired direction. Therapy should include a demonstration of the client's ability to implement a desired change. Therapy should end when the client knows what she needs to do and how to do it and has the resources to effect the change.

When changes do not occur that meet the client's expectations, she often views the therapy as less than successful. I believe this occurs because insufficient attention was paid to implementation of a desired change. Too often clients feel that understanding will make the change happen. I find it productive to help clients develop an operationally defined program for implementing change and a monitoring procedure to ensure that it happens.

A simple illustration occurred in a client who was having difficulty in a work situation because he frequently answered questions with "I don't know" or "I'll have to think about it" to protect his vulnerability to criticism. He knew this was creating a problem for him and was clear that he needed to modify this behavior. He was confident that he would do it and rejected my suggestion for a defined way to accomplish the change. We ended the discussion on this point and went on to other concerns. A few weeks later when we reviewed his progress, he was embarrassed to report that he did not get very far with his efforts. We defined a strategy that included a method for monitoring progress; I suggested that he set aside a few minutes each day to monitor how well he did that day in accomplishing his goal. When he was successful, it reinforced his continued behavior. When he failed, it gave him an opportunity to correct it the next day or experiment with ways to help incorporate the desired behavior. This procedure was also helpful because it kept the issue in conscious awareness. Successful change was accomplished in a short period.

Belief System

Reasons Clients Seek Therapy

Some clients present themselves with a symptom such as depression or anxiety. After evaluation, it becomes clear that their real agenda is to change someone else's behavior or to get them into therapy. I saw one woman who presented symptoms of depression. After reviewing her situation, it became clear that she thought her husband should be in therapy. Her presumption was that if he changed then she would not have any problems.

Sometimes people seek therapy because they are alone and lonely. I saw an elderly widow whose children lived in other parts of the country. She had had a successful experience in therapy many years earlier. She presented symptoms around a difficulty in her relationship with her children. After discussion, she acknowledged that there was nothing wrong with her relationship to them except the distance between them. She needed to talk and felt that this would be an appropriate entrée. Her fantasy was that I would help her find a way to get her children to move back to the same city.

Presenting Problem Is Not Always the Source Problem

A common occurrence is for a child to be presented for therapy with some form of school problem or behavior problem, only to find that it screens a marital or other family problem. I described earlier how I got started in family therapy through such a situation. A variation on this situation was the couple who came in seeking help on how to manage a difficult child. It turned out that they were more comfortable focusing on how to deal with the child's problem than on facing the problems in their marriage.

In another type of case, a man presented problems in his difficulty with making a commitment to get married to a woman with whom he was very much in love. He raised concerns about his discomfort with certain personality traits and with certain of her family members. Evaluation revealed that the underlying problem was that marriage meant changing his relationship to his mother.

Best Results When Therapeutic Learning Practiced Outside of Therapy

The therapeutic experience is like any other learning. A given behavior becomes an integral part of a person's repertoire when it is sufficiently practiced that it does not require conscious direction to occur. Too many clients approach therapy with the passivity that just talking about a problem will change it. This tendency is enhanced when the therapist colludes by not putting more responsibility on the client to play a more active role in incorporating the new learning.

Clients will Stay in Therapy When Benefits Exceed Frustrations

I believe this to be a truism for any behavior. The challenge for the therapist is to understand what constitutes a benefit or a cost for a client in the therapeutic relationship. It is not safe to assume that what constitutes a positive or negative experience for one person will have the same meaning for another person. I saw one client who was comfortable getting criticism because this was the major way he received attention. Much as he wanted positive acknowledgment, he felt uncomfortable getting it because he felt unworthy of it.

People's tolerance for dealing with gratifying and painful experiences varies greatly as a function of their past history and may be very specific to particular behaviors or affect a wide range of behaviors. One man grew up in an environment where his physical and emotional needs were generally indulged. This generalized to an attitude of entitlement that he expressed in all his relationships. His charm and competence further reinforced this indulgence. Frequently this would go too far, leaving him confused and angry when people rejected him. His low tolerance for dealing with this kind of pain got expressed in blaming other people for their shortcomings and turning to other relationships where he was still able to get what he needed.

In another situation a woman was physically abused by an alcoholic mother on a daily basis when she was growing up. She learned to tolerate the pain without showing any outward appearance of how it affected her. She was determined not to give her mother the satisfaction of knowing that she was being affected by the abuse. In her adulthood, this generalized to her difficulty in not letting people know how she felt or thought. This became established to the degree that she often had to work hard at determining for herself how she felt about many things.

Therapy Outcome Function of the Problems, Characteristics, and Available Resources

In developing a treatment plan, I learned to be more concerned about the balance between the severity of a problem and the resources available to cope with it than with severity alone. A minor problem with limited resources available can be as challenging as a major problem where there are many available resources. I saw a man who came from an environment in which he was grossly overprotected with the result that he had very limited skills for coping with relationships. Coping with everyday problems was frequently overwhelming. Problems that most people solve for themselves consumed much time, patience, and effort in the process of helping him to develop more adequate basic coping skills.

In contrast, I saw a family with multiple problems where there was the potential for developing many resources for coping with their problems. Therapy focused on helping them discover and learn how to use these resources. The therapy lasted about ten weeks, during which time a great deal was accomplished. Therapy ended when it was clear they had the tools to solve the outstanding problems. A six-month follow-up proved this to be the case.

"Client Resistance" Reflects Therapist's Difficulty in Addressing Client Needs

During part of my training, I often heard that clients dropped out of therapy because they were resistant to the process or they did not want to face their problems. I soon learned to view such situations in a different light. It became increasingly clear to me that clients often dropped out of therapy because the therapist was not able to relate to them in ways that felt safe. Lack of safety got expressed in various forms: using an unfamiliar language, feeling blamed, too much interpretation, not feeling they were understood, feeling judged, overly high expectations, or moving too fast. The therapist has a responsibility to provide an atmosphere where the client can feel it is safe to be vulnerable and where they will be treated with dignity and respect. Failure to do so is not the client's failing but that of the therapist.

The presumption is not that following such considerations in therapy will always achieve its desired goals. If a client did not want to invest further in the therapeutic process, it could be discussed and respected. The client would be helped to make this decision by understanding the basis for it and the consequences that go with it without being judged, if she chooses not to follow the therapist's recommendation.

Clients Seek Therapy When They Have Exhausted Their Own Resources

Some clients seek therapy at the drop of a hat, whereas others go to great lengths before doing so. In the former case one task of therapy is to help clients discover and use their own resources. In the latter case, the therapeutic goal is to help them use existing resources differently or to develop new resources. I saw one family that was living a rooming house life-style. They largely lived parallel lives where everyone did their own thing and shared very little. A crisis developed when one of the adolescent children got into trouble using drugs. In family therapy they became aware of how distant they had become from each other. They saw how they had not been available to one another and how isolated and lonely it was. Therapy provided the opportunity for recognizing what they needed from one another and aided them in redefining their relationships.

Clinical Application

The objective in defining the dimensions of values and beliefs was to have an operational way to assess what accounts for the kind of values and belief structures that a person holds. Through such understanding a therapist is better able to determine the likelihood of accomplishing change and where to direct such efforts when change is desirable. What I do in practice is to develop a profile of significant values and beliefs, using the previously defined conceptual frame to develop a treatment strategy.

I will describe how these concepts were useful in helping a couple resolve an issue of much conflict between them over a period of years. I will start with a brief description of the couple and their background and then discuss the therapeutic intervention stemming from this analysis and provide a guide for the clinical application of these concepts.

CASE ILLUSTRATION

Presenting Problem

Susan is very resentful of the demands of John's work because she feels that it interferes with the marital relationship and often leaves her feeling very lonely.

Background Information

John, 35, is a lawyer who is very dedicated to his career. He works very long hours. He follows closely in the footsteps of his father, who also was a lawyer who modeled a similar dedication to his work. John's mother was devoted to supporting her husband's career. She made few demands on his time. She accepted responsibility for raising the children and managing the home. She was grateful for whatever time his career permitted him to be at home and participate in family life. Whatever resentments she had, she kept to herself.

John's younger brother, Sam, who is three years his junior, has successfully followed a career in business. The members of John's family of origin are close. Emotionally the family is organized around relating to the father's career needs. The expression of emotion and conflict is frowned upon.

Susan, 33, has her own career and is working on an advanced degree. She is primarily responsible for rearing their two children, ages 4 and 6.

John is a willing participant in child rearing when the demands of his work permit.

Susan has a sister who is two years her senior. Her father was a successful businessman who traveled a great deal. As a result, he was away from the family for extended periods of time. The emotional atmosphere in the family was a volatile one where there was much expression of anger and criticism.

Therapeutic Intervention Based on Value and Belief Assessment

From the evaluation of this family, I concluded that John was very entrenched in all aspects of his value and belief system regarding his commitment to his career and what he expects from Susan regarding it. Susan was very vulnerable because she was not as intense in her values or beliefs about the priority of her work relative to what John placed on his work. This was reinforced by the modeling she experienced in her family of origin, where women deferred to men.

Susan was also bucking the strong commitment and allegiance that John had to his father and the expectation that he had to live up to the model demonstrated by his father. His expectation for Susan was the model his mother presented, which was to be totally submerged in being supportive of her husband's career.

Complicating Susan's position was that her self-doubts got expressed in negative ways, such as complaining, that ultimately got expressed in angry outbursts that offended John's sense of appropriate communication. Her manner of expressing her anger then became the issue, often obscuring the issue that was the basis for it.

It ultimately became clear to Susan that there was not likely to be any significant change in John's value and belief about his work. She ultimately recognized that she would get more of what she needed if she focused on how best to relate to his position rather than on how to change it. When she shifted her orientation, she was able to get more of what she needed, even though the basic situation did not change. This resulted in John's being able to be more emotionally responsive to Susan's needs.

A GUIDE TO CLINICAL APPLICATION

1. Determine the values for each significant social unit using the following dimensions:
   - What are the primary guiding values for the relevant social unit?
   - What is the operating structure of values?

- What is the subject matter?
- To whom does the value apply?
- When does it apply?
- How consistent are they with behavior?
- How committed are they to the values?
- How specifically is the value defined?
- What is the source of the value system?
- What evaluation process is used for holding a value?
  - Flexibility—how subject to change is a value?
    From client's view
    From therapist's view
  - With what priority are values held?
  - What purpose does holding the stated values serve?
  - What are the consequences of holding the given value system?
  - Is the value system primarily guided by intellect or emotion?
2. Repeat this evaluation for beliefs.
3. How compatible are the values, beliefs, and goals?
   - How clearly are goals defined?
     - Do goals have priorities?
     - What is the availability of resources to accomplish goals?
     - How consistent are the goals with the value and belief system?
     - How is conflict in goals managed?
   - How do values, beliefs and goals impact on the family social unit?
   - Develop an intervention strategy in collaboration with the family for resolving differences and inconsistencies that require attention.
4. Considerations for the therapist:
   - Periodically review your value and belief system as a therapist.
   - How compatible is it with your personal value and belief system?
   - What are your goals for yourself in a given case?
   - How compatible are these with the client's needs?
   - Are there things you need to work on?

Summary

All therapists work with values, beliefs, and setting of goals in their work in whatever their theoretical orientation may be. The purpose of this chapter was to provide a way of conceptualizing and operationalizing an approach to working with these concepts that can be useful to the clinician. This applies to understanding her own values and beliefs and those of her clients. Operational definitions were provided for each of the concepts and illustrated in a case example. A guideline for the general application of these concepts was also provided.

CHAPTER SIX

Assessment of Resources

Successful outcome of therapy is more dependent on the resources in the client system than on the nature of its problems. I felt it would be useful to define explicitly the various forms that client resources may take. Such attention led to greater sensitivity and awareness in the discovery and utilization of available resources.

THEORY

The ability of a family, individually or collectively, to change is a function of the resources that are available within the system. A resource is any material entity or cognitive, emotional, or character trait that at least one person in the family possesses and that is useful in accomplishing therapeutic goals. A resource also includes the family's ability to mobilize resources outside the family from relatives, friends, social agencies, or others.

Material resources include money, equipment, tools, and reference materials. Cognitive resources include creativity, problem-solving ability, information, skills, ability to negotiate differences, and experience. Emotional resources include empathic ability, access to feelings, and the ability to express them in appropriate ways. Character traits include sense of humor, honesty, commitment, responsibility, and integrity.

Part of the therapist's role is to determine what resources can be available for use in therapy and how best to utilize them. He does this by helping a social unit achieve a desired level of functioning by determining what resources it needs, discovering and using the resources they have, and developing those they need but do not have. I will describe in this chapter those that I find clinically useful.

The evaluation encompasses six areas of the family life space: descriptive characteristics of the social entity, ability to communicate, ability to negotiate differences, the nature of their cultural context, ability for self-assessment, and influence of history and past experience. The evaluation

151

includes determination of what resources are available or potentially available, how receptive the possessing social unit is to utilizing it, and how well the social unit is able to implement them. A parent may understand the struggle his adolescent is having with identity issues but is reluctant to utilize this understanding because he feels inadequate in how to apply it.

Overview of Resource Categories

Descriptive Characteristics of the Social Entity

This category includes any descriptive attributes of individuals or other social entity that has potential as a resource.

Ability to Communicate

I will focus on four aspects of communication: communication patterns, use of power, possible ways to express affect, and the ability to empathize. These patterns involve who talks to whom about what subjects, how family members influence each other's ability to express feelings, and how well people listen.

Ability to Negotiate

Negotiation involves decisions about how people behave and how they resolve their differences. This includes how families accomplish a division of labor, areas of agreement and disagreement, how they resolve conflict, and how decisions are made.

Nature of Cultural Context

This refers to the established patterns that derive from ethnic origin and the social context in which a family lives. It includes understanding how these influences affect the development of problems, the role that rituals play, and how to implement them in family life.

Assessment Capability

An essential part of accomplishing change is the ability to critically assess one's own behavior, which includes accepting input from others, especially those with whom one is having a troubled interaction. This requires distinguishing between openness to hearing feedback as separate from having to agree or act on the feedback. This applies to all categories of social units. A parent who tries to comfort a child rejected by peers by telling him the others do not know what they are talking about is not helping the child to learn about self-assessment.

Another important component of self-assessment is the ability to accept positive feedback from others. Children need the modeling of parents who show them how to assess a problem and who demonstrate the ability to acknowledge when they are wrong.

Assessment without implementation is an exercise in futility. The assessment process also should include the social unit's ability to utilize resources. Having affection for another person is of little value if it does not get expressed.

Influence of History and Past Experience

A major determinant of a social entity's current behavior is the nature of past experiences and how they are interpreted. Such experiences can be the source of resource for effective coping or an obstacle to it.

Description of Resource Categories

Descriptive Characteristics of the Social Entity

Characteristics of individuals include such attributes as appearance, intelligence, personality traits, sense of humor, regard for others, and others. Characteristics of other social entities (marital relationship, various combinations of parents and children and the family as a whole) include who is involved in the social entity and the basis for it. An example is the social entity composed of a father and his two sons based around their mutual interest in the sons being hockey players.

Ability to Communicate

Communication Patterns
Communication patterns can be a resource or a handicap in determining the degree to which a couple or a family functions in a satisfying manner. These patterns define who talks to whom, under what conditions, and about what subject matters. I saw one family where the expectation was that all communication between the father and the children would go through the mother, except when the father was angry or when he could not avoid it.

Such restrictive patterns of communication commonly result in limited development of the social unit and in its ability to know and make maximum use of its resources. This is particularly the case when the person in the gatekeeping role — the mother in the current illustration — intentionally or accidentally distorts communication between members of the family. In a family where there were marital problems, the wife quoted the children's views about their father to him to gain leverage in her disagreement with her husband: "The children told me how mean you were not to let them take that trip." This was a problem in two ways. She was not getting the children to negotiate directly with their father, and she distorted what they said.

Frequently such a pattern is more subtly defined. In another family, the children learned they had a better chance of getting what they wanted if they got their mother to get their father's approval. This was a father who was ambivalent about having children and did not feel comfortable dealing with them.

More commonly, communication patterns are open and unrestricted regarding who talks to whom, on what subjects, in what manner, and for how long. Each family develops its own style in how to manage communication. Commonly, children learn to go to their mother for certain matters, perhaps those concerned with feelings and relationships, and to their father for others, perhaps solving problems with "things" and money matters.

I found a different pattern in another type of family where the parents grew up in a tightly knit ethnic community. The children learned to go to the oldest brother about concerns outside the family because their father did not have much need to interact beyond his ethnic world. It is not uncommon for an older sibling, of either sex, to serve in a parentified role to siblings and at times to one or the other parent.

Power

I define *power* as the ability of one social entity to influence the thinking and/or behavior of another social entity. Such influence can be accomplished directly or indirectly.

Direct Ways to Exert Power.

- *Legitimate — by agreement and acknowledged:* The power to influence is openly vested in a social unit and accepted by others. Examples of this are election to a political office, a management position in a business organization, informal consensus that one person is to act as leader, being a spouse and a parent, and the power that is given out of respect to an adult or elder.
- *By virtue of expertise:* When one social entity views other social entities as having expertise on a given subject and this expertise is relevant to accomplishing some needed objective. The doctor, lawyer,

plumber, and auto mechanic all achieve power by virtue of their expertise when the social entity needs such services.

Less clear is what defines expertise in a parent. Unlike other areas of competence, the only requirement needed to be a parent is the capacity to contribute to the conception that culminates in birth or to be eligible to adopt. The only accountability for adequacy of parenting is in extreme abuse, when social agencies may be called upon to evaluate the adequacy of parenting and to remove the child(ren) from parental care when deemed appropriate. Children see their parents as experts to the extent that parents behave appropriately and accept the role (however inadequate they may feel).

- *Expectations:* Statement of expectations is a way to influence the occurrence of desired behaviors and discourage undesirable behaviors. One determinant of successfully accomplishing influence is the degree to which expectations are clearly defined and communicated with consistency. Training children to behave in desired ways is more readily accomplished when a child knows what performance is expected, under what conditions, and what will happen with failure to comply. Failure in any of these steps is likely to lead to less compliance than is desired.

  I saw a family composed of a mother, a father, and an adolescent daughter, Susan. The mother complained that she was never able to get her daughter to behave as expected. Exploration of family patterns revealed that the mother always had great difficulty in making clear what behavior she wanted from her daughter. Her inconsistency complicated the problem even when she could make expectations clear. When the father got angry at the mother for her inconsistency, they got into an argument that took precedence over the issue with their daughter. This resulted in Susan's learning that she could manipulate around situations with which she was not happy. Failure to define and manage sanctions was a core issue in the chronic battle between Susan and her parents.

- *Ability to grant rewards:* A social unit will allow itself to be influenced to gain some desired benefit. A child behaves the way a parent wants to receive a desired toy, special privilege, or other favor. A sexually desirous male wines and dines the woman of his desires to win her sexual participation.

  Another family is an illustration of how power through rewards effects behavior. The mother did not want to deal with the hassle of trying to manage the trials and tribulations of adolescents. She negotiated with her husband that he would be responsible for dispensing rewards and discipline to their children. This arrangement was quite satisfactory until she discovered that her requests and concerns had little impact on her children except when her husband backed her up by providing incentives they could not refuse. Her self-inflicted humiliation motivated her to learn how to deal appropriately with her children.

- *Capacity to punish or discipline:* The ability to influence can derive from the anticipation that failure to perform or failure to perform as desired will result in some form of pain, such as rejection, deprivation, guilt, or being hit.

    A distinction should be made between punishment and discipline. For many people these concepts are synonymous. I prefer this distinction because they serve different functions. Punishment stems from the need to retaliate for felt injury or injustice, whereas discipline has as its goal educating how to behave. Such a distinction does not guarantee that the intent behind either approach will be heard in the intended way. Consider the parent who grounds a child for coming home too late. Whether this child experiences such action as punishment or discipline depends on how the restriction is imposed and the context of the parent-child relationship. A message communicated in a way that focuses on learning from the experience might be: "When you learn that there are consequences to breaking the rules, you will be more respectful of your curfew." The message of punishment might be: "I'm angry that you broke the rules and disturbed my sleep so now you're going to pay for it!"

    I frequently see family situations where a person gets so angry he wants to retaliate under conditions where he either does not control or does not desire to consider the consequences of such action. One couple had a long history of exchanging derogatory remarks about their respective families of origin. On one occasion the husband made an especially hostile remark about his mother-in-law. The wife reported reacting in blind rage: "When he said that, all I could see was red! I just wanted to hurt back and I didn't give a damn about anything else."

    In another family, the mother discovered that her son broke a favorite vase through careless behavior about which she explicitly had warned him. Her first reaction was to want to lash out in retaliation and break something of his that was important to him. Second thoughts led her to consider her priorities: Was her need to gain the satisfaction of venting her frustration more important than trying to teach her son how to be more responsible? She was so angry that she said, "The hell with teaching," and promptly broke one of his favorite airplane models. After the glow of retaliation dissipated, she was left with residual anger at herself, her son, her husband, and the whole world. Things worked out well because she and her son were able to review what happened and how it happened. From this they both gained a better way to communicate and resolve their differences.

- *Having necessary resources:* Power also derives from having the resources necessary to accomplish a given objective. When a family faces a crisis, the person or persons having the necessary resources or access to them to resolve the crisis will gain a position of power.

I saw a family that had an adolescent child who was arrested for involvement with drugs. The parents were distraught and felt helpless to cope with the event. The mother turned to her older brother for help. He consulted his lawyer, his friends at city hall, and contacts in the police department. By having and applying the needed resources, the adolescent's uncle was able to intervene on his nephew's behalf.

This was one of a number of situations in which this brother was able to help his sister's family at times of need. As a result he was very respected. His advice was often sought when major problems confronted the family.

- *Expression of affect-intense anger, love, anxiety, and depression:* It is not uncommon to find that tears or anger can be effective ways to gain power when the show of such behavior is uncomfortable to others. The same can be said for such other emotions as love, anxiety, and depression. Love for a divorced woman was attributed as the reason that King Edward VIII abdicated his throne. Intensity of love has caused people to lose fortunes, betray their country, commit murder, and achieve undying devotion.

Exposure to people with significant anxiety and depression can significantly influence the thinking and feeling of those who are subjected to it. Both feelings can have the impact of disrupting relationships or of being a means to control them. In literature and the movies we often see situations where the anxiety or depression of one person is used to control the behavior of another person.

I worked with a family in which the mother was subject to periods of depression. She, her husband, and two children colluded in organizing family functioning around her periods of depression. It became clear that when she could not get what she wanted she expressed concern about getting depressed or would get depressed. This organized the family to cater to her bidding.

- *Guilt:* A common stereotype in the ethnic literature (Jewish, Irish, and others) is the mother who uses guilt to achieve desired behavior in her offspring. When reasoning and pleading fail, guilt is often called to the rescue. Guilt refers to the failure to behave in the expected manner.

A classic example of this occurred in a family session. This was a Jewish family composed of two parents and three children. The mother was feeling very unappreciated and taken for granted. She was agitated because she wanted some help with a household cleaning project and nobody had the time. This led into a litany about all the things that she was doing for every member in the family. She went on to voice her sadness and anger that nobody was there for her when she needed help. Her sadness and anger mobilized the family to do her bidding.

Guilt is also an important tool in achieving comformity to institutional doctrine, such as in religion. I saw many situations where the pressure of guilt induction, especially in orthodox religions, resulted in immobilizing anxiety and depression.

I was working with a couple around sexual problems. The woman had much fear and anxiety about having sexual relations. Evaluation of her concern showed that she grew up in an orthodox Roman Catholic family where any thought of sex was a mortal sin. This was reinforced by her very authoritarian father who was cold and aloof, forbade any discussion of sexual matters, and prohibited any movies or television programs that were at all suggestive. Making the transition from this type of atmosphere to sex being acceptable in marriage was more than she could handle. She had strong anxiety and guilt when she attempted to engage in any sexual behavior.

- *Shame:* Shame becomes an issue when a quality of the social unit comes into question. It is an attack on the self. A child who is arrested for stealing would feel shame if he felt such behavior was a reflection on his character. The child's family as a unit might feel shame if the behavior of their son reflected on the integrity of the family or the competence of the parents. If the child did not think his behavior reflected on his character, then he might just feel guilty for poor judgment.

Parents often use shame as a way to get a child to behave in a desired manner: "You should be ashamed of yourself," "Aren't you ashamed," or "How could you do such a shameful thing?"

Shame may develop from within the social unit or be imposed from outside it. I saw a family around the issue of their only son and oldest child who just informed his parents that he was gay. The mother was particularly traumatized and felt great shame because she felt that this happened because of some defect in her. She also feared that other people would see it the same way.

- *Obligation:* A favor done one day often carries with it the verbal and nonverbal expectation of reciprocation that might not otherwise have been granted. This concept is a commonly used tool in politics: "You scratch my back, and I'll scratch yours." The same idea is found in the family situation where one child says to a sibling, "I did your chore for you yesterday, so now you do mine today."

Although guilt and obligation have in common a commitment to another person, they differ in that guilt derives from the quality of a relationship whereas obligation relates to a reciprocal exchange of deeds.

Indirect Ways to Exert Power. Indirect methods of accomplishing influence are more subtle because they are expressed by *not* acting or by acting indirectly. This is achieved through silence, indifference, incompetence, and obstruction.

- *Silence:* The response of silence by one social unit to another's effort to communicate can have a profound effect on the relationship between them. This occurs because silence leaves open to interpretation by the social unit attempting to communicate whether the receiving social unit did not hear the message, is angry and not responding, doesn't understand the message, or needs time to think about it. Quite different consequences can go with these alternatives. Silence complicates the communication process because the amount of anger that results from getting no response can be felt by the sender of the communication as being invisible, invalidated, nonexistent, and helpless. With silence the original message is overshadowed by the lack of response. This is the case with the child who ignores his mother's request to do something, the boss whose request is ignored by his employee, and the letter that is not answered.

  In some families, silence can be sufficiently uncomfortable for a person that he will go to considerable lengths to avoid having that happen. In my work with one couple, I found that when the husband got angry with his wife he would not talk to her. This would get so upsetting to her that she would do whatever she could to get him to talk to her.

  In other families, they manage anger by not talking to one another, which can go for periods ranging from hours to weeks. I saw a couple where the wife would not talk to her husband for periods as long as three weeks when she got really angry. Such behavior became the breeding ground for other problems between them and resulted in tension that got expressed in irritability and arguing between other family members. In both types of situations, silence was a means for manipulating a relationship.

  The opposite also occurs. Some families engage in constant pointless chatter to avoid dealing with anger or to avoid facing unpleasant issues. I saw one family where there was constant chatter with the resulting difficulty and frustration in dealing with matters of concern.

- *Indifference:* Indifference is a way to protect against vulnerability. An adolescent girl may pine for the attention of a certain young man. However, she feels she will be less attractive if she lets her feelings be known and does not want to risk the possibility of rejection. She feels she will be more attractive by appearing to be indifferent to him.

  In other situations, a hierarchical relationship gets defined by one person having access to resources that another person desires. The power derives from this imbalance. An example in marriage is the wife who presents an attitude of indifference to sex as a way to maintain power in the relationship. I saw a couple who had a good and active sexual relationship. When she got angry at her husband, she would become indifferent to sex. His first reaction was to attempt to overcome her indifference. Once he discovered the basis for her indifference, he retaliated with his own indifference. This became a standoff until the desire for sex in one or the other of the couple became more important than the power struggle.

Children also learn how to use the power of indifference. They quickly learn that to show interest in something that is desired makes them vulnerable to being manipulated by those in control of it. I worked with a family in which there was a son, 17, and a daughter, 15. She liked one of her brother's friends but knew that if she let her desire be known then her brother would use it to manipulate her. She dealt with the event by appearing indifferent to his friends but managed to get the desired introduction through an apparent display of altruism in helping her brother and his friends prepare for a party.

Indifference is also a way to express hostility by not valuing what somebody else cares about. I saw a couple where the husband was an amateur sculptor. He would spend as much time as he could in his basement on his labor of love at the expense of time with his wife. His wife admired his work but often would appear indifferent to it as an expression of her anger because of his neglect of her. Her cool reception to his request for her feedback became a source of many arguments.

- *Incompetence:* A good way to avoid doing an undesired task is to pretend to be or actually be incompetent in performing it. This is particularly potent when time pressure is critical and when quality of performance is important. A hassled mother wants a certain chore done. Her reluctant offspring seems all thumbs in trying to do the task, knowing that the mother's impatience or time pressure will soon result in her deciding to do it herself.

A variation of this manipulation is the acknowledgment that someone else does the task so much better. In the above example, the reluctant son might plead that his mother ask his sister to do the chore because she is so much better at it than he is.

Incompetence also can be a way to express hostility. Being incompetent may force another person to do an undesired task. In one family, the father was very particular about how his lawn should be cut. He taught his 12-year-old son how to do it to his satisfaction. In the course of a family session, it became clear that one way that the son had to express his anger at his father was to screw up the way he did the lawn, which resulted in his father having to do it over himself.

• *Obstruction:* Obstruction can be an effective way to influence another social unit. There are many ways to practice obstruction: withholding needed approval or resources, introducing distractions, negatively influencing others, or undoing what has been done, among others.

The withholding of approval or needed resources differs from the application of power through punishment. Punishment is a clear statement and overt in its intent; obstruction is a more covert act such as silence or inaction without an overtly stated objective. In one family I saw, the mother often would deal with unpopular requests by taking them under advisement and then not to anything—a pocket veto. In one instance she handled her daughter's request to have a party in this manner. Ultimately this led to a big argument between them, followed by the daughter modeling her mother's behavior when something was desired of her that she did not want to do.

In another family a son wanted to go to a college that was farther away from home than his parents liked. As it happened, the father had friends who were well connected at that college and told the father that they would be happy to help his son out. The father withheld the information to avoid facing a battle over what college the son would attend.

Obstructing by using distractions is a common tool of the toddler's parents. When the child is about to reach for an undesired object, the parent attempts to shift the child's attention to a more acceptable object. This method is not limited to toddlers. In one couple when bill-paying time came and the husband would raise questions about the excessive use of charges, the wife would do her best to distract him with family news or problems of concern with the children. At other times she would creatively distract him with other problems that involved large expenditures of money.

Negatively influencing other people involved in a decision is another variation of obstruction. This happened in the case of a 17-year-old high school student who wanted to take a trip with his girlfriend, whose parents were receptive to the idea. When his parents recognized they might have a battle on their hands if they vetoed the trip, they discussed their concerns with the girl's parents. They were able to convince her parents to their point of view, which resulted in the withdrawal of their support and the avoidance of a potential crisis.

Combining Types of Power.   These forms of power are not mutually exclusive but have considerable overlap. The degree of influence achieved becomes more powerful when multiple sources of power are combined.

Consider the case of the mother who is trying to get her reluctant son to clean his room. She has several options. She can use reward, punishment, guilt, anger, or obligation. Each one of these may be effective alone.

However, combining two or more is likely to increase the likelihood of compliance. She could reward him if he does it as requested and punish him if he does not do it. She could also invoke guilt by indicating that she would have to do it if he does not and how this would burden her. She could also express her anger or cry because she knows it bothers him. The combination of such efforts would be likely to get the room more readily cleaned as requested than if she used fewer options.

Expression of Affect

There is a wide range of values in our society on the acceptability of expressing affect, whether it is in the form of anger, fear, love, anxiety, or sadness. Cultures differ in the degree and type of affect expression that is acceptable and the conditions under which it may be expressed. Problems develop when there is a violation of norms within a culture or when the norms of two cultures conflict.

Ethnic groups tend to have characteristic ways of expressing anger and joy. This was the case in couple I saw where the husband was a Protestant of Germanic background and the wife was of Italian background. He was formal and aloof and showed very little of what he felt. The wife was very volatile and expressive. When she felt something, she expressed it with gusto. Their arguments were very frustrating to both. Her expressive manner, which he referred to as hysteria, bothered him. She objected to his aloof and distant manner and described him as a "cold fish." Of particular frustration was her inability to have any idea about what he was feeling.

Some cultures have the stereotype that for a man to cry or show his emotional vulnerability is a reflection on his manhood. In one family situation after a son committed suicide, the father was at work the next day. He discouraged any but the barest acknowledgment of the event and on the surface behaved as though the death had never happened.

Empathy Capability

An important contribution to good relationships is the capacity for empathy — the ability to appreciate how another person thinks, feels, or behaves. To have empathy does not imply agreement. It is different from sympathy, which involves feeling sorry for the plight of another person without any appreciation for what it is like to have that feeling.

A parent who disciplines a child to appease his own frustrations without adequate empathy for the child's feelings is contributing to making a difficult parent-child relationship. The parent who is able to show such empathy is better able to exercise discipline that both discourages the undesired behavior and contributes to building a relationship of mutual respect.

Empathy is an essential ingredient in the therapeutic process. The therapist who cannot empathize with his client will limit his ability to be an effective resource. The client who cannot empathize with another family member is likely to have a difficult time with therapy. In such cases one of the early goals is to help in the development of empathy. This becomes easier to accomplish once empathy is not equated with agreement.

I was working with a family where the parents were upset with their 14-year-old son's recalcitrant behavior. My attempts to help the father empathize with his son's point of view were seen as siding with the son and asking the father to legitimize the annoying behavior. Once he understood that this was not the case, we were able to make progress.

Negotiation Skills

Division of Labor

The survival of any social unit, the family in particular, depends on the performance of many tasks. In the family these tasks include obtaining financial resources to purchase needed goods and services, the physical care of the home inside and out, purchase and preparation of food, and child care. The priority that families attach to these needs and how they determine a division of labor contribute to understanding the unique character of the family's culture.

Other important characteristics include the manner and flexibility with which they manage the division of labor, how rigid it is, how responsive it is to changing needs and abilities, whether all members of the family participate in the division of labor, and whether there is a way to modify how the work gets done or who does it and how to manage and supervise it. Also relevant is whether the division of labor is a family affair or whether each person does his own thing. How are violations handled? Are chores involving children viewed as a means of getting a job done, or is the purpose also to use this activity as a means for teaching survival skills and responsibility?

There is much to learn from an understanding of how a family handles the division of labor. It is a useful and relatively nonthreatening way to gain information without the family being aware of the way in which they provide it. Information can be obtained on the use of power that is employed, the nature of cooperative versus competitive relationships, equity in division of labor, attitude toward work and satisfaction with performance, and attitude toward working as individuals versus as a group. An example of how the division of labor is utilized is provided in a case illustration at the end of this chapter.

Decision Making

The functioning of any social unit requires making decisions. It is not possible to avoid making a decision in any given situation. A person has a choice to choose among available options or to choose to take no action. To take no action is in itself a decision. A wife who is aware her husband is having an affair and chooses not to say or do anything about it is making a decision which has consequences attached to it. My interest is in how decisions are made, by whom, about what, when, and how they are communicated.

Overt versus Covert.   An overt decision involves a conscious awareness to act or not act on a particular matter before the action takes place. A covert decision is one where the behavior precedes the awareness or the acknowledgment of a decision to behave or not behave in a particular manner.

Consider the previously mentioned case where a parent is faced with a child who violated her curfew. An overt decision would be the case where the parent decides to discipline the daughter by grounding her and so informs her. It would be a covert decision if the parent did not tell the daughter she was grounded but would not let her go out the next time she requested it. Another form of a covert decision would be if the parent would not let the daughter go on a school trip and decided after the fact why she could not go.

Degree of Clarity.   A decision can vary from being very clear and specific in principle or in how and when a particular behavior should be performed. A mother may be very clear in telling her child she wants the child to clean his room but not indicate what she means by that. It becomes another level of clarity when she specifies exactly what should be done and how to do it. In the former case, a child may be behaving in good faith according to his own definition only to find that it does not meet the parent's undefined expectation. In the latter case, the same behavior conveys a different message — an intent to violate the required behavior.

Failure to specify how a decision should be carried out is an invitation to conflict. Families often have an easier time obtaining an agreement in principle on a decision than they do in determining how, when, and by whom it is carried out.

I saw one family that was very intellectually oriented. They were quite able to make decisions about chores, vacations, and other matters that affected the family. They ran into a lot of trouble in determining the details about how to implement the decisions. They would argue about who should do them, when they should be done, and the level at which they needed to be done.

Effective decision making requires agreement both at the conceptual level and in how it is translated into behavior.

How Considered Is the Decision?   The basis for a decision ranges from impulsive behavior to careful consideration. A couple may decide to buy a house that they fall in love with without adequately considering the soundness of the structure or whether it will meet their needs. At the other end of the polarity, a couple could obsess so long in evaluating information that they lose the opportunity.

I saw many marriages in couple therapy in which there was a history of significant doubt about the decision to marry. For various reasons the doubts were not addressed. In at least two situations, the man was about to tell his girlfriend that he wanted to break off the relationship. Before he was able to communicate his feelings, he was confronted with an unwanted pregnancy. That information ended the discussion about terminating the relationship. In both of these cases, the marriages were turbulent from the beginning and eventually ended in divorce.

In another situation, a man was about to get married for the third time. The week before the wedding, he had growing apprehension about the wisdom of his decision. It was too hard to cope with undoing the momentum that was generated, so he went along quietly but with nagging discomfort. Five years later he was in my office struggling with how to end the marriage, which was stormy from the outset. In relationships like these, poor decisions were made because significant variables were not adequately considered when approprite.

On the Basis of What Information.   How does a family determine what information is needed to make an appropriate decision? The first consideration is whether there is a need to make a decision. Following this, a determination is made regarding what information they need about what and from whom. To what extent should they define how to evaluate the obtained information and the assessment of consequences that might result from making the decision one way or another?

Parents may make a decision about the appropriateness of their child's extracurricular activity based on their own experience on the assumption that they have all the relevant information. What often happens is that parental anxieties, lack of interest, and the pressure of more pressing priorities get in the way of obtaining their child's perspective or analyzing the consequences of the decision. Failure to gain the child's point of view or to check out assumptions leads to relationship difficulties.

I saw a patriarchal family in which a 17-year-old daughter wanted to work as a waitress in a summer resort in a neighboring state. It was especially important to her because a group of her close friends were all planning to do this together. The father had an Old World view that it was his responsibility to protect his daughter's virginity. He viewed her request as grossly inappropriate and rejected it out of hand without seeking any information about it. What bothered her most about his position was that he would not listen to anything she had to say. Adding to her frustration was that this event was a familiar repetition of other events that involved her being in social situations away from the family. Ultimately she got pregnant by a boy considered undesirable by her father. She finally did get him to listen!

Who Makes the Decisions?   There are a number of commonly found ways in which families organize around decision making. There are patriarchal and matriarchal families. In some families we find the "apparent patriarchy" — the figurehead decision maker. This is usually in the form where the father appears to make the decisions. Behind the scenes the mother wields major influence in a way that does not disturb the appearance of a patriarchy.

There are families where parents collaborate in decision making such that neither parent dominates. Often who makes decisions is based on who is more knowledgeable about the content area rather than by role. There are also families where children have inordinate influence on decision making that rivals the power of the parents. In other family situations, extended family members such as grandparents have major influence on how decisions are made. In welfare families major decisions are influenced and sometimes made by social agencies.

A young married couple, Steve and Sally, in their late twenties came for couple therapy. A major problem for them was conflict with his family. Steve worked for his father, who was in a service business, as did his two brothers. The father claimed he was very respectful of each of his children's private lives. Yet he would get involved in where they lived and what type of house they would buy. Much of this manipulation was accomplished because he contributed to making the purchase possible financially. He also intruded in their lives because his business required coverage 24 hours a day. When it suited him, he would call on their services, often outside their established responsibility in the business.

For the most part his wife was hostage to the same behavior. When things really mattered to her, she would wage a campaign whereby she would get him to do her bidding but in a way that protected his patriarchal image.

Content of Decisions.   Many matters affect family life. Many of them require making decisions in situations where parents do not have a choice about whether to make a decision. Examples of this would be where the family will live and whether a child will go to school. There are many areas where a decision is not required. Which of these a family chooses to make decisions about and which they let evolve can be another determinant of a family's culture. Included in this category could be such matters as the life-style a family leads, how family members dress and behave, and whether and how they address their responsibilities.

I have encountered two kinds of problems families have with content related to decision making. At one end of the spectrum is the family where every facet of life is carefully considered before making decisions. A case in point is a family of two parents and two boys aged 7 and 9. The father was a computer designer and obsessive-compulsive in his behavior. He made lists for everything that needed doing. Every major or minor decision about the family had to be carefully considered. The couple came into therapy because of the tension and stress that resulted from such behavior.

At the other end of the continuum is the laid-back family that does not make any decisions it can avoid. An example of this is a family with two parents and three children aged 9, 12, and 14. The father was a carpenter and the mother an artist. They lived a rather chaotic life-style. Bills got paid when they got around to it; they were always receiving dunning notices. Meals were rather irregular. Housework was done when it could not be avoided. The family came into therapy because the 12-year-old was having difficulty at school. He was failing because he was not getting his homework done and was having trouble paying attention in class.

When Decisions Are Made.   Timing of decision making can materially determine the outcome or the validity of making the decision. Premature action can be a problem. One example would be making a decision without adequate information. A child may have an easier time accepting an unpopular decision when he feels all relevant information was considered, whereas the child's belief that the parent does not have adequate information can provide a basis for resistance and hostility by the child.

I came across a family situation where a 17-year-old desperately wanted to have a motorcycle. His parents took an adamant stand against it. He was equally adamant because he felt that fear was the basis for their decision. After much struggle, they were able to talk about the basis for their decision. The amount of effort the parents had invested to learn about motorcycles and get safety statistics surprised their son. Even though he was unhappy with their decision, he was much more able to accept it when he understood how the decision was made.

How Decisions Are Communicated.   Effective implementation of a decision can be materially affected by how it is communicated. It can be done in a way that enhances or stresses the relationship. A junior in high school had had her heart set on spending a semester in France since she started French in the seventh grade. Her parents hoped to send her, but financial resources did not make this possible. They were able to communicate their decision in a sensitive and caring way that enabled their daughter to cope with her disappointment in a supportive way. Her reaction would be quite different if they presented their decision in a context of criticism and guilt for putting such a burden on them.

How Decisions Are Modified.   A fair assessment of the adequacy of a decision can be done only when it is based on the data at the time it was made. People often unfairly judge in retrospect. A good decision is one based on adequate information that gives equitable consideration to the interests of all who are affected by it and the possible consequences that result from making it. A decision that looks good at the point of making it can look bad when the projected outcome does not occur. What often gets overlooked is that it was not the original decision that was faulty but the way it was implemented or the occurrence of unforseen events.

Changing conditions are another reason why what started out as a good decision can turn into a bad one. To minimize this possibility requires openness to receiving or seeking new information that may warrant a change in the decision. It is also desirable not to view changing a decision as necessarily an indication of a mistake or as a measure of incompetence.

Problems are likely to result when decisions are rigidly held in spite of new information or when they are too easily changed with or without the introduction of new information or changing circumstances. Either of these conditions would suggest insecurity in the decision makers and thus carry with it the likelihood of trust issues in those who are affected by such decisions.

A typical example is illustrated by a couple I saw who kept blaming their current marital difficulties on the mistake they made in getting married. After much discussion, they realized that the problem was not in their decision to marry but that they made it knowing too little about each other. In addition, they did not have the skills or maturity to respect their differences and explore ways to find mutually compatible solutions.

Adequacy of Carrying Out Decisions.   Decisions are important to the extent they lead to appropriate action regarding implementation. Failure to do so undermines the quality of the relationship in which such decisions are made. Under such conditions, the making of decisions ceases to have any value, and if they continue to stand may have a negative value because they are likely to be seen as empty and meaningless gestures. A husband with a drinking problem tells his wife he has made a decision to stop drinking. The joy a wife may have in hearing this soon turns to hostility when he does not make any demonstrable effort to carry out the decision, such as not buying liquor, going to Alcoholics Anonymous meetings, or rejecting drinks where he normally would not.

How Decisions Are Evaluated.   The decision-making process, like any skill, improves by learning from experience. It is likely to be most effective when how it is accomplished changes with changing needs and abilities. The style for making decisions when children are young will not work well when children are teenagers. If accommodation is not made with changing needs and abilities, the family is headed for trouble.

When a family is open to looking at the way it makes decisions and is open to making changes in the process as appropriate, they are likely to enhance their skill and comfort as a unit. Failure to do so can lead only to reinforcement of the status quo and it increases the probability of difficulty.

One family I worked with consisted of a father, a mother, and two teenage children. When they married, the husband was the confident protector. His wife was barely out of her teens, naive, and insecure. She was happy to have someone take care of her. Children arrived soon after their marriage. During the early years of the marriage and of the children growing up, the father was the primary decision maker, to the general satisfaction to all concerned.

Once the children started school, the mother decided she wanted to get a college degree. Through her exposure to college, she gained a great deal of self-confidence. As she did this, she increasingly wanted to play a more active role in decision making. Her husband did not take kindly to her wanting to change the decision-making process. Their conflict was enhanced further when the children followed their mother's lead as they got older. The father's rigidity in making the transition to the changing needs of other family members caused a lot of tension and resulted in the family seeking therapy.

Areas of Disagreement

Evaluation of areas where there are agreements and disagreements is a vehicle for determining vulnerabilities and strengths. Evaluation of the degree to which there are commonalities across different areas of disagreement can provide insight in diagnosing problems of a more generic nature. Of concern is the distinction between disagreements that are issue focused and those that are process focused. A husband may disagree with his wife when she spends too much money on clothes for the children. It becomes a different matter when he objects anytime she behaves in an assertive and independent manner.

Further insight can be gained by attending to what types of coalitions develop on what issues. Coalitions develop for two reasons. In some families, the coalitions vary with the issue. In other families, maintaining the coalition is a higher priority than the content of the disagreement. In a family where gender issues are important, it may be more important for the women to stick together than to be divided by the content of the issues. The fear is that even a temporary breakdown of the coalition will weaken the ability to work together on other issues.

I saw a family where there were five children, two boys and three girls. Individually, the girls were manipulated by their brothers. They discovered that by sticking together they could prevent this from happening. In another family, when the mother felt her husband was being chauvinistic, she would side with her daughter and use such instances to deal with her own gender issues with him. The coalition of the females would also come into play when the daughter would support her mother in disputes with her father.

Another contributing problem to family tensions is failure to define clearly the content of the disagreement. Both sides may believe they are disagreeing about the same issue, only to find that they are talking about different issues. Failure to clarify such distortions leaves both parties to feed on their projections and distortions and to feel justifiably upset with each other.

How Conflict Is Resolved

The general idealized assumption in our culture is that a happy family does not have real problems. Past television programs such as "Father Knows Best" and more recently the TV "Cosby Show" only further reinforce such idealism of quick fixes for short-term problems. Such distortions in the media can lead families to set unrealistic expectations for their own functioning, particularly when problems are chronic.

Is a disagreement a conflict? A disagreement is a difference of opinion. It approaches a conflict when a single course of action has to be taken or when having a disagreement is a problem. I define a *conflict* as that situation where two or more people have different views on an issue and it is important or necessary to arrive at a single perspective. The problem is not in the presence of conflict but in the absence of adequate means to resolve them in a mutually significant way. When this is not the case, it becomes a goal of therapy to help a family develop such tools.

A family is in denial when it claims not to experience any conflict. When this is the case, there is a suppression of differences, and the conflict that goes with it will ultimately erupt in difficulty when the pressure of the underlying problems breaks through the family's defenses.

Competence in coping with conflict resolution includes:

1. The ability to exchange views in an empathic manner. Effective communication depends on the ability to hear another person's point of view in a constructive manner. This entails willingness and ability to understand the merits of a point of view independent of how acceptable it is to the receiver of such a perspective.

2. The definition of differences that leads to an attempt to convince one another to his point of view. This involves the determination that differences exist that are not the result of assumptions or inadequate information. This is followed by each participant's attempt to convince the other participant of the merits of his point of view. At some point it becomes clear that both participants are committed to their respective points of view.

3. When it is clear that a single point of view cannot be found and the discussion did not deteriorate into a hostile confrontation, the parties to the conflict are guided to shift their orientation from whether they should have differences to mutual acceptance and respect that they do have them. The goal is to focus on finding a solution agreeable to both parties that reflects significant aspects of each of their points of view. To accomplish this requires each person to be as concerned about the satisfaction of the other person's needs as he is about his own. Workable solutions include: a third alternative to the two originally proposed satisfactory to all concerned, taking turns with each person having their choice in serial order, one person chooses how and the other person when a solution will be implemented, and the proverbial flipping of a coin to avoid the power and competition issue.

This concept of constructive conflict resolution does not include expressed or implicit coercion. On the surface such situations could have the appearance of mutuality. Agreement to a solution because a person does not feel he has a choice does not meet the crucial criterion that the solution be mutually acceptable.

Further understanding of the conflict resolution process is gained by evaluating what issues are of concern to the participants. A determination needs to be made as to whether the conflicts are personality differences or whether issues are the focus. Conflicts that are ad hominem are destructive as they do not lead to solutions but only to heightened tensions. Conflicts that focus on issues have the possibility of being resolvable to the satisfaction of all concerned.

A couple came in for one of their regular sessions. I was alerted to what was coming when they started an argument as they came through the door. Harry and Sara were exchanging invectives. Harry was saying "You are as big a nag as your mother"; Sara returned the compliment with "You are as stubborn and bullheaded as your father." With the help of some outside perspective, they were able to see that were not going to accomplish anything constructive by exchanging attacks on one another. They were then able to appreciate each other's frustration, even though they disagreed with the basis for the other's feelings. After further discussion, they recognized that neither point of view was going to prevail. Once this was determined, they were able to focus on finding a solution that made sense to both of them.

An added consideration is to determine what purpose a given conflict serves, particularly if the conflict is repetitive and does not appear significantly related to issues. This is the case where the same issues continue to be of concern over time and after they appear to reach agreement. One possibility in such cases is that the conflict serves the purpose of keeping emotional distance.

One of the underlying reasons for the argument between Harry and

Sara was that he was angry with her for a variety of reasons and did not feel very close to her. Resolving a particular issue would bring them closer together. They would go through the cycle of having an argument. After a while he would appear to agree only to end the argument. The next time the issue came up, he would be back to his original position. Understanding this process enabled them to resolve the underlying issue of unresolved anger. Once this was done, it allowed them to deal with a particular problem without the baggage of previous issues.

Another perspective is gained by comparing how family members deal with conflict within and outside the home. It is common to find that people behave differently in different contexts. It is always irritating for a parent to hear that their annoying and recalcitrant child at home is very accommodating and reasonable outside the home. Another is the case of the father who is the essence of conciliation in the outside world and intractable at home.

Cultural Context

Ethnic Considerations

Effective communication depends on some shared frame of reference. People from different cultures can have very different ways of viewing and valuing the same behavior. A therapist is wise to determine the family's cultural background and value system early in the assessment process and be alert not to violate their cultural norms or values. Getting information about ethnic background is a way to join with a family and facilitate their cooperation in an interview. Areas of potential difficulty include:

Respect Values of the Family.   Families come to therapy with a committed value system. This may or may not include clearly defined roles and generation boundaries. If a father sees himself as head of the family and does not feel that the therapist respects this, then the therapy will be a short-lived experience. The same would apply in making light of family traditions.

I once saw a Catholic family that was very committed to their religion, in which there was a very clearly defined family structure. The father was the patriarch, and the mother was submissive and supportive to him. The family almost left therapy when I inadvertently violated the family structure by encouraging family members to express their views in a way that father perceived was contrary to his sense of propriety. I had to backtrack quickly to negotiate an acceptable way that we could work on the presenting problems that did not violate the family code.

Use of Language.   Establishing rapport is in large part determined by the therapist's ability to use language with which a family will feel comfortable. A therapist will make his job easier when he is able to do this. Use of familiar language facilitates the joining process. This also would include determining their familiarity and comfort level with the language styles of the day in the general culture. A therapist should keep in mind that different ethnic groups may have different meanings for commonly used words. This is most likely to be the case with ethnic groups who live in a homogeneous enclave or who recently emigrated to this country.

A good example of this is the use of profanity. Some families and therapists use such language comfortably and freely; others would be very offended by it. Failure of the therapist and family to relate in a language style that is comfortable to both is likely to result in a fragile therapeutic alliance.

Sensitive Areas of Discussion.   Not all topics are open to discussion for families. This may be due to unique value systems or as a product of their ethnic background. A therapist is well advised to determine appropriate boundaries for discussion. This is accomplished through knowledge of the ethnic or religious background and established value system. Beyond this, the therapist does well to be alert to verbal or nonverbal signals regarding which are acceptable areas of discussion.

In one family that was of a fundamentalist background, there was an issue about the father's heavy-handed and arbitrary use of his authority. The children also had similar feeling about their experience in the church. The father was adamant that religion was not an acceptable topic of discussion. Therapy was a touch-and-go process until we found a way to talk about issues related to authority in a way he could accept.

Use of Gestures.   Gestures are another form of language. A therapist needs to be sensitive to the style of the family and to communicate acceptance of their behavior, especially when it is markedly different from his style. A therapist who is very comfortable with the liberal use of gesture is going to have difficulty in working with a family that is uncomfortable with this kind of communication. The same could be true in the reverse situation.

Expression of Affect.   Cultures also differ in the acceptability of expressing affect. The challenge to the therapist is to determine what is the acceptable mode for such expression and to develop a way to use it to accomplish the therapeutic goals. This is particularly challenging when the family's values discourage expression of affect and where the presenting problems relate to the inability to do so.

I saw a family where the norm was to communicate at an intellectual level. A raised voice or other show of emotion was considered most inappropriate. The presenting problem was an acting-out adolescent. The way he expressed his frustrated rage was not an acceptable form of expression in the family. It was only through the pressure resulting from the adolescent's trouble with the police that the parents were willing to consider modifying family standards to permit anger to be talked about in a more open and direct manner.

Physical Contact.   A therapist should understand what limits exist regarding physical contact. This is relevant both in the therapy setting and in the family members' contact with one another. Any kind of physical contact may be offensive to one family, whereas it might be quite acceptable and desired in another family. For some such families, rejection of an embrace would be considered a rejection.

A hug can be a potent way to give support or show caring. It will have such an effect only when both parties are comfortable with this form of expresion. This is particularly the case between a family member and therapist. When a therapist participates in this form of expression, he needs to be sensitive to the possibility that the hug may have other meanings to the participants than what may be intended. Such considerations are part of determining whether such behavior is appropriate.

Physical Distance between Interviewer and Family.   People differ in their comfort levels regarding the physical distance between themselves and the people with whom they speak. Some ethnic groups have the reputation of talking to people on a relative nose-to-nose level. Other people are more comfortable with a lot of space between them and the person with whom they speak. This preference may stem from an ethnic background or may be idiosyncratic.

Physical distance also has potential use as a tool in the therapeutic process. I find it useful to determine what defines the comfort level of family members regarding physical distance between me and them. Such understanding can be a resource. Changing the physical distance is a way to heighten or lower the level of intimacy. This can be a useful contribution to guiding the emotional tone of an interview.

Family Rituals

Rituals are one way a family expresses its values and beliefs and provides information about their culture in ways that are difficult or impossible to get in the traditional interview.

There are two kinds of rituals. One kind relates to rites of passage: communion, bar mitzvah, graduation, and weddings. The other kind marks significant events such as religious holidays, birthdays, anniversaries, and special occasions.

Determining which of these events are significant to a family provides useful information about family structure and the quality of relationships: who values them, who organizes them, who participates in the preparation and in the event, and how much emphasis they place on performing the ritual compared with mutually enjoying the experience.

Stability-Change Balance

People vary in their attitudes toward stability and change. For some people, keeping things the way they are is the desired orientation in managing their lives. Such people find comfort and security in following the same routine day after day. In one family, a wife said of her husband, "You can set your clock by when my husband gets up, eats, goes to the bathroom, and when he goes to bed." Other people enjoy the familiar routine of the same restaurants, movies, and vacations. Still others need and thrive on change. For them the preferred way to live is to seek, accomplish, and adjust to change. These people resist doing the same activity twice in the same way. They vary their routines, vacations, and how they spend their time.

Between these two polarities are various combinations of coexisting attitudes toward change and stability. People may be very open to change in some areas and want to maintain the status quo in other areas. Preferences for stability and change also may vary with time circumstances. What is desirable at one time may not be at another. Difficulties may arise when a person is in conflict so that he may profess change on an intellectual level but resist it on an emotional level. This commonly happens in therapy when a client wants to change certain behavioral characteristics yet his behavior suggests the desire for things to stay the way they are. This could happen when a husband enters therapy to please his wife but has no underlying desire to make any changes in the way he functions.

At times, people have the option of to what degree they wish to seek change. At other times, there is no choice such as in developmental changes in the life cycle, leaving high school or college, dealing with retirement, having children, or death.

Although some people have difficulty coping with change, others have difficulty maintaining stability when it is appropriate and resisting the desire to change: maintaining a job, staying in school, or carrying on a family tradition. For some people, seeking change is a way to cope with frustration that does not seem resolvable. This is expressed in the adage that "The grass is always greener on the other side of the fence."

Either state can be a problem when it avoids dealing with an appropriate reality. One way to deal with relationship problems is to run from them. I worked with a man who was very successful in relationships with women. He always had many relationships open to him. This was both a blessing and curse to him because this success made it easy for him to avoid dealing with his problem with intimacy. When a relationship got too close, he would terminate it and shift to one of the other relationships immediately available to him.

A way to avoid the challenge of adjusting to a new situation is to stay with the existing one. An adult child continues to live at home because of the anxiety that would have to be faced in moving out.

Assessment Capability

Self-Assessment Capability

Basic to the survival of any social functioning entity is its capacity to evaluate itself either through self-assessment or by receptivity to information from within and outside its own system. This applies to all levels of social units. In the family it applies to individuals, parents, any subgroup, and the family as a whole. This evaluation provides information that enables the social unit to take corrective action that may affect physical and emotional survival.

The focus in the assessment of a social unit is to determine from what sources they obtain information, how they obtain it, how they evaluate it, and how they implement changes. People vary in the degree to which they will be self-critical. Some people verge on preoccupation with self-assessment; others are allergic to it. People also vary in the degree to which they will accept information about themselves, both in terms of how much they will accept and from whom. In therapy, it is not unusual to hear the frustration of one spouse when the other spouse accepts a recommendation from the therapist that was rejected when presented by the spouse.

People also have their tolerances for how much input they can accept at a given time, independent of the source or the value of the input. Too high a rate of feedback is threatening and overloads the social unit's capacity to process information constructively. The qualitative basis is likely to be more threatening if it challenges too many aspects of the social unit's concept of itself too quickly. The experience of overload kicks in the defensive system, which may take one or more forms of denial, such as attacking the source of information, defending the social unit, and distraction to other subjects.

I worked with a couple where the husband presented a very strong sense of his own identity. He had a relatively low tolerance for feedback. In one session, the woman was bothered because her husband had not spent enough time with her in the past month. He was able to accept her feedback and promised to be more attentive. Encouraged by her success, she broadened her complaint to include more time with their children. He responded sympathetically but with noticeably less enthusiasm, which she missed. She continued by complaining that he was too involved in his work and left too much responsibility on her for managing the house. It became increasingly obvious that he was on overload. His body tightened up. His face became more drawn.

Gone was the invitation for feedback. He shot back criticism about her being too demanding and not appreciating how hard he had to work.

Another consideration is how the social unit obtains information. Is it sought after, or is it obtained only when someone else volunteers it? Some people can accept feedback better in writing than they can accept hearing it directly from the source. This is not surprising because most nonverbal behavior is not communicable in written material. The how, when and, where of responding are left to the individual receiving the information. I saw one couple where the husband rarely sought feedback but was generally receptive to considering it when it was volunteered. His wife respected that he did best when she left him notes about her concerns.

How is the obtained information evaluated? Does the person or social unit evaluate by emotion, intellect, or both? Does the social unit seek corroborating information, or does it use only the presented information? To what degree does the person challenge the information or just accept it as fact? The more assertive social unit may also choose to test the information before deciding to accept or reject it. In one family the mother was getting feedback from her family that she was being too picky about cleanliness in the house. She felt she was being unfairly judged and defended her position by comparison to other families and by noting how many compliments she received from visitors.

Once feedback is accepted as relevant, how does the social unit approach its implementation? Does it develop a strategy for doing so in a disciplined manner, do they assume that it will just happen because they want it to happen, or do they assume that someone else will be responsible for making it happen? Once implemented, does the social unit have a means for monitoring the degree to which it works?

In a therapy session, a family accepted feedback from me regarding why they were having trouble working together as a family on chores. They developed a system for improving things and left feeling proud of themselves. They came back two weeks later disgruntled because their plan did not work very well. Discussion disclosed that they did not develop any procedure for monitoring how and when things would get done.

Modeling

Modeling is a mechanism for self-assessment. One social unit observes another social unit's way of behaving that appears attractive and seeks to incorporate what they observe into their own behavior. Modeling also occurs when information is needed in how to behave in a new situation. Learning from example is a major way that children become socialized. Assessment of the models that family members had and do have available to them provides insight into the range of resources available. Modeling is not a time-limited experience confined to childhood. It is an ongoing process throughout life. Because modeling is a potent source of influence, I routinely determine the predominant modeling influences in a family.

In some families parents often have a lot of investment in how other people outside the family think, feel, and behave when they are insecure about their own abilities. Such perceptions become strong influences on the expectations parents place on their children. In the course of therapy I often hear such references as: "What will the neighbors think?" "Why can't you behave like. . . ?" and "At the country club they said. . . ."

The world of advertising makes great use of modeling. We are forever bombarded with sales pitches by successful people in one field or another. Movie stars and sports figures are the most common examples. Modeling is a potent force in either positive or negative ways. It will be a reference point for similar behavior in the modelee when there is a positive identification with the model. It will have the reverse effect when the identification is negative.

Small children present a clear example when a little boy wants to know when he will be able to shave like daddy. A mother may cope with her son who doesn't want to eat his vegetables by urging him to "Eat your vegetables like Daddy does so you will be big and strong like he is."

In other situations modeling issues become more complicated. Parents smoke and drink while exercising prohibitions that their children not smoke or drink. Another example is the father who brags about his success in cheating on his income taxes or about his successful deception in business but gets indignant at his son who gets caught cheating on an exam or stealing from the local candy store.

Modeling may be at a conscious or unconscious level. It is likely to be at an unconscious level when a person is immersed in a situation where he needs to cope with his environment but is not clear how to do so and where there is incentive to behave like others around him. One illustration is the young child who grows up in an environment where his only exposure is to family members and where there is a reward for behaving as they do.

Conscious modeling occurs in many situations. Any time a person is in an unfamiliar situation, he is likely to model the behavior of those around him. This could be the situation in a foreign country, a new job, or membership in a new organization. Conscious modeling is also a way to manipulate a situation. This may happen when a child is chastised for drinking or smoking. One defense for the child is to respond, "You smoke and drink. Why can't I?" Teaching situations are commonly based on conscious modeling. The teacher demonstrates how to perform, and the student is expected to copy the teacher's behavior. As noted earlier, problems are likely to develop when there is a contradiction between what the "teacher" says and does.

Influence of History and Past Experience

The influence of history refers to material gained from a genogram and includes significant events in the life of the family. Past experience refers to events directly experienced by the social entity under consideration. An adolescent may have been exposed to the lost love of a sibling, but experiences a very different impact when it is his experience. The objective in resource evaluation is to determine what resources from the past can be drawn upon for application in therapeutic situation.

Influence of History

A social entity's history provides a context against which to interpret the entity's current experience. Such evaluation permits identification of the patterns of experience that have developed over time and the purpose they served. Understanding such patterns provides the therapist with some indication of the likelihood that change can be accomplished.

Past Successes

Past successes are a valuable resource. Knowledge of past accomplishments provides clues to information and skills that get lost under the pressure of new events. This is the case when they occurred in the distant past, when these events were undervalued, when the utility of such accomplishments for present application is not seen, or when the pressure or anxiety of the present interferes with the ability to reflect on drawing upon past resources.

In a family therapy session, the parents were upset with their son, who was a junior in high school and was having difficulty in keeping up with his homework. Added pressure came from their concern about his getting into college. He was distracted by his interests in sports and socializing. As a result, he fell behind in his academic skills. He felt defeated and did not think he could catch up. In the course of discussion, the parents talked about how pleased they were when he learned to play the saxophone in grade school. They were impressed with the disciplined way he approached it. The family mood shifted to a positive one as they encouraged him to draw upon those skills he developed earlier and apply them to his current problem. He gradually became more receptive and hopeful as he and his parents reminisced about his past successes. This led to discussion about how to adapt those same skills to cope with his academic difficulties.

Past Failures

Past failures can be a resource when properly considered. This is particularly the case when failure is defined as not learning from experience. Such failures can be useful when they help the experiencing social entity (individual, couple or family) better understand their capabilities and limitations. Such understanding can contribute to defining more appropriate and realistic goals.

I saw a young couple about to be married who came in for pre-marital counseling. They were glowing with the ideals they had for their relationship and the family they hoped to have. They were enamored with the idea of such counseling than the substance of it. I saw them three years later in the throes of disappointment from their lost ideals about being a couple and as parents of a two-year-old child. Work in therapy on how to benefit from their felt failures contributed to their defining more realistic goals and developing the relationship tools for accomplishing them.

Talents, Skills, and Interests

Competence in any past or present activity is a potential resource that can be drawn upon in solving family problems. This includes a talent or skill in any activity. Among the areas that should be considered are academics, sports, arts, leadership ability, organizational ability, music, hobbies, and politics. A goal for the therapist is to help the family identify such resources and utilize them in the resolution of family problems.

I saw a family where the parents were having a very difficult time coping with their adolescent children. Both of them felt impotent and defeated in their attempts to cope with the developmental crises of their children. As I searched my memory for information that might be useful, I recalled the father telling me about when he ran away from home at 16 because of what he considered intolerable family tensions. He was away for two years, during which time he learned how to survive under rather overwhelming circumstances. I had him retrace these experiences with the goal of reminding him of the skills he acquired then and how he might apply those same skills in his current situation. He was quick to see how these forgotten skills could be applied to his present dilemma. A month later the parents proudly reported that they had made significant progress in coping with their children. They were still anxious about the long-term outcome but felt more confident that they could cope.

Resources outside the Family

Thus far the discussion has focused on resources within the individual or within the family. Another major bastion of resources is outside the family. This includes friends, relatives, social agencies, clergy, the medical community, and the psychotherapist.

The survival of families with limited financial or emotional resources often depends on assistance from outside the family. This happens when insufficient income involves a family with welfare. This also occurs when relationship or behavior problems are not manageable, child abuse occurs, school problems develop, or there is involvement with the criminal justice system.

Application of Resource Assessment in Clinical Practice

Thus far I have defined the concepts I find useful in clinical practice. I will now discuss ways of gathering the material and how it may be used in clinical practice.

Format for Gathering Information

A structured format is one way to gather family culture information. In this approach the therapist proceeds through each of the items in sequential fashion by addressing the family as a group. This is a way to gather valuable information regarding the pattern of responses in who answers what questions. Families quickly demonstrate interaction styles by who answers what questions and the responses other members make to such revelations.

I experimented with two ways of conducting the interview in this fashion. One way obtains brief information on each item without delving into the many possibilities the responses may suggest. This assessment can be accomplished in one or two hours and provides a broad overview of the family structure and dynamics. It also provides information on the priority of issues gained from themes across different content areas. This approach tests the discipline of the therapist to stay focused on therapeutic goals and not get sidetracked into pursuing attractive issues and themes along the way.

Another benefit can accrue from gathering information in this focused form. I tape the session both for my own reference and for the family to review as homework. The experience of hearing themselves often provides a new and helpful perspective for the family. I give instructions for the family to listen to the tape and discuss it to the point where the discussion breaks down into nonproductive arguments. If this should happen, I ask them to bring the arguments to therapy.

One of the problems with this approach is that the interaction is primarily information gathering. This could have the impact of slowing down the development of rapport with the family because they are giving a lot of information and not getting much back. Another disadvantage is that adhering to a highly structured format can get wearing and boring for the therapist and the family.

Another approach is to de-emphasize getting through the whole assessment in the first one or two sessions. In this approach, I take each item and spend as much time as needed to get background information and work with any issues that require attention relevant to the presenting problem. The disadvantage to doing this is the perspective that may be lost from not having the benefit of the larger context.

Both approaches are useful. Which way I go depends on my mood, my sense of the family, and the nature of the presenting issues.

This assessment process may seem very cumbersome and impractical if performed as described. The value for me in using this framework is that it provides a lot of information in a focused and organized manner. Different parts of it have different degrees of relevance for different families and different settings. I recommend its use as with any instrument: to know its potential and to use it in part or whole and adapt its use as the needs of each situation warrant. When used in conjunction with the genogram, it provides a very powerful assessment tool.

Another way to use the assessment of resources is as a guide for obtaining useful information in the normal course of interviewing. In this form it provides a frame of reference for systematic collection of data on the family.

I have also experimented with gaining information via a self-administered questionnaire. In an earlier version of the questionnaire, I adapted the information gathering to a checklist series of items. Pilot data indicated that this is a viable way of gathering information, particularly when it is used as a basis for screening and the development of hypotheses for further exploration.

CASE ILLUSTRATION

The Harder Family

Mr. Harder, age 45, an electrical engineer, was a short, stocky man with auburn hair and metal-rimmed glasses. He always came to therapy in a three-piece suit. Mrs. Harder, age 41, a school nurse, was a pleasant-appearing brunette who was significantly overweight and who always came to therapy dresssed in slacks. Carl, 15, was a high school sophomore. He was short for his age and had a strong facial resemblance to his father. Katherine, 12, a sixth grader, was a slender brunette who was tall for her age. She had a strong facial resemblance to her mother. The family resided in a suburb north of Boston. Mr. Harder was a man of few words who revealed little of himself except when asked direct questions. He appeared to treat communication like a game of chess — a contest in which someone wins and someone loses.

The family's contact with therapy started with a referral from Mrs. Harder's physician because she was unhappy in the marriage and concerned that her unhappiness was getting expressed in too much dependence on her daughter.

Assessment of Resources

Communication Styles

The primary channel for communication in the family was through the mother. Mr. Harder withdrew from responsibility for child rearing because he felt his wife did not pay much attention to what he said. Because of this, most communication between the father and children went through her. When he did communicate directly with his children, it often contained some form of teasing, criticism, or sarcasm.

Direct Ways of Exerting Power

Legitimate Power.   The parents exercised the legitimate power that comes with being parents. They had limited respect for each other's adequacy in the parenting role. She thought he was too insensitive and demanding. When their son came home with a report card with As and Bs and one D, the only comment the father made was about the D. "If you had worked harder, you wouldn't have that D." He thought his wife infantilized their daughter: "You treat her like she's 5 years old. How do you ever expect her to grow up?"

Expertise.   Neither parent derived any power on the basis of perceived expertise. Their ongoing exchange of insults about their respective lack of competence as parents left both children with very mixed feelings about which parent to trust. Katherine knew her mother babied her but was unable to discourage it, especially when she was overloaded with anxiety.

Expectations.   Mr. Harder was very clear in defining the standards of behavior he expected from all members of the family. He thought his wife should be stricter with the children, do better at housekeeping, and work part-time. He often complained that she did not earn her keep.

He expected his son to excel in his grades and be an athlete. He gave him nonverbal messages to treat his mother the way he did. One way Mr. Harder did this was by saying nothing when Carl was berating his mother with profanity in his father's presence.

Mr. Harder had similar expectations for Katherine regarding academics and in her sports activities. He wanted her to be more self-sufficient but gave up on changing the relationship between mother and daughter.

Mrs. Harder wanted her husband to be more sensitive to the emotional needs of their children. She wanted him to be as concerned with praise as with criticism. She also wanted him to treat her with more respect. She wanted her children to do well in their various activities. She had a hard time being clear and consistent in her expectations and behavior. She wanted her daughter to be more mature in her behavior yet regularly undermined it by lying down with her when she went to bed and in helping her dress in the mornings.

Ability to Grant Rewards.

Mr. Harder exerted power through his ability to grant rewards. He made very clear that he earned the money that supported the family and used this to gain desired behavior. He also granted rewards to his son by playing tennis with him and with his daughter by attending her field hockey games.

Mrs. Harder granted rewards by being loving and actively supporting all of her children's activities. She did a lot of chauffeuring of the children and was an avid spectator in their sports activities. She was very attentive to their interests and needs. The positive ways she had of responding to her husband was through the meals she cooked and as a sex partner.

Capacity to Punish or Discipline.

Mr. Harder's capacity for criticism and harsh judgment had a great deal of influence on how all members of the family behaved. Punishment was the primary mode he used to gain desired behaviors. Sarcasm and withholding were common ways in which he communicated. He taunted his wife with "My retirement money is for me. If you're around, you can have some of it."

Mrs. Harder's efforts with the children were oriented primarily toward discipline. Her corrective efforts were inconsistent but served the function of discipline. When one of the children did something wrong, she related to their feelings and attempted to show them the correct way to behave: "Katherine, honey, let me show you the right way to solve that problem." The response to her husband was quite different. When he did something to annoy her, she fought back in kind or retaliated in other ways, such as not cooking for him when he came home late or withholding sex. During the course of therapy she stopped working. This enabled her to get back at him by refusing to get part-time work.

Having Necessary Resources.

Mr. Harder's major contribution in his mind was in providing financial support for the family. Mrs. Harder's major resource was her ability to be attentive, available, and loving. He was very reluctant to help the children with homework in the belief that this would not help them: "They have to learn to do it for themselves. Nobody did it for me." She functions in the opposite direction by becoming too involved in Katherine's homework. She thought she had to make up for her husband's neglect. When Katherine's report card arrived, he would ask Mrs. Harder, with a smirk and in a sarcastic manner, what grades she (the mother) got.

Expression of Affect.   Mr. Harder displayed a narrow range of affect. His affect came out mostly in his sarcasm and profanity and the way he laughed when he made a point, usually in a negative context. Mrs. Harder was very volatile. She responded in a range of emotions. When anxious, she spoke in a nonstop, rapid-fire manner. Carl mimicked his father's way of expressing affect. Particularly bothersome to the mother was her son's use of profanity toward her. Katherine was a cross between her mother and father. She expressed herself in the narrow affect range of her father but had her mother's ability to speak her mind.

Guilt.   Mr. Harder used guilt to remind family members that he supported the family in order to get them to respond to his wishes. This was likely to come up when he thought he was not getting the attention or respect he thought appropriate.

The wife justified infantilization of her daughter as an expression of her guilt to make up for the nasty way her husband treated Katherine and her inability to interrupt it.

Shame.   Mr. Harder attempted to use shame to get his wife to stop infantilizing their daughter and to go to work. He did this by telling her there was something wrong with her character. She retaliated by trying to shame her husband into treating her and the children differently by telling him there was something wrong with him and that he had no compassion.

Obligation.   The husband frequently used obligation as a way to relate to his family on a quid pro quo basis. Providing the family's income entitled him to the respect he desired. This included requiring his wife to be the kind of housekeeper and mother he expected and for her to work, part-time at least. The children were expected to respect his wishes and behave accordingly.

Indirect Ways of Exerting Power

Silence.   Mr. Harder withdrew into silence when he thought he was not able to get his wife to pay attention to his concerns. This happened in the case of child rearing. He had a different view on how to raise the children. When they could not agree and he could not get his point of view acknowledged, he gave up and retreated into silence to let her do what she wished.

Carl was the only other family member who used silence to any significant degree. When he was angry with his father and reluctant to risk expressing it, he retreated into silence. This regularly happened when Mr. Harder did not acknowledge positive accomplishments and only criticized shortcomings. An example of this was described earlier regarding Carl's D on his report card.

Indifference.   This form of influence was not utilized in this family to any significant degree.

Incompetence.   Katherine used incompetence to manipulate her mother into doing things for and with her such as homework and going to bed on time.

Obstruction.   When Mr. Harder did not approve of how his wife was managing money, he would take his time getting her car repaired or putting money in her checking account when she needed it. In another situation he kept the family financial records in his office so that she would not know their financial status.

Combining Types of Power
Mr. Harder wielded a great deal of power in his family because of his ability to utilize many of the direct and indirect ways of exerting influence. In contrast, Mrs. Harder was not very effective in utilizing any of the aforementioned forms of power, either because she was not able to exercise them or was inconsistent or unclear in their use.

Expression of Affect
Mrs. Harder was the one family member capable of expressing anger or affection when she felt it. Her husband and Carl did not easily express affection. Both quite readily expressed dissatisfaction when they felt it, usually in the form of hostility and sarcasm. Katherine was more likely to express her feelings in behavior such as becoming anxious, having a hard time going to sleep, and difficulty doing her homework. She could express her anger at her father to her mother but not to him directly. She frequently would say, "Why don't you divorce him?"

Empathy Capability
Mrs. Harder and Katherine were the ones in the family who were able to show any significant ability to empathize. They were able to do this with each other but not with the men in the family. Mrs. Harder had difficulty defining the boundary between her needs and those of Katherine. At times it was not clear how much of her empathic behavior was appreciating Katherine's situation and how much was a projection of her own needs.

Negotiation Skills

Division of Labor
There was a very clear division of labor in this family that was primarily defined by Mr. Harder. He provided the family income. Maintenance of the

home and raising the children were Mrs. Harder's responsibility. He paid some attention to the physical maintenance of the home at his convenience. He expected his wife and the children to finish tasks it was not convenient for him to do. The children did not have clearly defined responsibilities for contributing to management of the home.

Decision Making

Overt versus Covert.   Decisions on noncontroversial matters tended to be made overtly. This included routine daily matters of how to get children where they needed to be, curfew times, permission to visit friends, and recreational activities. One long-standing controversy involved a covert decision made by Mr. Harder regarding money Mrs. Harder inherited and gave to him to invest. He made the decision not to keep her informed of the status of any of their finances, based on his belief that she would handle such information irresponsibly. The decision was made covertly. He promised to show her the records he kept in his office but never managed to get around to doing so.

Degree of Clarity.   For the most part, their overt decisions were clearly stated. Curfew hours were clearly defined: social activities were not permitted on week nights and there was an 11:30 P.M. curfew on weekends. The same applied to getting homework done. Both children understood that postponing homework to another day was not acceptable.

How Considered Is the Decision.   Mr. Harder tended to give careful thought to decisions he made, especially those related to finances. This was not the case when it came to decisions related to emotional issues. He came to conclusions about how his wife managed the home and the children based more on emotion than on consideration of relevant information.

Mrs. Harder tended to make decisions more on emotion than on the merits of the situation. Her anger at her husband frequently affected her decision making. At these times she was likely to retaliate impulsively. On one occasion when he took the checkbook away from her in anger, she charged a number of purchases to get back at him.

Carl's way of decision making was like his father's, and Katherine's more in the model of her mother.

Who Makes the Decisions.   Mr. Harder was the primary decision maker in matters related to finances. Mrs. Harder made decisions for herself and the children. The children often gained the power to make decisions because of Mrs. Harder's difficulty in setting limits.

Content of Decisions.   Generally the Harder family made decisions in appropriate areas based on relevant information. This included decisions about money management, home maintenance, and raising children.

When Decisions Are Made.   The Harder family usually was able to make necessary decisions when needed. This involved decisions about the mechanical aspects of daily living such as paying bills, getting repairs done, doctor's appointments, and getting people where they need to be.

How Decisions Are Communicated.   When decisions were made about curfew hours, getting homework done, and needed chores, they tended to be directly and clearly communicated from parents to the children. They were less able to communicate decisions in a clear and direct manner with each other. He persistently communicated his concerns about standards of housekeeping and child rearing; she was very direct in her decisions regarding what she would like from her husband, but she was not very successful in getting the desired response.

How Decisions Are Modified.   Mr. Harder had a hard time modifying decisions. He tended to think he had all the information he needed and was not too open to input from his wife. Both children had a tendency to respond to the father's model in responding to information from others. Mrs. Harder had a tendency to behave in the same way but was more open to modifying her decisions when presented with a basis for doing so.

Decisions in the Harder family got modified in two ways: by edict and by coercion. When Mr. Harder thought it was appropriate to change a decision, he was likely to just pronounce it. There was little discussion about it. Any attempt at discussion was quickly channeled into implementing the change.

Mrs. Harder could be quick to change her own decisions. Her major way to get other family members to change their decisions was through coercion. She would persist until she got what she wanted or until her frustration level got too high and she quit her pursuit.

How Decisions Are Evaluated.   Mr. Harder carefully evaluated his decisions when they were business related and clearly definable. Decisions involving emotions and relationships were evaluated more on the basis of impulse and his mood than on logic. When he was angry, he would swear at his wife and feel perfectly justified in doing so: "It's what she deserved."

Mrs. Harder was more inclined to evaluate her decisions on an emotional basis than from an intellectual perspective. The intensity of her emotions tended to distract her from adequately evaluating the merits of a given situation. On one occasion she was offered a part-time job that had very flexible hours. In her enthusiasm to take advantage of this opportunity, she overlooked adequately assessing other responsibilities she would have that she did not like. As a result, she quit her job two weeks later.

Adequacy of Carrying Out Decisions. Mr. Harder was consistent in carrying out decisions he made that were meaningful to him. This was not the case when he gave the impression he was making a decision that resulted from Mrs. Harder's persistence. In such events he did this to interrupt her pursuit of him: "After a while I go along just to shut her up!"

Mrs. Harder was quite distractible in carrying out her decisions. This was partly due to conflicting commitments, her personality style, and the anticipated reaction of her husband. The children dealt with implementing decisions more like their father's model than their mother's.

Areas of Disagreement

The major areas of disagreement included management of money, Mr. Harder's complaint about the level of housekeeping and discipline of the children, and Mrs. Harder's complaint that her husband set standards too high for the children and did not give them adequate positive feedback. She was also bothered by the disrespectful way he treated her in front of the children, his lack of affection, and his refusal to follow through on his commitment to let her know about the financial status of the family.

How Conflict Is Resolved

The Harder family did not do well with conflict resolution between members of the family. Each person tended to do his own thing. Problems that required some form of joint solution tended to be made unilaterally by one parent or the other. At times she prevailed through dogged persistence to her point of view. Her ability to prevail usually was around matters related to the children. At other times he prevailed through unilateral declaration. Often joint decisions were not made when a single decision was not required. Individual decisions made in parallel were tolerated, resulting in a chronic undercurrent of tension and dissension in the family.

Cultural Context

Family Values

Mr. Harder had a strong commitment to the work ethic and a tightfisted attitude toward the management of money. Important values for him included: you should earn whatever you get, strong negative feelings about any person who does not carry his own weight, not a good idea to show your feelings, children need strong discipline, and coddling does not help children to grow up.

Mrs. Harder's values included having a supportive and caring relationship. Maintaining an intact family unit was very important to her. Both children placed a lot of value on participation in sports. All members of the family saw education as a high priority.

Use of Language

Mr. Harder frequently expressed his frustration in profanity. Carl followed his father's model and frequently expressed himself in a similar manner, to the annoyance of his mother, especially when it was directed at her. Her husband showed little appreciation for the impact of the language he used. When challenged, he would respond, "She deserves it."

Sensitive Areas of Discussion

The most sensitive area of discussion for the parents was the status of family investments. Also difficult was discussion of the failings of their respective families of origin. The parents frequently exchanged barbs about each other's family. Mrs. Harder's concern about her husband's lack of positive feedback to the children was an ongoing dispute. There was anxiety about Katherine's sexual identification because she talked about wanting to be a boy and dressed in ways that kept her sexual identity ambiguous.

Use of Gestures

Mr. Harder had a poker-faced presence most of the time. He made little or no use of gestures. Mrs. Harder made generous use of gestures. She was quite expressive in facial expression and body language. When annoyed with her husband, she would point her index finger at him and tell him how she felt about his behavior and character. Both children were restrained in their expression, with relatively flat affect and little use of gestures.

Physical Contact

Physical contact was a familiar way of relating in the Harder family. Mrs. Harder was free to show affection both verbally and physically. Her husband was much less demonstrative but made physical contact by having the children sit next to him when they were watching television. On occasion he also made physical contact in playful interaction with the children.

Physical Distance

Close physical proximity varied in comfort level in the Harder family. In the therapy interview, Mrs. Harder sat close to the therapist and often would reach over and touch the therapist to emphasize a point. Mr. Harder tended to take the chair farthest from the therapist. The children did not appear to have a preference.

Family Rituals

One of the deficiencies in the family was the absence of meaningful rituals, such as holiday meals or celebration of special events.

Stability-Change Balance

Mr. Harder valued keeping things the way they were. He did not acknowledge to his family any areas of his own vulnerability or anything that he needed to change. He was quite clear about what changes he expected in other family members, particularly his wife. Mrs. Harder was more open with her vulnerabilities. She sought a lot of change. She wanted her husband to treat her with more respect, spend more time with the children, be less critical of them, give them more positive recognition, keep her informed on the status of their finances, and be more of a companion.

Carl appeared comfortable coping with developmental changes and demonstrated a good balance between coping with existing situations and openness to changes.

Katherine had a more difficult time dealing with changes. She had a hard time becoming independent in dressing herself and in going to bed by herself. This was largely due to her mother's difficulty in establishing limits. Katherine was also having a difficult time with puberty. Her identification in the past was more with males than with females. To a considerable degree, this was the result of the way in which her father was very critical of her mother in the presence of Katherine and because the power in the family was clearly invested in males.

Assessment Capability

Self-Assessment Capability

Mr. Harder had limited ability to assess accurately his own behavior and the impact it had on family members. The fleeting moments when he showed such awareness were quickly followed by clouds of distortion that resulted in holding other family members, primarily his wife, responsible for problems that developed.

Mrs. Harder had a far better ability for self-assessment but demonstrated limited ability to implement behavior consistent with the assessment. It did not take long for her to become aware of the degree to which she was infantilizing Katherine, but it took a long time for her to change her behavior appropriately and stick with it.

Carl was more age-appropriate in his ability to assess his own behavior. Katherine had more difficulty. The intensity of her relationship with her mother interfered with her developing the ability for age-appropriate assessment. She agreed that needing her mother to lie down with her when she went to bed was not appropriate but showed little desire or ability to change it.

Modeling

Mr. and Mrs. Harder provided a confusing model for their children to follow. He modeled rigid, self-righteous, overly critical, and uncompromising standards that showed little regard for the individuality of the person who was the object of his judgment. In his model of marriage, the husband was king and the wife was there to serve him. The husband defined clear expectations for his wife and believed he should let her know her shortcomings whenever they occurred and in front of anybody.

She modeled loving and caring that in Katherine's case was smothering. She also demonstrated that it was appropriate to accept the kind of verbal abuse she got from her husband. At other times she modeled setting standards and limits that she was not able to consistently follow, such as taking a stand on Katherine's going to bed by herself, doing her own homework, or getting dressed by herself.

Carl modeled, for his sister, the competent athlete and student who got considerable recognition for his efforts. The model was confusing for Katherine because she did not get the recognition from her father that her brother got for similar accomplishments. Her mother's efforts to make up for her father's deficiencies came across as distortions, resulting in further confusion, rather than as helpful.

Influences of History and Past Experience

Past Successes

The Harder family had its share of past successes. Mr. Harder had a successful career in the service, was graduated from college, and was enjoying a successful career in business. Mrs. Harder graduated from nursing school and had been successful in her professional field when she was employed.

Carl achieved success both academically and in athletics. Katherine achieved success in academics to a lesser degree than her brother. She received recognition for her talent in field hockey. Both children continued to enjoy their successes in academics and in athletics.

Past Failures

Mr. and Mrs. Harder have had chronic difficulty in establishing a constructive way to communicate or resolve conflict. Emotional abuse in Mr.

Harder's childhood left scars that made it difficult to trust or allow himself to be vulnerable in a relationship. Mrs. Harder's emotional deprivation in her childhood resulted in her developing a strong need for nurturance and reassurance that became overwhelming for Mr. Harder. Their respective limitations made it very difficult for them to risk gaining the needed tools that would lead to a more satisfactory relationship. They were able to engage in therapy to the extent of understanding the nature of their problems but had great difficulty translating this understanding in new behaviors.

Resources outside the Family

The Harder's did not have many resources to call on beyond their immediate family. Mr. Harder's family of origin was in another part of the country. He did not feel comfortable calling on them for any assistance. He had a friendly but distant relationship with them.

Mrs. Harder was an only child. Her mother was dead, and her father was quite ill. She did not have any family to whom she could turn for help, companionship, or assistance.

The Harders did not have close friends. They did not have any sufficiently significant relationships to whom they could turn for help or comfort.

Talents, Skills, and Interests

Mr. Harder had interests in gold and in following the stock market, which he did avidly with significant success. Mrs. Harder's interests revolved around her children and their activities, particularly those of Katherine. She attended every one of Katherine's field hockey games. Outside school, the children's major interests were in their sports activities.

A GUIDE TO THE CLINICAL APPLICATION

Evaluate the resources of the relevant social entities.

1. What are the abilities of the social entities to communicate?
2. What major communication patterns are used?
3. Which of the following types of attempts to influence behavior are used in the family?
   - Direct attempts to influence behavior:
     - Acknowledged right to influence
     - By virtue of expertise
     - Through expressed or implied expectations
     - Granting of rewards
     - Ability to punish or discipline
     - Access to needed resources
     - Ability to express affect

           — Use of guilt
           — Use of shame
           — Imposition of obligation

- Indirect
  - Silence
  - Indifference
  - Incompetence
  - Obstruction
- In what ways are combinations of power used?

4. What is the family's ability to express affect?
5. How able are they to be empathic?
6. How able are they to negotiate?
7. How well do they manage division of labor?
8. How do they cope with decision making?

- Overt versus covert
- Degree of clarity
- How considered are the decisions?
- What is the basis for making decisions?
- Who makes the decisions?
- What is the content of primary decisions?
- When are decisions made?
- How are decisions communicated?
- How are decisions changed?
- How effectively are decisions carried out?
- How are decisions reviewed?

9. What are areas of disagreement?

- How is conflict resolved?

10. What is the cultural context of the family?

- Ethnic considerations
- What family values are unique to a particular culture?
- Are there particular prohibitions or requirements around the use of language?
- Are there areas of discussion that are uniquely sensitive for a particular ethnic group?
- Are there gestures that violate an ethnic group standard?
- Are there specific ethnic requirements for the expression of affect?
- What kind of physical contact is permitted?
- Are there customs regarding appropriate physical distance for communication?
- What family rituals are important to the family?

11. What balance in stability versus change does a family value?
12. What is the assessment capability of this family? How realistically are they able to assess their own capabilities?

13. What patterns of modeling are provided in the family?

14. What kind of past successes and failures has the family experienced?

15. What kind and range of talents, skills, and interests are held by family members?

16. What resources are available outside the family?

Summary

In this chapter I provided a framework for assessing resources in four areas: communication style, ability to negotiate, cultural context, and ability for self-assessment. The application of this framework was exemplified with a case illustration.

CHAPTER SEVEN

Developmental Sequences

The literature contains various views on developmental stages. On the individual level, there are the historic work of the psychoanalytic view and the work of others such as Erickson and Piaget. Other work has been done on group development and family life cycle. I found the information insufficient in its explanation of developmental sequences of a given social entity. I also found insufficient perspective on how the interactions of various developmental sequences of family members affect one another. Such considerations gave rise to this chapter, which is concerned with characteristics of developmental stages and how the circularity of an individual's cumulative experiences in multiple developmental stages affects other members in the family and in turn is affected by theirs.

THEORY

As therapists, our goal is to help our clients find solutions to problems that bring them to therapy. This involves defining a treatment goal and a strategy for achieving it. An initial step is gathering information about the present situation and relevant past history. Some organizing framework of theory, as described in Chapter 3, is used for determining what information is sought and how to organize it.

An approach common to clinical practice is to view the collected information as a series of relationships and events that affect one another. Such interactions give rise to feelings and in turn are affected by them. Over time I found two general problems with this approach: It does not adequately make use of the available information, and it does not adequately reflect the sequential impact of how one experience affects succeeding experiences. This awareness led me to the concept of developmental sequences (DS). A DS is that series of experiences that a social entity (individual, couple, family) encounters in pursuit of a goal. It may involve a task or a relationship. Commonly each experience sets the stage for the next and often involves increasing complexity. I do not call these *stages* or *phases* so that my usage is not confounded by the different ways other authors use these terms.

I find the concept of developmental sequences useful because it dynamically organizes information in relationship to goals. People engage in various behaviors to accomplish particular objectives: career, marriage, children, friendship, athletics, and the like. Each of these objectives is achieved by going through a series of experiences. Each experience sets the stage for the next. The characteristics of the DS are a function of the complexity and importance of the goal. The DS of the goal for a friendship will be much less complicated than the DS for seeking a spouse.

A man and woman explore having a relationship. If they experience compatibility, the relationship broadens and becomes more complex as they explore the various aspects they feel are important to make a marriage work. When the compatibility and attraction reach an adequate level, marriage may be the consequence unless other considerations interfere. When it becomes apparent that a satisfactory level of compatibility is not likely to be achieved, the relationship will be terminated. This process will be hastened if other parallel relationships hold more promise, for example, "being dumped for someone else." It may also be the case that a relationship that started with the goal of marriage is replaced by the goal of friendship when it becomes clear that the level of compatibility is not appropriate for marriage but is suitable for friendship.

Often a particular experience has implications for multiple goals. Consider the event where a child lies to her parents about skipping school. The immediate context is that the child's behavior violates a family value and a goal about honesty. Such behavior also interferes with the goals of getting a good education and behaving in a responsible manner.

Behaviors that are common to multiple DSs quickly become the focus of attention when they deviate from expectations. People who get into trouble because of insensitivity to other people's feelings will be pressed to attend to the problem when it gets in the way of DSs such as relationships at work and with family and friends. The concept of developmental sequences applies to all social entities: couple, family, and any significant relationship grouping within the family or outside it.

In this chapter I discuss characteristics of developmental sequences and show how these concepts have clinical applicability in a case illustration.

Characteristics of Developmental Sequences

As the goals of the DS gain in importance, the social entity develops sub-DSs that become more specific, both in pursuing the process of performing the developmental task and in the goal itself. For example, a person starts out with a developmental sequence aimed at marriage with a vague idea of how to accomplish it and a general idea of what is involved in being married.

As experience is gained, the person gains clarity in the various dimensions that comprise a successful relationship. As each dimension becomes defined, it leads to its own DS, both in the steps to be performed and the goal to be achieved. When an adequate level of accomplishment is achieved in a sufficient number of dimensions (e.g., compatibility in values, beliefs, and the ability to resolve differences), it results in marriage.

Origin of DSs

A social entity's (individual's, couple's, family's) experience of a developmental sequence may be self-imposed, imposed by others outside the social unit, or imposed by natural occurrences.

Self-Defined
A self-defined DS occurs by the choice of the social entity. Examples include choice in friendships, athletic pursuits, occupational choices, selection of mate, and parenthood.

One consequence of self-imposed DSs is the option for termination. The degree of choice diminishes as the social entity becomes more entrenched in them. A person who commits to a career choice and marriage theoretically has the option to interrupt them at any time. Financial limitations or emotional commitments may limit the degree to which this is possible. People often stay with jobs because they feel trapped by fear of the loss of security. People stay in unhappy marriages out of commitment to children or fear of being alone.

Imposed from Outside the Social Entity
A mother may decide that her child should develop certain skills such as playing a musical instrument, dancing, or athletics. The child may not be able to resist the pressure of parental expectations, particularly if the child shows talent and interest in a specific direction.

When a person is incarcerated in jail or committed to a mental hospital, she has a DS physically imposed on her. Her goal becomes how to survive the experience and preferably to terminate it.

Imposed by Natural Occurrences
Another exposure to DSs results from naturally occurring events. This includes coping with aging, accidents, illness, death, and natural disasters. In each of these cases, the social entity does not have the option of whether to cope but only how to manage the experience.

Categories of DSs
DSs are in service of four objectives.

Definition of Self. This category is basic to the others that follow. Inadequate accomplishment of DSs necessary for a positive sense of definition of self, couple, or family interferes with the ability to set or achieve goals. A person who has an inadequate sense of self will have difficulty in pursuit of social relationships, an occupation and other interests. A family that does not develop a positive definition of their family concept will have difficulty functioning as a unit. The stability and integrity with which the DS is defined is a function of the available opportunities and resources necessary for its development. The bright child who is permitted or coerced to put all her energies into a single interest such as music or dance can be deprived of the range of other DSs necessary to be a balanced and functioning adult. In a similar fashion, a child who is not permitted to learn how to deal with expressing her feelings is likely to be handicapped in social relationships as an adult.

An abused child's experiences will interfere with normal DSs. The degree of impact it has will depend on the nature and severity of the experience. This occurs because such abuse affects how the self is viewed, how the external world is viewed, and the ability to form relationships.

A couple that does not develop a positive couple concept will have difficulty relating to each other and to their children.

Social Relationships. Social relationships encompass a broad range of DSs that occur in some combination of family of origin, friendships, marriage, nuclear family, occupation, recreation, and community. People differ in the degree of complexity of DSs they are able to manage. People who had insufficient or traumatic socialization experiences will encounter difficulty in DSs that involve intensity or intimacy. Such people may cope by keeping social relationship sequences few and superficial.

Occupation. In this context the first DS is determination of what occupation fits the interests and talents of the individual. This concerns the process by which one acquires the necessary knowledge and skills to perform in that occupation. Most occupations require some form of academic or vocational training which itself becomes a DS. Following this the pursuit of an appropriate job opportunity becomes another DS. Once a job is acquired, the DS evolves to some form of career goal. One example is the accountant who starts by working for a firm with a clearly defined path for acquiring training and experience that will lead to passing the CPA exam and then to the ultimate goal of her own business.

Other Interests. This grouping involves a broad range of different interests that includes practice of religion, participation in organizational and community activities (Masons, League of Women Voters, etc.), avocational interests (arts and crafts, music, bird watching, etc.), and athletic pursuits as spectator or participant.

DSs Have a Beginning, Middle, and an Open or Closed Ending

The beginning or ending of a DS may be spontaneous or marked by some ritual. Friendships, hobbies, recreational interests, and accidents are examples of DSs that usually start in a spontaneous manner. The more important a DS is, the more likely it is to start with some form of ritual. Examples are marriages, ordinations, bar mitzvahs, baptisms, and oaths of office.

The same considerations apply to endings. A spontaneous ending of a relationship may occur when one of the participants chooses to end it. A person gives up her interest in playing an instrument when she recognizes that practicing becomes too much of a burden.

Rituals mark the end of many significant experiences: graduations, divorces, retirement parties, and funerals. Such endings give rise to DSs whose focus is in mourning the endings.

Some DSs are time-limited. Getting a formal education is identified with a specific period. The experience is over when a specified number of credits are successfully accomplished. Vacations are usually time-limited, with a clear beginning and a clear, however undesired, ending. In the business community, many organizations foster retirement independent of the individual's capacity to perform.

There are also DSs that have less clearly defined endings. The ability to participate in sports is possible as long as a person is able to perform adequately. Uncertainty about doing something places a lot of stress on fulfilling the goal of the DS. Some athletes go well beyond the usual norm. In baseball, a professional career usually ends somewhere in a player's thirties. On occasion a player is able to play into his forties.

Many significant DSs are open-ended. They have the potential to continue for as long as the participants desire. These include marriages, friendships, and avocational interests.

There can be significant psychological implications attached to the form that beginnings or endings take. Unexpected events that occur for a person who needs structure, order, and time to prepare will present difficulties. The star athlete faces a difficult emotional adjustment when she is no longer able to compete without the help of some form of transition experience.

Open-ended relationships have their own difficulties. They do not have the protection of ending by some external requirement such as a contract that defines a termination date. This is commonplace in marriages when two people are not happy in their relationship, but where initiating a divorce is too threatening. It becomes easier to tolerate the difficulties than to face the pain of ending the marriage.

DSs May or May Not Be Anticipated

Most developmental experiences can be anticipated that relate to education, friendships, occupation, marriage, and the like. Difficulties often come from those that are not anticipated, such as accidents, illnesses, or results of natural disasters like fires, storms, and earthquakes.

Problems also develop for social entities when events that could have been anticipated are not, and the failure to do so results in significant problems. This happens with social entities who put a higher priority on living for the moment than on long-term financial planning. When the consequences of such a choice occur, they are faced with major difficulties such as loss of home, possessions, and bankruptcy. It also happens with the spouse who engages in extramarital affairs without attention to the potential consequences of such an act.

DSs and Goal Definition

A person may seek to get an education for a specific occupational outcome, such as doctor, lawyer, or engineer, or get a degree that does not prepare the student for a specific occupation, such as a liberal arts education. In the former case, there is a clearly defined end point; in the latter case, the goal is ambiguous. The oft-heard refrain from the liberal arts graduate is, "What am I going to do with the rest of my life?"

An adequate operational definition of goals is needed to achieve a successful DS. A parent may desire to have her child pursue a musical career. If such a goal is sought, the parent needs information on what success in that career entails and whether her child has the talent and motivation to pursue it. Failure to do so may result in an aborted and unpleasant DS for the child and strain on the evolving quality of the parent-child relationship.

Sometimes friendships are developed for very specific goals such as financial or career advancement. The developmental course of such a relationship is likely to take a different course than when it is guided just by the merits of the experience.

Marriage provides another illustration in which most couples tend to approach the DS of marriage with vaguely defined goals or just the sense that it is the expected thing to do. When too little attention is paid to a couple's evaluation of their compatibility in marriage, they heighten the potential for a troubled relationship. Such inattention may result from lack of knowledge or lack of motivation. In either case, the results may be the same.

DSs and New Information

DSs may vary in the degree to which they are open to new information and modification in how they progress. At one extreme, biological DSs such as adolescence are genetically determined and are not subject to change except under extreme conditions of environment or illness. Resistance to change also can occur when a social entity is locked into a negative mind-set: "What was good enough for my grandfather is good enough for me." Some parents impose standards on their children that were relevant for their growing up that do not allow for cultural changes in the present. A case in point is the attitude towards pre-marital sex or living together before marriage. The other extreme is characterized by the attitude that rejects tradition and guides DSs solely by the present need.

DSs Are Not Necessarily Mutually Exclusive

There is a tendency to discuss DSs as though each one operates in a vacuum free from the influence of any other sequence. This is generally not the case because the same experiences may have an impact in more than one sequence of development. Behaviors that impact on high-priority DSs become highly valued. This significance becomes increasingly meaningful as such behaviors have major impacts (positive or negative) on increasing numbers of DSs.

An example is the physician who learns from relationships with her patients in such a way they may have impact on other relationships with her colleagues and her family. This can also work in reverse, where experience gained in her family can improve the capacity to function in her practice.

DSs May or May Not Be Compatible

It would be ideal if experiences in one DS were compatible with the needs of other ones. Often this is not the case. The result is a challenge in how to confine skills appropriate to a particular DS and not to others. A man learns that success in the business world demands toughness. Problems develop if the same approach is inappropriately applied in the family setting. The challenge to the father-businessman is to have the ability to develop appropriate skills in each DS relative to each family member.

DSs May or May Not Involve Increasing Complexity

DSs commonly increase in complexity as they become more relevant to a social entity. Relationships usually start at the simple level of acquaintance. Deepening a relationship involves an increased range of behavior; and with it, greater exposure to emotional vulnerability. In a good relationship the complexity matures and the relationship can continue indefinitely. It will begin to deteriorate when the compatibility between participants begins to erode and then begins to end when mutually satisfactory corrective actions are unsuccessful.

There are times when DSs do not get more complex. They may start at a simple level and stay that way until they terminate. Examples of such stages are casual acquaintances that occur at work, neighbors, and fellow members in an organization. These kinds of relationships occur because the purpose for which they originate does not require development beyond its initial level. This reflects the underlying premise that the complexity of DSs is a function of the priorities and goals they are intended to serve. One of the problems that leads to the interruption of a DS is that its goals change over time in a way that makes its continuation no longer viable.

A couple may marry with a set of common goals in mind. Over time, maturity and changing needs and desires lead to redefinition of goals that are not mutually compatible. The result is an end to the relationship, divorce. A variation on this theme is the couple who divorce for this reason but maintain a good friendship relationship because of the common goals relating to their children or because they wish to maintain a level of friendship outside marriage.

Circular Relationship between DS Status and Social Entity Status

A social entity's emotional status is, in part, determined by the success each member is having in accomplishing her own developmental tasks. An example is the degree to which a family has worked on how members spend their time together in a way that is mutually satisfactory. This would apply to vacations and other times they do activities as a unit. This would include how maintenance functions are handled in the home. The emotional climate is enhanced when the division of labor for chores is mutually agreed upon.

Contributing to a social entity's emotional status is the degree to which its members are successful in traversing their individual DSs and the extent to which doing so does not conflict with those of the larger social unit. A common illustration is the father who is so invested in pursuing his career goal that he is not often enough available for participation in family activities.

Valences and Priorities in Voluntary DSs

Sometimes there is a choice of whether a social entity participates in a DS, such as whether to pursue a particular relationship, activity, or goal. A contributing consideration in making such a choice is the level of attraction (valence) held in engaging in the DS. Another factor is the priority such participation carries relative to other DSs. As noted earlier, participation in some DSs does not carry the option of choice. This is the case in aging, management of health and survival issues, and earning a living.

However, often DSs that technically are voluntary are actually not because they are attached to other sequences. An illustration is the spouse who feels an obligation to get along with his in-laws even though he does not like them. Given his own choice (low valence and no priority) he would have no relationship with them. Pursuing it gains a higher priority (with no higher valence) because it is tied to the marriage, which may be a high priority.

When this is not the case, it becomes a contributing factor to the deterioration of the relationship.

Requirements for Progression Through Developmental Sequences

Successful performance in going through a DS requires definition of the goals to be accomplished, motivation to do so, needed resources, information processing, a strategy for coping with developmental tasks, and a means for defining and measuring outcome.

Definition of Goals

Goals refer to definable steps of achievement that result in the outcome of a DS. Getting good grades is a goal in service of the outcome of graduation. Being able to express feelings directly and constructively is a goal in service of better relationships.

The goal may be consciously defined by an individual, such as following a particular career; be involuntary, as in the case of physical maturation; or by the course of some external event, such as getting fired or a natural disaster. DSs may vary in length from minutes to the full life span. Usually the complexity increases as each experience increases in its depth, intensity, or breadth of exposure. Every person is necessarily engaged in parallel developmental sequences that may be complimentary or conflicting. The distribution of energies is not a fixed process but varies with changing needs and circumstances.

The priority of these needs significantly affects how a social entity relates to its goals. Education through high school is a requirement for all in our culture. Those with greater emotional, intellectual, and financial aspirations go to college. A still smaller group continues on to graduate and professional schools. Most people marry but not all choose to have children or are able to have them. Some social entities put a high priority on addressing spiritual needs, whereas others vary in the degree to which this is important.

Setting Subgoals

Subgoals are useful in cases where the outcome is at some future point from when the process starts or in cases where the DS is complex. Graduation is an example of the former case and achieving a good relationship is an example of the latter. Setting subgoals is very useful in providing reinforcement that the long-term goal is appropriate, realistic, and satisfying. When this is not done, there is the possibility of losing one's perspective. The task becomes even more complicated when experience leads to redefining the long-term goal. This is another reason why the use of subgoals is helpful.

One of the reasons that marriages have difficulty is that they define the relationship in vague terms such as to be "happy" without being very clear about what behaviors and experiences would result in achieving such a goal. When this is not done, it increases the probability that two people may agree on a goal of happiness but have rather different ideas on how this is achieved.

I saw one couple who were very much in love who felt compatible when they got married. The glow of romance overshadowed any necessity for thinking through compatibility on specific issues, such as management of money and life-style. By the time they got to therapy, the glow was long gone, replaced by the cold reality of how incompatible their life-styles and goals were. He wanted to live in the inner city with all its activity and excitement, whereas she preferred the rural setting and small town or suburban living. She was very conservative in fiscal management; he was more into spend today and worry about the bills tomorrow.

Motivation

Motivation derives from the clarity of a goal, the desire to achieve it, and the means and the opportunity to pursue it. Clarity, in such conditions, becomes blurred when conflicts exist in other areas of the social entity's life space. This can interfere with fulfillment in the first area.

A man may have a clear image of the kind of father he would like to be. He may have the resources to do so but insufficient opportunity because the demands of his job require a great deal of traveling.

Availability of Needed Resources

This includes any mental, emotional, material, skill, experience, or physical entity that is needed to accomplish a given goal. The aforementioned father might not be able to achieve his parental goal even if he had the time because he lacked the necessary social skills and experience for being a competent father.

Ability to Process Information

One significant influence in how a social entity approaches a DS is the way it receives and processes information. Social entities that are fragile and insecure in their felt competence may be threatened by any information that is different from what is familiar to them. This may occur even when change is desired. A couple may seek counseling yet resist taking in new information because of the fear that may go with the consequences of changing behavior or fear of losing identity. Oftentimes clients are reluctant to resolve painful memories, particularly traumatic or long-standing ones, because in doing so they fear the loss of part of their identity.

A couple that is open to information to gain the approval from another social entity (parents, friends, individuals) can run into trouble when the new information is not compatible with their goals. This is the case of the couple who try to please their therapist or the wife who caters to her husband to gain his approval and favor. In the latter case, this may work until her failure to pay adequate attention to her own needs gets expressed in resentment, which runs the risk of undermining her original goal.

Social entities who process information on too concrete a level can get into trouble when it is taken too literally. The problem gets worse when they are unable to discriminate between information intended to be symbolic and that meant to be literal. An illustration is the mother who takes the teacher's suggestion to help her son with his homework and then helps him every night with every subject.

Another difficulty in processing information occurs when the social entity receiving it is unable to show its vulnerability in asking for clarification or elaboration for fear that the question will be viewed in a negative light. This is the student who is afraid to ask questions for fear she will look stupid, or parents who are afraid to ask their pediatrician for help with their child's sleeping problem.

Strategies for Coping with Developmental Tasks

Every social entity has the task of defining what strategy is most appropriate to follow in coping with each DS. A child does not have the option of whether she will attend school but does have the choice about how she will approach doing so. When a couple decides to get a divorce, each spouse has the choice of how to approach the experience. Ideally, it is best done in the friendly context of two people who share responsibility for a marriage that is no longer viable. More often, couples approach it as hostile adversaries who exchange blame.

Other options for a strategy to cope with DSs are to accept definition of how to proceed from another person or to develop a strategy as the experience unfolds. An example of the former case is where a talented athlete allows an invested parent to determine how she should pursue her athletic ability; this is in contrast to allowing, if not encouraging, the child to be more responsible for deciding how and to what degree she wants to pursue her athletic career. An example of the latter is the student who makes no a priori decision about how much she will develop her athletic career but decides to play it by ear — to decide how far she will go depending on how well she does and what other competing priorities evolve.

Outcome

Social entities vary in the degree to which outcomes for a developmental sequence are defined. There are a number of considerations that affect outcome.

Definition of Outcome

Outcome refers to the end state of a developmental sequence. Graduation, getting married, or having a baby are examples of clearly defined outcomes. Other outcomes, such as having a good relationship, being successful, or staying healthy are more difficult to define as clearly. Complicating such determination is that the definition may gradually shift with changing circumstances, often without the awareness of the social entity experiencing it.

Conditions That Affect How Outcome Gets Defined

Importance and Priority of Outcome
The more an outcome is desired, the more likely is both its careful definition and the mobilization of all necessary resources.

Setting Priorities
Because every social entity is always in multiple DSs, there is an ongoing competition for resources and the assignment of priorities to goals. Every social entity (individual, couple, or family) has to make decisions on a daily basis for such allocation. The absence of clearly defined goals and their attendant priorities can lead to anxiety and confusion in attempting to sort out competing needs, especially as the point of intellectual and emotional overload is reached.

When both parents in a family have dual commitments to family and career, they have an ongoing challenge to juggle priorities between their respective careers and commitments to each other and to their children. Such a family situation can be quite workable when the parents have established a mutually satisfactory way to make decisions and set priorities. When this is not done the result can be a family situation fraught with shifting and often confusing or unpredictable priorities. This can result in competition, tension, anxiety, and the development of problems that ultimately will impact negatively on their careers. Taken to the extreme, this can lead to the deterioration of family relationships, resulting in high risk for divorce.

Distance from the Outcome

An outcome that occurs at some future time may not lend itself to more than a general definition. Contributing to such an occurrence are unforseen circumstances that intervene in the interim. This includes the possibility that the intended outcome may not continue to have the same value. In one situation, a man was working on his Ph.D. At the same time, he worked for his father on a part-time basis to help pay for his education. In the course of this work, he became increasingly interested in the world of business. He eventually gave up his pursuit of the Ph.D. in favor of a career in business.

A similar process occurs with a couple who enter matrimony with the general desired outcome to have a happy marriage without being very clear about what that means in operational terms. As they progress over time, they develop an increasingly specific idea of what constitutes a happy marriage. When this appears attainable, they are likely to invest the needed time and energy to accomplish their goal. In those marriages where it becomes clear that they are not able to do so, they may shift their energies to other more productive pursuits outside of the marriage. This dilution enables them to maintain a tolerable relationship.

Knowing What the Outcome Should Be

Oftentimes the form that the outcome of a DS should take is not clear. This would be the case of people who enter marriage with poor role models or lack of clarity in what they would like it to be. A similar situation occurs when a person enters a new job situation when there is not a clear definition of what kind of performance is expected. There are companies that as corporate policy intentionally do not set expectations for their professional staff. The guiding belief is that greater productivity will be achieved when employees define their own roles and outcomes within very broadly defined boundaries. For some, this is a challenging environment. To others, it is confusing and anxiety-provoking.

Clarity of Outcome

Many outcomes are difficult to define clearly, such as having a good relationship, being successful, or staying healthy. A complication is that the definition may gradually shift with changing circumstances, often without awareness of the social entity experiencing it.

It follows that the more vaguely defined the desired outcome, the less likely that it can be effectively accomplished. Such definition may occur due to lack of desire, interest, fear of outcome, or uncertainty on how to define the outcome. When there is lack of desire or interest, the social entity will tend to avoid the DS. When participating in such a sequence is not a matter of choice, such as in the case of being vocationally successful, then a diminished outcome may result in part from a lack of definition. When a person does not have a clear goal for how to achieve her physical well-being, then she will not pay attention to diet, exercise, or physical abuse, such as use of drugs, use of alcohol, or physical exertion that is damaging, including work in a hostile environment involving exposure to toxic materials.

Whether the Outcome Is Finite or Open-Ended

Outcomes such as weddings, graduations, births, and elections to office all are finitely defined. They occur at a specific time with clearly defined beginning and end points. Other outcomes like a good marriage, success in work, and health do not have a clearly defined starting or ending point. Experiences such as marriages or jobs start evolving approximations to outcome shortly after the experience begins and continue as long as the relationship continues. These two types of outcome in the DSs present very different challenges to the special entity. In the case of the finite ending, resources can be focused until the desired event occurs. Under such conditions the social entity can endure unpleasant circumstances because there is a finite point when it will end. In the case of the open-ended outcome, such as a marriage or a job, there is the requirement for continued attention to maintaining the desired outcome.

When Outcome Is Defined

For the obsessively inclined, outcome will be defined well in advance in great detail. For the more casual social entity, it will not be defined any sooner or with any more detail than is required by circumstances. In the case of the former, the desired outcome for a wedding would be planned in minute detail far in advance of the occasion. In the latter case, those aspects of a wedding that did not require advance planning would not be addressed in advance, or only when the needs of others required it. Implicit in the casual approach is the expectation that whatever happens can be managed and that the consequences of being casual are not sufficiently threatening to warrant greater attention.

Who Defines the Outcome

A goal that is defined by the social entity for itself will have a better chance of success than one that is imposed on it by others or circumstance. Court-ordered therapy is often an exercise in futility for all considered. The client involved may have little choice in accepting the requirement but have little or no investment in the process. A similar result can happen when one member of a couple coerces the spouse to participate in therapy.

How Realistic Is the Defined Outcome?

Pseudo-outcomes often are proposed by one social entity as a means to avoid confrontation by another one. This happens when a woman presses her alcoholic husband to stop drinking. Classically, the husband swears that this is what he will do. At best, he may mean it, and at worst it may be just a way to get her off his back. If he does not view himself as an alcoholic or has little interest in stopping his drinking, he will view the imposed outcome as unrealistic. Outcomes become unrealistic when they exceed the means for achieving them or when they are unlikely to be accomplished under even the best of circumstances. It is useful to make the distinction between what is the desired outcome, what is a realistic outcome, and what is pseudo-outcome used as a manipulation.

Conditions That Affect Accomplishment of Outcome

Availability of Needed Resources

A desired outcome is most likely achieved when the needed resources are available, and there is both the ability to apply them and stay focused. Failure to achieve this can lead to being mired at some step in the DS. A number of things can happen at this point. If the DS is an important one, then resources may be drawn from other DSs. If it does not carry a high priority, then the sequence can be put on hold or canceled. If resources are drawn from other sequences to the degree that it significantly interferes with performance in that sequence, then a domino effect can occur that would lead to increasing interruption of the social entity's functioning. In the extreme case, it would lead to a total breakdown of the social entity's ability to function, for example, a psychotic break.

Appropriate Feedback Mechanisms

Effective performance is dependent on the social entity's developing and utilizing adequate feedback as it progresses through the DS. This is necessary for the social entity to stay on course and adjust to changing circumstances to achieve a desired outcome. Failure to do so will create an environment detrimental to the integrity of the social entity. A case I saw for marital therapy is typical of what often happens. The husband had agreed to pay attention to feedback he got from his wife when she got frustrated with him. However, he did not take his commitment seriously. He paid lip service to her complaints with little response in behavior. He was flabbergasted the day he was served with divorce papers. He never thought she would go that far.

A dual-career family I saw provides another good illustration. The father was an executive in a large corporation and very involved in climbing the corporate ladder. His wife was a therapist who also traveled on a regular basis to give lectures. They had two children, a son of 14 and a daughter of 11. Both of them, like their parents, were heavily involved in many activities. For a number of years, they managed to juggle all their respective priorities in a way that was satisfactory.

Trouble developed when both parents were confronted with crises in their careers at about the same time. Both of them needed to invest a lot more time and energy in their work. This destabilized the family and resulted in competition between them as to whose needs should prevail. The children got caught in cross fire, which in turn affected their ability to function in their world. The family situation rapidly deteriorated, because their previous ability to keep their priorities in reasonable balance and their ability to adjust to one another's crises broke down. It took a number of months for them to get their various developmental sequences back on track.

Evaluation of Outcome

A key part of the developmental sequence is the ability to evaluate progress toward an outcome at various parts of the sequence. Development of a realistic capacity to do so is essential in determining whether and how to proceed and whether changes in the long-term goals are warranted. Failure to do so leads to self-delusion. Such confrontation can be devastating, depending on the degree to which it impacts on one or more social entity.

I saw a couple who felt they were doing well in their marriage in spite of the many problems they encountered. Once they got past an argument, they had a way of dismissing the significance of their dispute and viewing it as part of reaching their ideal of a marriage. This worked until the woman discovered that her husband was having an affair. The mechanism for dealing with past disputes no longer worked. This resulted in her putting past disputes in a very different light. She became aware of how she distorted many of the past conflicts. His efforts to continue to get her to follow past patterns did not work, and the couple ultimately divorced.

Evaluating the Developmental Sequences of the Family System

Most of the time people function in the context of a larger social unit. It may be in the context of the family, the work place, an organization, or the community. How well a person or other social entity progresses in a particular developmental sequence is the product of a number of factors. If the social entity has the necessary resources to accomplish the needed tasks, then the probability of successful completion is high. A case in point is the child who is able to do her schoolwork without outside help. If this is not the case and she needs input from others, then her success will in part depend on whether she is able to get it. The child who needs tutoring, and is not able to get it will do poorly and ultimately could become a dropout.

The reverse procedure also applies. If a social entity has what is needed for its own progression in a DS but is either forced or chooses to use its resources to help another social entity who is in need, then its progress in its own DS will be interrupted or, if necessary, terminated. This would be the case of a mother who is involved in a career, but who chooses to give it up to be more available to help her sick child.

Families are systems in which all the participants are involved in a myriad of DSs and are at different places in the process: starting, somewhere in process, or mourning the ending, and/or anticipating the start of a new DS. Usually there is enough ebb and flow so that when one family member is in need of help in traversing a DS, other family members have the resources to help out.

Crisis develops when all members may be in need at the same time and no one has the resources to help one another. It is at such times a family may be most motivated to seek outside help. One such family came for therapy when the alcoholic father was out on a binge, there was no money for food, the teenage son was arrested for shoplifting, and a 15-year-old daughter announced she was pregnant. Usually the mother was able to juggle family crises, but when all these events occurred within a few days she was overwhelmed and did not have any other resources available to her.

CASE ILLUSTRATION

The Application of the Developmental Sequence Process in Therapy

This case involved the Kane family of five members: father, 45; mother, 44; Susan, 22; Brad, 18; and Cheri, 15.

A social entity will function well when it has been able adequately to traverse necessary DSs. A family evaluation includes an assessment of DSs of family members: as individuals, as subunits (couple, parent-child combinations, sibling group), and the family as a whole. Consideration is given to whether the necessary DSs are being adequately accomplished and with what level of consequences.

The predominant social entities in the family were: the five family members, father and mother, mother and the children, and the two younger children. The major areas of DSs are shown in Figure 7-1.

FIGURE 7-1 • *Developmental Sequences of the Family at the Start of Therapy*

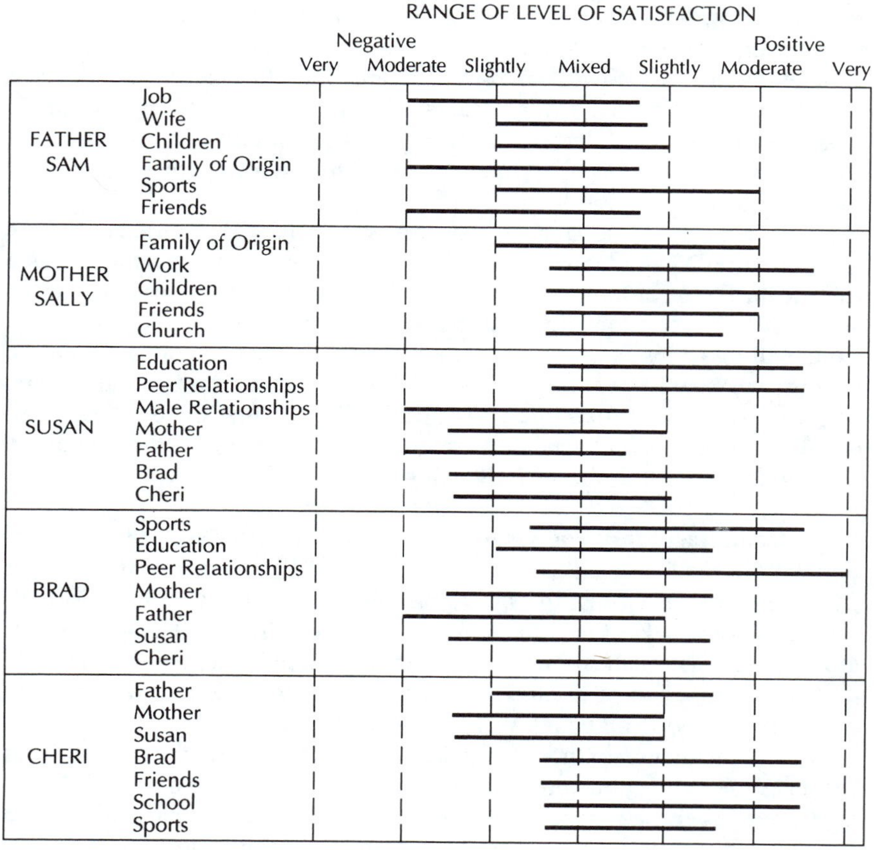

RANGE OF LEVEL OF SATISFACTION

		Negative					Positive	
		Very	Moderate	Slightly	Mixed	Slightly	Moderate	Very

FATHER SAM	Job Wife Children Family of Origin Sports Friends
MOTHER SALLY	Family of Origin Work Children Friends Church
SUSAN	Education Peer Relationships Male Relationships Mother Father Brad Cheri
BRAD	Sports Education Peer Relationships Mother Father Susan Cheri
CHERI	Father Mother Susan Brad Friends School Sports

Characteristics of Significant Family DSs

Father

The DSs in which the father was engaged were primarily self-imposed and assisted by support from his wife. His DSs focused largely on his occupation. There was insufficient address to self-definition and social relationships. His primary work DSs were moving towards premature closure, as he perceived it. He felt he had achieved as much as he was able since no further advancement was possible. This preoccupation was reflected in his attitude toward his work, his concern about the future course of his relationship with his wife, and the realization that the childhood phase of his relationship with his children was over. His apprehension about whether adult relationships would be any better with them only added to his inability to control the future. His work DSs were all anticipated. This was not the case with his children's DSs. The pressures of work and his lack of comfort in personal relationships interfered with his taking advantage of his newly found awareness, of how his work interfered with his involvement in family relationships.

His general goal at work was to be as successful as he could be. Failure to define the DS for his work in a more concrete and focused way was a significant factor in limiting his success. The same problem was even more apparent in his relationships with his wife, children, and extended family. Contributing to his failure was his inability to be open to new information over the years. When concerns about relationship were raised over the years, he gave them only lip service and superficial participation. Another contributing factor was his feeling of inadequacy in dealing with the children as they got older and more challenging.

Requirement for Progression through the Father's DSs.   As a general orientation, the father did not have clearly defined goals in any of his major DSs. He came the closest to doing so in his career, but even here his goals were ambiguous. He knew he wanted to be successful and make a lot of money. He was much more vague in defining relationship goals. This, in part, was a function of limited motivation and a conflicted history of relationships and poor modeling in his family of origin.

A consequence of not doing well in defining goals for his DSs was vagueness in defining outcomes. In his career he did not have any clear definition about when he reached a desired level of income or when he arrived at a desired position. In relationships he had no ability to define when a satisfactory state of relationship was achieved.

Mother

Her DSs were primarily self-imposed (working, children, friends). She was satisfied with her progress with the exception of her relationship to her husband. She felt comfortable about her part in trying to make their relationship work. She viewed the difficulty as being largely his.

She was doing well in the balance she has achieved in developing appropriate DSs in each category of definition: self-definition, her newly evolving occupation, and her social relationships. She understood that her children felt she can be too intrusive. She was making progress in modifying her behavior in those areas where she agreed.

Part of the reason she felt a sense of balance in her life was that the significant DSs were at different points of development: her work gave her an opportunity to achieve a new dimension in her self-definition. She also had made new friends through her work. Her marriage continued on a stable level, although not the way she would like it. Her DS as a mother of minor children was rapidly coming to an end.

She felt good about her ability to anticipate the need for participating in the DSs in her life. She looked forward to marriage and children and was reasonably well prepared for them when they occurred. Her anticipation of her children leaving home was an important consideration in the development of a new DS in the business world.

She viewed her general satisfaction with life as attributable to having defined goals that were clear and attainable. An important contribution in this effort was openness to receiving new information. She is unclear about the outcome of her marriage but felt optimistic that it would improve. She began to talk to her husband about what goals they will pursue in the next stage of their life.

She was fortunate in experiencing minimal conflict between her various DSs over time. The one major conflict was during the early years of having children, when her husband felt in competition with them for her attention. She tried to keep a balance in her priorities between her relationship with her husband and that with her children but was not as successful as she desired. At times, her own needs got lost in her efforts to pay attention to everybody else's needs.

Requirement for Progression through the Mother's DSs. Although she had clear goals in what she wanted from her marriage, she was less clear in defining what specific form the outcome would take. She was more clear on what outcome she did not want, which was her husband's inability to express his feelings. She approached raising her children with broadly defined goals and a sense of outcome. These became increasingly well defined with each child.

She had more masterfully defined both the goals and form of outcome in her new career in that she had a clear idea of what position she wanted to achieve and what outcome would go with it. She had a clearly defined salary and work schedule to which she aspired.

Susan

Her DSs were self-imposed (college, friends, hobbies). Adding pressure to her own definition were the expectations to make the most of her innate abilities from her parents and the school community. She felt comfortable in the DSs she was pursuing in self-definition and in her occupation. She was not sure whether she would become a lawyer but felt confident that this would be clear by the time she finished college. Her DSs in social relationships were more of concern to her. She responded to pressure to get more involved in social relationships, especially dating. She tried, but seemed to have difficulty in sustaining relationships with men for reasons that remained unclear to her. She had an easier time with women but would like to feel more at ease in these relationships.

Susan was at a time in her life when major DSs were just beginning or early in the phase. Exceptions included the change in relationships with her family and the friendships she had ended or would never be the same. Susan always had an eye on the future, so there were few surprises in anticipating the evolution of new DSs. This went along with her ability to define realistic, clearly focused goals. She usually was open to listening to other people, but at times her vulnerability made it hard for her to take in new information.

Requirement for Progression through Susan's DSs.   Susan had clearly defined goals in becoming a lawyer and what she would do once she got her degree. She had a clearly defined goal in the kind of relationships she would like to have and struggled with a definition of what form the relationship should take. Her defined problem in having significant relationships with men continued to confuse her. Also of concern was how to achieve the desired outcome of the goal to have a comfortable relationship with her mother. The same was also true for relationships with her brother and sister.

Brad

For the most part, Brad's DSs were self-defined. The major exception was the pressure he felt from his father to be the accomplished athlete that his father aspired to be but did not achieve. He felt he was on track with the DS regarding what occupation he would pursue. His DSs in social relationships were going well. If anything, they are going too well. At times they became a convenient way to avoid facing problems in other DSs.

Brad was at the crisis point that comes with the changes in DSs that go with graduation from high school and departure for college. He was uncertain about the degree of impact this transition will have on his DSs. This included new directions in family relationships, endings or changes in relationships with his friends, and endings that went with leaving home and going off to a new environment. One of the things that made it harder for him to make the transition to new DSs was having to give up the athletic and social successes he knew so well. Any new DSs would have an unknown outcome.

Leaving home for college left him uncertain about what kind of goals to pursue at college. He knew he would have to put a higher priority on his academic work. Because of this, he was not sure what kind of goals to set for his athletic interests. He was concerned that he might not be able to put the time in to achieve the same athletic accomplishments that he did in high school. Brad was good at staying open to receiving information from others. The major exception to this was his difficulty in accepting input from his father, since Brad felt his father did not pay much attention to what was important to him. He was pretty open to input from his mother, except when she got too intrusive.

As Brad prepared to leave home for college, the major DS concerns and priorities were coming to terms with the various endings or changes he would have to face. He also was concerned about getting established at college both socially and academically.

Requirement for Progression through Brad's DSs.   Brad's biggest struggle was narrowing his focus on what career he wanted to follow. He had a lot of pressure to be a lawyer. At first glance, this made sense because it sounded like something he would enjoy. His uncertainty stemmed from not having a very clear idea of what outcome he would like. He did not feel pressed at this time to make getting more information a priority.

His success in social relationships with his peers continued to go well because he had a good sense of the goals and outcomes he wanted. He had male and female friends that he found satisfying. He was having more difficulty in his family relationships in achieving his DS goals. The previously described difficulty stemmed from not being able to find a way to get his father to acknowledge his own needs and views. He sought assistance from his mother and siblings but with little change in the outcome. He had a similar but lesser problem with his sister Susan.

Cheri

Cheri's self-defined DSs included achieving the kind of relationships she wanted both within and outside her family. She also had the DS of deciding what her commitment would be to her studies. These choices resulted from the interaction of her values with those of her parents. She had well-established DSs in social relationships.

For the most part, she was in the early part of the DSs in her life. The two significant areas of change were leaving junior high school and her brother's leaving for college. Both of these events aroused apprehension. Cheri tended to stay focused on the present. As a result, she did not do well at anticipating change.

Cheri varied in her ability to define DS goals. Once she was clear in her definition, she could become very single-minded in her efforts. This was the case when she wanted to be able to have a better relationship with her brother. She got him to teach her to play tennis, which she knew was a favorite sport of his. She worked like a beaver to become good enough to play with him. She accomplished her goal; and through it was able to establish an improved relationship with Brad. Once she set her mind on a goal, she was very open to input from any source. There were no significant incompatibilities between her various DSs.

Her DS priority was making the adjustment to leaving junior high school and going to high school. She felt generally positive about all of the changes that confronted her.

Requirement for Progression through Cheri's DSs.   Cheri had done well in progressing through her relationship DSs. This was the result of her having both the motivation and personality style to accomplish it. Also contributing was her ability to have focused goals and a defined sense of the desired outcome; that is, she knew what she wanted in relationships and was able to make it happen. Her major concern in family relationships was the anticipated difficulty that would result when her brother went to college. She was concerned about being able to keep the positive evolving outcome in her relationship with her mother from shifting to a more negative one if her mother became too intrusive and dependent on her. She had no significant problems in DSs in her academic work because she had the necessary resources and definition of goals and outcome.

DSs of Husband and Wife

Their major DS categories were values, communication, sexual relationship, children, and finances. They were able to come to agreement on the basic values that defined their relationship. They did well in defining DSs on an intellectual level. They ran into trouble when dealing with the emotional component. This had created problems in the DSs concerned with communication, their sexual relationship, and dealing with the children. As described earlier in the introductory case material, all members of the family were bothered by the father's emotional remoteness.

They were well into their DSs in the previously defined areas. In the not too distant future, they would be in the ending of the DS related to children being at home. This would be replaced by a DS concerned with relating to the children as adults. For father, a major change was adjustment to the DS of his wife having a career and the impact this would have on their relationship. For mother, there would be the continued ability to anticipate changes in the family. One exception to this was her unanticipated success in entering the business world.

The couple did well in defining goals when they did not require significant dealings with each others' feelings. The couple were able to exchange views and felt heard otherwise. They had trouble finding a balance between meeting the financial needs of the children and their own needs.

The major DS concerns for the couple were around communication of feelings and the adjustment to the changes in their relationship as a result of the wife's work. The deterioration of the husband's work situation had made communication more difficult because he tended to withdraw when struggling with internal turmoil.

Requirement for Progression through the Couple's DSs. They were having difficulty in their DS concerned with communication because they jointly lacked the resources for defining a mutually satisfactory way to define common goals and the desired form of outcome. As a result, the husband's motivation dwindled while the wife pursued solutions to their problems. This only increased the husband's frustration. This stalemate ultimately was one of the reasons the family found their way to family therapy on the initiative of the wife.

Mother and Children

There are four DSs involving this mother and children: mother with each of the children and mother and children as a group. The mother entered a DS with the birth of each child as an outgrowth of the general category of DS concerned with raising children. At this level she developed general goals for each child that translated into specific ones as each grew. These DSs became significant because there was a shared mutual interest between mother and children in their further development. This was in direct contrast to the DSs that never developed beyond a relatively superficial level with their father.

The DS of childhood ended with Susan when she went to college and this was about to be the same for Brad. With these two children, the mother was at the beginning of the DS of mother and adult children and the relational transition in this context. These DSs were anticipated and welcomed by all concerned. It was not clear whether the children and the mother had the same goal in mind. Susan had some concern that her mother expected to have a closer relationship than Susan would have liked. At times they got into difficulty when the residual tensions interfered with the exchange of information about one another. There was some incompatibility in their DSs. The mother placed a higher priority on the DSs with these children than they did with her.

Requirement of Progression through Mother and Children's DSs. The prognosis for satisfactory definition and implementation for new DSs with Susan and Brad was good because they collectively had the motivation and resources to redefine mutually satisfactory goals and outcomes. They had adequate ability to exchange and process their respective views and to problem-solve differences. The prognosis for modifying the DS between mother and Cheri also looked good for the same reasons. The shifting family structure would likely create problems between them, but resolution was within the range of their resources.

Brad and Cheri

This relationship was the only other significant DS in the family. Their mutual interest in tennis expanded to doubles matches and the evolution of limited common friends. Cheri was very pleased with the shared relationships. Brad was, at best, lukewarm and anticipated that this DS would diminish once he went off to college.

Requirement for Progression through Brad and Cheri's DSs.   There did not appear to be any significant problem in Brad and Cheri working out their differences in their joint DS. Cheri had more difficulty with the transition, because of the loss in the relationship. The problem was short-lived, as she had many other compensating relationships and the ability to create new ones.

Father and Brad

The father very much wanted to develop a significant DS with Brad but was unable to achieve it. As noted earlier, Brad felt too much expectation from his father without an accompanying acknowledgment of what Brad wanted. The result was a friendly, distant relationship.

Requirement for Progression through the Father and Brad's DSs.   The prognosis for Brad and his father to improve their mutual DS was poor because they did not have the resources, particularly the ability to express, respect, and deal with differences about their feelings. Their goals were similar, but their definition of outcome was quite different. The kind of behavior they desired from each other did not meet the needs of the other person.

Clinical Intervention

The information described in the case illustration and shown in Figure 7.1 was obtained by the procedure described in the following section on clinical application of the DS concept. Several significant developments resulted from this procedure.

A number of distortions and problems were defined and clarified. Among these were:

1. Family members did not appreciate the level of the father's pain.

2. The father was surprised in finding out how much guilt his wife felt over her successes.

3. The mother realized how hard she was working to distract her husband from his depression about his job.

4. The father was surprised and hurt about the distance Brad felt in their relationship.

5. The mother heard how her intrusiveness got in the way of relationships.

6. Brad and Cheri became aware of how Susan felt left out and envious of their relationship and their ability to socialize.

Such developments helped the family to understand their relationships better as an ongoing dynamic process rather than as a series of discrete events. It also helped them to appreciate the way in which family members cope with their respective DSs. It helped them to see how one or more relationships may consume available energies with a deficit in another relationship. They expanded their understanding of rejection in the larger family context of competing relationships and DSs. Felt rejection (intentional disregard) must be distinguished from needed relationship resources that are not available.

A GUIDE TO THE CLINICAL APPLICATION
OF DEVELOPMENTAL SEQUENCES

I use the following method in the application of the DS concept:

- Early in the course of therapy I have each family member review the major DSs in which they are engaged and how they evaluate where they are in its development. Usually this is done in a family session but may be done differently to meet specific needs. In any event the outcome of this evaluation is shared with the family whenever possible.
- I have each member describe the level of satisfaction and concerns about each of these DSs.
- Then the person is asked to compare where they are relatively across all of their DSs (beginning, middle, end).
- I then ask them for an evaluation of how the state of progress of DSs affects one another and the consequences that result from such an evaluation.
- Comments from other family members are invited.
- After this process is completed for each family member, I invite them to participate in a process of looking at how each person's DS status might affect the DSs of others or in turn be affected by them.

- Ultimately the results of such discussion are related to the presenting problems in the course of going through the above steps.

This process is accomplished by evaluating DSs with the following considerations:

1. To what extent are the DSs defined by the social entity or imposed on it?
2. To what degree are social entities at a similar point in different DSs, for example, ending DSs or beginning many of them at the same time?
3. To what degree are the DSs anticipated?
4. To what extent does the goal for a DS remain fixed, independent of the way it is progressing? For example, a man stays in a job he hates.
5. To what extent are social entities open to new information on one or more significant DSs?
6. To what extent are the various concurrent DSs in which social entities are engaged compatible with each other? For instance, a man's job requires a lot of traveling, which interferes with his marriage.
7. To what extent are DSs progressing with increasing complexity?
8. What is the pattern of positive value attached to the range of DSs in which each social entity is engaged? A strong positive pattern would be a person who enjoys most or all of the DSs in which he is engaged.
9. Evaluate the extent to which social entities meet the requirements for progressing through DSs.
10. Are the goals for each DS clearly defined?
11. How motivated are social entities to accomplish their respective DSs?
12. How available are needed resources for accomplishing DSs?
13. How able are social entities to process information necessary for performance of DSs?
14. How adequately are social entities adaptive in overcoming problems encountered in progressing through their various DSs?
15. Evaluate considerations that affect outcome.
16. How clearly understood are what outcomes there should be for DSs?
17. How clearly and realistically are outcomes for DSs defined?
18. Are priorities defined for concurrent DSs?
19. How important are the outcomes for the various DSs?
20. To what degree are there problems in progressing in DSs because of the distance the current point is from the completion of the DS? For example, a woman is unhappy in her marriage but is committed to remaining until her small children leave home.
21. What is the proportion of open-ended versus finite-ended DSs?

22. At what point are outcomes defined for those DSs that have flexibility in defining goals? For instance, the force of family tradition requires that a student enter college, with strong expectations that she will become a lawyer.

23. Who defined the outcomes for those DSs for which a choice was possible?

24. How realistic are the defined outcomes?

25. Are the means for completing a DS adequately defined?

26. How available are the needed resources for DS performance?

27. How adequate are the feedback mechanisms for self-correction in achieving DS outcomes?

28. What is the basis for evaluating the quality of DS outcomes?

Summary

In this chapter I have defined and described the concept of developmental sequences by which the needs and goals of social entities are defined and achieved. Also highlighted is the critical factor of interaction between DSs. A case illustration was presented that briefly described how these concepts are utilized in clinical practice.

CHAPTER EIGHT

Transitions

A major source of vulnerability in life experience is how each social entity is able to cope with change and its aftermath. This chapter developed from my interest in acquiring a better understanding of these critical points and the impact they had in the therapy setting

THEORY

Our lives contain events and relationships that have a starting point, a period of time during which the event or relationship is experienced, and a time of ending when it comes to an end. Each of these transition phases presents a challenge. Success and happiness are significantly affected by the degree to which a person learns to cope with each of these transitions. In this chapter I discuss the process of transitions: how they are defined, how they progress, what functions they serve, and the consequences that result when they are not properly managed.

Overview of Phases

Transitions consist of five phases: anticipation, adaptation, stabilization and maintenance, termination and mourning, and integration. The anticipation phase occurs when a person attempts to anticipate a future event and may or may not include mental rehearsal for how to cope with it. During this time a social entity is usually in a heightened receptivity state for seeking and receiving new information relative to the anticipated event.

In the adaptation phase, the focus shifts to the implementation of adjustment when the event occurs. This requires the ability to receive information, assess it, and make appropriate changes in behavior on an ongoing basis until adaptation to the new event is completed.

The task of the stabilization and maintenance phase (SM) is to maintain the changes that have occurred. This involves accomplishing the shift from taking what is new or unfamiliar to making it familiar and doing what is necessary to maintain it. This presupposes that continuing in a given phase is desired or that if there is no choice to avoid the experience. A child does not have the choice of whether or not to attend school. The only feasible constructive option is to adjust to being a student.

The termination and mourning phase (TM) occurs with the ending of the SM phase. This may be by accident or design, desired or undesired, and temporary or permanent. The challenge in this phase is to adapt to the ending of an experience that permits the move to new experiences. Response styles to TM vary from hypervigilance and heightened activity to one of denial and refusal to relate to a forthcoming loss. The ending of this phase begins with the person's ability to accept the existing reality and become receptive to the anticipatory work of potential alternative experiences.

The integration phase dovetails with the ending of the TM phase. The major focus is on how a person utilizes the learning from a given experience and incorporates such learning for future reference and use. Failure to do this increases the probability that the same pattern of behavior will continue to be repeated.

Description of Phases

Anticipation Phase

The anticipation phase of a given event is not a necessary occurrence. There are times when events like the normal developmental experiences of births, graduations, moves, and job changes can be anticipated. There are also many times when events cannot be anticipated, such as accidents, illnesses, and unexpected deaths. There also are events that could be anticipated but often are not, such as being fired and getting divorced.

When an Event Can Be Anticipated

When the occurrence of an event can be anticipated, a social entity can make the determination of whether such an event warrants any preparation for it. How much anticipation work is done will depend on the following considerations:

1. The significance that is attached to whether or not the event occurs, for example, a couple who are having difficulty in their marriage and fear the possibility of divorce.
2. How such an event competes with the relative importance of other events that are occurring or may occur, for example, what priority is

given to improving the marriage relative to attending to career or the needs of children.

3. The degree to which resources are available for coping with the anticipated event, for example, does the couple have the emotional resources and know what they can do to change their relationship?

Anticipation work increases with the likelihood that an event will occur whose outcome will make a significantly positive or negative difference. In one family, a teenager was told not to use the family car when his parents were away over the weekend. He agreed, but as circumstances would have it, he needed to go somewhere and had no way to do it. He anticipated what would happen if he violated his parents' prohibition and decided he would take his chances with whatever consequences might result. Besides, there was always the possibility that he would not get caught.

When the Anticipated Event Is Desired.   When such an occurrence has significant positive meaning, the individual may engage in a mental rehearsal of the event. This may involve heightened anxiety and motivate the experiencing individual to behave in a way that would hasten the occurrence or quality of this event.

A couple with whom I was working wanted to marry but the man was separated, not yet divorced. This desire motivated them to do a lot of anticipatory work in how to effect a divorce quickly. This involved anticipating how to solve a number of problems with his wife so that she would cooperate in obtaining the divorce.

When the Anticipated Event Is Not Desired.   When the anticipated event is negative and significant, efforts will be directed toward avoiding or postponing the occurrence of the event and/or minimizing the negative impact.

The other side of the issue for the aforementioned couple who wanted to get married was that the wife who was being divorced did not share his enthusiasm for the event. She did not welcome the prospect of the divorce and devoted a lot of her energy to trying to prevent it. When it became clear that this would not succeed, she did all she could to delay its occurrence. During such efforts, it became increasingly clear to her that divorce was inevitable. This moved her to find other relationships to diminish the impact once divorce became a reality.

When an Event Cannot Be Anticipated

When the Event Is Desired.   Such an occurrence is likely to come as a pleasant surprise. This would be the case when dear friends who had not been seen in a long time drop in without advance notice. Under such conditions, the family's ability to adapt is tested. If this doesn't happen, the desired event can quickly become a problem.

When the Event Is Not Desired. The most threatening possibility is an unanticipated event that is very undesired. It might be a sudden illness or death, an accident, loss of a job, or a myriad of other possibilities. Such a situation does not allow for any preparation for what would be a difficult adjustment even if it were anticipated.

Ways of Dealing with an Anticipated Event

There are two general ways of relating to the anticipation of events: when and how the anticipation is accomplished.

When the Anticipation Work Is Done. This may occur far in advance of the event, when it becomes imminently relevant, and just before it is about to happen. I ran across an unusual situation many years ago when I was doing a workshop with a group of mothers of 4-year-olds. They were very concerned about getting their children into the right first grade that would assure the Ivy League college track.

Commonly, parents seriously begin to anticipate their children going off to college once they enter high school. Increasingly, comments are made such as "When you go to college . . ." and "Pay attention to your grades now because it will affect what college you get into." From the child's point of view, comments about anticipation include "I wonder wht college will be like" and "I'm going to miss my friends."

An example of last-minute anticipation is the student who is in a frenzy trying to complete his college application just before the filing deadline or the student who doesn't prepare for an exam until the night before. Such conditions can increase the difficulty in the adaptation phase and create problems for those people who are affected by the last-minute anticipatory work.

Way of Approaching Anticipation Work. People approach anticipation in a wide range of ways: ignoring it, minimizing it, dealing with it in broad general terms, or preparing for it in a detailed or obsessive manner. When a student is reminded of the need to begin to prepare for college, the reaction is to treat it as not relevant at the moment. The next level of reaction is to minimize it with the attitude that "it does not require current action," "there will be plenty of time to cope with it," or "there is not that much that needs to be done."

The next level is to anticipate in broad terms. This would involve defining a general idea of when to prepare an application and some thought about the type of college the student would like to attend. The next step would be detailed preparation that would include sending away for catalogues, getting information about colleges from peers and counselors, visiting colleges, and completing applications. For some, the last step may go to the extreme and become an obsession motivated by anxiety that gets expressed in being certain that each detail is properly attended to, often far in advance of the deadline.

Conditions That Influence the Response to Anticipation

Inability or Refusal to Anticipate an Event.   Inability or refusal to anticipate a forthcoming event does not allow for any preparatory work, which increases the difficulty in adapting to the event when it does occur. This is especially true in the case of trauma (such as unexpected death, natural disaster, or unexpected loss of job). When this happens, the pressure to cope may drain resources from other activities that could result in other problems.

I was working with a single woman who at age 35 had no prospects of marriage in the present or the foreseeable future. She was very clear that she wanted a baby with or without the benefit of marriage. Her desire to be a parent blinded her to suggestions of any anticipatory work regarding what consequences went with becoming a single parent and how this would impact on her career. Failure to anticipate the demands of motherhood resulted in her having a very difficult time coping with her daughter. This so preoccupied her that it left insufficient energy to function on her job. This resulted in her bouncing back and forth in her attempts to cope with the demands and crises of her child and her work.

Significance and Consequences of Anticipating Events.   The amount of energy expended in anticipating an event will depend on the significance and consequences of it happening. If its occurrence has little impact, then it will be low priority, and few or no resources will be utilized to address it.

In one case, a man was aware that he would be dropped from membership in an organization if he did not pay his dues. He meant to do so but was too busy with other concerns. He knew that he would be reinstated by paying his dues and a small fine.

If an anticipated event is perceived to have a major impact and a high probability that it will occur, attempts to assess the consequences would follow. If the event is positive, then efforts would be directed to maximizing its impact. When these consequences have significant negative impact, attention gets focused on how to minimize or eliminate them. If the perception is that little or nothing can be done to cope, the evolving anxiety can lead to adaptive behavior, such as numbing, which allows for survival. In this condition, the social entity is faced with limited ability to adequately process and act on information.

In one family, it became clear that the daughter, a senior in college, was involved in a destructive religious cult. The more the family learned about the situation, the more frightened they became about the consequences, which included a total cutoff from their daughter and the prospect that she would be involved in an arranged marriage. This awareness led them to make it a priority to mobilize all their resources to do what they could to extricate her from this group. In this case, the family was successful in their efforts. In another case, the family had more limited emotional and financial resources that resulted in a failure to rescue their son. They became depressed and functioned in a burdened and numbed state.

The process by which these assessments are made involves the emotional and intellectual preparation for anticipating the event occurring and the assessment of the ability to cope with it. The emotional preparation includes what kind of effect is attached to the event and whether the experiencing social entity feels it has the emotional resources necessary for coping. Also of consideration is whether the expenditure of emotional resources on this event will be in conflict with the emotional needs in relating to other events.

The intellectual process involves an evaluation of all the elements involved in determining what is likely to happen, what resources are needed for coping, and the perceived ability to do so. Under consideration are such questions as: What is the likelihood an anticipated event will happen and can anything be done to affect how, when, or where it occurs? If it happens, how severe are the consequences likely to be? What can be done to change or control the degree of consequences, and what is the likelihood of accomplishing it?

This process is facilitated by the use of mental rehearsal as proposed by Lazarus (1977). The success of this process will depend on the anxiety level being maintained at a level that does not interfere with the described analytical process. According to Lazarus, mental rehearsal requires the motivation and discipline to rehearse coping strategies in preparation for the forthcoming events. A number of important consequences can result from successful rehearsal according to Lazarus. Skill is gained in coping with the anticipated event at a level that approximates actual performance of the behavior. This is likely to heighten the probability of successful outcome. This in turn would contribute to an enhanced self-concept and ability to cope in other areas. Each such successful experience increases the repertoire of resources. If the rehearsal is unsuccessful and the forthcoming event is significant, a large increase in the anxiety level is likely, which would interfere with adaptation to the event.

Anticipation of a given event does not take place in a vacuum. It will be, in part, a function of what else is happening in the person's life space. If things are generally going well and there is a good supply of intellectual and/or emotional reserve, a social entity is likely to handle anticipation of an event in a different manner than if things were not going well in other areas of the life space. In such a situation, an additional stressor pushes the person's constructive coping capacity closer to the limit and the resulting dissipation of resources.

An added consideration that affects the way an anticipated event will be regarded is how compatible this event is to other events that could or will occur at the same time. This happens in two ways: (1) A particular event will happen outside the choice of the social entity. An example of this is the ending of a relationship where the woman wants to end it and the man does not. If he is confident that he can find other relationships, he will anticipate this termination in a way quite differently than if he felt this could not happen. (2) The social entity will have the choice of whether a particular event will happen. An example of this case is where a person anticipates having several attractive job offers. He is faced with deciding which one is likely to be the best career choice.

A social entity always has the opportunity to either anticipate a given event in the larger context of many other events or to view it in isolation. People who manage their lives in the latter manner run the risk of a more chaotic life-style.

In one case, a man always had his heart set on being a professional baseball player. He was single-minded in his dream and had initial successes. As he came closer to realizing his dream, he discovered that he had not anticipated other things that mattered, such as the travel, living in hotels, being away from family, and the many ways his life would not be his own. The dream lost its charm!

Adaptation Phase

Once an event occurs, the social entity experiencing it is faced with how best to adapt to it. Adjustment to an experience is enhanced when it is important and was anticipated, appropriate mental rehearsal was conducted, and needed resources were available.

Once a person is confronted with having to cope with an event, the challenge is to find a way to relate to it that is compatible with the person's needs. When a disruptive event does occur, it becomes a problem to the degree that it draws upon energies from other desired experiences or interferes with them. There was a case in which all the members of a family were actively involved in their various individual and joint activities. The father's unexpected unemployment and the prospect of the family having to move to a new city created a great deal of anxiety because of the impact on every family member's life.

One problem that interferes with the adaptation process is the difficulty in keeping energies constructively focused. This occurs when a person continues to focus on the past and what might have occurred rather than attending to how to cope with what has occurred.

Options in Coping with Adaptation

When a social unit is confronted with the onset of a new event, there are a number of options: adjust to it, resist it, fight it, or try to ignore it.

Adjustment. This includes the need to determine what knowledge, skills, and resources (time, money, assistance from others, etc.) are needed to adapt. Also of concern are the consequences that are like to occur. If the event is strongly desired or avoided, an added consideration is the impact of redirecting energies from other concerns to coping with the new event. The result of such collective evaluation determines the motivation for adapting to the new event. It also contributes to a decision about the costs and benefits of making adaptation a priority relative to other priorities of the social entity. A two-career couple want to have a child. They realize such a decision will significantly change their life-style. They are faced with making a decision about their priorities between career demands and having a family.

When exposure to events cannot be avoided and it does warrant the mobilization of resources to cope with it, a social entity has to then juggle available resources to minimize any unpleasant consequences that may occur. If the aforementioned wife got unexpectedly pregnant and there was no choice about whether to have the child, the issue shifts to coping with the impending birth.

Resistance. This option results when the occurring event is undesirable yet not sufficiently disruptive to warrant significant attention. The utilization of available resources now shifts from how to adjust to how to minimize its impact. In such cases, the resistance is likely to be more passive than active. In one couple, the wife's mother was rather intrusive and annoying to her son-in-law. When he got wind of an impending visit, he would grumble and then find ways to minimize spending time with her.

Fighting Back. The ante increases when the occurring event is considered more than undesirable and is to be avoided if at all possible. In such cases, coping efforts are more active and will likely take priority over other events in the social entity's life space. This involves marshaling resources and developing a strategy for interrupting the occurrence of the event or at least minimizing its impact.

In the case of the last example, the husband would make clear his objections and negotiate with his wife on how to change the nature of such visits or to cope with them differently.

In one family, a problem occurred in the neigborhood in which two younger children were bullied by another child. Efforts to get cooperation from the bully's parents failed. The parents involved the police, mobilized help from other affected parents, and helped the children learn how to cope with the bully.

Ignoring It.   This option is utilized when the occurrence of the event or its consequences are of little or no significance and do not warrant any attention. This would be the case in the example of the mother-in-law's impending visit, if her visit did not matter to the husband one way or the other.

Immobilized.   When the need to adapt is great and there are grossly insufficient resources or when efforts to adapt have met with repeated failure, a social unit can become immobilized and cease to cope with the occurring event. If this event is of sufficient consequence, it could result in the total immobilization of the social entity, as is often the case in severe alcoholism.

Each new experience provides an opportunity to gain new resources in the form of new understanding and new skills. Even the most worthy experience can be a problem if the demands of adjusting to it put the person in overload with the potential for disrupting the person's functioning in one or more areas of his life space. This often happens with the workaholic.

Stabilization and Maintenance Phase

Once adaptation has been achieved, the challenge is to maintain a satisfactory level of continuing performance. Whereas the adaptation stage requires the conscious and focused energy that goes with facing any new situation, the stabilization and maintenance phase (SM) involves getting the new behavior to the point where it becomes sufficiently overlearned that it ceases to require the conscious and deliberate monitoring that goes with new behaviors. Accomplishing this objective frees up psychic energy that can be directed to other pursuits.

An illustration of this process is seen in the courting relationship. At the start of a new relationship, a lot of attention is focused on discovering what the new person is like and finding ways to adapt to each other's behavior in some mutually satisfactory manner. As this gradually happens, less and less conscious attention is addressed to managing the relationship.

Another illustration is coping with the arrival of a new baby. Initially the new parents can feel overwhelmed in the challenges and anxieties of learning to care for the baby. Gradually and as each task is mastered, the anxiety level decreases, and more and more is done with less effort, concern, and deliberate awareness. Once this is accomplished, a level of comfort settles in until a new stage in the development occurs. This might be when the child starts to walk or until some other significant change occurs that requires adaptation to another set of circumstances. This can happen when a mother is faced with how to cope with child care when she goes back to work or how she will deal with a second child.

Definitions of Stabilization and Maintenance

A distinction should be made between stabilization and maintenance.

Stabilization.   Once a social entity has achieved a satisfactory adaptation to an event, the task is to develop the capability to keep functioning at the new level. This involves gaining sufficient knowledge and skill so that the desired behavior continues to be accomplished on whatever basis is needed. This involves sufficient learning so that appropriate performance does not require constant conscious focusing.

Maintenance.   When there is a deviation from the desired level of behavior, a social entity will take corrective measures that are necessary to bring behavior within the desired range. In one family situation, the parents anticipated how they would permit their teenage son use of the family car when he was old enough to drive. When that time came, the parents and their son, Rick, adapted well to the event. After some discussion, they worked out the ground rules for how and when the car would be used. The next concern was to develop a way to supervise this activity so that Rick's behavior stayed within appropriate limits. This involved the parents developing a monitoring procedure so that the rules were not eroded (stabilization). They also decided how they would cope when slippage or violations occurred in a way that would get Rick back on track with a minimum of difficulty for all concerned (maintenance).

Problems in the adjustment to changing circumstances need to be anticipated so that preparations can be made to accommodate them with a minimum of threat to those involved. Life becomes especially difficult for those people for whom change is threatening. When this threat occurs, available energy increasingly gets drained from current functioning to unproductive anxiety. This interferes with the present level of functioning and the ability to anticipate and prepare for forthcoming changes. Such events only further reinforce anxiety about change.

Consider the case in which a mother has adapted and stabilized in her ability to manage her first child. As her next pregnancy develops, and she anticipates the birth of a second child, she begins to worry how she will manage a second child when she feels she has all she can to do to cope with the child she has. This problem is further enhanced as she becomes aware that her first child's needs will be greater as he becomes increasingly mobile at the same time that the new baby will be arriving. If these anticipations exceed her perceived ability to cope, then she runs the risk of becoming increasingly anxious, which gets expressed in a greater level of irritability and less tolerance for coping with the existing stresses. This can lead to a distorted anticipation of the difficulties in coping with a second child. This heightened level of anxiety can also be expressed in the marital relationship, which if not properly managed can sow the seeds for ongoing marital tensions.

Considerations That Affect the Functioning of the Stabilization and Maintenance Process

Desirability of Functioning in a Given Area.   A social entity that copes with SM with a negative attitude will have greater difficulty in maintaining satisfactory performance in this phase. A parent who views dealing with his children's adolescence with trepidation will have a harder time than the parent who looks forward to it. The former parent will also have a much harder time when deviations occur that have to be corrected (maintenance). It follows that the emotional energies will be sufficiently taxed so that any added demand will become overwhelming.

This was the case for a mother I saw who was very threatened about dealing with her soon-to-be adolescent daughter. She was worried about her getting involved with drinking, drugs, sex, wrong friends, and other problems. At the least suggestion that something was wrong, she would go into a panic. It was no surprise to find that this daughter's adolescence was a trying time for all concerned.

When Stabilization Is Achieved and Is Unsatisfying.   When a social entity's social experience is found deficient, it has the option to terminate the experience and cope with the relevant mourning. When terminating the experience is not desirable, possible, or feasible, the social entity has the challenge of developing ways to make the experience more palatable. This becomes a maintenance function. This happens to marriages that cease to be satisfying. When the discomfort becomes too great and the ability to find ways to make the relationship more satisfying does not develop, termination via divorce becomes an option. A problematic state is when the situation was not improved and divorce was not an option. Such marriages become stabilized at a negative level where all participants become chronically unhappy.

Availability of Needed Resources.   SM is enhanced when the needed resources are readily available. When they are not as available as desired and when continuing with the existing behavior mode is required, the social unit becomes stressed in its search for the needed resources. Such stress, when not abated, leads to a crisis in the existing behavior mode or it can interfere with other behavior modes, resulting in additional crises.

I saw one family that had a stable financial history. Then at the age of 51, the father, the primary breadwinner, lost his job and was not readily able to find another one. This interrupted the financial stability of the family. As months passed, the stress built up as financial reserves were depleted and relief was nowhere in sight. The stress from this situation gradually permeated all other areas of the family's life: Marital tensions increased, school performance in the children deteriorated, and social relationships with friends were also affected.

Limited Ability to Cope with Change.   Many people are comfortable with the security of established ways of behaving and are threatened by change. Such people become upset when circumstances interrupt their tranquility. When this happens, their difficulty in adapting to change creates a narrow window for stability. When the changing circumstances exceed their tolerance, the social unit becomes dysfunctional and goes into oscillation, which is characterized by repetitive nonproductive behavior. Under such conditions, it is not able to utilize the feedback generated from its own behavior.

In one family, the father was very rigid. He had clearly defined patterns of behavior. There was a family joke that you could set your watch by the time he went to the bathroom every morning. When family members got in his way and interrupted any of his routines, he would get furious and was not very receptive to reason. When set off this way, he would rant and rave about all the ways people are insensitive to the little things he asks of them. At these times, he is closed to accepting any apologies or attempts to correct the situation. He was able to be more reasonable after a period of venting.

Ability to Anticipate Threats to Existing Stability.   One way to avoid a disruption to an existing state of stability is to be able to anticipate and prepare for events that may cause disruption. One approach used by the aforementioned family to cope with the rigid father was to anticipate events that would interfere with his routine and do whatever they could to avoid such disruptive behavior. Among the things they did was to make sure they were out of the bathroom when he would want to use it. They did not keep him waiting when they were all going somewhere together, and chores were done as expected.

When There Is Conflict about What Defines Stability.   This may occur within the individual or between any two or more social entities. This is the case when the social entity is not clear on whether being in a particular experience is desirable or whether there is question about how to achieve stability.

This was illustrated in the case of a couple who were disappointed to find that the relationship following their marriage wasn't what they thought it would be. At that point they were not sure what form it should take; they just knew they did not like it the way it was. After experimentation and a course of therapy, they found a way to define their relationship that was mutually satisfactory.

In another context, a man who was promoted to a new position was anxious about how to face the challenge of his new responsibilities. Once he discovered what it took to succeed, he found himself in conflict between what he had to do and what he felt comfortable doing. This realization created a lot of anxiety and interfered with his ability to adjust to his job. Ultimately, he found a way to resolve his conflict that produced stability in his job.

When Change in the SM Becomes an Adaptation Issue.   A social entity's life circumstances are always changing. A distinction should be made between a change that is within the normal experience of coping in the SM phase and when the orientation of the adaptation phase is required.

One way to make the distinction between deviations that are managed within the SM phase and those that require adaptation phase behavior is by the degree of conscious focused attention required to maintain the change. Adaptation phase behavior is likely to involve added resources, new learning, and a significant amount of time to make the needed adjustment.

Each social entity develops its own distinctive way of coping. Social entities may differ in the variation they can tolerate in their natural behavior patterns. Some people are able to cope with wide variations in their behavior without considering it a crisis or a threat. Other people have a low tolerance for variation so that small deviations arouse great anxiety.

I saw one family that was very flexible. It was their view that any problem that arose was grist for the mill and something to be solved. They did not feel that their competence for coping was at risk. After they had their first child, she developed a significant illness and had a series of accidents during latency. For this couple these events were upsetting but treated as the normal expectation of parenthood.

Another family had a very low tolerance for change. Anything out of the ordinary aroused a level of anxiety and became a crisis. When their daughter came home with poor grades, it became a crisis that warranted a reorganization of the family's routine to ensure that she got better grades and raised considerable anxiety in the parents about the intellectual capability of their daughter. When she missed her curfew on a date, it aroused a lot of anxiety about her judgment and trustworthiness. She was grounded for a month, and her curfew was made earlier.

Developmental Needs Change. Changes in transition phases result from the shifting needs of the social entity. This may result from changes in physical or emotional maturity, a decrease in physical capacity as with advancing age, and loss of resources. These changes will either interrupt the need for continuing in the SM phase and precipitate the onset of the mourning phase or alter the way in which the SM phase is managed.

An example of transitions resulting from physiological changes is the girl who approaches puberty with anticipation of starting her menstruation. This is followed by learning how to adapt to the experience. Once this is achieved, she will develop an established pattern for stabilizing and maintaining appropriate behavior. When her biological clock dictates the end of her menses, she will be faced with adjusting to its termination and the work of the accompanying appropriate mourning.

Events That Interfere with Comfort Zone of Functioning. Many kinds of events occur that may interfere with the SM process. Among these are changes in availability of needed resources, motivation, goals, and priorities. Needed resources may include money, time, and physical or emotional ability to function. Changes in motivation may result from changing need. This would be the case of a person who presents an air of superconfidence to the world to defend against feelings of inferiority. As the person overcomes the problem, he no longer has the need to behave in the same way.

Other reasons for change in motivation include a change in goals for a particular behavior such as a shift from a stressful job that is financially very lucrative to one that pays less but is more enjoyable. Priorities also may change over time. A mother may make it a priority to be home for her children after school. When her children are older or after they graduate from high school, her priorities are likely to change, and career or other interests will become a higher priority.

A frequent occurrence is for a couple in a troubled marriage to stay together to maintain an intact family until the children finish high school. Once the "nest" is empty, the priority on maintaining the marriage is no longer relevant.

Family life-styles are largely determined by family income. Any radical change in income will have a profound impact on the family. I saw one family in which the father was a senior executive with a company for 30 years. When the company was sold, he was suddenly without a job at age 55 and with little prospect that he would get another one that would approximate the same income. This resulted in a marked shift in the family's life-style and goals for the future.

The death of the breadwinner in a family also would have a significant impact on interrupting the various stages of development of all members of the family. The surviving spouse would have to become the breadwinner and one or more of the children may have to curtail their education in order to help support the family or care for younger siblings.

Termination and Mourning Phase

Definition of Mourning
Termination and mourning refer to the process of coping with the partial or total interruption of an ongoing experience. Such interruption may be temporary or permanent and with or without the choice of the social entity experiencing the change. The significance of the loss is a function of the discrepancy between the severity of the loss and the available resources for coping. Another significant consideration that affects coping with loss is the potency of familiar ways of behaving and the meaning that goes with its interruption.

Description of the Mourning Process.   The TM process involves recounting the memories of the event and related feelings that were part of the experience. It involves adjusting to the absence of the experience, feelings that result from the change, and judgments about why the change resulted and who has responsibility for its occurrence. The final challenge of TM is addressing if, when, and how replacement will be addressed. There is a clear beginning to the period of mourning such as a wake for Christians or sitting Shiva for Jews. This may also include a fixed time period for restricted behavior following burial as an expression of respect for the dead that may range from 30 days to a year.

The TM phase may include acute and prolonged periods. The acute period ranges from very brief to months, depending on the significance of the change or loss. At worst the TM phase may be unending. A simple example of the former would be a lost possession that is readily replaced. An example of the latter would be the death of a loved one.

The intensity and difficulty in dealing with the TM phase will be affected by the manner in which it comes about — through choice of accident and whether it was anticipated. When the mourning results from choice, such as resigning from a job, it carries with it the element of control over the event. This facilitates adjustment to a loss, even when the choice was an ambivalent or undesirable one.

The unexpected significant loss is generally the most debilitating and can be totally disruptive in all aspects of the life space. Commonly, death of a loved one, especially when unexpected, totally disrupts all aspects of the mourner's life for at least the mourning period and, for many, often well beyond this point, depending on the meaning of the loss.

When a loss can be anticipated, it provides an opportunity to prepare for the event and thus contribute to a less painful adjustment. A common example is the person who is terminally ill over an extended period of time. In such situations time provides the opportunity to prepare somewhat for the anticipated loss.

A less dramatic example is graduation, which has a clearly defined timetable. Even though it is for the most part a positive and sought-after time it still may involve giving up many positive experiences and relationships that were very meaningful. The mourning of this loss is enhanced when it goes with the uncertainty that many graduates face with respect to the undetermined future that lies ahead.

Characteristics of Losses That Affect the Mourning Process

Permanence of a Loss. The degree of permanence of an undesired loss significantly affects the adjustment to it. Consider the case of an adolescent who loses the privilege of using the family car because he violated his curfew. He will be a lot more comfortable enduring the deprivation for a specified time such as a weekend. He will be very unhappy if it is for some protracted period like weeks or months. However, this is still more tolerable than an open-ended deprivation: "You will get the use of the car when we think you are able to responsibly manage it."

Tolerance for a temporary loss will be intensified if such a loss interferes with some important activity. If an adolescent is grounded from using the family car when it interferes with going to his senior prom, he will have a lot harder time dealing with it than if it interfered with going out on a routine Saturday night.

A far more difficult problem exists when it is clear that the loss is permanent, such as loss of a job, a limb, a relationship, or a death. In this case the focus is on coping with the permanent reality of the loss and learning how to adjust to it. The impact will be tempered by the degree to which the loss played a significant part in the social entity's life.

Speed of Onset. As noted earlier, losses that are gradual in their development provide an opportunity for those affected to prepare for them and to initiate any mourning that may be indicated. A prime example of this is an illness that evolves over a long period of time. Cancer and Alzheimer's disease are two common examples where the onset of the loss may be very slow.

Losses that are sudden and unexpected do not provide any opportunity to prepare for experiencing the loss or the opportunity to develop alternative ways to cope with whatever deprivation may occur. The faster the onset of a loss, the less likely an opportunity to prepare for it. If the discipline was imposed precipitously, the adolescent referred to previously would not be able to make alternative plans for going to the prom in a way that would also be face-saving.

How Clearly the Loss Is Defined.   A social entity may experience losses that are not always clearly defined. There may be a clear sense that something is missing but what it is may not be clear. A person may have the strong impression that his reputation was tarnished but not be able to be clear about how it occurred or to what extent is has happened. In other situations a child may feel rejected by a parent or significant other and may not be clear about what caused it or the extent to which the loss will be experienced. When a child is getting caught in a lie and told he cannot be trusted, it leaves him uncertain about the extent to which he will be punished or how to regain trust.

Centrality of Loss.   The more a loss is confined to one segment of a social entity's experience, the less impact it is likely to have. The death of a parent will be pervasive in the life of a child, whereas the loss of a pet will affect only one part of the child's life. This is likely to be the case even when this loss is devastating to the child. Such loss will not affect the stability of the other parts of the child's life in the way that the death of a parent would.

Severity of the Loss.   The reaction to a loss is affected by how deeply it is felt by the social entity. One aspect is how much the loss hurts. A couple's loss of a child will have a far greater impact than being evicted from their apartment, which is in turn more stressful than pressures of work that require cancellation of a vacation.

Another aspect of severity is the time to which a social entity is exposed to a loss. Being fired from a job is an intense experience in itself. However, the severity of the experience may increase geometrically if failure to find another job goes on for an extended period and carries with it the prospect of running out of funds.

Degree of incapacity is another contributing factor to severity of loss. A married couple may find over time that the breadth of their shared relationship shrinks. Whereas initially they shared most interests, they find over time and with the presence of children that they developed individual interests and lost interest in formerly shared activities. In a relationship lacking adequate strengths, an increase in different interests becomes a potential breeding ground for significant marital problems.

For many people, aging or a decrease in their physical capabilities becomes a significant loss when their identity heavily depended on these characteristics. I saw a woman who in her youth was a June Taylor dancer. During her twenties and thirties, her identity was largely defined around her attractiveness and dancing skill. By the time she reached 40, she realized that she was losing these valuable assets. At that point she saw herself as "a pretty package with nothing in it." For her, aging brought with it a profound feeling of inadequacy and incompetence.

Meaning Attached to the Loss. The "objective" consequences of a loss can have little to do with the meaning that a social entity attaches to it. This was the case with the aforementioned dancer. In her eyes leaving her thirties was a little like dying. She had a hard time appreciating that she had other talents and skills that were not dependent on her physical attributes and capabilities.

Many people attach symbolic meaning to things or events that may be routine to other people. This is the man who gets panicky when he discovers the first sign of creeping baldness. I saw one man who treated such an event as the sounding of the death knell of his ability to attract desirable women.

An approximate measure of the significance of a loss is the difference between the severity of a loss and the confidence and resources for coping with it. The loss of a job will not have a lot of significance when the prospect of getting another one is high. If the loss of a job carried the prospect of being unemployed for a long period of time, then it would be a very significant one. The loss of a loved one, such as a child, is particularly devastating because it cannot be replaced.

When the Loss Was Experienced. Reaction to a loss is affected by the context in which it occurs. Often the same loss experienced under other conditions is experienced differently. A man who loses his job in the context of having several alternatives available to him will experience the occurrence quite differently than the man who does not have any prospect of finding another job.

The same holds true with relationships. A person who loses a desired relationship without having others available will fare differently than the person who has no doubts about being able to find another one. I saw a woman in her forties who had always found it difficult to develop significant relationships with men. She had an important relationship that lasted for several years. She was devastated when her lover left her for another woman. The pain of the loss was compounded by her feeling that this had been her last chance to have an intimate relationship.

How the Loss Was Experienced. Losses can be viewed as temporary setbacks that can and will be overcome, however painful or disappointing, or they can be viewed as irretrievable disasters, as was the case of the rejected woman described in the previous example. Attitudes about one's self-worth and competence are critical determinants in how one experiences loss.

Consequences of the Loss.   The way a social entity views the consequences of a loss sets the context for how to relate to it. If a loss is viewed
as irretrievable and its occurrence is devastating to the social entity's life-
style, then it will be viewed as a traumatic event. This in turn is likely to
interfere with functioning in other areas, which only adds to the impact of
the loss. When the loss is viewed as more manageable, it may lead only to
temporary disruptions and disappointments. This will occur until the social
entity is able to reallocate resources to adjust to the loss and achieve a new
level of satisfactory functioning. A good illustration is how different couples
cope when one person has an affair. In one couple, the affair violated the
foundation of trust in the marriage and resulted in a precipitous divorce.
In another couple, under relatively similar circumstances, the affair was
recognized as symptomatic of a problem and the couple entered therapy to
see if they could resolve it.

Likelihood of Replacement.   A major influence in how a loss will be
perceived is the likelihood of replacement. When replacement is viewed at
worst as an inconvenience, then the loss will have a minimum impact. The
negative impact will increase as the likelihood of replacement decreases. This
was the case with the woman described above who felt she lost her last chance
at a relationship or the finality in the death of a child.

Control over the Loss Occurring.   The reaction to loss begins with the
awareness that it might occur, whether immediately or in the future. When
there is the perception that the loss can be avoided or its effects minimized,
the social entity affected is likely to initiate action to cope with the anticipated
loss. When the loss cannot be avoided, the social entity may inappropriately
and prematurely begin the mourning process. For other social entities the
course of action may be denial, with the attendant anxiety getting expressed
in indirect ways.

I saw a family where there was a distant relationship between the
parents. The mother dealt with her felt deprivations by investing her emotional energies in her adolescent son. When he entered the tenth grade, she
realized that it would not be long before he would leave for college, and she
would be alone. This thought stirred up a lot of anxiety because she felt there
was nothing she could do about his leaving or in developing a suitable replacement. When she talked about it, she got shut off by all who heard. She was
put down for being hysterical for something that was a long way off. She
stopped talking about it and gradually became more depressed, anxious, and
developed various somatic symptoms.

Categories of Losses.   Losses occur in a number of different areas:

- *Self-Worth:* This involves a loss of self-esteem. It occurs when the balance of life experiences shifts from being positive to negative over a significant period of time.
- *Relationships:* This ranges from loss of a friendship to death of a significant other.
- *Material Resources:* Loss of resources becomes significant to the degree to which the losses are central to a sense of self-worth or to achieving the success to which a social entity aspires. This includes such things as money, possessions, and physical abilities.
- *Vocation:* Because material well-being is dependent on a person's vocation, its loss becomes a traumatic event for the individual losing it and the social units of which he is a part. The loss of an athlete's ability to participate as required and the doctor or the lawyer who loses his right to practice his profession are examples of this loss.
- *Position:* The loss of the position of parent can be very difficult. This is especially the case for mothers who have defined their lives around raising children. An emotional vacuum is created when all the children are grown, out on their own, and no longer dependent on their mothers. For many women this is a most difficult loss to overcome when they have not adapted and found other avenues for feeling fulfilled. It becomes a problem when these mothers attempt to deny the reality and attempt to maintain their children's dependence on them. Such efforts have become a major source of marital strife as the result of the adult child's conflict between allegiances to spouse and mother.
- *Status:* Status in the eyes of others is an important component of any social entity's self-definition. This can be lost in many ways: the beautiful woman and handsome man as they age, the politician who is voted out of office, the respected citizen who is found to be corrupt, the individual who is asked to take early retirement.
- *Vision or Ideal:* Visions have led many people to seek goals and overcome obstacles not thought possible. Such visions can be driving forces to the extent that they leave little energy for other aspects of life. When such visions are achieved or are found to no longer be relevant, the loss that is experienced can leave a great void in a social entity's life.

   This is the case of a couple who enters marriage with an ideal of what it will be like. When it becomes clear that their goal is not attainable, the vision needs to shift to one of survival and the investment of energy elsewhere.
- *Ethics:* One source of satisfaction for social entities is to live by valued ethics. When this is violated for reasons beyond the control of the social unit, it results in a significant sense of loss. This happens in such situations as when a person is coerced to lie to back up his employer, when a spouse feels that the ethics of the relationship have been violated by infidelity, or when lying is used to gain ends not otherwise attainable.

Losses May Involve Any Combination of Affect. Implicit in this discussion is that losses may be positive, negative, or a combination of the two. Positive mourning would result in happiness about a negative experience ending, such as graduation, getting out of the army, or a divorce. Examples of negative mourning include the loss of a positive experience, as in the death of a loved one, loss of a job, or the loss of a significant relationship. Many situations, such as graduations, involve both kinds of feelings. The kind of affect generated by the loss will influence the kind of mourning but not whether mourning needs to be managed.

Potential for Replacement of Loss. Suffering a loss is bad enough, but it gets worse when the prospect for replacing it does not look possible or can be accomplished only with great difficulty. Loss of a job can be devastating, but its impact is tempered when there is confidence that another one can be had. Loss of a long-term relationship can also be devastating, but it becomes more so when it is accompanied by the presumption that another relationship will never be possible.

Loss History. A person who experienced many losses over his life and learned to cope with them is likely to cope differently with a new loss than a person who experiences his first significant loss. Prior history with loss can either facilitate or hinder adjustment to future losses. The greater difficulty will come when past losses were not adequately resolved. The addition of new losses adds to a sense of increasing futility and diminishes resources and the ability for coping with new ones.

I saw a woman who suffered many significant losses during her lifetime. This included her parents, a sibling, a very close friend, and a child. At age 52, her husband, with whom she was close, died suddenly. She was totally devastated, went into a deep depression, and felt no purpose in continuing to live.

Combination of Losses. When too many losses occur in a short period without adequate time to adjust to one before another occurs, there comes a point where the accumulation becomes overwhelming, as was the case of the widow just mentioned. This can result in the social entity's diminished capacity to cope to the point of being immobilized. When this happens, it is likely to trigger losses in other areas of the life space.

Coping with Mourning

Anticipating a loss facilitates adjustment to it when it does occur. As parents anticipate the loss experienced when their child goes to college, they are able to prepare for both the positive and negative experiences that will result, such as freedom from child care responsibilities and missing the child's presence.

The situation is more difficult when the loss can be anticipated but where there is the belief that nothing can be done to prevent the loss or to adjust to it. Such circumstances get expressed in either denial, "It won't happen," or "I will deal with it when I have to." What often happens is that mourning proceeds on an unconscious level.

I worked with a couple where the husband had a terminal illness. At a conscious level, his wife presented the view that he would recover from his illness and spoke of it as a transient occurrence that would pass. It was clear from her behavior that she was gradually pulling back from the relationship. She started to share less of her feelings with him. She began to engage in activities she postponed doing in the past and increasingly found it difficult to help care for him.

Another woman coped with a similar situation in an opposite manner. She became more attentive and more involved in her husband's life than she ever did before. This included her doing things with him such as watching sports events on television that she abhorred doing in the past with the conscious belief that her interests had changed after 35 years of marriage.

Kubler-Ross (1979) has articulated the stages that are experienced when a person is faced with impending death. These include: denial and isolation, anger, bargaining, depression, and acceptance. There is a counterpart set of stages for the person experiencing the loss of a significant person or other experience. These stages include reactions of shock, denial, anger and guilt, depression, and acceptance.

Shock occurs when the loss is unexpected, as in the case of a sudden death or an unanticipated firing. Denial may follow as a defense against the resulting loss. Once the denial wears off, anger may be expressed at the cause of the loss. Guilt will be involved to the extent the person feeling it believes he contributed to it in some way. In one case where there was a suicide, each member of the family felt some guilt for the death and punished themselves with all the things they might or should have done.

Sadness that may lead to depression is likely to result as the full impact of the loss is experienced. As a person adapts to the reality of it, attention gradually turns to acceptance of the loss. From this emerges the realization of how to cope with the resulting changes. This process is facilitated as the mourner is more able to find an acceptable way to replace or develop alternatives for coping with the loss.

Variables That Affect Adjustment to the Mourning Process

Familiar versus Unknown. I am always impressed to find how powerful is the pull of the familiar, even when it involves painful or undesirable experiences. It is common to find people who stay in jobs or relationships that are unsatisfactory or even painful. It appears that the security of knowing how to cope with the familiar often outweighs the uncertainty of the unknown, even if it may hold promise for a more satisfactory outcome.

People also mourn the loss of painful experiences. They may relive the events and struggles they experienced and the relief in having survived, and at the same time have guilt for having survived. Holocaust survivors show a wide range of experiences, including survivor guilt, nightmares, and difficulty in adapting to the past painful experiences.

Emotional Vulnerability.   The process of mourning is affected by the value system held regarding the acceptability of showing one's emotional vulnerability. At one end of the spectrum are the stoics who view showing emotional vulnerability as a sign of weakness and inappropriate behavior. At the other end of the spectrum are those who express their pain in volatile and dramatic ways over a long period of time at any thought or mention of the loss.

Whether or How Loss Can Be Replaced.   A necessary part of the mourning process, at some point, is facing whether and how the loss can be replaced. This may take the form of either a similar replacement or some form of substitute. A similar replacement would be replacing a lost love with another one. An example of a substitute would be when the loss is replaced by getting invested in work, a hobby, or an organization. Which direction a social entity takes in mourning will depend on such variables as motivation, emotional needs, needed skills, and available replacement resources.

Risk of Further Losses.   After suffering a significant loss, a person may have little or no desire to become vulnerable again and risk another loss. Even if a person has the motivation to replace the loss, he may not feel he has the necessary information, skills, or opportunity needed to accomplish it. I often hear this in the case of couples who divorce after many years of marriage. "It's been so long that I was in the dating scene I wouldn't know where to start, nor do I have the skills I used to have."

The situation is even more dire if the person was never comfortable in the dating context. An added problem occurs with the perception that replacement opportunities are not available. This confronted a divorced woman who got to the point that she was ready to date only to find that she had no acceptable opportunity to meet appropriate eligible men. She had little contact with men in her work. Those she did meet were much too young for her. She lived in a neighborhood of couples and families and did not have other activities that put her in touch with suitable prospects. The option of dating bars or singles events was not comfortable.

One motivation that affects the desire for replacement of a loss is the benefits that may accrue from it relative to the pain involved. Once there was adjustment to the pain, the benefit side may surface. In one case a woman who spent most of her adult life feeling constrained by the responsibilities of a couple relationship began to enjoy the freedom of not having to account for herself to another person after she got over the pain of the divorce.

Inability to Accept a Specific Loss.   The stages of mourning do not occur in clearly defined ways, either in the way they begin or in the way they end. In many situations they may occur over a long period of time. In extreme cases the mourning process may never terminate. This was the case with a woman who lost her 2-year-old son in a freak drowning accident in a birdbath when she went to answer the telephone. This woman never was adequately able to resolve the mourning over this child. Forty years later she continues to be racked with guilt in a way that has prevented her from resolving the loss and not permitted her to cope with other relationships.

Reminders of Losses.   After the acute mourning has ended, people commonly may reexperience the loss at significant times that remind them of it. In the case of a death, this would be at holidays, birthdays, weddings, anniversaries, graduations, or at other events where the absence of the deceased person is felt. Such experiences are not limited to deaths. The same feelings can occur with loss of a job, loss of physical abilities, or loss of status.

Ability to Replace Losses.   A frequent pattern after the initial mourning period is for the intensity and frequency of such experiences to diminish gradually over time. How long such experiencing will have a significant impact on the function of a social entity will depend on its maturity and the ability to find a replacement for the loss. A person who has not been able to replace a lost love relationship will have a harder time dealing with mourning than one who is able to find such a replacement. The football player who has the opportunity to move from the playing field to the broadcast booth has the ideal situation where he continues to participate in his sport with an open-ended opportunity.

How the Mourning Process Affects a Social Entity.

- *When It Affects Part of a Social Entity:* When a part of a social entity is engaged in mourning, it generally does so in the context of a supportive environment. When the loss is significant, it will likely disrupt its ability to function. Support for coping with the mourning will come from significant others—other members of the social entity who are less affected or unaffected—and from those outside the social entity such as co-workers and friends. The ability to cope with the mourning will be influenced by what losses are being experienced in other parts of the social entity's life space. When too many losses are experienced at the same time, they can affect the ability to deal with any or all of them. Further complicating this process is what other past losses, resolved or unresolved, are reexperienced by the current losses.

I saw one family in which a close friend and mentor of the father at work died. The rest of the family knew him only on a casual basis. To this father the emotional impact was similar to the loss of a combination of a father and a brother. He was very upset at the loss. He was unable to adequately concentrate on his work for weeks. He shared his grief with other members of his work team. Other fellow workers were able to be supportive, as were his wife and children. His mourning affected his relationship with his family when it extended beyond the expected period. They became concerned about his difficulty in recovering. What no one was aware of was the unresolved mourning of his father's and brother's death that was reexperienced by his current loss. His brother died when he was 10 years old in an accident where the father felt some responsibility.

An additional contribution to this mourning came from the coincidence that the father was experiencing other significant losses in his life at the same time. He had recently injured his elbow and was not able to play tennis, which he dearly loved and played frequently. It was near the anniversary of his mother's death; and additionally, he also was in the throes of anticipatory mourning of his son's leaving for college in a few months.

- *When the Losses Affect the Whole Social Entity:* There are some added considerations when the whole social entity is jointly involved in mourning a loss. There may be little or no ability to support one another in the grieving. It may also occur under such circumstances that the mourning is complicated by the expression of one member's grief that tends to intensify the experience of others, resulting in a contagion that complicates the grieving process.

The possibility of developing secondary problems may result when the social entity is not able to perform necessary maintenance functions. The event of multiple mourners increases the probability that other losses current and past may add to the difficulty in coping with the current mourning. In the extreme, this would result in the social entity becoming dependent on outside resources for its continued survival.

The impact of such a situation was graphically demonstrated to me in a family where the second oldest of four children committed suicide at the age of 13. The children ranged in age from 9 to 15 at the time. Compounding the problem was that this child was the one who seemed the most together, the most amiable and accomplished one. The shock of his death totally derailed the family. They were all devastated and unable to be of any comfort to one another. This was particularly difficult on the children because of their age and the social modeling of the parents, who followed the cultural value of not showing grief openly. Further complicating their mourning was the contribution of other losses, both past and present.

This loss reactivated the mother's unfinished mourning of the death of one of her siblings when she was a teenager. The father was in the midst of a significant business crisis. Fortunately, there was enough support from extended family and friends to aid the family in coping with the death until they were sufficiently able to cope with their grieving to regain their ability to function.

Considerations That Affect Resolution of Mourning.

- *Mourning Does Not Exist in a Vacuum:* How a person relates to a particular loss will in part depend on what else is going on in their life space. The adjustment will be far more difficult if many losses in important areas are happening at the same time. Conversely, when most things in a social unit's life space are going very well, more resources will be available to cope with mourning.

  In one case, a woman was so distraught in mourning the loss of her child that she withdrew from her job and her husband, with the result that the marriage ultimately ended in divorce. From the husband's point of view, it was as though his wife had died with the death of their child.

- *Inability to Face Reality of Loss and Consequences That Result from It:* I worked with one woman who could not cope with the death of her husband because of the major changes that resulted from it. The cataclysmic event of his stroke jolted her from her protected life. All of her needs were managed by other people; she did not have to cope with any problems. After his death, she was suddenly catapulted into having to face the management of a whole array of personal and financial problems. She went through a period of numbness during which she could not accept the reality of his death because to do so confronted her with overwhelming pain.

- *Ability to Replace the Loss:* After the early phases of experiencing a loss, the social unit is confronted with whether and how to replace the loss. This goal is eventually achieved when the social unit possesses the motivation and necessary skills to accomplish it and when replacement objects or experiences are available.

In one case a couple had a relationship over a number of years and reached the point where they were contemplating marriage. One source of reluctance for the man was that this woman did not match the level of intellectual maturity and social skills he felt were important for the social interactions his professional career involved. He vacillated in his commitment to the relationship and after a few trial separations broke off the relationship.

He struggled for some time with his desire to return to it. Eventually, he decided that it was not meant to be. This did not stop him from thinking a lot about the parts of the relationship he missed. These thoughts were tempered by his being free of the tensions that went with her overdependence. As he became more resolved in his decision, he was able to turn his attention to developing other relationships. This process was facilitated because he was attractive and socially skilled and made relationships easily.

Integration Phase

Integration refers to the process of incorporating the learning from the transition phases into an integral part of the social entity's way of functioning. When this occurs, the new learning becomes part of the social unit's repertoire that enables it to improve its future coping ability.

When the new learning contradicts the preexisting and established patterns of behavior, the social entity is faced with how to resolve the conflict or whether to eliminate either the new learning or the preexisting behavior.

Interaction between Phases

Each social entity is undergoing transitions in multiple areas of their lives at the same time: work, marital relationship, extended relationships, friendships, aging, raising children, and others. There is interaction between phases in these various areas in two ways: the competition for available psychic energy and how the experience in one area of behavior affects another. When too much energy is required in coping with transitions in one or more areas, the remaining energy may not be available to conduct the work of transitions in other areas. This will result in elimination of low-priority behaviors or develop problems in areas that cannot be eliminated. Success in coping with transitions has generalizability. When a social entity successfully copes with adaptation in one area, it contributes to the confidence in adapting in other areas.

The interaction between phases becomes more complicated when it is going on simultaneously in each member of a family and in every combination of relationships: individuals, couple, dyads, and family as a whole. Beginnings and endings are constantly involved in an ongoing circular flow. Problems can develop when the demands for one kind of transition are too great and are not offset by the balancing benefits of other transitions. A common occurrence is when a social entity is faced with many losses and too little opportunity to develop replacements, and/or there is difficulty in the SM phase.

This would be the case when a woman is coping with onset of menopause, her last child is going off to college, she feels taken for granted by her husband, and she has to cope with the increasing demands of aging parents in ill health.

Counterbalancing these experiences are the support of her friends, satisfaction with her children, and the prospect of returning to the labor force. However, if the drain from issues of mourning is not sufficiently balanced by the excitement of adapting to a job, she could become depressed. This could also be the case if she is not getting enough support in the stabilized relationships with her friends. Once the depression sets in, it can feed on itself and lead to further deterioration in her ability to deal with mourning issues and inhibit the development of positive reinforcing experiences.

The aforementioned woman who was experiencing many losses might make the transition through this period without too much difficulty if other members of her family system are supportive, at least on a temporary basis, until she is able to reestablish a workable balance. This could be the understanding husband who is able to provide his wife with the kind of caring and support that would enhance her self-image and her importance to him. Further help could come with his helping her cope with the problems of her aging parents. Support from him could include active participation in maintaining a positive relationship with her mother.

This situation would be quite different if each member of the family was in the same state of unbalance—experiencing a similar overload on mourning issues and having too little resources to counterbalance it. In such a case each member is needy of input from others, and sufficient support is not available within the family. At such times, the family would need to turn to outside resources such as therapy and help from relatives and friends until they were able to regain needed resources for a more balanced level of functioning.

More needs to be said about the way in which transitions occur. They commonly do not happen in a nice, orderly fashion but undergo a variety of patterns. Often this involves moving from the SM phase back to the adaptation phase when circumstances change, then back to the SM phase, and then to the mourning phase.

At times the mourning is aborted, and the social unit is kicked back to the adapting phase or to the SM phase or some variation of these processes. In the dynamic reality of a job, marriage, raising children, or other life experiences, all aspects of the transition process are ongoing at the same time. In the course of a marriage, a couple are anticipating in certain areas, while adapting in some areas, functioning in a stabilized manner in others, and mourning the losses of various changes.

This process is illustrated in the case of a couple who were anticipating the purchase of new furniture and departure of a child to college, adapting to the move to a new house, and mourning the loss of the old, while the wife is adjusting to a new job. They are enjoying the positive stability in their relationship. The husband also experiences stability from his job. Meanwhile, they are mourning the loss of their old neighborhood and friends and the absence of their college-bound child.

Consider a hypothetical situation in which a couple coped with the revelation that the husband had had an affair. If the wife had some suspicion of this prior to the revelation, she would be likely to have an easier time adapting to it. If she had no anticipation of it, then she would be likely to have a much harder time coping with it. Let us suppose that the adaptation involves the wife expressing her anger and feelings of betrayal and the husband acknowledging his guilt, asking for forgiveness, and promising not to continue or repeat the behavior. If he is accepted, an adaptation period would be followed by a stabilization period. The process starts with the wife accepting his commitment and the couple jointly working to establish a comfortable redefined relationship.

However, the course will not be smooth because periods of doubt periodically surface. During this time she anticipates that her husband may not be able to honor his commitment. This unsettles her efforts at stabilization and puts her back in the anticipatory stage. This leads her to a new stage of adaptation, which requires adjusting to the possibility that he will try to honor his commitment but may not be able to so. This leads to a more uncertain and shaky period of stabilization because of the couple's shaky confidence in his commitment. As a result, efforts to accomplish a period of a comfortable and stable relationship are intermeshed with anticipatory periods of mourning. As these efforts continue, she begins to contemplate that their relationship cannot return to its earlier level.

At the same time she has periods of hope in which she can anticipate that things can be better. This reverberating process can continue; there is a shifting back and forth from one point of transition to another. This state of instability can continue indefinitely, with its attendant anxiety and the consequences that stem from it, or until a new level of confidence is achieved that permits a more confident and trusting period of satisfaction. Under such conditions the anticipatory periods of mourning will diminish. If the new level of confidence is not reached, then the relationship will ultimately result in divorce, especially if the wife develops other options for herself.

Consequences of Distorted Involvement in Phases

Too Much Concentration on Anticipation

This happens when a social unit becomes stuck in the world of fantasy. This may occur because the SU is fearful of facing reality and when the generated level of anxiety is immobilizing. It is also a problem when there is uncertainty about how to proceed or what course of action to take. It also can be the case when going beyond anticipation is of low priority. An example is the man who spends a great deal of time fantasizing about dating a desired women but would not attempt to ask for a date for fear she would refuse.

Too Little Attention to Anticipation

This can occur if the need for anticipation is underestimated or if there is no reason to expect a particular event to happen. It can also occur as a way to deny facing the reality that a given event could or is likely to occur.

The result of too little anticipation leaves the social entity more vulnerable to difficulty in adapting to the occurrence of events. This can lead to developing problems, depending on the consequences of having done too little anticipatory work. In addition, it can detract from performance in other areas.

Problems also occur when a social entity has too little confidence in being able to adapt to a new situation or when other pressing priorities do not permit addressing adequate resources to the task. A case in point is the man who is promoted to a new job. His anxiety about whether he could do the job interfered with his ability to apply his experience and skills.

Whether it is a case of lacking confidence or competing priorities, the result is likely to be some degree of failure. In the former case it will further undermine the man's confidence level and ultimately be expressed in his lowered self-esteem.

In the latter case, it likely to be a source of annoyance or inconvenience. The significance attached to this will depend on the importance of the failure to adapt adequately. It will tend to be of less significance as long as there is confidence that the adaptation can be accomplished if it is of sufficient priority.

Too Much Focus on Adaptation

This could happen when the occurring event is of high priority or is life-threatening and there is anxiety about the ability to make the necessary adaptation. It could also occur in social units where the preference is for dealing with new and challenging situations in preference to dealing with the familiar, such as encountered in the SM phase. This is the case with the man who enjoys the chase in his relationship to women but runs into trouble in making a relationship work.

Social units in this difficulty tend to live with more chaos in their lives because they do not develop the skills or satisfaction in the SM phases. As a result, they run the risk of living a shallow life characterized with many superficial relationships.

Too Much Emphasis on Stabilization and Maintenance

This occurs when the social entity has anxiety about coping with new situations or fears the loss of what is familiar. One example is the woman who struggles to hang on to a bad marriage for fear of having to find a new relationship. Overemphasis on the SM phase also may occur when a social entity has resources too limited to cope with more than established necessities.

The result of such a situation is that the social entity may not be able to accomplish appropriate developmental shifts. The failure to do so is likely to lead to the point where the existing stabilization is disrupted, thus forcing attention to a new level of adaptation. An example is the mother who tries to inhibit her daughter's attempt to become independent and seeks to maintain the dependent relationship she has with her. When the child ultimately rebels to gain her independence, the mother is forced to face an adaptive situation to replace the loss or to run the risk of further alienating her daughter.

Too Little Attention to Stabilization and Maintenance

This occurs when the SM phase becomes boring and ceases to address the social entity's needs. It also occurs when the satisfactions that made it a positive experience lose their value out of familiarity and/or the lack of challenge.

The consequence of such occurrence leads to an unstable system and the seeking of change. This happens when a couple ceases to work at their marrriage and the resulting path takes them to divorce. The situation gets more complicated when there is a desire for change and a fear of coping with it.

Too Much Attention to Termination and Mourning

This occurs when a social entity lacks the confidence to replace a loss. This is the case of the athlete who becomes obsessed with hanging onto his diminished athletic prowess. He finds it difficult or even refuses to address the reality that his athletic career is over.

Too little attention to TM also can occur when the termination of an event or a relationship will create problems in other ares. Such preoccupation can also be disruptive to existing SM phases to the point where it can lead to additional undesired losses. When too much of this occurs, it can ultimately lead to immobilization of the social unit. This would be the case when the last child goes to college, leaving the parents to face a troubled marriage that evaded attention as long as they were focusing on the needs of their children.

Too Little Attention to Termination and Mourning

This occurs when a social unit finds facing loss issues too painful or is too preoccupied with other priorities to adequately attend to facing losses. It could also result from not wanting to cope with the consequences of attending to terminations. This is often the case of the couple who are not able to face the impending end of their relationship until they are suddenly faced with the reality of it.

Under these conditions a social unit will have a more difficult time coping with losses once they occur. It also heightens the possibility that attempts will be made to avoid dealing with mourning, with the likelihood that future relationships will be affected by the unresolved mourning. Such attempts to avoid facing mourning issues can interfere with functioning in other areas of the life space.

Too Much Attention to Integration of Transition Experiences

This occurs when there is a preoccupation with how to integrate new learning. Such efforts can be driven by concern over not repeating past mistakes. Excessive focus on such learning can lead to problems that result from not properly attending to current issues. This occurred in my work with a couple. They got so involved with practicing new communication skills that they failed to recognize that their way of doing it was causing problems in relationships with other couples.

Too Little Attention to Integration of Transition Experiences

This can occur when the social unit is preoccupied with other priorities or may presume that integration takes place by itself. The consequences of not adequately attending to integration affect the likelihood of repeating the same mistakes and the resultant undermining of self-confidence and definition of self-concept.

Clinical Application

I will now illustrate the clinical application of these concepts.

Step 1: Take a history of the family as individuals and for each significant social unit, including the family as a unit.

Step 2: Determine the distribution of transition states of relevant social units in the family. Determine to what extent and with what priority family members are involved in each of the transition phases. The goal is to determine the distribution of transition states across social units within the family.

State 3: Evaluate the successes and failures in coping with the transitions of the various social units involved and how they impact on one another. This is done both to identify resources for their application to the resolution of areas of difficulty and to identify the nature and degree of problem areas. This process will lend itself to identifying recurrent patterns, either for a given social entity or across social entities. For example, does one person tend to repeat the same pattern of difficulty in coping with certain kinds of experiences such as destructive relationships with the same or opposite sex? It might be the case that the same destructive pattern is common for more than one family member.

Step 4: Develop an intervention.

CASE ILLUSTRATION

Description of Family

This case involved the Kefer family, composed of five members: the father, Victor, 52; the mother, Helen, 48; Victor, Jr., 17; Sara, 15; and Claudia, 11. The Kefer family was a cross-cultural family: the father was from the Middle East, and the mother was American. The mother came to this country when she was 10, and the father when he was 18. Both are naturalized citizens. He was an engineer in a high-tech field, she was a hygienist. Victor, Jr., held a favored position in the family as the only son. He was outspoken and well rounded as reflected in his academic, social, and athletic success. Sara was the quiet one who also had her share of academic and social success. Claudia was mature for her age and, like her brother, made her views known; she also did well academically and socially.

The couple came to therapy because of tensions in their relationships. They reported difficulty in their ability to communicate and deal with resolving family issues in a mutually satisfying manner. The marriage was stable but not close, largely due to the father's distancing workaholic tendencies.

At the time of entering therapy, there was a history of two major traumatic events for the family and the anticipation of the forthcoming departure of Victor, Jr., to college.

Five years before, the mother had developed a serious, life-threatening intestinal illness that required several operations over a period of a couple of years. During this time, the father and the children carried on the normal maintenance functions of the family when the mother was not able to do so. During the last three years, she returned to relatively normal functioning with her illness under control. The long-term prognosis indicated that she should be able to live a relatively normal life, with the probability of a less than normal life expectancy.

Another significant event was that two years ago Claudia was molested and about to be raped. The attack was interrupted by her call for help, which attracted passers-by. She was unharmed physically. The mother took the initiative in helping Claudia deal with the psychological trauma. There was much discussion and support for her within the family. The mother was concerned that it be sufficiently talked about so that Claudia would not bury the pain.

One significant finding from the evaluation was the family's difficulty in dealing with the mourning issues related to the mother's illness.

Review of Transition Phases

In the interest of brevity, I will limit this illustration to transitions as they are relevant to the mother when she entered therapy.

Anticipation Phase

The mother initiated couple therapy because she recognized that she and her husband were stabilized in a communication pattern that was unsatisfactory to her. She was also aware that she was not able to move to an adaptive phase to achieve a more satisfactory relationship.

She anticipated that making this transition might not be possible. She was clear that she could not stay in the negative stabilization phase in which they were living. This led her to anticipate that at some point she might have to consider divorce. This thought led her to some anticipatory mourning, which upset her and got expressed in the determination to get into therapy.

Her illness was another source of chronic anticipation. The uncertainty of how long her remission would last and what course her illness might take left her with anticipatory anxiety about how little she could do except to follow the prescribed medical regimen. Adding to her discomfort was the unspoken anticipatory anxiety she sensed from other members of the family.

An added dimension to this anxiety was her concern about what would happen to the children if she became critically ill before they all became adults. She knew that Victor meant well but doubted that he would be able to adequately cope because of his work pressures. Periodically, she gave thought to what she might do to prepare for this possibility. The increased anxiety that such thoughts aroused and the absence of any ready solution led her to avoid such thoughts.

Concern about the implications of Claudia's having been molested by a stranger was never far from her mind. She worried about the unknown implications of how this might affect Claudia's development and to what extent she would be permanently emotionally scarred by the experience. She gave a lot of thought to what she could do to ensure this did not happen.

Helen always had a close relationship with Victor, Jr. In his adolescence she was able to talk to him about things for which her husband was unavailable, such as some of her concerns about the future. She realized that their relationship took some of the pressure off the communication problems with Victor, Sr. She increasingly got into anticipatory mourning about the loss of the relationship to her son when he went to college and how she would cope with the resulting vacuum.

Her husband's involvement in his work left her with a lot of loneliness. Oftentimes she felt like a single parent. She frequently spent time anticipating what she might do to gain more of his attention but without much success.

A long-standing issue for Helen was her husband's commitment to his family of origin, especially since his father's death. She painfully anticipated that it would not change until his mother's death. She also wondered to what extent that same commitment would transfer to his siblings once his mother was gone.

Adaptation

Therapy represented an effort to break out of the negative stabilization pattern in their marriage and to replace it with a level of stabilization that would be satisfactory to both. Helen attempted to deal with her anxiety about the poor communication between father and son by trying to get her husband to be more responsive to their son's needs. Her failure to accomplish this was another contributing factor for entering therapy.

Another negative stabilization pattern for Helen concerned her husband's unavailability when she needed him, which was the case with Claudia's attack. He was preoccupied with letting his mother know what happened to Claudia ahead of his wife's needs. This tied in with her long-standing resentment at her husband when he consistently put his mother's needs ahead of their family needs.

Stabilization and Maintenance

Helen was in a satisfactory stabilization phase in areas that included her relationship to her children, the current status of her occupation, her relationships to her parents and her friends, her status in the community, and her volunteer work.

Termination and Mourning

Helen was in a chronic state of underlying mourning for her health, which could deteriorate precipitously. For the most part, she had managed to relegate it to the back of her mind so as to maintain her daily functioning. The worry and anxiety intensified under heightened conditions of stress.

She had prepared for the possibility of her death by ensuring that her children had the skills necessary for their independence. She was doing the same with her husband, including her support and expectation that he would remarry after her death. Dealing with this goal gave rise to ambivalence because she tried to be less close to him so that his loss of her would be less painful. This was in contradiction to her need for closeness for herself. Further complicating the situation when she became too upset with the status of the marriage was whether divorce would accomplish anything. At times she wondered whether the state of her health contributed to her husband's distancing. She was not sure because he was not that different before her illness. She was actively adapting to her son's approaching departure for college. She increasingly distanced herself from him.

Integration

Helen's illness led to a shift in her values. She learned to live more in the present by making the most of her daily experiences, with less emphasis on planning for the future. Claudia's traumatic experiences coupled with her own led her to value relationships in a more compassionate way.

Implications in Pattern of Distribution of Energies

Viewing family relationships from the perspective of the pattern of psychic investment in the various transition phases provided added perspective on the degree to which there is emotional balance for each social unit.

I refer to balance in terms of how much emotional drain there is in a person's life relative to how much nurturing is available from all sources.

I drew a number of conclusions from Helen's situation. She was heavily invested in anticipation although not much could be done about her health problems, so this concern became a constant negative drain. Only a limited amount could be done about her son's leaving for college, about Claudia's traumatic experiences and how they will affect Claudia in the long run, and the course of Helen's marriage.

A saving grace for Helen was the number of areas in which she is in a positive stabilization phase: friends, the relationship with her children, extended family and job. This contributed to her ability to invest her available energy into a more satisfactory stabilization phase.

Her mourning work was, in part, a reflection of her anticipatory work. Just as some of her anticipatory work was open-ended, some of her mourning work was of the same nature, namely, that related to her illness.

In summary, it was clear that she was not getting enough nurturing from her marriage. This was complicated by the ambivalence created by her illness and her attempt to find a balance between meeting her needs and those of her family.

A GUIDE TO CLINICAL APPLICATION

Evaluate how social entities cope with anticipation phases.

1. How often have significant events been anticipated?
   • When the events were desired
   • When the event was not desired
2. To what degree was the anticipation work done when it should have been?
3. Did social entities adequately evaluate the significance and consequences of anticipated events?
4. Evaluate how social entities cope with adaptation phases. In which of the following ways are SUs coping with adaptation issues?
   • Adjusting to it
   • Resisting it
   • Fighting it
   • Ignoring it
   • Immobilized by it
5. Evaluate how social entities cope with stabilization and maintenance phases.
   • How much do social entities desire to be in this phase?
   • How well do they cope when they are unhappily in this phase?

- Do they have adequate resources for coping with this phase?
- Are they able to cope with change?
- Are they able to anticipate threats to existing stability?
- Are they able to cope with ambiguity in what is needed for stability?
- Are they able to adjust to changing needs?

6. Evaluate how social entities cope with termination and mourning phases.

Evaluate losses:

- What are the social entities history with losses?
- When were the losses experienced?
- Was there any control over whether the losses occurred?
- In what categories did the losses occur?
  - Self-worth
  - Relationships
  - Material resources
  - Vocation
  - Position
  - Status
  - Vision or ideal
  - Ethics
  - Spirituality
- How were they experienced?
- To what extent are they permanent or replaceable?
- What was the speed of onset of the losses?
- How clearly is the loss defined?
- How central is the loss to the social entity's life space?
- How severe are the consequences of the loss?
- What meaning is attached to the loss?
- How likely is the replacement of the loss?

Evaluate the ability to cope with mourning:

- Which of the following variables affect the social entity's ability to cope with mourning?
  - Fear of the unknown
  - Emotional vulnerability
  - Ability to replace losses
  - Whether or how loss can be replaced
  - Risk of further losses
  - Inability to accept loss
  - Reminders of losses

Evaluate how losses in part of a social entity affect the functioning of the larger social entity. For example, how does a significant loss in one member of a family affect the functioning of the family as a unit?

Evaluate how a social entity copes when a significant loss affects the whole social entity.

Evaluate how well social entities are able to resolve mourning issues.

7. Evaluate how the social entity accomplishes integration from transition phases.

Summary

In this chapter I described five transitional phases that are common to the life experiences of social entities: anticipation, adaptation, stabilization and maintenance, termination and mourning, and integration. I also discussed the interaction between these phases and the consequences of negative investment in these phases. A case illustration was presented to demonstrate the clinical applicability of these concepts.

CHAPTER NINE

Benefit-Cost Balance

As I listened to clients, I was struck by how much their behavior is determined by two joint considerations: what benefits are derived from a given action relative to the expenditure of resources, and what deprivations are necessary to accomplish it. The development of these concepts is the subject of this chapter.

THEORY

A fundamental driving force of human behavior is to seek and maximize desired experiences at the least possible cost in time, energy, money, stress, and distraction from other activities. Such experiences may be voluntary or imposed, such as illness, aging, or having to work. If voluntary, the social entity makes a choice about exposure to a given experience. The choice is based on an assessment of whether the benefits gained warrant the cost required to achieve it. In the case of imposed experiences, the challenge is how to adapt best to the ordeal—to maximize what can be positive and minimize the expenditure. In the case of voluntary experiences, a social entity, such as a couple, will generally not engage in marriage unless the perceived benefits sufficiently outweigh the attendant costs.

A major determinant of such assessment is the benefit-cost balance (B/C) as perceived by the experiencing social entity. This balance concept is equally applicable to the range of social entities—individual, couple, family, and significant subunits.

This concept is applied with varying combinations of analytical assessment and "gut level" experience, that is, what feels right. When the analytic and experiential assessments lead to the same conclusion, the decision is easily made. When they are in conflict, a struggle ensues. In such situations the resulting decision will be ambivalent. At these times cognitive dissonance comes into play; those characteristics that support a decision are emphasized, and those that contradict it are minimized. This is an ongoing process where the comfort in the decision that is made will vacillate during a given experience and even after it has ended. A person may continue to have ambivalence about staying in a relationship even after it is over.

In this chapter I discuss the variables that affect how benefits and costs are determined and applied. A case illustration is provided to demonstrate this concept.

Characteristics of Benefits

Definition of a Benefit

A benefit is any emotional, physical, or material occurrence that is considered desirable by the social entity experiencing it. This could take the form of acquisition, of giving up something undesirable, or of maintaining the status quo. Acquisition could include gaining a desired relationship, money, power, material possessions, prestige, or the high from drugs. Giving up something undesirable could include such things as responsibilities, a drug habit, pain, a bad reputation, or a bad marriage.

Who Benefits from the Occurrence?

Ideally it would be great if all involved in an experience benefitted. What is a benefit to one social entity may be a loss to another. In most social environments there is a competition for available material goods and access to power. In most family situations there is an ongoing process of how to allocate limited emotional, financial, material, and power resources among shifting needs of family members. Disagreements about how this is accomplished become the source of family conflict that often finds its way to the therapist's office.

To adequately appreciate how to evaluate a benefit, it is helpful to know the context in which it occurs. A family member who gains a positive experience, supported by family members and not at someone else's expense, is in a different context than when the same benefit is achieved at the expense of one or more other family members. This would be the case of a family who puts all its financial resources into supporting one member getting a college education. The rest of the family combines their collective earnings to make this possible and to support maintaining family needs. This happened with many immigrant families in the early part of the 1900s. This also occurs when a wife works to support her husband while he attends college or gets established in business. In between these extremes, family members jockey to balance meeting their own needs with those of other family members.

What Form Benefits Take

Beneficial experiences may take many different forms, as referred to previously. These possibilities warrant a more detailed description.

Psychological Benefits.   These refer to desired experiences gained from relationships. This includes feeling loved, being consulted for advice or help, being desired as a companion, and having one's views or needs be respected.

Physical Benefits.   These include any experience that affects physical well-being, particularly the absence of pain. Also included would be anything that contributes to physical health, such as food, lodging, exercise, and medical care.

Material Benefits.   This includes possessions of any desired material object, including house, cars, clothes, property, books, or a television. This is particularly relevant for people who measure their success by the quantity and quality of their material possessions.

Spiritual Benefits.   This includes any experience or frame of reference, often in a religious context, that provides an ethical context for how a person guides her behavior and gains a state of serenity in how to view and relate to the human condition.

When Benefits Occur

The time frame for experiencing benefits may vary from immediate to years later. Benefits may be multiple and occur at different levels. For example, eating may have the immediate positive benefit of a good experience. The quality of food eaten may result in a contribution to longer-term good or poor health. This is reflected in the current social concerns about low fat, low cholesterol, and healthy diets in general.

A woman has a range of positive and negative experiences that occur with the onset of pregnancy and continues to the ultimate birth of her child. This exemplifies the case where there is a long time period between the time an experience starts (pregnancy) and the time when the sought-for benefit is achieved (birth). A variety of differing discomforts are experienced in pursuit of the objective. Getting an education is another example where there is a long delay in obtaining a benefit. In the case of the economically disadvantaged, the delay may be too long, and the cost, financially and emotionally, be too great for an uncertain benefit.

Duration of Benefits

Benefits may vary in duration from a fleeting moment to open-ended. Examples of increasing duration range from telling someone off, going to the theater, vacation, taking a course, going to school, having a job, a friendship, and marriage.

Intensity of the Benefits
Benefits vary in intensity from minimal to very intense. At the minimal end, the benefit barely provides a feeling of satisfaction. This might be a low level of interest or satisfaction in reading a book, or a pleasant meal, so-so enjoyment of a vacation, and a relationship that is little more than tolerable.

A more intense benefit might result from reading a good book; getting a desired gift; having a good experience at the theater, museum, or stadium; getting a good bonus; having a great vacation; enjoying a relationship; or performing in an occupation.

Under What Circumstances
Experiencing benefits may depend on who else is involved, such as being alone, with someone else in general, or with another person in particular, or a benefit may depend on a particular time or place. The benefits of going to the theater, a sports event, or a vacation are likely to be quite different when a person goes alone or with someone else. Getting a college education from an institution of limited means in the middle of a large city will be different from a well-endowed college in a small town.

Source of Benefit
Benefits may derive from a social entity's own efforts or from another source. This is of particular significance when a social entity does not feel able to achieve desired benefits on its own and is dependent on others or on circumstances to do so. This is the case when parents pay for a child's education or for the wedding of a daughter.

Another variation is when a social entity can provide benefits only for others and not for itself. This would be the case when a patron commissions an artist to create some art object. Another example is the parent who did not have an opportunity to get an education but is able to provide it for others.

At the extreme is the social entity who concentrates on deriving personal benefits and has little interest or concern for participating in the benefit of others. This can occur in circumstances where a social entity is involved in pursuit of a goal that totally occupies the social entity's energies, such as a person running for political office who is totally absorbed in doing what will further her campaign. This would also apply to the company that seeks to maximize its profits without paying adequate attention to the way such efforts abuse the environment.

The meaning of a benefit may be defined more by the source of it rather than by the benefit itself. A compliment is a good example of this point.

Coming from the wrong person it means little, and from the right person a great deal. A mother telling her son he is a good athlete may carry little weight, whereas it will mean a great deal when it comes from his coach.

Another example is the developing artist whose total energies are directed in pursuit of developing her talent to gain needed recognition. This often happens in a family situation where one or both parents foster this kind of commitment. It also happens in families where a child displays a particular talent in music, art, or athletics.

Characteristics of Costs

Definition of Cost

A cost is the desired or undesired expenditure of any resource — emotional, financial, physical, or intellectual — in service of a particular benefit. The expenditure of money for a particular reason may be desired, but it still depletes the amount of money available for other purposes. The same is true for energy or any other limited resource.

Expenditure of a resource that results in little or no benefit creates problems, especially when the resource is jointly owned. This would be the case when a person invests time and money in a venture that fails. The situation becomes worse when such a loss results in other undesirable experiences. This happens when a bad investment forces a family to change its life-style. The seeds of further difficulty surface when an investment is viewed as an error in judgment rather than as a bad break. The same could apply to a relationship. A bad experience in a love affair results in a person's reluctance to risk having another one.

One exception to the problem of an expenditure of resources without a redeeming feature is when a social entity intentionally expends resources or professes to have done so to avoid a distasteful experience. This is the case when the child manages to come home too tired to do her chores, homework, or any other undesired experience. The same could be true of the man who comes home and claims to be too tired to cope with any family problems.

Cost to Whom

The cost for gaining a benefit may or may not be at the expense of the person gaining the benefit. The situation may vary from the case where the benefit and the cost are totally borne by the same social entity, such as the person who earns the money to take a vacation. This varies on a continuum where the cost is shared in varying degrees with other social entities. This would be the case when family members each contribute what they are able for a family vacation or the child who contributes to the cost of her college education by working part-time and summers.

At the other end of the continuum is the case where one social entity gains a benefit with no cost to itself. This would be the case of a person whose college education is paid for by parents or a scholarship. The only potential loss would be the lower priority of income lost from not having worked, had she not gone to college.

Cost in What Form
The description of the forms that cost can take, which was referred to earlier, warrants further discussion.

Emotional Costs.   The emotional cost can potentially take different forms. It can involve the emotional drain to do something desired or undesired. This could result from an intense argument: The positive side of the drain is to face up to an issue; the undesired part is the unpleasantness that was involved in doing it. It can involve worry about adequacy in doing something or the fear of judgment by others. It can involve worry about what is not being done for self or others as the result of participation in a particular event.

Financial Costs.   The financial cost occurs at two levels: the direct expenditure of limited funds and the lost opportunity to generate income as the result of participating in the occurrence of a particular event. This is the case of the father who pays tuition for his child to go to college and then takes time off from his work to visit his child.

Another source of cost is the indirect financial expenditure. A child who helped out in his father's business prior to going to college has to be replaced at some increased expenditure. This is in addition to having to pay for chores that were done by his daughter.

Physical Costs.   Physical costs involve expenditures of physical energy to contribute to the development of a benefit. In extreme form this may become detrimental to physical health as a result of such participation. Mothers are often in the position of putting excessive drain on their physical energies, at times to the point of becoming injurious to their health. The possibility of this occurring is enhanced when a woman has a career in addition to carrying the major, if not total, responsibility for maintaining a home, ensuring adequate child care, and attending to her husband.

Spiritual Costs.   These costs become involved when a social entity, usually a person, feels obligated to violate her ethics or standards of behavior in service of gaining a benefit. This would be the case when she feels the need to lie about family income in order to help her child obtain a scholarship or get some other form of financial aid. Another example is the person who lies to save embarrassment. The spiritual cost in such cases is the loss of self-respect.

Intellectual Costs. These occur in various forms. One form is the person who is not able to go to college because her earning power is required to help support her family. Another variation is the person who is not able to pursue her intellectual interests, such as reading, taking courses, or engaging in hobbies, because the demands of work and family responsibilities do not permit enough time to pursue such pursuits.

Conscious or unconscious distortion of reality by way of such mechanisms as rationalization or intellectualization in service of protecting a desired image is done at the expense of intellectual honesty. When such experiences become within awareness, there is the added cost of a diminished self-image.

Significance of a Cost

The significance of a cost may vary from being trivial to having great impact. A child may not mind being prohibited from watching television as a punishment because she has other interesting things to do. A student who fails a course for cheating on a final exam experiences multiple costs: the stigma of being caught cheating, having to repeat the course, having her record blemished, and having to deal with the ire of her parents. When a family member commits a major crime, it not only reflects on the individual but also affects other family members.

When the Cost Occurs

The cost for achieving a particular benefit often is not apparent until well after the benefit was experienced. The various forms of cost that go with being a parent are not emotionally and intellectually realized until well after the benefit started. In the case of parenthood, the cost fluctuates in varying degrees. During times of joy, a parent may not experience any sense of cost. At other times, the many demands that go with child care may feel very costly especially when it interferes with a parent pursuing her own needs. The cost is even greater when children develop problems that deviate from the norm, such as physical illness and emotional and antisocial problems.

In the case of college, the emotional costs are likely to be greatest in the first and second years because of the demands of adjusting to a new and more challenging environment and the challenge to begin to make career decisions. The emotional cost may again peak in the senior year, when consideration has to be given to what future course to follow.

Secondary Costs

A secondary cost occurs when the immediate cost associated with providing a particular benefit interferes with experiencing another benefit; that is, participating in one activity prevents participating in another one. This is a common occurrence for mothers, who in providing benefits for their families often do so at the expense of attending to their own needs. A man may stay with a secure job to provide for his family at the cost of not being able to pursue a risky business venture.

How Long the Cost Will Last

Costs vary from being momentary to being open-ended. The pain a child feels from a reprimand for raiding the cookie jar might be momentary. An adolescent who violates her curfew may get grounded for a month. A person who causes another person a permanent injury may have the pain of guilt forever. The impact of divorce can affect family members indefinitely.

Benefit-Cost Balance

Who Makes Allocation Decisions?

Decisions regarding pursuit of benefits are made in different ways. At one end of the spectrum, such decisions are made by the individual that pertain only to herself.

The process is more complicated in a larger social entity such as the family. Families vary greatly in how this is done. A common pattern in the traditional family was where the father made decisions pertaining to finances and maintenance of the home, and the mother made decisions about housekeeping and raising the children. A common approach in contemporary families is for these decisions to be more shared, particularly when the wife has her own career. In dysfunctional families, children may be given inappropriate power for making such decisions. Children may pressure to buy things or engage in activities the family can ill afford.

How B/C Balance Decisions Are Made

In some famiies decisions about the pursuit of benefits are made in a unilateral manner, commonly by the father. In other families this may be done by the wife when the husband is passive, otherwise preoccupied, or delegates such responsibility to her. In situations where a couple are in conflict, their differences are often expressed in the context about who will make such decisions and how.

Nature of the B/C Balance

The nature of the B/C balance is a major determinant in what course of action a social entity will follow. I will discuss examples at three levels: where the benefits by far outweigh the costs (direct or indirect), where they are about equal, and where the costs far outweigh the benefits.

Balance Is High

An example of a B/C balance that is high is a couple who have a very happy marriage because they derive many positives from the relationship that far outweigh the significance of any negatives. The same would apply in a family where members find that the benefits from being part of the family by far exceed any detracting qualities.

Approximate Equal B/C Balance

Under these conditions, whether the benefit occurs is unclear and will more likely depend on the circumstances of the moment. Such benefits will have a low priority for resources. A frequently heard comment on family outings is that the enjoyment was not worth all the hassle in preparing the picnic lunch and having to cope with keeping the kids from doing one another in. This perspective may well be gone by the next time a suggestion for a family picnic comes up because at the moment of making the decision, the allure of going to the ocean, at least momentarily, overshadows the negative aspects. If the suggestion for such a venture had come up at the time when the parents were at a low point of frustration tolerance, the memory of the process in previous outings would be more prominent and the suggestion for an outing would be scrapped.

Low B/C Balance

Under these conditions the benefit would not occur or at best would be very unlikely to happen. Beneficial events can occur under these conditions when there is a desire or need for an event to transpire, independent of the cost of having it happen. This is the case of marriages that stay together for the benefit of children, even though the parental relationships border on the intolerable. Another example is the person who stays in an undesirable job for the security and the fear that she would not able to get another job.

Making B/C Decisions Relative to Other B/Cs

Families often get into difficulty when they get preoccupied with making a particular B/C balance decision without adequately considering how it will affect making such decisions in other areas. In one family, the parents were so preoccupied in sending their first child to the alma mater of both parents that they neglected to adequately consider how this would impact on providing the desired college education for their other children. Nor did they pay adequate attention to how the pressure to generate the additional income would impact on them and their life style.

When Only the Benefit or Cost Is Considered

There are times when the immersion in making a decision focuses on only the benefit or the cost involved. Most families will do whatever is needed to cope with a health problem without much attention to the cost. A couple in the throes of a whirlwind romance marry without adequately addressing how their lives may change in undesired ways. I saw a family where the parents grew up in abject poverty and vowed that they would do whatever necessary to be financially secure. When they had to make a decision about where to live, they made it solely on the basis of finances, which resulted in their living in a high-risk neighborhood. They presumed they could manage any problems and that financial stability would result in the desired quality of life. They were very disheartened when they realized they had underestimated the negative impact that the neighborhood would have on their children.

When a Benefit Is Not Needed

Parents are often besieged by their children for benefits of one kind or another. When they place a low value on the subject of such requests, the decision is easy and is based primarily, if not totally, on cost considerations. Many family problems result from debates around the importance attached to a particular benefit. This commonly occurs in conflicts between parents and their adolescents. Adolescents often behave as though their very survival depends on attaining a certain benefit that seems totally unnecessary and trivial to the parents. This happened in a family where a 15-year-old daughter was totally committed to the belief that her social survival depended on getting a particular kind of haircut. The request was rejected as a waste of money.

Application of B/C Balance to Family Therapy

The B/C balance concept provides a useful way of understanding family dynamics because it aids in the concrete definition of the issues that are important to how family members make decisions. As noted earlier, most conflicts arise about differences in how individual members define benefits and costs. Also involved are how determinations are made about different priorities. Problems between adolescents and parents are generally over differences stemming from how this balance is viewed. A case in point is when an adolescent is certain that she can manage many different projects without any difficulty. Her parents have a different view based on past experiences when she had tended to minimize and overestimate what was involved.

Problems often develop in families around how priorities are set in the allocation of resources among family members. This involves not only who gets the benefit of what resources but also at what cost to the individual receiving it and at what cost or deprivation to other family members. The difficulties develop more from the process by which these decisions are made than by the decisions themselves.

One step in the process is how the family determines need. What criteria are used and how is the decision made as to who benefits and who does not? Who gets the new clothes or goes on the school trip, and who will have to do with less or without to make this happen? In a new couple, a wife may forgo her own pursuits to support the couple to enable her husband to finish his education.

Oftentimes parents lose their perspective by an imbalance in catering to the needs of their children relative to their own needs. Such an occurrence is likely to carry the implicit unilateral expectations by the parent for the sacrifice. Failure to be aware of what is being transacted by the parent and failure to include the recipient in the B/C process provide the breeding ground for relationship problems. Best results are achieved in situations of very limited resources when all those affected by B/C issues feel that their needs were considered in the process, even if they do not get their needs met in the desired fashion.

The B/C balance is an expression of the values, beliefs, and goals of a family. Lack of clarity in defining them and in setting priorities contributes to the possibility of impulsive behavior in dealing with B/C issues and the possible problems that may result from it.

CASE ILLUSTRATION

Background Information

The Green family consisted of the father, Paul, 50; the mother, Colleen, 48; Evelyn, 22; and Mark, 20. The father was a high school teacher who enjoyed his work and was very dedicated to it. Colleen had been an English teacher and was then trying to develop a career as a free-lance writer. Evelyn was a junior in college who had a hard time focusing on what kind of career she wanted to pursue. Mark was a sophomore in college who was doing well and had a career path aimed at being a lawyer.

The parents came to therapy as a result of conflict in their marriage around issues of money, communication styles, and competition in their careers.

Paul got his graduate training after they were married. Colleen was very supportive of this effort and worked to make it possible for him to complete his degree as fast as possible. They both agreed in principle that he would do the same for her sometime in the future.

One source of tension in their relationship was the difference in their personality styles. Paul was laid-back in his manner and analytical and liked to ponder over decisions until he was comfortable that the necessary considerations were addressed. Colleen was quite the reverse. She was high-strung and quick to assess and react to a situation, with little patience for dwelling too much on details. When she was bothered about something, she would not hesitate to make her feelings known. She was pleased with her forthrightness.

Paul liked to avoid conflicts and arguments. When they got into arguments about issues of who was going to do what, he would tend to go along just to avoid the hassle. In so doing, he would commit to things he would get around to doing after other more important things had been done. This would infuriate Colleen, who interpreted his behavior as dishonest, and so the arguments continued.

They got into a constant struggle around whose career should get priority at a given point. They were each in search of validating their identities through their careers. This conflicted with their desire to be supportive of each other. Their conflicts also got expressed around their differences in how they related to their children. Differences around child rearing practices often got viewed as power struggles about whose view was more valid.

They were always overextended financially. This led to ongoing disagreements about how their financial resources should be allocated. They shared similar values about life-style, child rearing, and intellectual and cultural interests. Legitimate needs always exceeded their financial resources so that defining priorities was always a struggle. They did reasonably well when it came to defining priorities between the children relative to theirs. The situation was different when it came to allocation of resources between Paul and Colleen.

Application of the B/C Balance Concept

Family Definitions of Benefits

Father.

- Time to do his work and writing
- Make decisions in his own time frame
- Avoid hassle and conflict

- Being nurtured and validated by his wife and children
- To be together as a family
- Intellectual achievement of his children
- Have his wife and children be happy
- Be free of financial worry

Colleen.

- To be successful and able to pursue her career
- Have her children be successful emotionally and intellectually
- To feel loved and respected by her husband and children
- When she and her husband can resolve their differences and he follows through on what he promises to do when he says he will do it
- To feel good about herself
- To be financially secure

Evelyn.

- To get a good education
- To be respected by her parents
- To be socially successful
- Not be drawn into parental battles
- Have close friends she can trust
- Get along as a family
- Have a good relationship with her brother

Mark.

- Get a good education
- Participating and being a spectator in sports
- Be respected by his parents
- Be able to enjoy doing things with his father
- Enjoy his pursuit of music
- Be socially successful

Ability of Family Members to Know Each Other's Definition of Benefits and Costs

The members of this family have a good understanding of each other's feelings and needs regarding what are benefits and what are viewed as costs. The father was not aware of the benefit value that Mark placed on having a relationship with him. Part of the process in therapy is to help family members define what experiences constitute benefits and costs for themselves and for each other. Such knowledge eliminates the problems that come from lack of information and heightens the possibility of being able to be responsive to one another's needs.

B/C Balance in Relationships
It is helpful to understand the B/C of the major SEs in the family, which include the marital relationship, each parent with the two children, father with Mark, mother with Evelyn, and the family as a whole.

The Marital Relationship.   At the time of entering therapy, the B/C balance of the couple relationship was in trouble. The cost of maintaining the relationship outweighed the benefits obtained from it. In their better moments they were about equal, with occasional times when the relationship was positive on balance. The pain and struggle of their arguing was not offset by the times when they felt positively connected. They both shared the same view.

Father with the Children.   From the father's point of view, the benefits of the relationship exceeded those detracting aspects. The enjoyment of the times they spent together was not significantly diminished by their negative and rebellious behavior. The children shared a common and somewhat different perspective on their relationship. For them the balance between benefits and the cost of maintaining the relationship tended to be about equal on the average. The good times were offset by the frustration and annoyance of the times he was not available when they needed him. Adding to their frustration was the father's tendency to be emotionally remote when he was absorbed in his work.

Mother with the Children.   Colleen felt the benefits of her relationship with her children were clearly more positive than were the negative aspects of their relationship. They were able to enjoy being together even more since they both went away to college. The tense moments when they get into unpleasant arguments tend to be short-lived. At times they gang up on her and come off in an entitled way that is very irritating. This behavior is diminishing as they are living in the real world and becoming more realistic and independent. Most of the time the children feel that the benefits clearly outweigh the negative aspects of the relationship. They have the most difficulty when she gets in the middle of their arguments and attempts to impose her solution. Happily, this occurs less and less often as they are better at setting limits and are becoming more independent.

Father with Son.   The father and Mark are similar in personality style, which gets in the way of having a more positive relationship. For the father the cost-benefit balance is about equal. He would like it to be more positive, as would Mark, but each seems to wait for the other to take the initiative. They both have a low threshold for being rejected by the other.

Mother with Daughter. From the mother's point of view, the benefits outweigh the tensions in their relationship. The balance shifted in a positive direction since Evelyn went to college. Prior to that the balance was in the other direction. From mother's point of view, Evelyn was aloof and distant most of the time. Colleen could not account for this behavior so she presumed it had to do with her getting ready to leave home.

Evelyn shares her mother's point of view about the current status of the balance in their relationship. She has a different view about their relationship prior to her going to college. She experienced her mother as being uptight and intrusive. She protected herself by keeping her distance when she sensed her mother was not in a good mood.

Family as a Unit. The balance between the benefits and costs of being together as a family was pretty equal. They frequently were able to enjoy being together as a family for short periods of time. Their different personality styles and interests usually resulted in tension developing after a short while. The exception to this sometimes occurred when they were away on vacations. Being away from the pressures of work and home seemed to make it easier to get along. Under these conditions they had more tolerance for coping with their personality differences.

Application of This Perspective in Therapy

Introduction of the perspective of the balance between benefits and costs was helpful to the family in understanding their relationships in a new way. It also gave them a tool to use in coping with tension when it developed. When things got difficult, they found it useful to think in terms of what was going on in the balance between what they were getting out of the relationship and what it took to make it happen. It shifted the tendency to focus on judging the other person to a broadened perspective. They felt more in control in deciding whether what they were getting from the relationship was worth what it took to accomplish it. When they decided the balance was too negative, they would back away from it. This perspective made it easier to determine when it was better to quit than to keep investing in a relationship that was too draining.

A GUIDE TO CLINICAL APPLICATION

The method I use in applying the concept of benefit/cost balance consists of the following:

Step 1: For each of the areas of concern, I have the family members consider what are the attendant benefits and costs to each person involved in the problem.

Step 2: I have them look at how each of their perspectives on the B/C balance affects other family members.

Step 3: We then consider how to negotiate an adjustment in B/C balances so there is some harmony between the needs of the significant social entities (individuals, couple, prominent sub-groupings of family members such as siblings or a parent and a child, and the family as a whole).

Step 4: Once the resolution of a particular issue is solved, I encourage generalization of the method to other areas to enable making needed changes in B/C balances and provide flexible options as circumstances and needs change.

This process involves evaluation of the benefit/cost balance for significant events from the following points of view:

1. Define the major events for the primary social entities.
2. For each of these events evaluate what the benefits are and who benefits.
   - What is the source of the benefit?
   - What form do the benefits take?
     - Psychological
     - Physical
     - Material
     - Spiritual
   - When do the benefits occur and with what consequences to whom?
   - What is the duration of the benefits?
   - What is the intensity of the benefits?
   - Under what circumstances do they occur?
3. What are the costs that go with each of the benefits with respect to
   - Who pays a cost?
   - What form does the cost take?
     - Emotional
     - Financial
     - Physical
     - Spiritual
     - Intellectual
   - When does the cost occur?

Summary

In this chapter I described the concept of the balance between the benefits of participating in a particular experience and the emotional or other costs that went with it. Variables that affect this balance were described. A case was provided to illustrate the clinical applicability of this concept.

CHAPTER TEN

Definition of Problem

When I first started clinical work, I though that the definition of a client's problem was a relatively simple matter. My experience soon taught me this was not so. I found that clinical practice can be enhanced by greater attention to the variables that are involved in defining a problem. The results are described in this chapter.

THEORY

One of a therapist's responsibilities is to help clients find solutions to the problems that lead them to seek therapy. To do this, he needs to determine what problems to address. These may be the presenting problem(s) or other issues outside the client's awareness. This process is based on understanding what constitutes defining a problem from both the client's and therapist's points of view. For whom is the situation a problem? What is the set of life circumstances that warrants the label of "problem"? Why is it that the same set of circumstances can be a problem at one time and not at another time?

Another responsibility of a therapist is to engage the family in therapy. A number of considerations will determine whether and how effectively this takes place, depending on the characteristics of the family and the therapist.

In this chapter I discuss the definition of the problem to be addressed in therapy and considerations that affect whether a family enters therapy.

Variables that Affect Problem Definition

What Is a Problem?

At its core, a problem exists when a social entity's (individual, couple, or family) desire to cope with its environment is blocked by someone or something. This can occur in different ways: (1) A person is unhappy with his self-concept, which is expressed in symptoms of depression, anxiety, or inability to function at work. (2) A person desires to relate to another social entity in a particular way and is not able to do so; for instance, a parent is concerned about his inability to cope with his child's unacceptable behavior, or a couple is having marital problems. (3) A person desires to relate to an idea, value, or belief; for example, a person desires to practice a certain religion and is prevented from doing so because of religious prejudice. (4) A person desires to relate to some thing(s), such as a 9-year-old boy who has his heart set on making the Little League team and is rejected.

Variables that contribute to the definition of a problem include:

Developmental Changes

It is common for people to be impatient or fearful in coping with developmental changes. Such concerns range from the child who cannot wait to grow up to the man who has a lot of anxiety about the prospect of retirement. It could also take the form of a parent who is concerned that his 2-year-old child has not started talking.

Coping with Time Limitations

People frequently have to cope with accomplishing certain tasks within a fixed time limit. The level of anxiety that accompanies such concerns is a product of the consequences of not meeting the time requirement. A mother is concerned about her 4-year-old son's bedwetting and wants to resolve the problem before he starts school.

Failure to Adjust to Needed Changes

When all possible efforts to find a solution are exhausted, there is a reluctance to adjust to the existing situation. A parent cannot accept that his child has an emotional problem after all physical findings are negative. Failure to do so prevents addressing the source of the problem.

Failure to Agree on the Presence of a Problem

What is a problem for one person in a relationship may not be a problem for another person. It could also be the case that the participants in a relationship agree that there is a problem but disagree on what the problem is. A married couple are not getting along with each other and efforts to resolve their differences end in failure. Contributing to this failure is their inability to agree on what the problem is and who should take what responsibility for areas of conflict.

For Whom Is There a Problem?

In the marital situation, a philandering husband may not have a problem with his behavior, but it would be very much of a problem for his wife.

In a similar vein is the adolescent who is quite satisfied to have his room look like a disaster zone, which is a major problem for his mother. I find it useful to make a distinction between problems that are defined within the family by one or more members and when the problem is defined by someone outside the family system such as the school, neighbors, or the police.

A problem defined from within the family is operating from a common cultural base. Differences result from how values are expressed, not what they are. An adolescent may argue about what time his curfew should be, not whether he should have one.

A more complicated problem develops when a member of the family introduces values from another culture into the family. This is the case of the adolescent who adopts values of his peer culture that are alien. The problem now becomes a difference in values. A child who grew up with respect for his religion now sees religion as irrelevant and refuses to participate in the family's religious practice.

Added complexity develops when the problem is defined from outside the family by the school, court, physician, clergy, social agency such as welfare, or any other source that has power over the family. The level of problem becomes more complex to the extent that cultural or ethnic differences result in conflict between the family and an external source. The conflict results from their differing definition of whether there is a problem or what it is. An example is people who vent their frustrations on immigrants from other countries. This creates a bewildering and frightening problem for people who are in an alien culture and language.

I saw an immigrant mother who was upset because the school was critical of the way she disciplined her child. The presenting problem of the child's behavior in school had to be secondary until they were able to resolve the cultural differences between the mother and the school about how to discipline children. Another example is the middle-class social agency representative who, with good intentions, attempts to impose on a welfare family middle-class values that are irrelevant to them when their primary concern is physical survival.

When there is a difference in whether and how a problem is defined between the family and external sources, the relative power relationships become an issue. When a welfare agency has a different standard about how children should be treated, the parents run the risk of losing custody of their children, if the welfare agency considers the differences of sufficient importance. When a parent is at odds with the school in the definition of his child's problem, the parent is left to his own limited resources if he is not able to convince the school to change its perception of the problem. Such an occurrence places an additional burden on the parent.

Differences in Problem Definition between Referrer, Identified Client, Family, and Therapist

Every participant in the referral process — referrer, identified client, family, and therapist — is likely to have his own perspective on why the referral is made and what the nature of the problem is. Such occurrences complicate the process of problem definition. A frequent result is that the client's needs get lost in disagreements between the caregivers involved.

Consider the case when a school guidance counselor refers a child for therapy for behavior that neither the parents nor the child considers warrants therapy. Such parents would either reject the referral or present themselves in therapy with resistance to the process. This difficulty increases if the therapist's judgment differed from that of the family. The problem for the therapist becomes twofold. One is the parents' feelings about considering participation in therapy; it is intertwined with their problems about the basis on which they were referred.

I saw a family where a 9-year-old boy was referred for therapy because his behavior was disruptive on the playground and in the classroom. He was aggressive and often got into fights. The father was upset at the school after hearing about the referral. He said, "What's wrong with that school? They are trying to make a pansy out of my kid. I always taught him to stand up for himself and not let anyone push him around. He didn't do anything wrong!"

His wife did not share her husband's view, as she experienced some of the same difficulty with her son. She prevailed on her husband to go for the evaluation. He expressed his concern to me as previously quoted and challenged me to agree with him. It took a while to deal with the father's concerns before we were able to address his son's behavior at school. Ultimately, I was able to deal with the father's underlying insecurity and how it was being handled in a way that only created further problems. The child's behavior showed quick response once the father's attitude was addressed. The father continued on in individual therapy to work on the way his aggressiveness created problems for him.

Who Is Involved

The nature of the reltionship between people involved in a problem situation can significantly affect the approach to coping with it. Problems with peers present different issues and opportunities than if the participants to a problem have a hierarchical relationship, as in the case of parent and child, student and teacher, or employee and employer.

Part of considering who is involved is to understand what alliances exist, how their existence affects the problem under consideration, and how subject to modification the alliances are. There was a family situation in which the parents were in the process of getting a divorce at the initiation of the husband. Their two daughters were aligned with their mother, who was in the victim position. They expressed this by wanting nothing to do with their father.

It was clear that the alliance between the daughters was an important influence in the relationship between their parents. It was also clear that the alliance would not be subject to change until the parents resolved their differences.

It is not appropriate to assume that all parties to a problem have the same investment in acknowledging the problem or in resolving it, independent of how it is presented at first view.

In the example noted previously, it was clear that each of the parents and the daughters had different ideas about what constituted the problem. The daughters saw the problem as the father's lack of caring about them. The wife saw the problem as her husband's lack of commitment to the marriage and the family. The husband saw the problem as incompatibility between him and his wife. In addition, the family had rather different ideas about how to resolve the problem.

Why Is It a Problem?

Why is the behavior that brought the family to therapy a problem? In what way is it dysfunctional? How many people does it affect, and in what way? Why does it become a problem at the point that it does, especially when the behavior under consideration was present for a considerable time? Is the presented behavior the core problem, a symbolic statement of the problem, or a distraction from the real problem, which is too threatening to present? These types of questions are necessary to understand the significance of the presenting and underlying problems.

Many families live with a great deal of pain over long periods of time without seeking outside help. People will seek help when one of two conditions exists: sometimes they are coerced by some external force such as the school, an employer, or the courts. The second and more frequent reason is that the family is at the point where the consequences of their problems exceed available resources within the family, and the resulting discomfort is not tolerble (see Chapter 8).

I worked with one couple who were battling for years in a very stormy marriage. At times they talked about getting therapy but never felt strong enough pressure to make therapy a priority. It was only after the wife discovered that her husband was having an affair that devastated her that she took a stand and declared either they go for help or the marriage was over. Because her husband was not ready to leave the marriage and they exhausted their own resources for resolving their differences, they entered therapy.

Content of the Problem

The focus of problems can be classified as follows:

Self-Content
A person may be dissatisfied with his competence, body image, how he is seen by others, or the like.

Feelings
A person may be struggling with how to express anger or have difficulty in expressing feelings. He may also be depressed or have immobilizing levels of anxiety.

Things
A parent finds a child with possessions not considered appropriate, such as sexual material, weapons, alcohol, or drugs.

Ideas
A child presents a value system contrary to the parents' values, or a husband and wife have differences about priorities in the use of money or in the management of children.

Behavior in Relationship to Things
A child steals or does not do his homework or his chores, or a husband is angry at his wife because she spends too much money. A wife is angry because her husband drinks too much.

Behavior in Relationships
A husband and wife are hostile to each other and are not able to negotiate acceptable expectations from one another. The adolescent does not feel understood by his parents.

Motivation and Intent
Problems develop when people hold one another accountable because of the hostile motivation they assume underlies an undesirable behavior: the husband who assumes his wife is trying to punish him when she refuses to

have sex, or the adolescent who gets angry at his parents in reaction to undesired limit setting.

What Purpose Does the Problem Serve?

It becomes easy to assume that problems are solely dysfunctional and serve no useful purpose. Often, this is not the case. Problems are often in service of meeting important needs. As noted earlier, one of the reasons I got started in family therapy was the result of working with an 8-year-old boy around his anxiety in school. It became clear to me that there were other issues bothering this youngster. I called the parents in for consultation and found that there was a lot of tension in the marriage and that there was risk of a divorce. At that point it seemed quite likely that the child's problem was more a statement about his parents' marriage than about him. This led me to shift my attention to helping the parents deal with the marriage. Their commitment to do so was enhanced when they realized that conflicts were affecting their son's school performance. Therapy terminated after several months. A follow-up after six months revealed that the relationship between the parents was better and that the child was doing well in school. Quite often one problem is created to avoid another or to relieve frustration in the inability to cope with another problem. A woman might drink as a way of coping with rejection by her husband.

Motivation to Solve the Problem

One of the things a therapist learns early in his career is that he cannot assume a client who seeks therapy is motivated to change. This is better understood by considering what affects the motivation to change in the therapy environment.

Politics of Participating in Therapy

Assessing motivation in family therapy is complicated because it involves the motivations of each person, which are in part a function of the interaction between family members. A child's motivation to participate in therapy might be based on bribery, coercion, threat, guilt, obligation, desire to be part of a family activity, or identification with an older sibling. A family member's motivation to participate in therapy may be obscured by conflict with another family member. I saw a family where an adolescent gave the impression of being very committed to being in therapy. I later learned that he did not want to be there and did not think that the process made any sense. He gave the appearance of wanting to be there because if he cooperated, his father would buy him the car he desperately wanted.

In another family a husband gave the initial impression that he was not enthusiastic about participating in therapy but did so at the behest of his wife. It later turned out that he was very desirous of the therapy but did not think it was a good idea to acknowledge it because he felt that doing so would negatively affect his wife's motivation. He felt that she needed to feel that she was in charge and responsible for the therapy.

Severity of Consequences

Anyone considering therapy implicitly if not explicitly goes through an evaluation process. This involves contrasting the consequences of to what degree getting help would be productive at what emotional and financial expense. When the combination of positive consequences of going into therapy outweighs the combined anticipated negative consequences of *not* going into therapy plus the negative aspects of being in therapy, the social entity (individual, couple, or family) will seek therapy. (See Chapter 9 for a more detailed discussion.)

Another consideration in determining motivation for therapy is whether there are qualitative or quantitative consequences. Will the existing situation change or will it just become more tolerable?

In one family the parents were on the verge of divorce, and there was great animosity between the parents and the children. It was clear that the family situation would deteriorate further if they did not get help. They were fearful of getting into family therapy because they anticipated it would only heighten the tensions that periodically got out of control. The initial interview was critical in helping the family see that the therapy environment was a safe place to work on their problems. They got more invested in the process as they began to see that qualitative changes were possible.

Another family I saw struggled with the decision to go into therapy. The Zep family consisted of a mother, 50; her second husband, 55; and the woman's daughter, Wendy, 15. Mr. Zep's children from his first marriage were grown and on their own. He was happy to be free from that responsibility and was unhappy at the prospect of coping with another teenager.

When he came to the evaluation session, he was quick to let me know that he did not believe in therapy but that he was caught between the negative emotional drain of therapy and the negative hostile environment at home. The severity of pain in the home outweighed the negative prospect of being in therapy. He agreed to go along for the time being to see if life could become more peaceful. The presenting problem centered around Wendy's recalcitrant behavior and the recent incident in which she had a big party in her parents' absence in violation of their explicit rules. She was very angry at her mother's ambivalent way of relating to her and wanted little to do with her stepfather. An underlying issue was anger at her mother's remarriage.

Wendy also was ambivalent about therapy. She did not want individual therapy and did not want the family to be seen without her. She had a real struggle between seeing therapy as a way to get her mother to put less pressure on her and her fear of being held more accountable than she wanted. She agreed to participate in therapy because the potential for a positive outcome outweighed the negative environment at home and the challenging aspects of therapy.

Mrs. Zep was the clearest about her motivation for therapy. She was caught between the pressures of her daughter and her husband, who were pulling her in opposite directions. She felt overwhelmed and frustrated. For her the severity of her pain in the family outweighed any reluctance to participate in therapy.

Degree to Which Severity of Consequences Gets in the Way

A strong motivating factor for therapy is when the evolution of problems significantly interferes with day-to-day functioning in personal relationships, work, and the necessities of daily living. Conflict about therapy is likely to be high when the disruption in mood or success in work or social relationships is high enough to be annoying, but not enough to put therapy as a top priority. The presence of sufficient physical or emotional pain will interfere with any pursuit until the pain is reduced to tolerable levels.

Therapists commonly hear in their intakes comments like "I've wanted to get into therapy for a long time but didn't get around to it until the crisis happened." I saw one family that was living with a chronic degree of tension for a period of years that included major periodic blowups. They often talked about getting into family therapy but never got around to it until the youngest child made a suicidal gesture.

Consequences of Removing a Problem

Chances for effective resolution of a problem are enhanced when consideration is given to what consequences are likely to result when the presenting problem is resolved. If this is not done, then the purpose the problem was serving will not be resolved, and the likelihood is great that the problem will be expressed in another way or the person displaying the symptom will regress after a period of time.

In one family I saw where there was a significant marital problem, the mother invested her energies in her children and her 10-year-old daughter, in particular. She still helped her get dressed and walked her to school. My early attempts to interrupt this pattern and allow her daughter age-appropriate independence failed. She could agree with all that I said, but then was not able to translate it into behavior. This was in part due to her inability to find more appropriate ways to meet her needs. Significant progress was not made until this woman was able to find more appropriate outlets for frustrations and disappointments in her marriage.

How Treatment Orientation Affects Definition of the Problem

Some therapists and agencies organize their services around providing a particular method of treatment, such as hypnosis, behavior modification, and brief therapy. Other service providers organize their services around particular problems, such as depression, sexual dysfunction, and behavior problems in children.

Each of these orientations contains its own theory and set of techniques of implementation that provide a heightened sensitivity and context for how to define and diagnose problems that are presented for consultation.

Some therapists limit their practice to a single theoretical model and method of practice, such as psychoanalysis or contextual or structural family therapy. In such a situation, a therapist approaches a problem from the orientation of a particular method with the goal to see how this method can help a client resolve the problems of concern to them.

In contrast, other therapists approach therapy with an eclectic background in both theory and application. Such therapists are capable of providing services in different methods. In such cases, the therapist approaches a presenting situation by attempting to determine which method is likely to help the client most effectively cope with his problem(s).

Considerations for Engaging Clients in Therapy

Do the Therapist and the Client Agree on the Definition of the Problem?

When the therapist and the client do not agree on what problem to address, the viability of the working relationship is at risk. This occurs when the therapist behaves in a way that makes no sense to the client or if the client does not feel validated that the therapist respects his perspective of the problem. The therapist may have his own view of the problem underlying the presenting problem but needs to start by respecting what the client presents. Once he has established rapport and obtained data to support his perceptions, he will be in a position to renegotiate the definition of the problem so that both the client and the therapist are working towards a common goal.

A frequent occurrence is exemplified by the case of a couple who sought therapy because of their different views about how to discipline their children. They resisted any effort to redefine the problem. After appropriate attention was given to their concern and a good relationship was established, they were able to accept that the conflict about discipline was a screen to avoid facing the more threatening issue of their battle for control in the relationship.

Do the Therapist and the Client Agree on the Goals for Therapy?

It is not uncommon for clients to set unrealistic goals for therapy. The goals may be unrealistic in terms of the time the therapy will take or the changes to be achieved. Clients often come to therapy with a time frame in mind for solving the problems they present. The working relationship becomes at risk when the therapist and the client are not able to agree on a realistic time frame for the goals set for therapy.

The same thing applies in defining the goals for therapy. A common occurrence in couple or family therapy is for each person to view the goal as getting someone else to change. An immediate challenge to the therapist at the initiation of therapy is to help the client develop realistic goals for what needs to be achieved and is likely to be achieved in therapy.

Are Needed Resources Available to Resolve the Problem?

A family usually seeks therapy to learn to cope better with or eliminate a dysfunction in a part or in the whole system. In Chapter 3, I discussed the assessment process that focused on how a therapist's theoretical orientation gets expressed in the way a diagnosis is made and how a treatment strategy is developed.

Implicit in this process is the necessity to assess various aspects of the problem, as described in this chapter. A key consideration in developing a treatment strategy is to determine what resources are needed to resolve the problem. Such definition provides a guide to the therapist as he attempts to determine whether the needed resources are or can become available as described in Chapter 6.

In one family, the mother was primarily responsible for discipline of the children. As the children reached adolescence, she had increasing difficulty in setting limits. An assessment of resources showed that the father was quite capable of setting limits. This was evident from his work, the self-discipline he displayed in his personal life, and the time he had responsibility for the children.

He was not more involved in disciplining the children because his wife was reluctant to ask him for help in that it would define her failure and because she feared his reaction. This pattern was interrupted when the youngest daughter acted out in ways where the father's involvement was required. One part of the therapy involved getting the father to help the mother with limit setting in a way where she felt supported and could improve her skills without feeling judged. A secondary benefit of this effort was an improvement in the marriage.

The task is more challenging when the needed resource is not available in the needed form. The therapist's job is to help the family identify existing latent resources or to help them develop new needed resources. A case in point was the family in which there was a discipline problem similar to the one previously described. The difference in this case was that neither parent showed any evidence of coping very well with limit setting and both reported feeling inadequate to the process.

In the assessment of resources, I found that both parents had satisfactory and successful experiences in team sports in high school. The mother also had a history of successful leadership in organizations. The father was a parts manager in a local auto dealership and had several people working for him. One aspect of therapy involved helping the parents to realize the ways in which they were able to exercise discipline and do it well in non-children related activities. Therapy also involved helping them draw upon those skills and apply them to discipline of their children.

Value and Belief System Regarding Therapy

Some people operate with the value system that they should be able to solve their own emotional problems. They view seeking therapy as a sign of weakness. These people have a difficult time when their participation is requested in another member's therapy such as a parent being asked to participate in a child's therapy. When this is the case and such a person does participate, the therapist is faced with overcoming the resistance to the process and preventing contagion from influencing other family members who might be vulnerable to such influences.

This was one of the problems I faced in engaging the Zep family described previously. Mr. Zep's immediate declaration about his attitude toward therapy did not give his stepdaughter a lot of confidence that the existing unresolvable problems would have much chance in therapy. This contributed to her reluctance to commit to the therapy process.

Likelihood of Outcome

Two of the concerns that affect how much attention a social entity pays to the consequences of any positive or negative behavior are the value placed on the behavior and how likely it is to happen. Children learn this concept early in life. They learn to assess how likely parents are to carry out their threats. When a low probability is determined, the child has license to pursue his desires. When there is a high likelihood that the parents will do what they say, the child is likely to be more responsive.

I worked with a couple that was experiencing chronic marital turmoil. Periodically the wife would threaten to get a divorce. At first, her husband took her at face value. After a few such events, he concluded that this was her way of expressing frustration and that there was little likelihood that she would do anything about it. When these threats continued, he paid little attention to them. One day he was rudely awakened when he was served with divorce papers as he entered work. In the course of reviewing past events, he became aware of how in his desensitized state he missed noting the change in the way that she made her threats to get a divorce.

Ability to Do the Work of Therapy

Fear of inability to cope with a task is a great motivator to avoid having to perform it. I periodically encounter people who desire to seek therapy but are fearful of their ability to cope with the therapeutic process. One of these concerns is tolerating exposure of vulnerabilities, especially when appearances and the opinions of others are an important concern in relationships. Another is fear of not being able to tolerate the emotional pain that is anticipated to be a necessary part of the therapy.

Some people harbor the fear that they will find out that they are "crazier" than they feared they were. For these people it is sometimes easier to live with the ambiguity that they might be more disturbed than they are than to risk finding out that their mental state is as bad as they feared.

Importance of Therapy to Others

There are people who have no particular aversion or attraction to therapy. Their only reason for engaging in the process is to help or please other family members or significant others who may request their presence.

In one couple the husband did not feel the need for therapy but participated to please his wife. In another situation, a child was referred for therapy because the quality of his work deteriorated, as did his relationships with peers. Initially, the parents did not see the need for their participation, but were quite cooperative when their participation was requested by the therapist for the benefit of their son.

Outcome of Therapy

How Being in Therapy Affects Other Aspects of Life

A major fringe benefit of therapy is that the skills that are learned have application to other parts of family members' lives, such as work, school, and social relationships. For some people therapy is a distracting interference from other concerns both in time and emotional energy.

A major deterrent to participating in therapy is cost. When money is very limited, it becomes an added pressure in competition with other needs and interests. This heightens the already existing level of conflict in how to allocate insufficient funds.

The same kind of tensions can also result from the short supply in schedules of available time. Taking time from an already overcommitted schedule creates its own problem and affects attitudes toward anything that requires a significant investment of time.

Nature of Losses That Can Result from Therapy Experience

Many fantasies abound about what happens in therapy. One kind of fear is that people will lose their creativity in the belief that somehow neurotic people are more creative than those who are happy. Another fear is that they will lose their sense of identity or they will have to give up things they enjoy. For many children and some adults, the idea that other people will know they are in therapy will cast a stigma on them. Another concern is that the emotional stress of therapy will interfere with their ability to function in other areas of their lives. People who struggle with their ambivalence about their own behavior often view therapy as a place to be judged and blamed.

I saw one man who had a hard time participating in therapy. One reason was his feeling that he would lose face in front of his family. Another was that he would be confronted with things he did not want to hear. The image of competing with the therapist added further resistance. He also enjoyed and valued the way the family worked out their conflicts with much noise and shouting as was the case in his family. In part, he did not want to be confronted with this in therapy because then he would feel some pressure to change his behavior.

Consequences of Solving the Problem

In the face of intense pain, all energy gets focused on eliminating the problem. It often is only after this is accomplished that there is the realization that more than the noxious situation was eliminated.

An issue that came up in one family situation was a 7-year-old who had a problem in school because he was being scapegoated by his peers. He responded well in therapy in learning what he did to encourage it and was happy when he ceased to be treated that way. Sometime later he expressed his unhappiness about an unanticipated consequence of no longer being scapegoated. When such events happened, he got a lot of support and attention from his teachers. He was disappointed that such nurturing was no longer forthcoming from them.

Types of Interventions Needed for the Family

A clear statement of the client's problem provides the basis for determining the intervention that is needed to address it. In this section I describe a range of options that are open to the therapist in developing interventions.

Redefinition of the Presenting Problem

Clients define presenting problems for seeking therapy for different reasons of which they may not be aware: it is the problem that needs to be addressed, it is the safest problem to talk about, it is the only problem that the client(s) is willing to talk about, it is a forum for punishing another family member, a way to gain support for a particular point of view, and a way to gain nurturing. These are only a few of the possibilities. One type of intervention is to redefine the problem in a way that provides a new perspective which enables the client to relate to their difficulty in a different way. This is commonly referred to as reframing.

One of the problems presented by a couple was the husband's complaint that his wife was always trying to manage him. Evaluation of his complaint disclosed that she was always criticizing him for his food habits and lack of exercise. When the problem was redefined as her concern for his health, he was able to see her behavior in a different light. When this happened she was able to express her concern in a way that communicated caring rather than a desire for control.

Sometimes the needed redefinition of the problem is not possible because it is too threatening for the client to accept. Under such conditions the therapist needs to work on the problems that the client is able to accept as a focus. The intervention becomes one of working on these problems in a way that builds a comfort level that ultimately enables the client to address the central issues underlying the presenting problems.

This is commonly the case in families that present problems in management of children. It often is quickly clear to the therapist that the underlying issue is a marital problem that is being expressed in disagreements about how to manage the children. In such cases, attention needs to be addressed to to child management issues before one or both of the parents feel safe enough to address the marital issues.

Providing Information and Skill Training

The least complicated interventions are in response to families that present problems resulting from lack of needed information and/or the skill to use effectively the information they already possess. Once they have such knowledge, they are able to cope as needed.

This frequently happens with parents and their first child. They may be alarmed by developmental issues and not know how to handle them. Once they are provided with the needed information, they are able to behave appropriately. Such families are likely to need brief periods of help as their children progress through their development.

A father came in concerned about his relationship to his 12-year-old daughter. They were always very close until she turned 11. He found that she appeared to distance herself from him and that he was not feeling as comfortable with her as he used to feel. Once he was able to understand the issues that go with how puberty can affect relationships, he was able to redefine how he related to his daughter in a way that was comfortable for both.

Skill Training

How to Function in a Given Role.   In large segments of our society, children are provided with little hands-on training in roles they are expected to perform as adults. Often lacking are basic skills in home management: the necessities of shopping, cooking, sewing, and use of tools in simple home repairs. Also lacking are skills in money management: budgeting, managing checkbooks, and obtaining loans. This often results from the emphasis on self-development and competence in education and sports. As a result, children are left to learn these skills as needed. This does not adequately prepare them for leaving home and living independent lives and for coping with marriage and children.

Another confounding problem, especially for women, is potentially contradicting role expectations. In our present culture, women grow up in a world dominated by the role expectations for men: get an education, succeed in a job, and support yourself. Then, when they get married and have children, they are supposed to forgo such interests and goals and devote all their energies to the wife and mother role. The other option is for them to do it all — wife, mother and career. This becomes a problem when husbands espouse shared responsibilities and have difficulty acting on it. The conflicts that arise from a couple's differences in such role expectations become the breeding ground for marital and family problems when they are unable to negotiate their differences.

How to Deal with Differences. When children are raised in environments that inordinately focus around their needs, they tend to grow up with a sense of entitlement. Such experience leads to problems in excessive expectations in relationships outside the family. This difficulty is enhanced when they have unique capabilities that invite special attention from the outside world. This would be the case with special talents such as music, athletics or academic achievement. In such cases, they receive special attention that encourages lack of consideration of other people's needs.

At the other extreme, difficulty in dealing with differences stems from having low self-esteem. For some people survival depends on catering to the needs of other people as a way to gain self-esteem at the risk of neglecting their own.

In both of these cases, providing information is not going to be sufficient to interrupt long-established patterns of behavior and the emotional investment in maintaining them.

How to Communicate Effectively. Effective communication requires respect for self, competence in listening skills, competence in the expression of one's own point of view, respect for other people's views, and a desire to have a relationship of some kind. Deficiencies in one or more of these areas are the breeding ground for problems that lead people to seeking therapy. As in the case of differences, providing information about such behaviors is a necessary part of therapy but in itself is not sufficient to resolve the problems that bring a client to therapy.

How to Manage and Resolve Conflict. A common problem in the therapy situation is the mismatch between family members in their ability to cope with conflict. This may occur for a variety of reasons: They may be threatened by the emotionality that goes with conflict; they may feel they do not have the tools necessary to present their views effectively; they may fear the consequences of conflict based on past bad experiences. Providing skills in conflict resolution is usually only one ingredient of the therapeutic process.

Time Management. The principles of time management are buzzwords in the business world but have escaped application in the family setting. I commonly find that families have difficulty in how they manage time. This is particularly the case with dual-career, achievement-oriented families. When they are asked to assign time frames to their various activities, they are surprised to find how much difficulty they have in managing their time.

Learning to set goals and priorities realistically, being accountable for commitments, and appropriate use of delegation of responsibility are important skills whose absence contributes to family tensions and sets negative role models.

I saw a dual-career couple in marital therapy that involved battling about who was going to do what and what was a fair division of labor. To their surprise, a time management review indicated that their commitments exceeded the available time by 25 percent. A result was that their time as a couple got low priority, leaving them one hour a week as a couple at best. They were usually too tired to take advantage of the time when it was available. Such awareness led to their appreciation that the time crunch was a significant contributing factor in their marital difficulties.

Learning to Take Risks and Make Commitments

Risk taking and making commitments are common subjects of discussion in therapy. It is useful to define what is involved in each of these behaviors.

Fear That the Desired Outcome May Not Occur

A major deterrent to taking risks is that the behavior under consideration may not result in the desired outcome and that the consequences that go with it are unacceptable. The concern could be either because of a possible negative outcome, the severity of the negative outcome, or the positive outcome does not meet expectations.

In one couple a man was struggling with feelings of inadequacy on his job. He was fearful of talking to his wife about it for fear that she would lose respect for him and/or be too threatened by it. He also feared that even if she was supportive on the surface that she would lose confidence in him.

There was a family situation in which an adolescent girl, Susan, was desperately in need of talking to her mother about a struggle she was having with her boyfriend about sex but could not take the risk of doing so for fear that her mother would try to cut off the relationship. She also had some fear that even if her mother was supportive that she would have less respect for her.

Also of concern is how the consequences of taking a risk in one area of behavior would affect other areas of behavior. In this example, Susan was fearful of talking to her mother about her problem with her boyfriend because it might affect her mother's relationship to her. She was also fearful that if her mother told her father about her concerns that it would change her relationship to him. It is easier to take a risk when it does not affect other parts of a person's life. In contrast, Susan did not have any difficulty discussing with her mother how to handle a conflict with a girlfriend.

Impact of Other Competing Risks

A person who does not perceive that he has the resources necessary to have a successful outcome will not take a risk unless he has no choice or unless failing is a lesser alternative to not trying. I saw a young man whose life was replete with many failures. He was open to trying many things because he had little expectation of succeeding. This was a more palatable alternative than the risk that went with not trying and being seen as lazy.

Whether a person takes a given risk is also going to depend on what other risks and vulnerabilities coexist. Other higher priorities may affect taking a particular risk more than the circumstances surrounding that particular risk. One man I saw was in a difficult situation at work where he was faced with making choices, each of which carried significant risks. At the same time he was struggling in a relationship with a woman. He was conflicted about confronting issues with her that bothered him for fear it might jeopardize the relationship. Dealing with both at the same time was too much for him to risk. He chose not to confront the relationship issue until he resolved the work situation.

Degree of Exposure in Risk Taking

Risks also vary in their degree of exposure. They may be for a brief moment or for indefinite periods. They may involve emotions, time, energy, and material resources such as money. A man may take the risk of irritating his wife by going on a hunting trip if he felt she would tolerate it. The situation is quite different if he felt it might be the last straw that would jeopardize the marriage.

Definition of Commitment

I think of a commitment as a risk over an extended period of time, such as in a marriage. The longer a person is in a committed relationship, the more entrenched he becomes and the harder it is to change the commitment, except when the discomfort of staying in the relationship exceeds the pain of terminating it. A frequent occurrence is the divorce that comes after the children leave home. In such cases the priority shifts from the children's needs to dealing with discomfort of staying in the relationship.

Redefining Relationships

A major concern of families seeking therapy is the repair of dysfunctional relationships. In the social psychology literature, role theory relates to positions in society such as police officer, doctor, lawyer, teacher, and parent. Society defines appropriate behaviors for a person performing in each position. These behaviors are in three categories: required behaviors, permissible behaviors, and prohibited behaviors. Parents are required to be responsible for the physical and emotional care of their children. They are prohibited from abusing their children. Otherwise, there is a great deal of latitude in the way they carry out this responsibility.

In the business world, a contract is a legal concept that refers to a binding agreement between two parties that defines what each party is expected to do and prohibited from doing and the compensation that is derived from performing in the agreed-upon manner. Family relationships commonly involve informal contracts. They run into trouble when they do not adequately negotiate what they expect from each other. These "contractual relationships" evolve over time as experience warrants. They usually are not explicitly defined and vary with changing circumstances, such as children's changing needs and abilities as they mature. A frequent source of friction in families is that the implicit contracts that evolve may be mutually satisfactory at one point in time but not at another time. When such changes take place, it involves each party to the original implicit agreement defining the desired changes. Unresolvable significant differences become the breeding ground for chronic problems.

A parent and child develop a mutually satisfactory caretaker-dependent relationship. As a child matures, his evolving needs for independence do not match the parent's need to maintain the dependency relationship. Similar situations occur between husband and wife. A couple may start out with an implicit contract that he will be the major decision maker. As she gains more experience and maturity, she gradually moves toward a shared decision-making responsibility. When this is not acceptable to the husband and they are not able to find a mutually satisfactory resolution, conflict develops. When this exists over time and spreads to other aspects of the relationship, they wind up in the therapist's office or the divorce courts.

A common task for the therapist is to help families be aware of the implicit contracts that exist, and redefine relationships to be mutually satisfying, and change them as the need warrants. This may involve dealing with defining and eliminating distortions, identifying and changing patterns of behavior, learning to cope with feelings, dealing with vulnerability, and understanding the relationship between the past and the present.

CASE ILLUSTRATION

This case involves the Minler family. John, 52, was a salesman of financial services and in his second marriage for five years. He had been divorced seven years ago after a marriage of 22 years. The marriage had faltered for a long time and resulted in divorce at the initiation of his first wife. There were three adult children from that marriage. He continued to have a good relationship with his son but a distant one with his two daughters.

Martha, 50, was a homemaker who was also divorced and had three adult children from her former marriage. Both reported that the current marriage was a good one.

The presenting problem was John's depression after he lost a lot of money on a bad investment. John's performance at work deteriorated greatly. Their income was in jeopardy because he got paid on a commission basis. They came in as a couple to learn how to cope jointly with the problem.

It was clear to me from taking a history that the presenting problem was a trigger that released a lot of guilt he felt about a number of things in his first marriage. When I suggested this possibility, he got annoyed and said, "I didn't come here to get shrunk. That's not the problem. Don't make a big deal about this. You shrinks always make a big deal out of any problem. I just want to get out of my blue funk and get to be productive again."

It was clear from these comments that I went too far too fast. I backtracked and focused on the problem with which he was prepared to cope. As we talked further, it became clear to him that there was more to this problem than he originally thought. I was able to bridge his immediate problem to earlier problems by tracing the similarities of disappointing situations in which he made a big investment.

One purpose the problem served for John was to distract Martha's attention away from his error in judgment and appeal to the nurturing side of her. He feared that the major loss of their investment would change her trust and affection for him. The prospect that he might face a second divorce was very threatening and immobilizing. Once he felt safe, he was more able to face the underlying issues when he felt her support and acceptance of the financial loss.

Part of what contributed to John's being able to respond in therapy was to draw upon his past successes and put the present situation in a more balanced perspective. Instead of being a failure, the current setback was viewed in the context of the many successes he had had that far outweighed his failures.

I also was able to draw upon the many difficult situations he had successfully faced in the past. The recovery of resources helped him to regain a more balanced and appropriate self-concept. This enabled him to take the risk of facing underlying problems that he had avoided confronting.

A GUIDE TO CLINICAL APPLICATION

Make the following evaluations:

1. What problems are presented?
2. For whom are they a problem?
3. Which of the following considerations are involved in the problems?
   - Developmental changes
   - Coping with time limitations
   - Failure to adjust to needed changes
   - Inability to agree on whether there is a problem
4. Are there differences in the definition of the problem between client, referrer, and therapist?
5. Who is involved in the problem?
6. How much motivation is there to solve the problems?
7. Why is there a problem?
8. What is the content area of the problem?
   - Self-concept
   - Feelings
   - Things
   - Ideas
   - Behavior
     - In relationship to things
     - In relationship to people
   - Motivation
9. What purpose does the problem serve?
10. How severe are the consequences of the problem?
11. What are likely to be the consequences of resolving the problem(s)?
12. How does the therapist's theoretical orientation affect the definition of the problem?
13. What is the therapist's skill and comfort level in dealing with the presented problems?
14. How do the presented problems relate to the therapist's diagnosis of the underlying problems?
15. Are the therapist and the client able to agree on the definition of the problem?
16. Are the resources available to resolve the problem?

Summary

In this chapter I considered a variety of factors that affect the definition of problems that are presented in the therapeutic context. I also discussed a number of variables that affect success in engaging a family in therapy. A case illustration involving a couple was given to illustrate some of the principles described in the chapter.

CHAPTER ELEVEN

Process Family Therapy Method

The preceding chapters discussed basic concepts and aspects of method that are an integral part of Process Family Therapy. I felt a chapter was needed to describe the basic philosophy of this approach and specific methods for applying it to clinical practice.

Introduction

In Chapter One I described how the early origins of Process Family Therapy got started around 1959. I also described the variety of sources that led to this eclectic approach to family Therapy. My initial guiding ethic was that whatever I did had to be pragmatic, respectful, and sensible to both me and the clients. In this chapter I discuss the basic philosophy of Process Family Therapy. I will draw upon concepts described in preceding chapters in addition to concepts not described earlier.

All therapeutic approaches have implicit or explicit value systems. I believed a therapist would function best when she had an explicitly defined set of values, beliefs, and goals for her work. I will describe those that have evolved for me and the methods that I use in accomplishing therapeutic goals. Such definition is never finished and always subject to review and modification, as ongoing analysis of experience and the evolving maturity of theoretical formulations dictate. This book represents the view from a point of reflection as I continue on the path of further clarification and development.

Guiding Philosophy in Conducting Therapy

Values

As defined in Chapter 5, values are the social entity's statement of how it should think and behave. In this book is my view of what values apply to Process Family Therapy.

1. A basic objective of therapy should be to assist clients in developing basic coping skills that are applicable to any problem.

2. Therapy should, implicitly and explicitly, seek to aid clients in achieving respect for self and for the needs, feelings, and behavior of others for the benefit of all concerned.

3. A social entity (individual, couple, or family) should be accountable for its behavior as separate from the outcome of that behavior when variables beyond its control influence the desired outcome. An athlete who played well in a game that the team lost should be able to feel good about his performance and sad they did not win. A participant in family therapy who feels she performed well should feel good about her performance even though the therapy did not accomplish the desired goal.

4. Therapists should consciously monitor that their gender does not inappropriately influence the diagnosis or way in which therapeutic intervention is managed (McGoldrick, Anderson, & Walsh, 1989); Van Den Bergh & Cooper, 1986; Reiker & Carmen, 1984). This applies to both men and women. Both are capable of introducing distortions through the lens of their own gender. Men have been more obvious and guilty of doing this; women are also capable of these same distortions, either in reaction to male distortions or by reflecting the biases they have learned on their own or from their mentors.

5. A preferred approach to therapy is from an eclectic point of view. Each perspective of individual and family therapy adds its own unique contribution to understanding and relating to observed behavior. The multidimensional lens will provide a perspective with more depth than any one orientation, Process Family Therapy included.

6. For some therapists the therapeutic relationship is defined in a hierarchical fashion where the therapist is the knowledgeable one in charge of the proceedings and the client has little to say about what happens. I find it more effective to view therapy as a partnership in which therapist and client work together to help the client learn how to cope with the issues that brought her (them) to seek therapy. This approach has the advantage of encouraging more responsibility on the part of the client and contributes to minimizing the development of nonproductive dependency. In so doing, it provides an added basis for the client to take ownership of what is accomplished in therapy.

7. A therapist should communicate a sense of impartiality to the family over the course of each session. In the process of doing this, it may be necessary and/or desirable to be partial to one or another subunit during the course of the session. This is consistent with Boszormenyi-Nagy's (Boszormenyi-Nagy & Krasner, 1986) concept of multilateral impartiality.

8. A therapist should not make decisions for clients except under unique circumstances of incapacity, such as need for involuntary hospitalization,

or when clients are otherwise not able to function. Such responsibility should be terminated as soon as the client is able to make decisions for herself.

9. A therapist should seek to understand and respect the cultural framework of the family. It is the therapist's responsibility to develop a therapeutic framework that is compatible with both the family and the therapist as described in Chapter 2. When this is not possible, the family should be referred to another therapist. If this should occur, the inability to find a common culture should be understood as a joint responsibility by the family and the therapist. It should not be viewed as the family's failure with the "resistance to treatment" label or any other one.

10. All actions by a therapist should be performed only if they are in service of the client social entity. A therapist needs to have an ever-present self-monitoring system or some form of consultation relationship to ensure that this value is practiced.

11. A therapist should know her vulnerabilities and blind spots so that she can protect the social entity from having therapy compromised by them.

12. A therapist must not exploit her client social entity or subject it to any form of physical, emotional, sexual, or material abuse.

13. A therapist is obligated to respect the confidence of the client social entity. Information gained from one social entity should not be shared with another one without express permission for what is shared.

14. A client should be free to express whatever thoughts or feelings she may have without having to feel judged or responsible for the feelings of the therapist.

15. The length of the therapy session should be determined by the need of the client social entity, their ability to function in a given time frame, the comfort level of the therapist, and the practicalities of available time.

Beliefs

In Chapter 5, *beliefs* were defined as a statement of a social entity's perception of reality. In this context they refer to my beliefs about the conduct of therapy.

1. People usually seek therapy when they have exhausted their own resources for coping with their problems, except when therapy is mandated by others, such as the courts or schools.

2. Every action has an emotional and an intellectual component. With rare exceptions, emotions will be the primary determinant of behavior when they are sufficiently strong and in conflict with intellect. In effect, feelings will short-circuit rational processing when they become too intense for the client social entity's ability to cope with them.

3. Every person functions in multiple modes: individual, spouse, family member, occupation, friend, athlete, organizational member, and so on. People may develop difficulties in how to function in a particular mode and, very commonly, in how to behave in multiple modes in a way that is compatible with other modes (see Chapter 4). Problems also develop when people have trouble switching from one mode to another, for example, a father who is in trouble making the transition from his work mode to being husband and father. The problem is more difficult when needing to operate in two modes that are incompatible.

4. The way a social entity relates to coping with current needs, resources, and abilities is filtered through the lens of accumulated history, its "experience reservoir." This may be with conscious or unconscious awareness.

5. Therapy has a greater likelihood of being successful when the therapist is able to ask which method is needed to best help the client social entity resolve its problems rather than how to use a particular method to accomplish the same objective.

6. Two sources of problems social entities encounter are ambiguity in their value and belief system and difficulty in resolving conflicts in these systems. When this happens, people become vulnerable to being unduly influenced to behave according to the values and beliefs of other people. When such vulnerability is exploited, people are subject to varying degrees of dysfunction: physical and emotional abuse, cults, and exploitation by others.

7. Every social entity develops its own map for how to perceive and interpret life experiences. Problems develop when these maps are in conflict with one another and when one social entity attempts to impose its map on another one.

8. Clients will respond to a therapist who provides a safe environment in which they can say what they think or or feel without feeling judged or having responsibility for the therapist's feelings.

9. People will gain self-confidence and self-respect when they are able to hold themselves accountable for their own behavior and not judge themselves by desired outcomes that involve behavior or circumstances they do not control.

10. People will leave therapy for a variety of reasons including when their needs are met, they feel judged or shamed, more is asked of them than they feel they can give, too much is asked too fast, they are asked to face something they cannot or do not want to face, they are not validated or acknowledged, they experience undue partiality over time, there are not results, they experience pain without seeing it leading anywhere, or they otherwise feel disrespected.

11. Transition points in life experience are times of particular vulnerability (Chapter 8). Failure to manage them successfully will lead to dysfunction.

12. A major determinant of behavior is the benefit-cost balance as described in Chapter 9.

13. The balance in developmental sequences between validating experiences and those that are invalidating (Chapter 7) is an important determinant in how a social entity perceives itself.

14. For me, the advantages outweigh the disadvantages for one therapist to see different social entities in the same family. Such an arrangement permits the benefits gained from each therapeutic unit to benefit the other. This may be done directly or indirectly when confidential issues are involved. Working with multiple social entities in the same family is a circular process. Material gained in couple therapy can be utilized in individual therapy to help the client understand what she does to get into trouble. The reverse is also true. The therapist can assist the client to apply understanding gained in individual work to couple therapy as needed. Such possibilities become more cumbersome, if even possible, when each treatment modality has a different therapist.

The same principle applies when working with a family with the addition that the number of treatment possibilities multiply. In a family of four the treatment entities that are often relevant are the parents singly, the couple, one or both parents with one or more of the children, the children alone, or some other combination of children.

To work with more than one social entity in a family effectively requires that the therapist be comfortable in these multiple treatment relationships. One challenge in doing so is not to get too identified with one treatment entity. When engaging in such therapy, there is the potential problem of dealing with secrets. I deal with this in the following manner:

   a. I do not carry messages from one person to another. My responsibility is to help people learn to speak for themselves.
   b. When people have secrets, I help them decide whether to share them with their spouses or other family members. This involves evaluating the consequences of when it is shared and when not. Secrets that involve suicidal intent or plans to harm another person are stated to the client as exceptions as required by law or out of concern for the client.
   c. If I am not comfortable knowing a secret and fear that I might inadvertently reveal it in some form, then I do not do both individual and couple work. Except in rare cases, I do not find that working with clients both single and jointly interferes with therapeutic outcome. Quite to the contrary, I believe the reverse is true. A tenuous level of trust by one member of the client social entity is a contraindication for such a therapeutic program. Another case is when the therapist would be too uncomfortable to work both individually and jointly.

15. A major way to effect change is to change the context in which

a given behavior is evaluated. A man may interpret his wife's suggestion as nagging when he considers her as hypercritical. The same behavior might be interpreted as supportive if he considers her as a caring person. This formulation is the basis for the concept of reframing.

16. Familiarity is a powerful determinant of behavior. Many people prefer to continue to behave in less than desirable experiences that are familiar rather than risk the uncertainty of the unknown.

17. Once a behavior pattern is established, it may not respond to modification once the cause is eliminated that originally gave rise to it. Changing such patterns of behavior may be accomplished using methods for modification of undesirable habit patterns.

18. The therapeutic process is most effective when it is integrated in the total life experience. In most cases, I liken it to an educational model. The therapy hour is like the classroom where the goal is to understand the concept and how to relate to it. The homework done outside the classroom is when learning really is assimilated. The same applies to therapy. The therapy hour is where the underlying sources of dysfunctional behavior are understood and the means for correcting them are gained. Such learning becomes best integrated into a person's behavior when it is actively applied to all relevant aspects of client's life space.

Goals

These are the primary goals of therapy:

1. To help clients define their problems, define what options for coping with them are available or attainable, define what consequences go with each of these options, evaluate priorities, arrive at a decision they are willing to take as their own, and learn to cope with undesirable consequences that cannot be avoided.

2. To help clients acquire needed resources, within themselves or from others, for coping with problems.

3. To gain the ability to generalize the learning from therapy to apply to solving other problems.

4. To learn how to communicate effectively one's feelings and to be able to hear the same from others.

5. To gain needed skills in how to avoid emotional and physical abuse.

6. To define clear boundaries in relationships that are open to information flow both ways and with a clear definition of what is acceptable behavior.

Process Family Therapy Guidelines

First Telephone Contact

1. I prefer to do my own intake because the relationship starts at this point when people are often most vulnerable.

2. I generally do not get very much information on the telephone. At minimum, I obtain basic identifying information that includes who they are and the general nature of the problem. How much I get depends on the stress level of the person calling, how ready she is to talk on the telephone, and information needed for making an appointment.

3. I let the caller decide who should come in for the first session after discussing the options. If they do not have a preference, I request that the largest relevant social entity attend: individual, couple, family, or any other appropriate subunit of the family, or other relevant people outside the family.

First Phase of Therapy

The first phase of therapy may be accomplished in one or more sessions. The goals for this phase include:

1. Definition of the presenting problem in behavioral terms and what kind of behaviors are a problem and for whom.

2. Definition of the core problem. Oftentimes social entities present specific problem issues that take many forms but are different expressions of the same underlying issue. A wife may complain about a variety of things that her husband does or does not do. The underlying issue may be that she does not feel loved by her husband or that his behavior activates the unresolved anger she has at the way her father treated her. Attempts to focus too much at the manifest level can contribute to an unnecessary dependency and minimize development of the competence to cope independently with underlying issues.

3. Definition of what resources are needed to cope with the diagnosed problems. This includes who should be involved, how available they are for participation and to what extent they have the motivation and skills for participation in therapy (Chapter 1).

4. If sufficient resources are not available and not obtainable, therapeutic goals will need to be modified accordingly.

5. Determine the basic working contract regarding fee, use of insurance, length of session, who attends, and the like, as discussed in Chapter 2.

The length of my sessions are regulated and commonly go for one or two hours. I arrived at this approach because I found people vary in what is a productive work segment. In my experience this varies from half an hour to four hours on a regular basis. When needed, the length of the first appointment is longer than the usual. This is often the case when it involves family members traveling from a long distance or when it is likely that a certain degree of work needs to be done in the first session. Another option when family members come from a long distance is to meet in an open-ended session, usually on a weekend.

One format is to meet for the morning, break for lunch, and meet in the afternoon for as long as needed. The break for lunch serves two purposes: to recharge energies and to reflect on the proceedings of the morning. I also usually give some task for the family to discuss over lunch. I will not do this if too much stress was generated in the morning.

The second format is also done on a weekend. It involves the same kind of morning session as in the first format. We break after the morning session. I give the family a task to work on for our meeting the next day. Another reason for the extended break is to provide the family the opportunity to see if they can work on the discussed issues on their own. If this is successful, they get positive reinforcement and confidence in their ability to cope better with their relationships. If they got stuck, it provides an opportunity to help them find ways to cope with such conflicts while the issues are still very current. Before the family leaves after the second session, I do whatever I can to be sure that sufficient closure was achieved for family members who could attend only these sessions.

6. Determine the nature of the family's value and belief systems. This should also include a determination of the family's cultural background and how to relate to it in a way that is respectful and in service of therapeutic goals. Doing this provides needed insight in understanding the family's map for interpreting their experiences.

7. Determine to what degree all of the participants, including the therapist, are talking about the same problem in a language that is understandable to all concerned.

8. Develop a therapeutic plan with the family's participation for coping with defined problem areas.

Middle Phase of Therapy

The therapist is in an ongoing process of making decisions of how to proceed in some combination of three areas: to what degree to focus on process and/or content, whether to work with the literal or symbolic content, and what combination of focus on affect and intellect to follow.

Implementation of an intervention and evaluation procedure is a circular process following the model described in Chapter 3. This involves the cycle of observation, hypothesis formulation, intervention, evaluation, modification of hypothesis, more data gathering, and so on and continuation of this cycle to a successful conclusion.

Various therapeutic tools are used to accomplish therapeutic goals, which are described later in this chapter. Clients are aided to define destructive patterns and to develop procedures for replacing them with constructive patterns of behavior. Assistance is provided in defining and implementing a way to monitor that the desired changes are happening. The work of therapy is not always done in a continuous block of time. Some families intentionally or unintentionally accomplish their goals in steps. They accomplish a certain amount in therapy and for one reason or another interrupt it and then return at some later time for additional work. The return is usually prompted by a new crisis or slippage of the attained progress.

As the major objectives of therapy approach completion, the therapist begins to prepare the client entity for functioning on its own.

Closure Phase

As the family increasingly demonstrates effective incorporation of new behaviors, more time is given between sessions to gain added confidence in applying their new learning and to determine areas or conditions of potential vulnerability. When an appropriate comfort and confidence level is reached, this phase is concluded with one of two options: return for additional therapy is placed on an as-needed basis or a follow-up or checkup session is scheduled for some time in the future, such as six months, at which time retained progress is assessed and the need for any further therapy is determined.

An additional task of this phase is to review the therapeutic experience. The first part is done with the client and includes the client's and therapist's views of the positive and negative aspects of the therapeutic experience. The second part is the therapist's private assessment of the pros and cons of the therapeutic experience and what learning can be gained for application in her future work.

Therapeutic Tools

In the course of practice, every therapist develops her own array of tools for accomplishing therapeutic goals. In this section I will describe tools I find useful. Some of these are variations of what other therapists do, and I developed the others. When I have used or adapted the work of others, I indicate the source from which I drew it. Otherwise, I developed the tool myself. I have not listed another source necessarily if I have developed a tool in parallel to another therapist. These tools are listed in seven categories based on the primary purpose they are intended to accomplish. This listing is over-simplified in that these tools vary in the degree to which they apply to more than one category. The following categories are used:

1. Diagnosis
2. Expression of feelings
3. Improve awareness
4. Improve the social unit concept
5. Improve communication skills
6. Improve coping skills
7. Integrate learning

Diagnosis

Autobiography or Time Line
One aspect of clinical training was the importance of good history tak-ing. At times taking a history became rather tedious. I began to wonder whether there were other ways to accomplish the same thing. It occurred to me that having people write autobiographies would be useful to both me and them. I ask them to describe significant positive and negative emotional events in their lives. For those people who found such writing too demanding, I asked them to do a time line of the same emotional highlights. This involves listing these significant events in chronological order with some minimal description. Almost everyone was able to do one form or the other of this task.

These methods were useful in two ways. I had not fully anticipated that clients would find it as useful to review their history as I expected. My con-cern that the task might stir up too much anxiety was unfounded. When this did happen, it facilitated their getting involved in therapy. At times it helped overcome anxiety about therapy because it focused their attention on a clearly defined task. What also helped in this process was that I would review the autobiography or time line material in therapy. Doing so helped me get in-formation quickly in a way that was of interest to the clients and that also gave information about their emotional priorities.

Modified Genograms
I use modified genograms consistent with the basic principles described by McGoldrick (McGoldrick & Gerson, 1985). I found genograms useful in describing the skeletal structure of the family. The process of doing it led me to wonder what added insights the structure of emotional threads in the

family would add. To get this information, I asked the client to give a thumbnail description of each member of the family. Such descriptions provided information on the emotional profile of genogram constituents. Patterns usually emerged that showed characteristics that were shared by people across generations and within generations. Such findings give rise to insights and hypotheses about family dynamics. In one family the similarity in descriptions of the client, her mother, maternal grandmother, and maternal great-grandmother gave a clue to an important identification linkage that very quickly led to helping the client separate her own identity.

Positive and Negative Role Models

Much of the social learning is based on role modeling. I usually ask what significant positive and negative role models influenced a person and in what way. Often such conversation leads to discovery of influential role models of which the person was not aware. This is always part of the discussion in reviewing genogram and autobiographical material.

Evaluation of Family Direction and Resources

The material gained from the autobiography and the genogram is focused on a historical view of the family. I found it useful to add a cultural perspective that involved a brief review of the major family values, beliefs, goals, and resources that guide their behavior (see Chapter 5 and 6). Such information quickly illuminates problem areas and resources that may not otherwise be readily identified. The acquisition of this combined information facilitates the determination of what is needed to create a viable therapeutic culture.

Family Drawings

An excellent way to get a new perspective on a family is through the use of drawings (Landgarten, 1987; Snider, 1971; Kwiatkowska, 1967a and 1967b). This is particularly useful for families for whom discussion is not a comfortable way of relating. I discovered this method during my visit to the National Institute of Mental Health in Bethesda, Maryland, when I visited there in 1967. A sculptress, Hanna Kwiatkowska (1967b), developed a six-step experience for working with families. Each member of the family is provided with an easel, a large newsprint pad, and a box of colored chalk or marking pens. The easels are all in a circle where each person's work is visible to all of the others. Family members are asked to perform each of the following tasks:

1. Make a drawing of anything they wish to draw.
2. Make a family drawing of all members of the family, including the

person drawing it. They are asked to draw the full body; stick figures are not acceptable.

3. Make an abstract family drawing. Instead of drawing each figure as in step 2, they are asked to draw something that represents that person, something they think of when they think of that person.

4. They are instructed to close their eyes and make a scribble on the page. They are directed to look at the scribble and make a drawing from the scribble. They are permitted to add any lines they need and ignore any lines they choose.

5. They are directed to make another scribble in the same way as they did in the previous exercise. After this is done, the family members are instructed to look at each other's scribbles and choose one of them on which the family will work together as a group to develop a single drawing. This task provides a very useful perspective on family dynamics in a very unobtrusive way.

6. Repeat the first step.

After each task, each person describes to the others what she has done. The observing family members are given an opportunity to react to the presentation, which may or may not lead to a group discussion.

This exercise provides a great deal of information on different levels about each individual and how the family members relate to each other. It has the advantage of being a fun activity that does not focus on difficult subject matter and utilizes experiences with which all are familiar. It is difficult to censor performance because there is no obvious good or bad answer.

Information is provided on the following dimensions:

1. How each person related to the task, used the space, approached making her drawings, used color, saw herself in relation to other family members, described her drawing, and reacted to the description of others.

2. How family members interact during the exercise. Are they competitive, cooperative, supportive, or disruptive? In some families information gained from my observation of interaction is more informative than information gained from the drawings.

This exercise requires at least an hour and is comfortably done in two hours. The size of the family and its ease of communication will influence whether additional time is needed beyond the norm. The repetition of this exercise is also useful as a means to assess change. I use a minimum time interval of about six months.

Family Photos

Krause and Fryrear (1983) discuss ways in which photography can be used in therapy. The use of family photos is an easy way to get a good perspective on a family by asking an individual to bring in the family photo album. This accomplishes several purposes at the same time:

1. It provides a visual image of family members and significant others. It shows any abnormalities regarding physical appearance that might not otherwise be mentioned. It may also provide information about physical similarities between family members that may have dynamic significance.

2. It may identify people who are missing or who have had significant impact on the family in the past and otherwise might not be mentioned.

3. It may help to identify relationships that were different in the past than they are in the present. This is particularly the case when the anger and frustration of the present distort memories of what occurred in the past.

4. It may also provide information on changes in the family's economic status over time.

5. Photos can also help to trigger associations that otherwise might not be remembered. At times this can trigger blocked affect.

Interview without Questions

Some families find it difficult to talk about details of family life for one reason or another. Attempts to interview such families are difficult, frustrating, and sometimes not possible. I evolved a method for conducting interviews that did not require asking any questions. This method is also very useful with verbal families. I find that I can learn a lot about individuals and how family members interact within thirty to sixty minutes. There are two versions of this method. The process is the same in both cases, but the materials are different. One version is for families with latency-age children, and the other is for older children.

In families with latency-age children I use small blocks, Legos, or some similar form of materials. For other families I use a collection of miscellaneous materials that includes rubber bands, cups, string, hangers, ribbon, styrofoam balls, straws, paper bags, paper, paper clips, and any other materials that are handy. The tasks are similar for both types of families.

Instructions for Families with Latency-Age Children

1. The blocks are put in the middle of the floor, and the children are each asked to make something out of the blocks at the same time. The parents do not participate but observe the process.

2. The children are asked to agree on one thing that they will build together.

3. The children are asked to compete in seeing who can build the tallest building that can stand by itself in an allotted time. Pressure is added by making the task time-limited.

4. Step 2 is repeated with each parent included separately.
5. Step 2 is repeated with both parents jointly participating.

Steps 4 and 5 are included to see how each parent relates to the children in a joint task and how things change when both parents participate jointly. After each step the participants describe what they made.

Instructions for Families with Older Children
A box with all of the materials is placed in the center of the room.

1. All members of the family are asked to create something using the materials provided. Parents are included in this step because the task is more age-appropriate. (In retrospect, parents in younger families might also be given the opportunity to participate in the first step.)
2. The children are asked to create something jointly.
3. The children are asked to compete in creating something with the parents acting as judges.
4. Step 2 is repeated with each parent separately.
5. Step 2 is repeated with both parents jointly.

After each step the participants describe what they created.

Observation of families in this exercise provided very useful and largely uncensored information on self-concept, how people approach a task, ability to focus and work under pressure, how they deal with frustration, how parents relate to their children separately and jointly, and how children's behavior is affected by participation of parents. Additional information is gained when reactions to the experience can be shared. Such discussions provide valuable information about how people perceive themselves and their relationships with each other.

"Fly-on-the-Wall" Observation of Interaction
A frequent topic of discussion in therapy is the problem people have in talking to each other. Understanding the nature of this problem gets more difficult when family members do not agree on what happens. It remains unclear how much the presence and active participation of the therapist distorts the way family members relate to one another. I looked for a way to get to see how family members relate without therapist involvement.

I tried an approach that involved telling the family that it was difficult to get an idea of how they actually related to each other when I was part of the process. To overcome this I suggested they discuss any subject of interest to them as a family without involving me in any way.

In the absence of structure provided by the therapist, the "gravitational pull" of the family's natural style will come into play. This structure forces the family to relate in a more normal fashion. At first, the discussion is likely to be forced and awkward. Once they get into a specific topic, the relevancy of the topic and vested interests dominate, with the result that inhibitions commonly become secondary. This method provides the opportunity to make a number of assessments about family interaction in a very brief period that might otherwise be more elusive.

I found that couples and families get into styles of interacting that they describe as pretty typical of discussions they have at home. The degree to which this happens when the therapist is not part of the process is usually a surprise to the families because their initial response to the task is typically doubt that it would work because the context was too artificial.

After the discussions I ask them to reflect on their conversations. I then give my feedback on my observations. An added potent benefit is obtained when the discussion is taped by either audio or video. The use of this technique is discussed later in this chapter.

This exercise provides information on a number of variables: who takes leadership in defining the topic, the content of the topic, the degree of risk the family is willing to take in what they talk about, who participates, how they participate, styles of participation, expression of affect, kinds of conflict that arise and how they resolve them, what if any conclusions are reached, how they are accomplished, and the way the family assesses the discussion after it is over. A more detailed description of this process follows.

Selection of Topic.   The selection of topic may vary depending on the therapist's goals asnd the receptivity of the family to the task.

- *By the Client.* Selection of topic is made by the client when I do not have a specific topic I would like them to discuss, giving them control over the topic is important, or I anticipate that my giving them a specific topic might be difficult or threatening.
- *By the Therapist.* I may ask them to talk about a specific topic when the content has some particular relevance and when I feel it would be within their capability and emotional tolerance to do so. I may select a particular topic because it might shed light on how they get into unresolvable conflict situations.

Ground Rules for the Exercise.   I define the exercise subject to the following ground rules. The family is asked to:

1. Decide on a topic of current interest that is relevant to them as a group when the topic is their choice.
2. Discuss the subject in as natural a way as possible.
3. Do not involve the therapist in the discussion directly or indirectly:

avoid looking at her, do not direct any comments at her, and do not ask any questions. To facilitate this process, I tell them that I will sit out of their line of sight or observe them from behind a one-way mirror. To further assist in the process, I avoid any eye contact. Once the family gets going, I found that I could observe without distracting them from the assigned task.

4. Do not have any physical interaction. They are informed that violence or throwing things is not permitted.

5. Do not leave the room during the exercise.

They are told that I will terminate the exercise when I have the desired information.

Termination of the Exercise. I terminate the exercise under one or more of the following conditions: I feel I have obtained adequate information, the discussion is becoming nonproductive and at risk of becoming destructive, one or more of the members show signs of discomfort that are not being expressed or recognized, family members start to turn to the therapist either verbally or nonverbally, or they indicate a desire to stop the discussion.

The length of the exercise can vary. I found that a great deal of information can be gained in as little as five or ten minutes, depending on the family. A common workable range both for the therapist and the family ranges from five to twenty minutes.

Processing Reaction to the Exercise. After the exercise I process the experience with the family. I ask a number of questions that include how long they perceive the exercise lasted, how much the discussion was like what went on at home, how they felt about the content of the discussion, how they felt about the way they interacted, and whether they felt acknowledged by other family members. Having the observed interaction as a reference point tends to put the office interview in the perspective of what goes on at home. This exercise leads to a more open and less protective way of discussing what happens outside the session. I think this happens because the family experiences that the exposure of their vulnerability is not judged, and thus it instills some confidence that the therapeutic environment is a relatively safe place to take risks.

Variations in the Use of This Exercise. For some families this exercise can be used productively on some regular or periodic basis. It can be useful for families that get caught up in intellectual discussions. The heat of the here-and-now discussions works well in cutting through such communication styles. It can also be helpful in discussions where people talk about feelings rather than express them. This approach has the subtle impact of training a family in how to shift communication patterns in a way that emphasizes self-discovery as opposed to direction coming from the therapist.

Another variation of this exercise is to have one or both of the parents conduct a family business meeting as though they were at home. In this case, I ask the parents to run a business meeting of the family in the way they might do on their own. I define ground rules in the same way as described previously. This variation has the additional benefit of providing information on the way in which they approach the problem solving. I am interested in observing who provides the leadership and how they deal with power issues and division of labor. I am also interested in the way they deal with boundary issues in relating to their children. Also noteworthy is whether any triangulation exists between father, mother, and children. When it exists, I am interested in what form it takes and how it gets managed.

After the exercise, which would operate in the same time frame described previously, I process the experience with the family in the same manner that was described earlier. The ultimate objective is to aid the family in culling what learning they can identify in the experience that can be applied in their daily relationships. This includes a discussion of how to accomplish such generalization.

Messages from Significant Others

It is a common occurrence for people to assume that the way they interpret a message from another person is the way it was intended. One of the objectives of therapy is to help people understand how such an assumption can contribute to strained relationships. What I frequently do in a family session focused on conflict is to ask people what messages they got from what they heard. It never ceases to amaze me how differently people can interpret the same message, even though I can understand why this happens.

Asking this kind of question is particularly useful in conjunction with genograms or autobiographies. In doing a genogram, I will usually ask something like, "What message did you get from the way X person treated you?" or "What message did you get from that experience?" In the case of a couple arguing, I ask, "What message do you get from what X is saying and doing?"

It is not safe to assume that the context in which the therapist hears a person's history will be the same in which the reporting social entity experienced it. One client once described what sounded like an emotionally abusive relationship with her father. When I asked her what message she got from him when he behaved that way, she replied, "That's his way of showing he loves me."

Defining Common Map

It is natural to assume that the way a person perceives her environment and experience is shared by others. It is easy for a therapist to forget that people enter therapy with very different maps for perceiving life experiences. The same applies to how families relate to one another. In both of these situations and in any situation where people seek to communicate, the success of the interaction is going to depend to a significant degree on how well the participants are operating from a common map or understand in what ways they are operating from different maps. A classic example is the parent who expects or assumes that her adolescent child is operating from the same map as she is. Some semblance of a working relationship is achieved when both of them learn to find a mutually satisfactory map of their relationship. Accomplishing this is one of the tasks that is part of successful therapy.

Expression of Feelings

Art Making

Frequently people are at a loss to express what they are feeling in words. I found a way to help in such situations. I have an easel, a ready supply of newsprint pads, and marking pens. I ask the client to draw something that would express how they are feeling. The instruction may be feelings in general or specific to a particular situation.

I once saw a young man of 14 who was very tight-lipped and had a hard time verbalizing what he felt (Snider, 1971). On one occasion we were talking about his relationship to his father. It was clear that he had a lot of angry feelings toward him but was not able to express them. After being frustrated in various attempts to help him, the thought occurred to me that he might be able to express his feelings in a drawing. At first, I dismissed this because I thought it would seem a bit weird to ask somebody to draw something as vague as this. Because I had no better alternative, I decided to ask him anyway.

To my surprise, he thought for a few moments and then with more characteristic energy and attention proceeded to fill the page with lines and curves of different colors going in all directions. The visual image seemed to mirror his many different feelings about his father. After a while he stopped and stared at the palm of his hand as though in deep thought. After a brief period he put two or three different colors of pastel chalk on his palm and then in a sudden and abrupt movement smashed his palm into the middle of the page, which resulted in smudged prints of different colors. He said with an air of authority and finality, "That's what I think of my father." This opened the door to a fruitful discussion about their relationship.

Foam Rubber Bats

Foam rubber bats are useful in helping people who have difficulty in expressing their feelings. They are made of sturdy foam about two feet long and six inches in diameter with a handle at one end that is protected by a guard where it is held. One way it can be used is as a sword. It permits two people to hit at each other using large muscles without fear of hurting each other. As in a fencing match, the objective is to hit your opponent without getting hit in return. It can serve as a way of expressing anger at another person that is not otherwise possible. It can be a release for the person doing the hitting, and it gives the recipient some idea of the depth of feeling that was felt but not expressed. Oftentimes this comes as a great surprise. Such an encounter, which may only be a few minutes, can cut through resistance and open up new ways to communicate on an emotional level that was difficult if not impossible before the experience.

I was working with one family composed of a physician, his wife, and two sons, ages 10 and 12. In the weeks preceding the use of these bats, the father came across as a pleasant man with flat affect even during difficult discussions, which were usually on an intellectually level. I thought the bats would be useful to see how this family would handle nonverbal expression of their feelings. It was striking to see the contrast in behavior when the father picked up the bat. It was as though someone turned on a light in the dark. He became animated and highly energized as he swung his bat with erratic, sweeping, powerful moves. It shocked the other members of the family, who were both amused and frightened to see this kind of behavior unleashed with a vehemence they had not previously seen. This experience led to discussions of feelings in ways that were quite different than before the exercise.

Another use for these bats is to permit expression of feelings by using them to hit a chair or pillows. This works well when it is based on feelings toward a particular person or situation and is accompanied by what the person wielding the bat would like to say to this person or situation but never could. The expression of such emotion often permits discussion of the relationship in a more constructive manner.

Puppets

Puppets have long been a mainstay of play therapy. I found an additional use for them in families with small children where parents have difficulty in communicating with their children. I ask each member of the family to select one or two puppets and have a conversation between the puppets. I find such conversations revealing, both between different members of the family and also when they reflect intrapersonal issues (when one person has puppet in each hand). Puppets are useful in providing both children and parents a means to communicate in ways that otherwise are uncomfortable. In providing distance from their normal roles, it permits the participants to talk and disagree without control issues getting in the way. One of the reasons this happens is that the puppets provide a fun context and a way for discussion to be held in the third person, which provides enough distance to facilitate discussions that might otherwise be difficult. The subjects for discussion are drawn from the current issues in therapy.

Journals
The use of journals serves a number of useful purposes:

1. A means for recording feelings and events that might easily be forgotten.
2. A way to monitor progress on attempts at changing behavior.
3. A means for self-expression of uncomfortable feelings.
4. A means for measuring progress over a period of time. It is often hard to assess change when it occurs in small, often unnoticeable increments. It is useful and sometimes quite surprising for someone to realize how much progress she made when she is able to document change over a period of time.

Improve Awareness

Video Feedback
Video is an established tool for work with families (Berger, 1970). It is used in various ways: to review sessions in preparation for other sessions and for teaching, research, and demonstration purposes. To my knowledge little attention has been paid to use of video by the family.

A number of years ago I came to the realization that if video review is useful for therapists, would it not also be equally useful for a family to review? This led to the added reminder that each of us is capable of observing others, but we do not ordinarily get the chance to observe ourselves except in the occasional home movie or video. The same applies to the family as a unit. People commonly observe other families but usually do not have the opportunity to observe themselves in ways that would be relevant in therapy.

One day while I was seeing a family who had a very distorted view of how they related to one another, it occurred to me that it would be very helpful if they could see themselves in action. I asked for permission to videotape our sessions so they could see how they relate to each other from the perspective of an observer. They were intrigued by the idea and readily accepted the invitation.

Two variables that initially needed to be considered were how much to tape and how to handle the observation. A number of possible options were considered:

1. Tape a whole session and take the next session to review selected segments of the tape for discussion.
2. Tape a portion of a session such as half of it, and in the second half of the session review random or selected parts of the session for review and discussion.
3. Tape a session and stop for review and discussion after segments of particular interest to either the family or the therapist.
4. Tape a session and have a family come in and review the tape on their own for discussion at the next session. In this case the family would be asked to perform one or more of the following tasks:
   a. The family is asked to come to a consensus about the significant observations gained from the taped sessions. Doing so would provide interesting data on the content of their discussion and on the process they went through in arriving at their conclusions.
   b. Each member of the family is asked to comment on her own behavior. Each person is also asked to identify segments that were of particular significance to her and describe why she thought so. This could be done in two ways: One way would be for them to discuss their observations with each other. This has the disadvantage that those members of the family who did not trust their own judgment or who would be subject to influence or pressure from others would refrain from expressing their views, particularly if observations took the form of criticism and judgment.

      The other way would be for each member to watch the tape, make her own observations, and not discuss it with each other until their therapy session. This would provide some protection and a message to the more vulnerable members of the family that their views do count and that they can be heard.

As in other exercises, the ultimate objective is to assess what the family is able to learn from such observations and how they view applying such learning to changing current patterns of interaction.

Ways to View Video Tapes.   There are several ways to utilize review of video tapes. One way is to play selected segments and discuss them. I generally like to start off a review session in this manner. Doing this provides a base line for what follows. I next replay the video without sound and encourage comments about family members' observations as the tape is playing. Discussion as previously described follows such segments. This nonverbal review of the tape often provides startling revelations to family members such as "Do I do that? I never realized that I made those kind of gestures," or "I never appreciated how angry I can look." Such self-awareness, whether or not publicly acknowledged, is very powerful because it comes from the person observing herself and thus is not subject to the defensiveness that might be present when hearing it from others. The significant impact is that what is experienced is not something to debate, and the client is confronted with how to relate to the new information. Even when such observations become subject to suppression or denial, they still leave a mark and tend to lower the threshold for receiving future information that carries the same message.

This experience is followed up by the reverse procedure without video. The video portion is turned off and the family is directed to listen to the audio portion, similar to what would be done in reviewing an audiotape. The same procedure is followed as was described when viewing the video without sound. The results can be as revealing and useful in a somewhat less dramatic fashion.

Role of Devil's Advocate

Some client social units have difficulty in accepting any feedback that sounds negative or critical. One way that I found useful in diffusing such situations is to tell them that I would like to take the devil's advocate position. Doing this appears to shift the context from one of personal judgment to an exercise in exploring new ways to consider issues of concern.

I tell them I would like to help them expand their thinking by raising challenging questions about issues that came up in our discussion. I explain that the objective is not to be critical but to discover new options.

Story Telling

People vary in their comfort level in talking about their concerns. When this happens, I attempt to find if they have any other more comfortable means for expression. For some people this involved story telling (Stone, 1989). They are more comfortable giving history in the context of stories than by routine descriptions. I suggest to them that families have stories that they tell about each other around significant or humorous events. I ask what stories are told about them. I am also interested in stories that are meaningful about other members in the family. These may include stories about a favorite pet, a special relationship to a grandparent, special occasions, family rituals, illnesses, and humorous events. Such story telling is very useful because it provides a comfort level that enables a person to reveal their concerns without having to focus on problems.

Making Choices

It is often surprising to find how often people feel trapped in their life circumstances. One way this gets expressed is feeling victimized in situations where they have to cope with unpleasant situations and think they have no choice in what happens. It becomes refreshing to them when they appreciate how often they have more choices in how they can behave than they were aware. This can also be anxiety-provoking for those people who have difficulty making choices or taking responsibility for making them. For some people, living in a victimized position is safer than being accountable for their behavior.

Required, Permitted, and Prohibited Role Behavior

It is often helpful for people to realize how relationships get defined. The use of role theory concepts is helpful in doing this. I help people to recognize that relationships are characterized by three kinds of behaviors: those that are required for a relationship to continue, those that are prohibited if a relationship is to continue, and everything else that is permitted with varying degrees of acceptability. Marital relationships run into trouble when one member of the couple tries to change a behavior from one of these categories to another and the change is unacceptable to the other. At one stage in a relationship, a wife may consider her husband's drinking permissible. After suffering abuse as a result of his drinking, she redefines drinking as prohibited if the relationship is to continue. When this change is unacceptable to him, it becomes a major source of friction in the marriage that might ultimately jeopardize the relationship.

Improve Social Entity Concept

Creative Expression

People are often not aware of resources they possess that may be useful in coping with the problems that confront them. One way to explore such possibilities is to have them bring in any form of personal expression. This might involve painting, poetry, sculpture, photographs, scrapbooks, or stamp collections. Such exploration often reveals emotional sensitivity and understanding not otherwise evident. The therapist can often draw on these resources by helping the client social entity learn to apply them in coping with issues of concern. In one family, a father was seen as remote and not in touch with his feelings. One of his hobbies was oil painting. I asked him to bring in some of his work and was surprised to discover the sensitivity revealed in his art. It proved useful to help him learn to utilize this sensitivity in his relationships with his family.

If it is not possible for clients to bring their work to the office, I go to their home or other appropriate place, when possible, to learn about their interests. Such communication is useful in establishing rapport because it goes beyond normal expectations of a therapist and because it provides an opportunity to talk about something meaningful, positive, and special to the client in a positive context.

Ownership of Accomplishments

A major factor contributing to diminished self-esteem is the failure of a person to make the distinction between the quality of her own performance as separate from the outcome that involves contributions from other people. In doing this, a person loses the benefit of recognizing her competence, which could lead to further failures that would be based on an inaccurate belief. This is the case of a man who does an excellent presentation as part of his company's proposal for a new contract. When the company does not get the contract, he feels he failed. I work with people in learning to value their own performance and not allowing it to be unduly clouded by things they do not control.

Accountability to Self, or the Chameleon Personality

It is common to find that people define themselves by how others perceive them. When they get good feedback, they feel good; when they get negative feedback, they feel bad. Learning to be accountable to oneself is a very liberating experience because people gain a greater sense of control over their lives. Often people are amazed to find how vulnerable they were to being defined by others. I help people become accountable first with themselves for their own behavior. I suggest that when they get feedback from someone else, positive or negative, they put it through their own "intellectual and emotional computer" to decide whether it meets their own standards or ethics. If it does, then they should accept it, which may include feeling good or bad and any appropriate change in behavior. If it does not fit, then they are to comfortably reject it. To accomplish this usually involves either or both understanding the source of destructive patterns from the past and the desire to break current disruptive habits.

Cutting the Emotional Umbilical Cord

Sometimes people have difficulty recognizing how dependent they are on their parents or significant others for defining who they are and how they should behave. I find the metaphor of cutting the "emotional umbilical cord" useful. I suggest that people are born with two umbilical cords: one physical and one emotional. The physical cord is necessarily severed at birth, but the emotional cord need never be broken. Whether this happens is the individual's choice. The simplicity of the imagery seems to cut through what might otherwise seem a more formidable concept. The therapeutic work often involves dealing with unresolved dependency issues that tend to get intertwined with anxiety about incompetence.

Improve Communication Skills

"I"-"You" Statements
Difficulty in resolving relationship problems often results because people complain about the behavior of another person. The accompanying implication is usually that everything would be OK if the other person would change her behavior. Such positions lead only to the other person taking the reverse position. One way to avoid this problem is to help client social entities shift the form of communication from "you are" statements to "I" statements. It is the difference between "You are annoying me" and "I have trouble when you behave that way." Implicit in such awareness is the reminder that the only change a person can accomplish is in herself.

Listening Exercise
A common occurrence in couples with marital problems is their difficulty in sharing feelings. As tensions build, this form of communication gets increasingly constricted. I found a useful way to help such couples interrupt this process.

1. I suggest they find some time toward the end of the day when they can have ten or fifteen minutes uninterrupted.
2. One spouse describes the positive and negative emotional highlights of her day in all areas of her life in "I" statements.
3. The other spouse listens without comment. The only exception is for points of clarification. After the presenting spouse finishes, the listening spouse summarizes what was heard.
4. Steps 2 and 3 are repeated with the spouses reversing positions. The listening spouse now presents his emotional highlights of the day.

Any feelings or issues that need to be discussed that result from this exercise are dealt with at another time. It is important to provide a safe time where each person can be heard and validated without having to deal with decisions or resolution of conflict. The goal is to have this structured exercise gradually shift to a spontaneous interaction.

One client described his experience in the following way: "It remains an important tool that we use to ensure both people are aware of the other's emotional state. With this information comes a greater respect for the other person's position and concern for her emotional well-being."

Say It Another Way
People get used to saying the same thing in the same way. This familiarity carries with it an established way of interpreting the accustomed message. When this message is annoying or threatening, it tends to evoke and reinforce a familiar negative reaction. This begins what often becomes a circular

reaction that increases with negative intensity until it develops into a major argument or one of the participants gives up. One way of breaking this negative mindset is to ask the participants to restate the provocative statements using other words.

Improve Coping Skills

Checking Out Assumptions

For various reasons people often find it easy to treat their assumptions about other people as facts. This becomes a problem when these other people are held accountable for the assumptions that are being made about them. This usually occurs without conscious awareness. I find this particularly prevalent in marital therapy, but it occurs in all relationships. When I work with a couple and hear their complaints about one another, I determine to what extent they are aware of the assumptions they are making and how far they went in checking them out for accuracy. It often comes as a shocking revelation to discover the extent to which assumptions were equated with facts. Such awareness can lead to quick improvement in couples who have a good foundation in their marriage. In more difficult relationships, it facilitates getting to fundamental issues more quickly. In the process of doing this, it gives the couple some positive experience in clearing up some of their difficulties and distortions.

Manage Rather Than Judge

A common way that many people handle difficult situations is to react with judgment. It may be aimed at themselves with guilt, recrimination, shame, or all three. It may be aimed at blaming someone or something else. In such situations I found it helpful to give clients a phrase that helps them to identify and interrupt the process. I suggest to them that, when they find themselves in a difficult spot, "manage rather than judge." I remind them that judging is destructive. Such behavior does not solve any problems and only adds one that results from the judgment. I separate judgment from constructive evaluation of past experience. When faced with a problem situation, I suggest that the issue is not whose fault it is but recognition that something is "broken." Attention should then be directed at how to "fix it." The underlying objective is to shift the mind-set from responsibility for what is wrong to discovering resources from within or from others to resolve the presenting problem(s).

Replacing Destructive Patterns

Replacing dysfunctional patterns requires being able to identify the patterns and means to interrupt them. Identifying these patterns is relatively easy, providing the client social entity is able to tolerate such exploration.

If this is not the case, work must first be done to get to this point. Once this point is attained, the focus shifts to interrupting such behavior. Insight into what contributed to the dysfunctional behavior can be helpful but often is not sufficient for the desired change. One reason for this is that the client social entities may not have the needed skills or resources to accomplish it. Acquiring these needed skills is not too difficult if lack of information is the only reason for not having them. Complications occur when the dysfunctional patterns of behavior have developed a function autonomy; that is, established habitual behavior patterns become entrenched, independent of the original reason why they developed.

I found I could increase clients' confidence in their ability to effect change. I tell them that achieving change is within their ability if they will commit to exercising discipline in implementing the following process, which is done in collaboration with the client.

1. Define the behavior with the object of change in as concrete and observable terms as possible.
2. Define the new desired behavior in as concrete and observable terms as possible.
3. Define the means for implementing the change.
4. Implement the change. I educate the client social entity to accept that changes will only occur when the client is willing to invest the time and energy to make them happen. This often gets into a discussion of the client's fantasy that therapy is like taking an aspirin. You just swallow it and the rest is automatic.
5. Develop a monitoring procedure to insure that the desired behavior has replaced the undesired behavior. The need for this procedure resulted from my frustration in hearing people make pronouncements about the wonderful things they were going to do with the new understanding they had gained in therapy and which then never happened. Added to this frustration was that I was blamed when therapy wasn't working, while actually the client did not do her part. I made a major inroad in changing this situation by employing the concept of monitoring. I would discuss with client social entities that good intentions do not bring about change. Results would only happen if the client made a commitment to defining a specific way to bring about a desired change, and then monitor to make sure it happened. I emphasize my opening comments that the client social entity has the power and the choice to decide whether change takes place.

In one such situation, a woman decided she needed to be more assertive with her husband. She understood why she wasn't and vowed that she would change her behavior. When it didn't happen, I helped her to define specific ways to do this. One suggestion was that she not walk away from an event that bothered her without doing something about it, even if it only involved letting him know that she was bothered. I suggested that at the end of each day she review the events of the day and assess her performance. She could take pleasure in those times that were successful and reinforce her confidence. In those situations in which she did not behave as desired, she could look review and if possible go back the next day and correct her behavior. If this was not possible, then she could, at least, learn what happened and apply that learning to future situations. The added benefit of this monitoring process is that it keeps the desired issue in consciousness, thus increasing the potential for implementation.

Rituals

The dictionary defines *ritual* as a ceremonial act or action that contains any formal and customarily repeated acts or series of acts. Every culture has its rituals, which provide transitions between developmental events. Graduations mark the end of one level of education as a step to another level or other endeavor. Weddings mark the shift from single to marital status. Funerals are a means to acknowledging a death that helps to facilitate the mourning process. These are but samples of the many significant transitions that are part of any culture.

Another function of a ritual is a reminder to all concerned of the changes in values, beliefs, or behaviors that are an appropriate consequence of the ritual. The bar mitzvah boy is now treated as a "man" in the eyes of the Jewish community. In some families, men and women are not treated as having reached maturity until they marry.

A ritual can also be a vehicle for new learning. To gain a new skill usually involves a process of performing a series of acts or repeated acts in a particular manner. This applies to learning to read, drive a car, do math problems, and countless other examples. Once the desired behavior has been sufficiently learned, the ritual increasingly becomes irrelevant. Failure to sufficiently follow the defined ritual, such as learning a new skill, leads to ineffective performance.

Although the function of performing rituals is clear, there are many dimensions that define a ritual. Rituals vary in when they happen, how they happen, how long they take, who participates, when they participate, degree of complexity, degree of importance attached to them, how specifically they are defined, and how they are evaluated.

Rituals are used in two ways in family therapy. They can be used to assess family functioning, and they can be used as a treatment intervention. Any diagnostic test or structured task falls within the definition of a ritual. A standard procedure or series of specifically defined behaviors provides a reference point against which to compare different families as well as to compare the same family over a period of time.

Family therapists vary in the degree to which they conduct family assessments in a ritualistic fashion. Some have a very structured procedure in whom they see and in how they conduct the assessment. John Bell, one of the pioneers in family therapy, would see families only as a whole. He would not see members individually. If such a need was indicated, he would refer them to another therapist. Various schools of thought in family therapy have clearly specified do's and don'ts regarding permissible and impermissible behaviors in conducting family sessions.

Families vary in the degree to which they utilize rituals. The degree and form of a family's ceremonies provide a lot of information about the family structure and culture. It can be very useful as part of obtaining family background to determine what rituals and celebrations are important to the family, when they happen, how they happen, who is involved, who is responsible for ensuring they happen, how long they last, and how they are valued and by whom.

An illustration is the celebration of a holiday such as Thanksgiving. For some families it is the celebration of the year. It may be the one time everybody gets together. How it is viewed and managed gives important perspectives on both the nuclear family and the extended family.

Christmas is another holiday ritual that has the unique dimension involving the giving of gifts and the various ways in which this is managed. Rules tend to get defined as to who buys what kind of gifts for whom. Families tend to have clearly defined rituals for how and when gifts are given and opened. Such exchange of gifts carries with it prescriptions on how the acknowledgment of gifts is managed. It is not uncommon to find that the whole process surrounding the exchange of gifts results in a lot of discomfort because of the pressure and expectation to conform to the ritual of gift giving. For other family members the process is enjoyed and approached with enthusiasm. Accounting for the difference is a useful contribution and opportunity to learn about family relationships and values in ways that avoid the reluctance to discuss such matters when they are dealt with directly in the course of an interview.

Family therapists also use rituals as an intervention. One situation in which I frequently use a ritual is when a person has difficulty coping with a persistent negative aspect of their self-image. One example is to ask them to write down what they dislike about their behavior and in another place the way they want to behave. A recommendation is made to hold a ceremony in front of significant others to honor the occasion. The person is asked to burn or in some other way destroy the list describing the undesired behavior and with it to symbolically give permission to cease functioning in that way. The person is then asked to read to the assembled group what will be the replacement behavior. This ritual provides the support of a public commitment to change and raises the consciousness level for ceasing the old behavior and performing the new behavior. The public commitment also acts as a reinforcer to perform the new behavior. A therapist may also use a ritual to help a family learn new behaviors. An example is when I encourage a family to have regular business meetings. The details of this procedure are disussed elsewhere in this chapter.

Separate Feelings from Actions

People often get into trouble in discussions because they presume that the expression of feelings implies that some course of action should be taken in relation to those feelings. This creates problems when no action is desired or expected. The person expressing the feeling may not want or expect any action to be taken but just needs the opportunity to vent and let her feelings be known and validated. Unrequested or undesired actions can inhibit the opportunity to be able to express feelings. Such actions taken impulsively in reaction to the expression of feelings may be ill considered and add new problems because the actions were inappropriate either for the person expressing the feelings or for the recipient of such feelings. It also can shift attention away from the need to express feelings and to prematurely focus attention on how to cope with the actions taken in response to the feelings.

I find it useful to deal with this type of problem in the following way:

1. I suggest that people function on two channels simultaneously. One is on a rational level and the other is on an emotional level, and the rules are different for each level of functioning.

2. I indicate that most of the time our behavior is determined by some combination of the two.

3. I discuss that when feelings got too intense, they will short-circuit the ability to function on a rational basis. I give the example that when a person is in intense pain her only consideration will be to get rid of the pain—nothing else will matter. Such a phenomenon underlies the basis on which one spouse affects the behavior of the other. In one couple, the wife learned not to reveal her feelings on certain subjects to avoid the pain that would result from her husband's anger when he heard what she had to say. In such situations, the priority of avoiding pain was greater than the desire to have her views heard.

4. I suggest that communication will be most effectively received when a person who expresses pain has her feelings acknowledged, not how or why they got that way. A classic example is the parent who attempts to lecture a child about her misdeeds when she comes seeking help when hurt. Once the pain is attended to, the child will be much more able to deal with the rational message.

5. I recommend that when people have a hard time separating the expression of feelings from taking actions in regard to them, they indicate the need for time to talk about feelings. This is done with the understanding that the only agenda is to discuss feelings. No action statement is to be

implied or wanted in such expression. After feelings are exchanged, then joint attention is directed to what if any actions are desired.

Awareness of Contributions to Conflict

Most arguments involve an exchange of accusastions with the implicit assumption that if the other person changed everything would be fine. One useful way I found to interrupt this process was to help clients recognize that nobody changes another person's behavior. A person can change only her own behavior. I then work to get people to shift from what the other person is doing to look at what each person is contributing to the ongoing difficulty. This is useful because it shifts the focus from criticism and blame to a positive climate in which each person can better understand what she did to contribute to the problem. Such a shift enhances each person's ability to improve the situation.

Time Management

Many people struggle with how to manage time to accomplish all that they would like to do. Frequently individuals and couples present problems about being overstressed and not having enough time to do what they want or what needs to be done. In such cases I find it useful to run through a time management exercise. I conduct this with a couple. I ask them to:

1. List all of their daily activities from the time they get up till the time they go to sleep.
2. Designate the time it takes to accomplish each activity.
3. Assign a priority to each activity.

We then evaluate the data. This exercise is usually sobering to the couple. They often find that they are unrealistic about time commitments. When they run out of time, the first activity to suffer is time together. Such awareness provides insight on why they are having difficulty in the marriage. Other revelations occur when they realize that they differ in how they view the time it takes to do various tasks and in the priorities they attach to getting them done. Awareness of such differences adds insight on the basis of some of their arguments. Such discussion provides the opportunity for redefinition of commitments and how they will resolve differences. It is useful to repeat this exercise in a few months to determine what progress was made and to further clarify problem areas.

Changing Context as a Basis for Change

One of the difficulties clients experience in attempting to make changes in their lives is to try to do things differently. I saw a couple who were struggling in their marriage. They were both overcommitted in their individual pursuits. They were frequently in conflict and did not understand why they were having a difficult time. Efforts to improve the relationship only seemed to add to their problems. When we reviewed the context in which they were functioning, a number of things became clear. They set unrealistic goals and did not allow enough time for their relationship. Their high expectations always left them with a feeling of not making it, no matter how well they did. This awareness led to redefining the context, which involved setting realistic goals, measuring their accomplishments by what they gained rather than by what they did not achieve, and giving a higher priority to time they spent together. This change in the context of how they experienced their relationship led to a great improvement in their level of satisfaction.

In the case of ordinary conversation, how people interpret what they hear and experience is in part a product of the context in which they hear it. Often this is not clear. A man accused his wife of overreacting to his failure to fix a leaky water faucet, which he had promised to do. What he did not know was that this was about the fifth time she experienced this kind of frustration from family members in the past week. This incident with him was the last straw. This is the process that underlies the concept of reframing.

Two-Time Rule

A common occurrence in family meetings is to hear complaints in which one parent is accused of nagging. Parents also express their frustration at not being heard when they express what they consider to be reasonable requests of their children. To help them cope in this situation, I suggest implementation of the two-time rule, which is that a person never repeats the same request more than twice. When the second request does not get results, I recommend that something qualitatively different be done. When Johnny did not pick up his coat from the living room floor after the second request, the recommendation is for the parent to take him by the arm and say, "I've asked you twice to pick up your coat and you didn't do it at your convenience, so you will do it now."

This rule is not limited to parent-child relationships. When a wife asked her husband to fix a broken screen on two occasions and was told he would do it both times with no results, she held him accountable for his lack of performance by requiring a different kind of response, such as a commitment to a specific time when it would be done and what would happen if it was not done as promised. This way of handling such frustrations is very useful because it not only gets a desired task done but also avoids the demeaning experience of not being acknowledged and feeling helpless and angry.

Integrate Learning

Task Assignments outside Therapy

As noted earlier in the discussion on belief, therapy works best when it can operate from an educational model. The therapy sessions are like the classroom where concepts are learned. The major learning derives from the home in applying the new concepts. In this view, therapy is not viewed as something that only happens in the therapist's office. It emphasizes the need for the client to take more responsibility for the outcome of therapy.

The underlying assumption in insight therapy was that such awareness would lead to resolution of the underlying conflict. Experience demonstrated that this was often not sufficient to bring about the desired change. I also discovered there were times that change could come about without insight. This was usually the case where somebody was not able to function for lack of information. Once she gained the needed information, she was quite able to function appropriately.

Further analysis led me to the conclusion that therapeutic results would likely be best achieved when clients understood the nature and source of their problem, which led them to a specific way to interrupt the undesired behavior and replace it with a desirable behavior, as described earlier in this chapter in the section on replacing destructive pattern.

I saw a man who had difficulty in being more assertive. He understood the sources of his problem, but it did not help him change his behavior. The first thing we worked on was to define the assumptions he was making and to check them for accuracy. This involved clarifying unrealistic fears he had about what would happen if he said or did the wrong thing. Then we identified those times when it was a problem for him. He recognized that he experienced tension in his abdomen when this occurred. He made a commitment to assert himself at those times, rather than withdraw, and not to worry about the outcome. I instructed him to take a few minutes each day to review his progress on being assertive that day. Doing this would reinforce when he did well and clarify when he did not behave as he wanted. In these situations, he could correct his behavior the next day if possible. If that was not possible, then he could consider what would help in another situation. In our therapy session, I would review his experience and help him when he got stuck.

Another way to use assignments outside therapy was to interrupt established patterns in couples that were causing problems. A common phenomenon in couples is the wife becoming a social director and resenting that all the responsibilities for these activities falls on her. The first step is to help them understand how they both contributed to this arrangement. I then suggest a model for changing this that they can modify to suit their own situation.

I suggest that they set aside once or twice a week for "dates." Then they are to alternate responsibility for planning and implementing all aspects of the event, initiating the idea and making all the arrangements necessary to carrying it out, including getting a baby-sitter as necessary. The only restriction is that the event is not totally unacceptable to the other person. Usually this exercise brings into focus significant issues and provides a current forum for dealing with them. As needed, I help them refine the process when they get stuck.

Family Meetings

Many families who have trouble relating to each other also have great difficulty managing the daily tasks necessary to family functioning, such as division of labor, appointments that need to be made or kept, planning of family fun activities, and resolving routine conflicts. I suggest to the family that they hold family meetings regularly, such as once a week, at a time that is reasonably convenient for all participants. I also recommend that these meetings be made a high priority, which includes minimizing interruptions and preferably eliminating things such as phone calls or making other commitments. This works well when the time is negotiated. It also is important for the parents to clearly define and enforce the rules on which there was agreement. Everyone should be encouraged to contribute to the agenda. I also recommend that the meeting end with some kind of family fun activity such as singing, game playing, or telling jokes or stories.

A sense of security and trust are enhanced when each meeting is followed up with accountability for follow-through on what was discussed at the previous meeting. When families are able to develop such a process, it can provide a stable, cohesive family experience. This is particularly useful in families where they rarely find time to be together as a family and tend to live parallel lives. Such an exercise provides at least one time during the week when they can all count on being together in a constructive environment.

Frequently families do not know how to organize such meetings or find it too difficult to manage them and the conflicts that occur when such efforts are made. One way of helping families to accomplish the necessary skills is to have one or more family meetings in the office, as described earlier.

Summary

In this chapter I defined the values, beliefs, and goals that underlie the practice of Process Family Therapy. I also described a number of tools I found useful in assisting the achievement of therapeutic goals.

CHAPTER TWELVE

Circular Questioning

I found the Milan method of circular questioning a useful way to conduct a family interview. I experimented with ways to use it in evaluations. I found one method particularly useful, and it is the subject of this chapter.

THEORY

Prior to the Milan Group's contribution of circular questioning (Selvini Palazzoli, Boscolo, Cecchin, & Prata, 1980; Penn, 1982; Tomm, 1985), therapists asked clients questions primarily about themselves or how they related to others. In circular questioning, the emphasis is on asking for a person's views on the relationships and the differences between family members. Some of the ways in which this is accomplished are through "most" and "least" questions with regard to various behaviors and through focus on how one family member perceives the interaction between two or more other family members. They also utilize "what if" questions and "what would so and so" say about a particular behavior or event. In this manner they obtain an understanding of the family structure and family relationships.

I extended this thinking, particularly as it applied to diagnosis, by obtaining each person's view of how another family member would answer a structured set of questions, for example what the mother believed the identified client thought was the reason for the family being in the therapist's office.

Families often assume that because they have discussed a particular issue, they share a common view of the problem. Frequently this is not the case, especially in a relationship where different points of view are not easily tolerated. For people who feel more vulnerable, it is easier to go along and not express their views. This kind of interviewing procedure illuminates important differences between family members in a less threatening context than if people were asked questions directly, which often invites defensiveness and arguing.

Success with this approach led me to an additional variation that involves two levels of questions. At the first level, one person describes how he thinks another person would answer a question. As an example, a husband would be asked what he thinks his wife would say in answer to the question of why they are in therapy. The wife is then asked to confirm or correct his impression. The procedure is then reversed.

At another level, the husband is asked what he thinks his wife thinks his answer would be to the same question of why they are in therapy. The first level provides information on his level of understanding his wife's views. The second level of question provides information on how well he thinks his wife understands his views.

In one family situation, the mother was asked how she thought her daughters would guess she (the mother) would answer the question of why the daughter thought they were in the therapist's office. Mother reported that she thought her daughter believed she was there because she and her sister fight. When the reverse question was asked, the daughter said her mother believed that she (the daughter) thinks she is there because her mother does not know what to do with her.

I consider this variation important because it clearly exposes the way people deal with their projections. Suppose that because I think you believe or feel a certain way, I assume that it is the way it must be for you. In effect, my assumption is treated as your reality. When I do not check this out and hold you accountable for my projections, the situation is ripe for righteous indignation on the part of both people.

This procedure is not utilized with parents in families with small children (approximately 7 years old or younger, depending on the maturity of the child). In this chapter I describe how this method can be utilized with couples and families.

The method to be described expands the Milan concept by getting systematic feedback that provides information in a relatively comfortable context and also gives perspective on the family members' ability to be empathic, learn how each member is perceived by others on both positive and negative characteristics, be able to correct distortions held by others, and see how family members cope with what they hear. Initially, this form of interviewing gains information by focusing on characteristics of common issues of family interaction rather than on problems.

Couples and families usually find this an interesting process because it is unexpected and carries a certain degree of challenge and uncertainty and because they learn a lot about each other. It also provides an opportunity for family members to appreciate their strengths. They often hear themselves described in positive ways that they have not heard before.

There are different ways to ask circular questions. The underlying principle is that questions should be asked in a form that provides information about differences between the way the involved participants think, act, and/or feel.

Participants may be asked questions in one or more of the following categories:

1. How they believe another person would answer a question such as "How do you think person *X* would answer question *Y*?"

2. How one person reports on the behavior of others when a particular event occurs. This is in response to a question such as "How do family members react when persons *A* and *B* have a particular kind of interaction, for example, argue, show affection, or engage in a particular activity?" or "Who is most or least affected by event *X*, followed in decreasing or increasing order until all members of the family are included?"

3. How they respond to hypothetical questions such as "What would happen if event *X* took place?" or, in more focused form, "How would one or more members of the family react if *X* event took place?" or "What do you think will happen to a person, relationship, or event in the future?" Another variation would be to include "most and least" questions.

First, I will describe the introductions I use with couples and families and then describe a variety of questions I have found useful. It is generally not necessary to ask all of these questions. I utilize the subgroup that appears most relevant for the particular couple or family.

Opening Comments to Clients

With Couples

"I have a way of getting to know you that is a little different than you might expect. I would like you to introduce each other. Tell me what you believe would be useful for me to know about the other person." After one spouse is introduced, I ask that person to comment on the way they were introduced. "Was there anything you particularly liked or disliked about the introduction? Was there anything you feel should have been added or deleted?" The same procedure is repeated with the other spouse.

With Families

The only difference with families is that I ask each person to introduce the person next to them on one side or the other. I might start by asking for a volunteer, or I may select a particular person. I would start with a particular person if I had reason to believe that getting that person's response first would make a difference. An example would be to have the youngest child in the family start the introductions because younger children are often more likely to mirror what adults in the family have said.

Other possibilities include introducing other children in the family before the identified client as a way of diluting the focus on the symptomatic child. Selecting a particular person to start an introduction is also a way to ensure the participation by family members who might not otherwise volunteer any comments at all.

Selecting a parent to make the first introduction is one way to acknowledge the parent role when that appears to be needed. When family members are anxious, it helps to select a particular member who might more easily relate to the task. This provides a model for the more reluctant members to follow.

As is done with couples, each person in the family is given an opportunity to react to his introduction with additions, deletions, and any other comments. This provides an opportunity in a supportive atmosphere to correct any distortions that were heard, which might normally not be possible. It also provides a clue to those areas that are important to an individual in either a positive or negative way.

Asking for a volunteer has the advantage of seeing how families relate. Watching the pattern of who volunteers and the family reaction to it gives information about the structure and nature of emotional relationships in the family.

The way people respond in the family context is especially useful because it shows how members give and receive information in the presence of one another. With this method they come closer to demonstrating natural ways of relating than would be the case in the usual form of interviewing.

In the following section I describe the categories of questions that may be asked and the rationale for doing so. Which of the categories and the form in which the questions are asked depend on the style of the therapist and the nature of the particular interviewing situation.

The focus of the questions is on whatever social entity (individual, couple, family, or subunit of the family), as discussed in Chapter 4, is under consideration.

Categories of Questions Asked

Priorities in Life

Priorities are the guidelines by which people mobilize and direct their energies. When high priorities utilize all available resources, lower priorities are likely to suffer. It is the process of defining priorities and allocation of resources that so commonly becomes the source of intense conflict in couples. Does the husband or wife become so invested in career that there is too little time or energy left for the relationship? Is one of the couple so involved with his family of origin that too little commitment is made to the marriage?

Couples

One way of asking a question about priorities is "What do you believe are the major priorities in life for your spouse? Please give them in order of priority." The degree to which a person is able to describe the spouse's priorities in their order of importance provides an indication of how tuned in one spouse is to the other.

When the presentation is complete, the spouse being described has an opportunity to respond to the accuracy of the description by suggesting deletions, additions, or changes in the order of priority. This is followed by a reversal of the process with the other spouse.

The next procedure would be to ask each person to give his impression of how he perceives what priorities the spouse has for the couple. When the mutual exchange is completed and discussed, attention is then given to see if there are significant incompatibilities between individual priorities and those for the couple.

Families

The same procedure is followed for families. This procedure may present a problem in a large family. When this is the case, it may be necessary to concentrate on having the family define family priorities and the way in which individual members differ. Specifically, the family is asked to define what priorities the family has as a group. This is done by addressing the question to the group or asking a specific individual to describe a perceived priority. After the suggestion is made, other family members are asked to comment on the suggestion for their agreement or disagreement and the basis for it. When there is agreement, it is also useful to ferret out from such discussion for whom it is a greater or lesser priority. This can be done by asking the family to discuss for whom they feel the selected priority is most important and for whom it is perceived to be least important. Following this, the family members who were described are asked for their comments.

Focusing attention on family priorities as a unit often provides a good approximation of what would have been obtained if it were done on the basis of individual priorities. Indications that this is not the case are when family members do not very actively participate or there is a lot of criticism when suggestions and comments are made. Conflicts in such discussion provide added definition to understanding the nature of differences in the family. It may be necessary to include some focus on individual priorities to fully understand the issues. The development of such conflict provides a natural forum for the discussion of issues that cause tension in the family.

Self-Concept

A major determinant of the successful outcome of any therapy is the degree to which a couple or family's resources can be developed and utilized in service of therapeutic goals. A key step toward accomplishing this goal is the assessment of family members' self-concepts that includes both strengths and weaknesses. It is hard to negotiate a relationship when a person does not feel he has much to offer because he feels needy, inadequate, and unworthy.

Such assessment contributes to the definition of realistic treatment goals and the design of appropriate therapeutic strategies. The goal of helping a son improve his relationship with his father may be very desirable, but it would be self-defeating to set such a target when it is clear that the father has a poor self-concept and has neither the desire nor the skills to improve the relationship. This was the case of a workaholic father who had little time or energy for his family.

An initial step in self-concept assessment in the couple or family context would be with the question "How do you feel person X feels about himself?" The reverse question is "What does person X think you think about him?" This latter question is a more indirect way of determining how somebody feels about himself. A similar procedure could be followed in assessing the status of other social entities.

Performance

An important ingredient that contributes to the sense of worth of any social entity is feeling productive in a significant way. For the individual this may be accomplishment in work, school, athletics, or an avocation. For the couple it might be the ability to have fun together or to be able to solve problems in a mutually satisfactory manner. For the family it might be to have fun together, be supportive of one another, or to work together as a unit. All situations have in common a sense of making a contribution and in some form paying one's own way in economic or social terms.

Evaluation in this area may be in the form of a question such as how person C (or social entity) thinks that person Y (or social entity) views his competence (satisfaction, performance) in a particular area. The reverse question, how person X believes person Y thinks that person X rates person Y's performance, provides added perspective. How does a father think his son believes how he (the father) rates his son's behavior?

Expression of Affect

Social entities vary greatly in the way and degree to which they develop standards on whether it is acceptable to have certain kinds of feelings (anger, love, sexual, hate, jealousy, envy, etc.) and the permissible ways for their expression.

Affect assessment may focus on different areas. The concern may be about what feelings are acceptable to have, what a person feels about a particular subject, under what conditions it is acceptable to express feelings, or in what ways it is permissible to express a particular kind of feeling.

One way to approach this assessment is with a question related to how person *X* thinks that person *Y* thinks or feels about one of the content areas previously listed.

Family Relationships

The status of family relationships in the nuclear and extended family provides perspective on the way a couple or family relate to one another as individuals and as a group. This includes obtaining information about coalitions and adversarial relationships. The pursuit of such information generally reveals the presenting problem but in a different context than when this is directly the focus of discussion. When the problem emerges in this fashion, it evolves from the context of both positive and negative aspects of the family. This makes it easier for the family to examine their situation with new perspective when the need for defensiveness by family members is reduced.

A range of questions is useful in gaining this information. These include questions related to "most" and "least" assessments, such as the differential way family members respond to a variety of situations such as "Who is the first to notice or react when mother is upset?" "Who is best at expressing his feelings?" "Which parent is tougher on discipline?" "Who gets along best or poorest?" and "Who is closest to grandparents or other extended family members?"

Social Relationships

The nature of social relationships outside the family provides information on the degree to which family members depend only on one another for dealing with their interpersonal needs. This also provides information on the degree to which family members feel competent and confident to engage in outside relationships. It also gives some indication of the parents' ability and willingness to support such development and the degree to which they are emotionally dependent on each other.

Questions for obtaining such information may include "most" and "least" questions regarding the relative amount and kind of social relationships outside of the family. This might also include questions regarding how family members are affected by the nature of relationships that other family members have outside of the family. Also useful are the questions that focus on how one family member perceives another family member feels about social relationships appropriate to that person.

Presenting Problems

Each person who comes to therapy has his own idea about the nature of the problem. A couple or a family may agree that there is a problem. Beyond that, there commonly is little agreement about what the problem is. In many situations differences in perceptions of the problem get withheld or obscured because of the belief that to talk about them would lead to arguments and an exchange of accusations. The use of the format described here often facilitates revelations between family members about how the relationships are perceived.

The question for determining the perception of the presenting problem may be asked in the following form or some variation of it: "What problems do you believe your spouse [family member] thinks are the problems in your relationship [family]? Please give them in order of the priority you feel your spouse [family member] holds them." Effort should be made to get as concrete a description of the problem(s) as possible. The more observable the description of the problem, the better the likelihood of having a clear understanding and agreement about what the problem is.

It also is desirable to ask, "What do you think your spouse [family member] thinks you believe are the problems?" This question provides information on how the person reporting the information is sensitive to how he is perceived by others. This is helpful in understanding how accurately a person is aware of how he comes across to others.

Goals to Be Achieved in Therapy

It is easy to presume that once you know the presenting problems that the goals for therapy are obvious. This may or may not be the case. The therapist who makes the assumption that what makes sense to him will also make sense to his client(s) is likely to make his job more difficult.

Consider the family situation in which a 9-year-old boy's misbehavior at home and at school was the presenting problem. At one level the goal was to correct his misbehavior. After evaluation it became clear that the mother's goal in initiating therapy was to do something about the escalation of problems in her marriage.

Couple

I prefer to start with a broad question that provides the opportunity to see what frame of reference the respondent uses. Does he respond in terms of the self or in terms of the couple? When this is the objective, the question may be in the form of "What do you believe your spouse hopes to accomplish in therapy?" If the answer was in terms of self, then I repeat the question in terms of the couple. This might take the form of "What do you believe your spouse hopes to accomplish in therapy for himself?" or "What do you believe your spouse hopes to accomplish in therapy for the couple?" The reverse question may be asked: "What do you think your spouse thinks you want to accomplish in therapy?"

Family

The same considerations that applied to the couple would also apply to the family. In both cases the joint recognition about the difference in goals is often revealing and surprising to the extent that the presumption of agreement in goals is found to be quite different. One family I saw consisted of two parents and two teenage girls. They were all in agreement that the family had problems, but each saw the goal for therapy quite differently. For the father, the goal was for the mother to stop giving the oldest daughter such a hard time. The mother saw the goal as getting her daughter to be more cooperative. The identified client saw the goal as getting the parents to let her have her own apartment. The goal for the youngest daughter was to get more attention paid to her for her good behavior and less to her older sister who was always getting into trouble.

Resources

As noted earlier in the chapter on resources, I have learned to pay as much attention to defining the strengths in a family as to defining the problems. A therapist's preoccupation with developing a clear understanding of problems comnmonly leads to too little attention being paid to adequate assessment of resources available in or to a family. Prognosis for therapeutic outcome is more appropriately dependent on determining the combination of what resources a family has to deal with whatever level of problems they may have. A family with minor problems and few resources will likely have as much of a struggle to resolve their problems as another family who have major problems and a lot of resources.

Resources are gained from knowledge about an individual's characteristics and from experiences in relationships inside and outside of the family.

Relationship Experiences

One way to gain information on relationship experiences is the question "What do you believe your spouse [family member] feels have been the most memorable experiences in your relationship [family]?" I note the degree to which the experience was focused on the individual or on the interaction. On one occasion a husband said, "*I* enjoyed the times we went skiing." This was in contrast to another couple where the husband said, "*We* enjoyed the times when we went sailing." Noting such distinctions provides clues about whether a person views the relationship as a means to individual gratification or whether the joint satisfaction is the focus. In either case, such information is useful as a potential resource in helping a couple or family draw upon the ability to relate in positive ways that may have become obscured by disagreement and conflict. It can also provide information about skills demonstrated in one situation that can be useful in another.

In one family a couple worked very well in coping with their 8-year-old daughter's protracted period of illness and hospitalization. At the time they were able to nurture each other and make joint decisions. The history of this experience was utilized in helping them resolve a long-standing conflict that surfaced years later that centered on how they related to the wife's family. The earlier example of the hospitalization of their daughter provided a model they were able to draw upon in resolving this conflict.

Individual Characteristics

The same principle that applies to utilizing resources from relationship experiences also applies to utilizing resources from individual characteristics. One way to approach this is with the question "What do you believe your spouse [family member] most admires in you?" Such a question serves more than one purpose. It provides an opportunity for the couple or family member to have a more balanced perspective of their relationships and to give validation to one another in a context when this often has been overshadowed by the current tensions. This awareness and appreciation often are lost in the heat of conflict, especially when it has occurred over a period of time.

Dealing with Conflict

Family members often have different perceptions about how they, as a unit, deal with conflict. Often just talking about the subject becomes a battle because family members are quick to defend their positions.

The interview method under discussion provides a context for obtaining such information with a reduced risk of nonproductive discussion. I believe this happens because it focuses on process — how things happen, rather than on who is responsible. Any of the previously described styles of making inquiries would also be appropriate here.

Questions on conflict may be asked such as "Who is most bothered when your parents argue?" "Who is most likely to try to settle an argument when two siblings are fighting?" "Who is most worried about conflict in the family?" and "Who is least worried?"

Future
People who are depressed or feel inadequate are less likely to be giving much thought to the future. Gaining perspective on the family members' view of the future provides additional perspective on levels of competence, resources, and their degree of confidence about being able to cope with it.

The same form of questions described previously can be utilized here as well. An added dimension is provided by "what if" questions with the format of what would happen if a given event did or did not take place. Also included could be questions that relate to how other family members are perceived as anticipating the future.

CASE ILLUSTRATIONS

In this section I will illustrate the use of the modified form of circular questioning in excerpts from two cases. The first case demonstrates how the use of this method applies in a family interview in the way they introduce each other. Space limitations do not permit showing other content areas of questioning described earlier in this chapter with a family. However, this broader range of questioning can be illustrated with a couple, which is the second case illustration. I suggest the reader note the way in which this method of interviewing elicits a great deal of information that is relevant from the client's point of view with a minimum of hesitation and reluctance.

Borden Family Interview

The Borden family consisted of two parents, Jerry, 52, and Amelia, 53, and their three children, Jane, 23; Peter, 21; and Jeff, 18. Jerry was an engineer, Amelia was a homemaker, Jane worked in an insurance company, Peter was a college student, and Jeff was a senior in high school. This excerpt is from a family evaluation interview. The presenting problem given on the phone by Amelia was the family's difficulty in communication. Nobody had time for one another. The parents and Jane came to the first interview. The following excerpt is from the second interview in which all family members were present.

MS: I have a way to get to know you that is a little different than you might expect. I would like to ask you to introduce each other. I would like you to tell me anything you feel that would be useful to know about that person. I will ask one person to start the introduction. After that person is finished, other family members can add their own contributions. Following the introductions, the person who was introduced will have an opportunity to comment on the way he or she was introduced. The person may want to add something, modify something, or disagree with something.

One other thing before we get started. Since Peter will be going off to college shortly, this will be the only opportunity to have the whole family together for some time. Because of this, I have arranged my schedule so that we can have an open-ended session. This means we will continue till either you or I get tired.

During the course of our session I will talk with you in different combinations. We'll talk for a while with the whole family. Then I will talk with the children alone. I have already talked with the parents alone. We can also have any other combination of people that anyone may desire. The reason for doing the separate groupings is that sometimes it is useful to talk without having to worry about how other people might be affected by it.

Jane, would you start by introducing the person on your left or right? [Jane has the choice of her older brother Peter or her father.]

Jane: I'll introduce Peter. This is my brother, Peter. He is a student at Syracuse University; he is majoring in engineering. He recently was transferred from Northeastern University. It was recommended to him that he could better himself at a university more suited to his interests, so he transferred to Syracuse, where is is doing quite well. He just completed his first year.

Peter is a very sensitive person. He knows what he wants, and he is very accurate in going about it. Everything is very well organized and planned out in his head. If it is not in his head, it is on paper. He is moody. I think everyone is at times. Like I said, he knows what he wants, and he knows how to get it. If something gets in his way it upsets him, it frustrates him, whether that be family or someone at school, or things other than people that are beyond his control. He has a temper which at times he blows, and at times I think he holds it in a lot too. One of the reasons we are all here is because Peter thought that he should do something about our family communication and he discussed it with me, and we both decided that if it was agreeable with everyone that we should go for it. That is my brother Peter.

MS: Any comments from other members of the family?

Father: Yes. I think Peter needs us to assure him that he is doing the right thing. Sometimes he lacks a little self-confidence himself, but like Jane said, he has got enough drive, enough organization that he knows what he wants, and he knows how to go about getting it, but he also needs a lot of support. If we criticize too much, his feelings are hurt.

MS: Other comments? [None are forthcoming.] Peter, any comments on how you were introduced?

Peter: I think it was pretty sufficient.

Jane: Obviously there is a lot more we can say, in a few words that describes somewhat his personality.

MS: Those were the highlights?

Jane: Yes.

MS: Peter, now it's your turn. Would you introduce your mother?

Peter: She is the oldest one in the family, but she doesn't look the oldest. My mom is a very loving person; she sometimes needs to express that, and sometimes it is hard to let her do that because of personal.. . . . Mom is having a hard time with all of us becoming too independent, which is very understandable. I think she is the type of person that needs someone around to communicate with and to talk with, and I think she misses us while we are away. She always tries to get us home for dinner, and I think. . . . She also doesn't have that much self-confidence. I think she should; I just don't think she wants to do it, for whatever reason. Sometimes even the things that seem pretty simple to her seem difficult. When she resists doing them, it causes tension, because someone has to take up the slack. That is about it.

MS: Comments from other members?

Father: I think we all know Amelia is a very loving person. She is, in my opinion, most unhappy when she is at home, especially when I am around. I am not sure just why; she has problems with one member of the family, and right away she turns to befriend another one. As when she has an argument with Peter, she will discuss it with Jane. When she is having an argument with Jane, she will discuss it with Peter. When it is with me, she will take either one that is around.

MS: Are you saying that she asks people to choose sides?

Father: Yes.

Peter: I think Mom ends up being in the middle too much. I think because she is so caring, she will listen to people's problems, and when one has a problem, it could be the simplest thing. I mean, Jeff's car broke down; he couldn't get here today, so she went to get him.

Mother: I went to Nantasket Beach.

Father: And then she complains to me that she has to go, but she still goes. And yet, Jeff has no way of getting back in the morning, and she is always worried about that and how he will get back. And she is already asking me for my opinion about that. I think the reason why she discusses things with everyone is because she wants to do the best thing. She doesn't quite know how to hold on.

MS: Are you saying she doesn't know how to take care of herself?

Father: I wouldn't say that; I think she just doesn't know how to care for the entire family. I think she wants to give everything she can to everyone in the family, but she doesn't have the confidence to do that.

MS: Confidence? But is she realistic?

Jane: She knows what she can do. She knows exactly what she can do.

MS: But she is not realistic in what she does, or tries to do.

Father: I think she is always, more or less, on the negative side. Like, it just can't be done. Always the pessimist.

MS: The reason I was asking for clarification here was because I was hearing she doesn't address her own needs when she gets involved trying to take care of other people's needs. This gets her into trouble and gets expressed as negativism, and pessimism because she feels nobody is looking out for her?

We will come back to that. The question is — and I will just leave it for the moment — how much do you invite the response you get? OK, Amelia? [She nods agreement.]

Amelia, are there any comments you want to make about your introduction?

Mother: It is true. There are no comments.

MS: You don't have a quarrel about what people say?

Mother: No, it's true. I am always in the middle of everything.

MS: OK, no, the question is, Is there anything they should have added?

Mother: I don't think I am always moody. Who said I am always mad, unhappy? I don't think that is true. Jeff. Well, I can't say too much about Jeff, because Jeff doesn't communicate with any of us. He is a nice kid, and he never gives us any trouble; he never talks. The only thing I would like him to do is communicate. At suppertime he will come out; he is a very fast eater, and in five minutes he is away from the table, and even when he is there he doesn't talk. We have lost communication completely. We all have.

Jeff does not talk. He is a quiet kid. He only talks when he has to talk, such as "What time are we eating?" That is about it. They just don't do anything together. But, Jeff is a great kid. He never gives us any problems; he has lots of friends. And, I wish he'd spend more time with us. He has his desk downstairs in the family room, and he stays there all the time; we don't see him that much. He just comes up to eat.

MS: Other comments?

Jane: I think that when we had been here before we told you that Jeff was very quiet. We had a discussion about all the rest of us, and you had pointed out that maybe Jeff is quiet because he is being smart, he is staying out of it, he is not maybe as strong-headed as some of us, and he would rather take it as it comes, and not fight back. I think that is a very true point with him. I think that he is probably the least moody of all of us. He doesn't have mood swings as far as I can see. He, like Mom said, you ask him to do something, and he might not say yes or no, but he goes and does it. He is very easygoing and very accepting of what you ask him to do.

Mother: Peter used to work for his father out on the boat, and they didn't get along because Peter would get hurt. Jerry can do the same thing to Jeff, and Jeff doesn't get excited or doesn't get mad.

Jane: Let's put it this way, if it does faze him, he does not show it. We think it goes in one ear and out the other, but maybe it doesn't.

Father: He has shown it to me a couple of times.

Peter: Well, my dad gets a little high-strung when we fish. I think Jeff has been around long enough to see my sister and myself handle it. We figured it out this weekend; my dad asked me to do something and I said no. He didn't like that; I think he got offended that I talked back to him in front of others, and he got mad at me. And he told me I couldn't go fishing anymore, that kind of thing. I said, "Jeff, how come that doesn't happen with you?" He said, "When he tells me to do it, I just say yes and do it." Whereas when it comes to me, I say I am not going to do it if I don't want to do it. I think he does not know how to handle those situations.

MS: How do you not handle it, Jane?

Jane: I don't usually say no, but I make it known that I am not happy about what I am doing.

Jerry: She jumps the boat as soon as it docks.

MS: Any other comments on Jeff?

Jerry: Jeff, I won't say he is not ambitious, but he is satisfied probably less with material goods. He is satisfied much easier. He doesn't have the aggressiveness that Peter has. Jeff will be laid back, and if it happens, it happens. I think he lacks — I won't say ambition, he has ambition, he can do what he sets his mind to do — but sometimes I think he should set his mind on goals a little bit higher so he has something to strive for. He just does what he has to do, that is it. No more, no less. Most of the time, what I want, I have to ask for. But when I do, he does it. When I don't ask for it, it won't get done. He doesn't initiate it. Fifty-fifty.

MS: Jeff, do you want to comment on your introduction?

Jeff: I think it was pretty good.

MS: OK. Do you want to do the honors with your father?

Jeff: This is my father, Jerry. Most of the time, very demanding, but not all the time. Like, he is much more relaxed when he is fishing, on weekends, than when he comes home from work. I think sometimes he is a lot like Peter; if things aren't done the way he wants them done, he gets upset. That is about it.

MS: OK. Other comments?

Peter: My dad very rarely gives out compliments. And he rarely admits he is wrong. Even when he is wrong, he will continue to argue that he is right. And, he has a hard time coming to terms with my sister and I being educated and her having a college degree. He is still having a hard time talking to us. I think there is a fine line here to what I am saying. He is obviously still our father, and he talks to us like he is our father, but on another level, when someone becomes educated, to a certain point, there is a communication there that should be equal. He has a hard time dealing with that. Let's face it, my education is coming 30 years after his. Times have changed somewhat, and education has changed. Even with three years of college under my belt, I am never right. I shouldn't say in everything but most often, so even things that I have more knowledge about because of my education. Even things such as academic things, like the shingling on the house, and I shingled half a roof last summer — and I have learned through construction how to do a roof — after I did it, it was wrong, and he knew how to do it right. But, I don't know if he ever shingled anything, but I know he hasn't done it in the past 20 years or so, but yet, he still couldn't say it was a good job, it was done, it was complete, it wasn't going to leak, but yet, it is not done to his satisfaction. It kind of bothers me. He is an engineer, he hasn't shingled a side of a house in so long, what makes him such an authority? That is some of the things that bother me.

MS: Ladies, anything you want to add?

Jane: Just touching on what Peter said about being able to communicate on a different level, on a more adult, more mature level, I often wonder if that point will ever come. I picture myself getting married, and still being little Jane. I can picture myself having children, and still not attaining that level that I think Peter is talking about. I know with Mom, I could see her saying to me that I am not doing something right with my child, but with Mom, I could say, "This is my child." But with Papa, I can't see myself ever saying that. He is always right, no matter what. I just can't see myself getting to that level.

MS: It is not that you couldn't say it, it is just that you wouldn't be acknowledged.

Jane: Right. Exactly.

MS: OK. Is that it on Papa? OK, Papa.

Jerry: Let me first talk about myself. I think Peter has a conception about an education which doesn't fit the norm. Getting a college degree is not an education, it is a beginning of an education. What Jane has learned in college I have reason to doubt that she has the expertise that she should have. I have seen it in applying the simple rules of economics. I have talked to Jane about it a number of times. It chagrins me, that she has this college background and some of the fundamentals in economics are not really clear to her. This is not an education, this a process that she has to go through.

MS: Are you talking about managing money?

Jerry: Yes. Managing money, or interest rates, loans, other things we have talked about, tax returns, and stuff like that. They don't teach you that in college. But she took business administration course. And you know, she says that I don't respect what she has of the things and some of the decision-making process that she does, then I can see some achievements. In that sense, she has got a degree, but she doesn't have the education that you referred to.

Jerry: Education is a process. It is a foundation for which to build on. I also thought the same as you do, Peter, when I was 22. I had a lot of knowledge. I thought I knew everything.

Peter: I never said I thought I knew everything.

Jerry: I said I thought it at that point, OK? And then when you get 30 years on top of it, you say I am still learning. There are still things I know today that I didn't know last year. And there is still process dealing with people. Not just dealing with my kids, not just dealing with my wife, but in the business world, there are things I learn everyday. You will also learn, you will see it 10, 20 years from now, you don't really know a whole lot. You have some fundamentals, you have the basic intelligence to learn.

Now let me talk about carpentry. I was shingling houses, I built a barn practically alone for my father when I was before your age, and it is not going to leak. You are very sensitive because you have had some experience. You can do whatever you want, if you do it for me, fine, if you don't like it I feel I have a right to say it wasn't done the way I think it should be done. Fine. I didn't bawl you out, I didn't yell. One of the things I was unhappy about is that you should have used a wrecking bar to pry in those shingles so you could slide those things underneath. Somehow it wasn't important for you to do that. 'Cause that is the right way, I know it.

MS: Is there "a" way? Is there more than one way?

Jerry: There is more than one way to skin a cat. There is a shortcut, there is the right way. There is some way in between. I think Peter went maybe the in-between and the short way.

It will stay tight for a while, but that is not the way I think it should have been done. But it will work, it's better than I had the time to do it myself, so it is done.

Peter: It just seems to me that you don't have the time to do those things, and I did it for you. You should be content with that "this is not right." Why don't you say, "thanks for doing it?" That is all I am saying, that is the point here.

Jerry: Would you rather that I always say that I have done everything right, than to be truthful about the way I feel?

Peter: No, just once in a while.

Jane: Once in a while you can praise us.

Jerry: I have. You have done some great work.

Peter: When you do that like that, do you think I feel like doing anything else for you? I don't feel like doing any more things for you because I don't like the negative criticism toward the end.

MS: I wonder if what you are hearing is that there are two parts to what is being talked about. One is what you are saying; the other is how you are saying it.

Jerry: Ask Peter, did I say it in a gross, abrupt fashion, or did I just comment on that was not the way it should be?

Peter: Well, I think for me to bring it up here, I think it was obviously said in a way that sounded very critical. The fact is that I shingled half a roof last summer, and I was told that it was done right. It hasn't leaked since. It isn't going to leak because I did it the same way, so I can't understand how you can come in and make a judgment on that and say that it, you know, these are professional carpenters that I worked with. They said this is fine. You are an engineer, you haven't done carpentry since you were 18, or shingled since you were 18. And yet you still know more than these people who taught me how to do this last summer.

Jerry: I understand the dialogue on that point. I think the question that was asked is how was it that I said it, and was it in an abrupt, coarse criticism, robust in sarcasm, how did I explain to you that I wasn't really happy with it?

Peter: The same way you always do, you examine it and you kind of ignore who you are talking to as you are looking at the final details that, and you know, you just seem quite aloof. When I asked you how to do it the night before, I was trying to explain things to you and you didn't hear one thing that I said. Then you told me how to do it, then you walked away and you went to see Jeff. I couldn't finish my discussion with you, and I had other things to talk to you on, and yet I had to go to someone else's living room in front of other company to talk to you about these things. You have to say you don't listen to what anyone else has to say, and then you go about your business.

MS: Peter, do you feel your father competes with you?

Peter: Competes with me? I don't know. I never thought of it that way.

MS: You look like you have some thoughts on that.

Mother: Not on that point, on other things. I remember a time when Jeff was, over five years ago, he works on the boat, he cleans it, he scrubs it, everybody says they have never seen kids that work so hard. And he had been scrubbing this boat all day, I was there; Jerry came down the dock, the first thing he does is looks at this boat, and the boat was spotless except for one little spot that Jeff missed, and he didn't say the boat looked nice. He said, "You missed this, and why didn't you do this?" The bad part. I will never forget that. He can't praise you when you do something good. It is always the negative part. I felt so bad.

Peter: There is a point where in general, that there are certain group of fathers that want their children to do well, they are going to figure they are doing well enough not to strive for anything further. Yet some of my fraternity brothers, I will bring home a report card with two A's and two B+'s and a C, and instead of saying "Two A's, great," it will be "Why the C?" I mean, there is a point to pushing people to strive for better grades or better accomplishments.

MS: Jerry, when I was saying before how you said it, I wasn't limiting it to being gruff. I think it has to do with the point of the balance of acknowledging what is right with what you have a problem with. I don't think it is a question of if you should pretend what isn't, but rather it is more of a balance. What is your feeling about it?

Jerry: There are certain things that are obviously right, and naturally, I don't praise as much as I criticize. But then, I don't demand from any member of the family any more from them than I demand of myself. As a matter of fact, I demand more of myself than any of them. I would expect that they would at least follow me and try to do a little bit more than themselves. Jane, she is doing OK, Amelia. . . .

Amelia: Me?

Jerry: Amelia has got very little ambition of any in that respect. I work 12 hours, I leave the house before seven and don't get in before seven. I go for 12 hours working my ass off, I come home, they growl because I don't have time to talk with them. I am beat.

MS: Why is it that you work 12 hours a day?

Jerry: It takes me 45 minutes to get to work and I have a job to do and don't leave the office before my daily tasks are complete.

MS: How much are you expected to get done?

Jerry: To get my job done. I am general manager and vice president of this small busines, which we are trying to grow. It is very demanding. A lot of people report in to me; they depend on me. I have to have an even disposition with customers, with the ownership, the people working for me, and my family. Then I come home and I am faulted because I sit in front of the TV and I fall asleep. Then I wake up and I want to talk and they are all asleep.

Amelia: You don't wake up.

Jerry: I am saying that I don't demand that Peter says that I don't give any credit. I criticize a lot. I criticize a lot. I give compliments too.

MS: One of the things that I think we are talking about is different standards. For you it may be enough, for them it may be different. The question is, Can you respect that they maybe have different standards than you do without it being right or wrong?

Jerrry: I am not on Jeff's tail for being not as aggressive as Peter. I accept that.

MS: Do you feel he accepts it?

Jeff: I don't think I am as less aggressive as he thinks I am. If that makes sense. I am, but he doesn't really see.

MS: But, as Jane points it out, you have a different strategy for dealing. When you put yourself out there as a target, you see, these two make a real clear target. You give a very narrow target.

Jeff: But it is still there.

MS: The point is that we don't know it is there. So, you are perhaps correct that your father may be less accurate with you because you don't give him as much to work with. Those two are much more clear with where they are at, and how they feel. I am not saying good, bad, or indifferent here, I am just saying that may be part of the difference.

Jerry: The question was the standards that I established for myself, I shouldn't have to expect it from them. I said, with Jeff I know his esteem is lower than Peter's, but I accept it.

MS: What Jeff is saying is that may not be true.

Jerry: It doesn't reflect that he has. . . .

MS: You don't see it.

Jerry: I didn't say that he wasn't ambitious. I said he sets lower standards for himself.

Jeff: I don't think they are as low as you think they are.

MS: All we are able to talk about is perceptions. That is how you see it. What I hear between the lines here is that you put out a lot and you don't get too much back.

Jerry: First of all, I think Amelia can put a little bit more into it. I put out a lot more effort and work for the family than I perceive Amelia as doing or willing to do.

MS: Do you feel you get your due from your children?

Jerry: I think so. I haven't felt that they didn't respect me, or that they didn't give what I expect from them.

MS: So, your major beef is with Amelia.

Andrea and Edgar

Andrea and Edgar were a couple in their late twenties who had been married for two years. She was a dental assistant and he was employed in an auto parts company. Andrea was the second oldest of six children in an intact family. Edgar was the oldest of three children and had two younger sisters. His parents were divorced.

The following transcript is an excerpt from an initial interview that illustrates the application of circular questioning with a couple as described above.

MS: I would like to get to get to know you in a little different way than you might expect. I would like you to introduce each other by telling me what you think would be useful for me to know.
Andrea, would you like to start?

Andrea: Edgar grew up in Lynn, Massachusetts, with his family. He came out of high school and went straight into the Army for a couple of years. Then he went into the reserve Army for a couple more years, before we met. When I met him he was still in the Army reserve. We have been dating for six years. We dated for four and a half years before we got married. We have been together for six years. He is really nice.

MS: What does that mean?

Andrea: He is kind, he is considerate. He is generous. He is a loner. He likes to do things by himself. He is very talented when it comes to models and fixing things. He is very good with his hands. The difficulties we have been having as a couple sometimes center around Edgar having trouble managing his anger, and getting angry and saying things he doesn't mean.

MS: Edgar, do you have any comments about the way she introduced you? Anything to add, leave out, change?

Edgar: No.

MS: Do you want to introduce her now?

Edgar: It is kind of hard.

MS: What would be useful to me to know about Andrea?

Edgar: She is kind of innocent. She comes up strong, but she is kind of, needs to be protected like. She likes to read. She is a nice person. She would do anything for you, even if it puts her out.

MS: Are there any comments about what he may have said?

Edgar: She is a dental assistant. She is good at it. She likes working with people.

MS: Andrea, what you think are Edgar's priorities in life? If you could give them to me in order of what you think are important.

Andrea: I think Edgar's priorities are . . . he doesn't like aggravations, so he would like a peaceful life. He wants to own an old antique car and be able to play with it in the garage. We are so different. He does want to get his degree. What he would really like is a civil-service job. That is all I can think of.

MS: Where do you fit in?

Andrea: I think I fit in with the peaceful life.

MS: I mean, you didn't list yourself as a priority.

Andrea: I think that I am a priority.

MS: Where would you put yourself in the list of his priorities?

Andrea: I think most times first.

MS: What about family?

Andrea: Having a family between us?

MS: That's one thing. . . . Since you mention it, where would that fit in?

Andrea: It doesn't.

MS: And where would the families you grew up with fit in?

Andrea: I would say, I guess it would be first with his family, then the things he wants.

MS: Edgar, you had your priorities described; would you change it in any way?

Edgar: Yea, I think she is being kind of biased. Of course my priority is number one for Andrea.

Andrea: I just didn't think of it the first time. I was thinking of things first.

Edgar: She wants a house and kids.

MS: We are describing you first.

Edgar: Oh.

MS: She described your priorities. Do you agree or disagree?

Edgar: I think my first priority is her; my second is that I would really like to have a house. I want to get my college degree.

MS: Where would you put your family?

Edgar: They are important. I am married to her now. If you have to measure out people, she is number 1, my family is second, and then her family, do you know what I am saying?

MS: Let's do the reverse right now. Edgar, what do you see as her priorities, as she sees them.

Edgar: She wants a house. She wants kids. But I don't think she wants them all right away. Well, actually, she does. She wants a bunch of kids. I am afraid of that. You know, the price of things today. She wants to go back and get her master's degree. She wants me to get my degree.

MS: Where are you in getting your degree?

Edgar: I'm coming along, but I do it at night school. Night school is kind of bizarre.

MS: What else is a priority?

Edgar: Believe it or not, that is basically all her priorities. Priorities and goals, I kind of put in the same. . . .

MS: Priority is how important something is, a goal is what you are trying to accomplish.

Edgar: That is what I am saying. We are sticking in achievements, houses, kids, . . . so, I think her priorities are squared away.

MS: Andrea, what is your comment to this discussion?

Andrea: I agree with all of them. But he didn't put himself on the list.

MS: He did. He put you first and your family third.
     What do you think Edgar thinks is the problem as to why you are here?

Andrea: I think Edgar thinks that adjusting to marriage is hard for us. We are starting to settle down. We lived separately for a year in another apartment, then we moved back into my family's house just last summer. We have a separate apartment on the third floor away from everybody. I think Edgar is putting a lot of the blame on moving into my house and being around my family for making things in our marriage a goal. I think Edgar feels that he is responsible for a lot that has gone wrong in our marriage because he has a strong temper.

MS: What does he think you think is the problem?

Andrea: I think he thinks that I think it is him. All him. And I don't. It is a shared problem and it is 50/50. When it becomes more him than me is when he crosses the line and his behavior is outrageous. Then it is more him than me.

MS: Any comments Edgar?

Edgar: No, it is pretty accurate.

MS: Now tell me what you think she thinks is the problem.

Edgar: She just said it. Yea, we disagree big time. You see, when we live by ourselves, I am a weird kind of guy I'll admit it, I like things to be the same, day in and day out. It takes me a while to get used to things. Like, when I first got out of the Army I moved back home with my mother, which was probably dumb, then we started dating, and then I moved out of there into an apartment, because I was intolerable. My mother would drive me dizzy. Then I moved into this apartment. It was like living in a phone booth, and I used to have aggravation because of that. I used to attribute it to the apartment. I figured when I moved into a bigger place, I would be a little bit more settled, but it seemed like every time we moved. . . . I feel like a carpetbagger, the past few years I have moved three times. I hate that! So, I figured that once me and her were over it, we were on our own, and I was just starting to get . . . we had been there for a year, and I was just starting to feel at home, relax, I know that sounds crazy, but, taking time to get comfortable with something. Then it seemed like the minute I got comfortable, we are running home to the mess.

MS: Why did you do it?

Edgar: Because I thought it would make her happy. She wasn't too happy neither. I figured if it made her happier, well, then it would make me happier because she wouldn't be picking on me as much. It seemed like it didn't work. I guess I should have been different.

MS: OK.

Andrea: I think that the problems between us don't stem from. . . .

Edgar: Oh, Oh, I am sorry, you are right. No, it ain't stemming from, I might have misled you there. It isn't just from the apartment. I do have a real bad temper some times. But sometimes I get real, not physically abusive, but sometimes I say things I don't mean.

MS: What do you think Andrea would like to get out of therapy?

Edgar: Solve my temper. Not solve it, but control it.

MS: What do you think she thinks you want to get out of therapy?

Edgar: It is like walking on eggshells. I have blown up over the stupidest things.

MS: Do you agree with that?

Andrea: I think a little bit beyond managing his temper. I think that Edgar doesn't feel good a lot of times. Depressed, really irritable, and really unhappy. I think there is a lot of unresolved feelings about what a family should be like.

MS: From whose point of view?

Andrea: Edgar's.

MS: What do you think?

Andrea: Growing up, maybe, his family was tolerant of a lot of anger and depression toward each other. I think the both of us need to handle things a little more calmly. I do provoke it.

MS: How do you think Edgar feels about the division of labor you have in the marriage. About who does what?

Andrea: I think he is satisfied. I don't think there is a lot to do, really.

MS: Does he think you are satisfied?

Andrea: I think he thinks he should do more.

MS: Edgar?

Edgar: I think I should do more. I'll vacuum and clean the house, but she will do something really spontaneous, like lug two bags of groceries up the stairs. I think that should be my job. We live on the third floor, so I will try to beat her to it. Like, Saturday we were supposed to go shopping together, but if we don't go together she is going to have to lug the groceries up the stairs. So I got up real early and got the groceries and dingbat is out on the porch waiting for me.

MS: If you go shopping together, why does she have to carry the groceries?

Edgar: Because she is that way. You can't tell her not to do it. I came home and she is down there on the stoop waiting for me.

MS: Doing it together doesn't do it?

Edgar: It is three flights of stairs. So, I'll do it. I don't want her to have a stroke going up the stairs. I'll load the dishwasher and stuff like that.

MS: Andrea, do you think Edgar is satisfied with the way you deal with your respective families?

Andrea: No. I think he thinks I am too involved with my family. He thinks it is increased because we are living there now.

MS: How do you think he feels about the way you deal with his family?

Andrea: I don't see his family a lot, but I like them.

MS: I know, but how do you think he feels about the way you do it?

Andrea: I think he is comfortable with it.

MS: Edgar.

Edgar: She don't see my family enough to be involved with my family. So, they are not even a part of it.

MS: Is she satisfied with that?

Edgar: I wouldn't force my family on anybody.

Andrea: Edgar, they are not bad.

Edgar: They are just crazy.

Andrea: They are not. Maybe from your experience, but they are nice to me.

MS: Is she satisfied with the way you both deal with her family?

Edgar: No. I don't like going down to see them.

MS: So she is not happy that you don't like her family better.

Edgar: It ain't out of hate or anything like that; I like them all, but there is one brother down there. . . . He is just an arrogant little bastard in plain English.

MS: Which one is that?

Edgar: The 23-year-old Henry. He talks to you like you are a dog. I avoid him. I feel like if he is arrogant to me, I should be arrogant back. You are sitting there and someone is being arrogant to you. I have bit my tongue in the past and I have just let it go. To avoid the problem of having to put up with it and feel humiliated, I don't deal with it. Now I am living in their fort. It is very awkward.

MS: That is certainly one way to handle it. It is the safest way, probably.

Andrea: What upsets me is that you won't let me talk to him about it. I said to Edgar that he could say anything to him; if he is being a jerk to you, tell him he is. Edgar says no because once he starts, he will want to punch him.

MS: What stops you from saying something to your brother?

Edgar: I prefer her not to. I want her to stay out of it.

MS: Do you think he is aware of what he is doing?

Edgar: I don't think he has the brains for that. I think he could care less. I think he is driving at something. But he has no mentality to figure out what he is doing.

MS: If this bothers Andrea, not because she is taking care of you, but because it bothers her that her brother treats her husband like that.

Edgar: Does it bother you that he treats me like a jerk, or is it because you have to take care of me? Nobody got to take care of me.

Andrea: It bothers me. I would love to talk to Henry and knock it off.

MS: If you are doing it for you, it is one thing. If you are doing it to protect him, he doesn't need it.

Andrea: It would be both. It doesn't happen in front of me.

MS: Fine, but the point is Edgar doesn't need it for him.

Andrea: I just want it to stop. I don't care who I am defending.

MS: Andrea, do you think Edgar thinks that sex is a problem?

Andrea: Yes, sometimes. In the frequency.

MS: Does he think you think there is a problem?

Andrea: No.

MS: Edgar, do you agree, that you think that Andrea thinks there is a problem?

Edgar: She could live without it. I don't have a problem with it anymore. We were discussing it. I am starting to get more. . . . Don't put nothing behind it, I watched Oprah. I have mellowed out. I think she has gotten more like me, and I have gotten more like her. We have come to agree with it more like when we feel like it. I don't like talking about this at all.

MS: The only thing is that you need to talk about what the issues are. You are doing fine.
    The question is, is there a problem in who initiates it?

Edgar: Oh yea. Don't get me wrong, it is plenty. It is when we feel like it, but it is always me. Although lately, she has been saying, go take a shower. But things are really mellowing out. Do you have any problems with it? We had to come to an understanding, why should somebody have to submit to something like that all the time if they don't like it. But they feel uncomfortable. So, I figured I would go your way. I really have.

MS: Edgar, what do you think that Andrea feels good about herself?

Edgar: That she is kind. She likes her work. She is pretty. She is vain. She likes cutesy, cutesy things. She likes putting the drapes up, and picking the stuff that goes with it, to great lengths. She likes to have everything just the way she wants it.

MS: What do you think she thinks you like about her?

Edgar: I think she thinks that I like that about her. She is kind of cute, and sweetsy, sweetsy. I don't know what she thinks I think. . . .

MS: You told me what Andrea likes about herself. The other part of that is, what she thinks you like about her.

Edgar: I think she thinks I like the things that she likes about herself. I do.

Andrea: You don't like my job.

Edgar: It ain't that I don't like your job; I think sometimes your job gets you a little remote. A little intolerant. I don't want to sound like I am repeating myself. Am I supposed to have different answers?

MS: It doesn't matter whether you repeat yourself or not. It is whatever you think that is important, not whether you repeat.
  Andrea, let's reverse that. What do you think that Edgar likes about himself.

Andrea: I think Edgar likes the fact that he has a lot of pride in his workmanship. He likes the fact that he is funny and he is popular. He likes to know that he is a kind and good person. He likes the fact that he is strong.

MS: What about what he thinks you like about him?

Andrea: That he is kind. I think he thinks that I think he is attractive and handsome. but he doesn't think that about himself I don't think. I think he is a good person always. His strength.

MS: Andrea, how satisfied do you think that Edgar is when you settle your arguments?

Andrea: I don't think he is satisfied. Usually the argument is about something indirect, then it escalates. We don't even agree or disagree. It escalates and falls apart.

MS: Do you think he thinks you are happy?

Andrea: I think he thinks that all I want him to do is shut up. I don't want to fight. But sometimes I just want to stop it.

MS: Edgar, let's do the other side of that. Do you agree with what Andrea said about the way that arguments get settled?

Edgar: I just think that it is hard. I don't think I think too rationally. We grew up entirely different. When her family fights, they avoid each other for months. In my family you screamed, hollered, ranted, raved, stomped your feet until somebody says, alright, we will discuss it. It just doesn't work.

MS: So it is a matter of how you put the two together.

Edgar: For sake of mind, I would rather see it her way than my way. It is not healthy to do that.

Andrea: I will discuss something. He never would ask me to do that, but if he did, I could. But once he starts arguing, I just shut him off.

MS: What is the difference?

Andrea: He starts yelling.

Discussion

The case excerpts presented above illustrate how a form of circular questioning provided a great deal of information in a short period of time about the dynamics and relationships of a family and a couple. Obtaining such information would have taken longer in more traditional forms of interviewing. In both cases the presenting concern was a problem in communicating.

This method inspires balanced participation by all participants. In other forms of interviewing, Jeff's participation in the family would more easily have been obscured by other more vocal members in the family. This method also provides a safer atmosphere that facilitates taking greater risks in sharing information.

In the case of Edgar and Andrea, this method of interviewing minimized the defensiveness that Edgar would have felt if the focus was primarily on him. This form of interviewing provided a balanced context in which the contributions of both people could be addressed without one person feeling on trial.

A challenge to the therapist in doing this form of interviewing is to stay focused and not get distracted into working on problem areas as they are defined. This is not rigidly followed because there are times when the need to deal with an issue that surfaces should take a higher priority than the intended structure for the interview.

Otherwise, I feel it is preferable to stick with the format of the interview because it provides a useful experience for the client social entity to have this form of evaluation done in one interview. Often this is not possible, especially with a family. How long this process takes is a function of the size of the client social entity, the personality characteristics and emotional needs of its members. The outcome of this form of interviewing usually has the following characteristics:

1. Participants usually find the interview more comfortable than expected and are usually surprised at how much they have learned. It is not uncommon to have people say they enjoyed the interview.

2. There tends to be more balanced participation by all members once the introductions suggest a pattern for interaction.

3. The therapist gains a great deal of information in the review of the previously described areas of the social entity's functioning. In this context, people tend to provide revealing information that is less likely to be expressed in the context of problem-focused discussions.

Summary

This chapter illustrates a method of eliciting information from couples and families in a context that minimizes the stress that commonly accompanies initial or early interviews in therapy. This process also encourages family members to interact in familiar styles, which in itself is a useful source of data.

The concepts outlined in this chapter are intended to help a therapist develop a reservoir of various ways to interview a family by using the interviewing techniques described here, from which the therapist draws upon an appropriate subset tailored to the unique needs of the clients.

Glossary

Adaptation Phase   The adjustment to the onset of an event when it occurs. This requires the ability to receive information, assess it, and make appropriate changes in behavior on an ongoing basis until adaptation to the new event is completed.

Anticipation Phase   Takes place when a person attempts to anticipate the occurrence of an event and how to cope with it. During this time a social entity is usually in a heightened receptivity state for seeking and receiving new information relative to the anticipated event.

Attitudes   The heightened tendency that guides behavior to be an expression of both values and beliefs, for example, the predisposition to approach a given situation with honesty.

Beliefs   A social entity's perception of what was, is, or is expected to be, for instance, many people are dishonest when it suits their purpose.

Benefit   Any emotional, physical, spiritual, or material occurrence that is considered desirable by the social entity experiencing it.

Benefit-Cost Balance   The judgment a social entity makes regarding whether the benefits that are obtainable from a given experience are worth what emotional, physical, or material costs are required to obtain them.

Cost   Desired or undesired expenditure of any resource — emotional, financial, physical, or intellectual — required to obtain a particular benefit.

Countertransference   When the therapist's emotions interfere with his ability to apply his clinical skills.

Culture   The way in which a social entity defines the ethics, goals, customs, rituals, and rules of how they will relate to each other.

Developmental Sequence   The series of experiences that a social entity encounters in pursuit of a goal. Commonly each experience sets the stage for the next one and often involves increasing complexity.

Discipline   Attempts to modify behavior guided by the desire to teach rather than to retaliate.

Dynamic Equilibrium   When the state of ongoing activity continues within and between various social entity concepts with no significant change in their definition or in the relationship between them.

Emotional Umbilical Cord   The emotional attachment that a social unit has to another social unit, which interferes with its ability to function independently. This cord may never be cut, in contrast to the physical cord, which necessarily is cut at birth.

Empathy   The ability to appreciate how another person thinks, feels, or behaves. To have empathy does not imply any judgment.

Experience Reservoir   The collection of life experiences from which a social entity draws in coping with a new situation.

Genogram   A map of the family over as many generations as there is information for. It shows factual data on family relationships with dates of significant events, geographical location, and any other significant characteristics of family members.

Guilt   Feelings about the failure to behave or not behave consistent with personal values. It is a statement about behavior, not identity.

Integration Phase   Dovetails with the standing of the TM phase, where the major focus is on how a person utilizes the learning from a given experience and incorporates such learning for future reference. Failure to do this work increases the probability that the same pattern of behavior will continue to be repeated.

Material Resources   *Physical* resources include money, equipment, tools, and reference material. *Cognitive* resources include creativity, problem-solving ability, information, skills, ability to negotiate differences, and experience. *Emotional* resources include empathic ability, access to feelings, and the ability to express them in appropriate ways. *Character traits* include sense of humor, honesty, commitment, responsibility, and integrity.

Method-Oriented Approach to Therapy   The therapist considers how a preferred theoretical orientation and method of doing therapy can best be utilized for the resolution of dysfunctional behavior.

Permeability   The degree to which there is open communication across the boundary between social entities.

Power   The ability of one social unit to influence the thinking and/or behavior of another social unit. Such influence can be accomplished directly or indirectly.

Problem   Exists when a social entity's desire to cope with its environment is prevented from doing so by someone or something, either within the social entity, external to it, or both.

Problem-Oriented Approach to Therapy   The therapist considers which theoretical orientation and method of intervention is most likely to be effective in coping with the defined dysfunctional behavior. This presumes the therapist has skills in multiple orientations or that he is knowledgeable enough to make such an evaluation for appropriate referral.

Punishment   Behavior in service of retaliating for felt injury or injustice, with or without the hope that it will also lead to a modification in behavior.

Resource   Any material entity, cognitive, emotional, or character trait that one or more people in the family possesses that is useful in accomplishing therapeutic goals. Also included is access any family member has to outside resources.

Ritual   There are two kinds of rituals. One relates to rites of passage: confirmation, bar mitzvah, graduation, weddings, and the like. The other kind marks significant events such as religious holidays, birthdays, anniversaries, and special occasions.

Shame   An attack on the social entity's identity.

Social Entity/Social Unit   The identity that characterizes a social being, which may be an individual, a couple, a family, or any subunit of a family. This includes the way a social being defines itself and the rules by which its members relate to one another. It is a term for generic reference to any combination of people.

Social Entity Concept Balance   The balance of positive and negative experiences of a social entity that affects how it perceives itself at a given point in time. A particular form of balance exists over time and has the potential for changing how the social unit defines itself or is defined by others.

Stabilization and Maintenance Phase (SM)   The focus is on maintaining the changes that have occurred as a result of the adaptation phase. This involves accomplishing the shift from taking what is new or unfamiliar to what is familiar and doing what is necessary to maintain it. This is done on the assumption that continuing in a given phase is desired or where the choice to avoid the experience is not possible.

Sympathy   Feeling sorry for the plight of another person without experiencing the feeling.

Termination and Mourning Phase (TM)   Occurs with the ending of the SM phase. This may be by accident or design, desired or undesired, and temporary or permanent. The challenge in this phase is to adapt to the ending of an experience that permits the move to new experiences. Response styles to TM vary from hypervigilance and heightened activity to denial and refusal to relate to a forthcoming loss. The ending of this phase begins with the person's ability to accept the existing reality and receptivity to the anticipatory work of potential alternative experiences.

Therapeutic Culture   The working relationship that a family and therapist jointly define for the purpose of resolving the dysfunction that led the client to seek therapy. It is a product of family characteristics and circumstances, the orientation of the therapist, the goals to be achieved, and the environment in which the assessment takes place.

Therapist's Culture   The therapist brings to the therapeutic relationship a blending of two cultures: his personal experience and his professional training. The result is the therapist's culture. This represents the defined way that a therapist has learned to relate to clients from his professional training consistent with his personal history and experience. A therapist's culture is an evolutionary process that changes with changing needs and experience.

Values   Statements of what ought to be; a statement of ideals. A personal guide for a social entity's behavior.

Bibliography

Ackerman, N., *Treating the Troubled Family* (New York: Basic Books, 1966).

Bateson, G., *Naven* (Stanford, Calif.: Stanford University Press, 1958).

Bateson, G., *Steps to an Ecology of Mind* (New York: Ballantine Books, 1972).

Bateson, G., *Mind and Nature: A Necessary Unity* (New York: Dutton, 1979).

Berger, M. M., Editor, *Videotape Techniques in Psychiatric Training and Treatment* (New York: Brunner-Mazel, 1970).

Boszormenyi-Nagy, I., and Krasner, B. R., *Between Give and Take: A Clinical Guide to Contextual Therapy* (New York: Brunner-Mazel, 1986).

Bowen, M., *Family Therapy in Clinical Practice* (New York: Jason Aronson, 1978).

Bowen, M., Dysinger, R. H., Brody, W. M., and Basmania, B. *Study and Treatment of Five Hospitalized Families Each with a Psychotic Member.* Paper presented at the American Orthopsychiatric Association, Chicago, March 1957.

Erickson, M., "A Field Investigation by Hypnosis of Sound Loci Importance in Human Behavior," *American Journal of Clinical Hypnosis* 16 (1973), 92–109.

Framo, J., *Explorations in Marital and Family Therapy* (New York: Springer, 1982).

Gilligan, C., *In a Different Voice* (Cambridge, Mass.: Harvard University Press, 1982).

Guerin, P. J., Editor, *Family Therapy: Theory and Practice* (New York: Gardner Press, 1976).

Gurman, A. S., and Kniskern, D. P., Editors, *Handbook of Family Therapy* (New York: Brunner-Mazel, 1981).

Haley, J. "An Editor's Farewell," *Family Process* 8 (1969), 149–58.

Haley, J., Editor, *Changing Families* (New York: Grune & Stratton, 1971).

Haley, J., *Uncommon Therapy* (New York: W. W. Norton, 1973).

Haley, J., *Problem Solving Therapy* (San Francisco: Jossey-Bass, 1976).

Howells, J. G., *Family Relations Indicator* (New York: International Universities Press, 1984).

Jackson, D. D., Editor, *Human Communication,* Vol. 1: *Communication, Family and Marriage* (Palo Alto, Calif.: Science and Behavior Books, 1968a).

Jackson, D. D., Editor, *Human Communication,* Vol. 2: *Therapy, Communication and Change* (Palo Alto, Calif.: Science and Behavior Books, 1968b).

Keeney, B. P., and Ross, J. M., *Mind in Therapy: Constructing Systematic Family Therapies* (New York: Basic Books, 1985).

Krauss, D., and Fryrear, J. L., *Phototherapy in Mental Health* (Springfield, Ill.: Charles C. Thomas, 1983).

Kubler-Ross, E., *On Death and Dying* (New York: Macmillan, 1979).

Kwiatkowska, H. Y., "The Use of Families' Art Productions for Psychiatric Evaluation," *Bulletin of Art Therapy* 6 (1967a).

Kwiatkowska, H. Y., "Family Art Therapy," *Family Process* 6 (1967b).

Landgarten, H. B., *Family Art Psychotherapy: A Clinical Guide and Casebook* (New York: Brunner-Mazel, 1987).

Langer, E., *Mindfulness* (Cambridge, Mass.: Addison-Wesley, 1989).

Lazarus, A., *In the Mind's Eye: The Power of Imagery for Personal Enrichment* (New York: Rawson, 1977).

Lewin, K., *Field Theory in Social Science: Selected Theoretical Papers* D. Cartwright, Editor (New York: Harper, 1951).

Maturana, H., "Biology of Language: The Epistology of Reality." In Millar, G., Editor, *Psychology and Biology of Language and Thought,* pp. 27–63 (London: Academic Press, 1978).

McGoldrick, M., Anderson, C. M., and Walsh, F., *Women in Families: A Framework for Family Therapy* (New York: W. W. Norton, 1989).

McGoldrick, M., and Gerson, R., *Genograms in Family Assessment* (New York: W. W. Norton, 1985).

Minuchin, S., *Families and Family Therapy* (Cambridge, Mass.: Harvard University Press, 1974).

Minuchin, S., Montalvo, B., Guerney, B., Rosman, B., and Schumer, F., *Families of the Slums* (New York: Basic Books, 1967).

Murphy, G., and Jensen, F., *Approaches to Personality* (New York: Coward Press, 1932).

Murray, H. A., "Basic Concepts for a Psychology of Personality," *Journal of General Psychology* 15 (1936), 241–68.

Papp, P., *The Process of Change* (New York: Guilford, 1983).

Paul, N., and Paul, B. B., *A Marital Puzzle* (New York: W. W. Norton, 1975).

Penn, P., "Circular Questioning," *Family Process* 19 (1982), 267–80.

Reiker, P. P., and Carmen, E. H., Editors, *The Gender Gap in Psychotherapy: Social Realities and Psychological Processes* (New York: Plenum Press, 1984).

Rokeach, M., "Some Unresolved Issues in Theories of Beliefs, Attitudes and Values." In Howe, H. E., Jr., Editor, *1979 Nebraska Symposium on Motivation* pp. 261–304 (Lincoln: University of Nebraska Press, 1980).

Satir, V., *Conjoint Family Therapy: A Guide to Theory and Technique* (Palto Alto, Calif.: Science and Behavior Books, 1967).

Selvini Palazzoli, M., Boscolo, L., Cecchin, G., and Prata, G., "Hypothesizing-Circularity-Neutrality," *Family Process* 19 (1980), 3–12.

Sluzki, C. E., and Beavin, J., "Symmetry and Complementarity: An Operational Definition and a Typology," *Acta Psiquiatrica y Psicologica de America Latina* 11 (1965), 321–30.

Sluzki, C. E., "Marital Therapy from a Systems Perspective." In Paolini, T. J., and McCrady, B. S., Editors, *Marriage and Marital Therapy: Psychoanalytic, Behavioral, and Systems Theory Perspectives* (New York: Brunner-Mazel, 1978).

Snider, M., "Directed Art Productions as a Diagnostic and Treatment Aid." In Jakab, I., Editor, *Conscious and Unconscious Expressive Art,* pp. 152–59 (New York: S. Karger, 1971).

Stone, E., *Black Sheep and Kissing Cousins* (New York: Penguin Books, 1989).

Tomm, K., "Circular Interviewing: A Multifaceted Clinical Tool." In Campbell, D., and Draper, R., Editors, *Applications of Systemic Family Therapy: The Milan Approach,* (New York: Grune and Stratton, 1985).

Van Den Bergh, N., and Cooper, L. B., Editors, *Feminist Views for Social Work* (Silver Spring, Md.: National Association of Social Workers, 1986).

Von Foerster, H., *Observing Systems* (Seaside, Calif.: Intersystems Publications, 1981).

Watzlawick, P., Jackson, D., and Beavin, J., *Pragmatics of Human Communication* (New York: W. W. Norton, 1967).

Index